Taking a fresh look at the impact of non-state actors on world politics and on the foreign policies of states, this book revives the debate on transnational relations which started in the 1970s. This debate withered away in the face of state-centered approaches, but this book's new approach emphasizes the interaction of states and transnational actors, arguing that domestic structures of the state as well as international institutions mediate the policy influence of transnational actors.

Empirical chapters examine the European Economic and Monetary Union, US–Japanese transnational relations, multinational corporations in East Asia, Soviet and Russian security policy, democratization in Eastern Europe, and ivory management in Africa. The book concludes with chapters discussing the theoretical implications of the findings in the empirical studies.

CAMBRIDGE STUDIES IN INTERNATIONAL RELATIONS: 42

Bringing transnational relations back in

Cambridge Studies in International Relations is a joint initiative of Cambridge University Press and the British International Studies Association (BISA). The series will include a wide range of material, from undergraduate textbooks and surveys to research-based monographs and collaborative volumes. The aim of the series is to publish the best new scholarship in International Studies from Europe, North America, and the rest of the world.

CAMBRIDGE STUDIES IN INTERNATIONAL RELATIONS

Series list continues after index

Bringing transnational relations back in

Non-state actors, domestic structures and international institutions

Edited by
Thomas Risse-Kappen
University of Konstanz

CAMBRIDGE UNIVERSITY PRESS

Published by the Press Syndicate of the University of Cambridge
The Pitt Building, Trumpington Street, Cambridge CB2 1RP
40 West 20th Street, New York, NY 10011–4211, USA
10 Stamford Road, Oakleigh, Melbourne 3166, Australia

© Cambridge University Press 1995

First published 1995
Reprinted 1997

Printed in Great Britain at the University Press, Cambridge

A catalogue record for this book is available from the British Library

Library of Congress cataloguing in publication data

Bringing transnational relations back in:
non-state actors, domestic structures, and international
institutions / Thomas Risse-Kappen.
    p.   cm. – (Cambridge studies in international relations: 42)
Includes index
ISBN 0 521 48183 X (hardback) – ISBN 0 521 48441 X (pbk.)
1. International relations. 2. World politics – 1989–   .
I. Risse-Kappen, Thomas.   II. Series.
327'.09'049 – dc20   95–866 CIP

ISBN 0 521 48183 X hardback
ISBN 0 521 48441 3 paperback

Contents

Contents

Tables

Contributors

David R. Cameron	Professor of Political Science at Yale University, New Haven, CT, USA
Steve Chan	Professor of Political Science at the University of Colorado, Boulder, CO, USA
Patricia Chilton	Senior Lecturer in European Politics in the Department of Politics and Philosophy at the Manchester Metropolitan University, Manchester, United Kingdom
Cal Clark	Professor and Head of the Political Science Department, Auburn University, Auburn, AL, USA
Matthew Evangelista	Associate Professor of Political Science at the University of Michigan, Ann Arbor, MI, USA
Peter J. Katzenstein	Walter S. Carpenter, Jr., Professor of International Studies at Cornell University, Ithaca, NY, USA
Stephen D. Krasner	Graham Stuart Professor of International Relations at Stanford University, Stanford, CA, USA
Thomas Princen	Assistant Professor of International Environmental Policy in the School of Natural Resources and Environment, University of Michigan, Ann Arbor, MI, USA
Thomas Risse-Kappen	Professor of International Politics in the Department of Administrative Sciences, University of Konstanz, Konstanz, Germany
Yutaka Tsujinaka	Associate Professor of Political Science at the University of Tsukuba, Tsukuba, Japan

Preface

The end of the Cold War and the dissatisfaction with prevailing approaches to international relations have opened new spaces for theorizing about world politics. This book attempts to revive a subject that rose to a certain prominence during the early 1970s, but then withered away, while state-centered approaches to international relations carried the day. Pronouncing the topic of transnational relations dead, we argue, has been premature. This volume takes a fresh look at the impact of non-state actors on world politics and on the foreign policies of states. In particular, we look at the interaction between states and transnational relations in various issue-areas and conclude that domestic structures and international institutions mediate the influence of networks among non-state actors in international society.

The idea of bringing transnational relations back into the debate about international politics originated in conversations between Matthew Evangelista and myself when the "earthquake" of the end of the Cold War hit us in 1989–90. Matt and I then organized a first panel on the subject at the Annual Convention of the International Studies Association in Vancouver, BC, Canada, in March 1991. Matt, Daniel Thomas, and I presented papers, while Robert Keohane served as a commentator. The response by the audience was sufficiently enthusiastic so that I decided to pursue the issue further. Yale's International Studies Program and Cornell's Peace Studies Program, particularly the two directors, Bruce Russett and Judith Reppy, became interested in the topic and offered to host two project workshops. The first took place in New Haven from May 8 to 9, 1992, the second workshop followed in Ithaca from November 13 to 15, 1992. In between, we presented the project at the 1992 Annual Convention of the American

Political Science Association in Chicago and at various universities. This book is the result of our discussions.

Funding for the project workshop was provided by Cornell University's Peace Studies Program, Yale University's International Security Program, the MacArthur Foundation, and the Social Science Research Council. I gratefully acknowledge this support.

This book would not have been possible without the continuous backing and critical input of many colleagues and friends to whom I am enormously grateful. Bruce Russett and Judith Reppy have already been mentioned. I also thank the contributors to this volume for their inspirations, comments, and their preparedness to make this a truly collaborative enterprise. In addition, many scholars commented on the project along the way. I am particularly grateful to Valerie Bunce, Thomas Christensen, Daniel Deudney, John Duffield, James Goldgeier, Judith Goldstein, Isabelle Grunberg, Peter Haas, G. John Ikenberry, Robert Keohane, Audie Klotz, David Lumsdaine, Michael Marks, David Meyer, Ethan Nadelmann, John Odell, Gail Osherenko, T. J. Pempel, M. J. Peterson, Chris Reus-Smit, Steve Ropp, Kathryn Sikkink, Shibley Telhami, Janice Thomson, Alexander Wendt, Oran Young, Michael Zürn, and several anonymous reviewers. Steve Smith encouraged me to submit the manuscript to Cambridge University Press and offered very helpful advice along the way. John Haslam guided the book through the editing process and Jean Field did a great job as the copy-editor. Finally, I thank Susanne Kupfer, Birgit Locher, Klaus Roscher, Heike Scherff, Claudia Schmedt, and Hans Peter Schmitz for research assistance and help with preparing the index.

Thomas Risse-Kappen

Abbreviations

ABM	Antiballistic missile
ASAT	Antisatellite weapon
AWACS	Airborne Warning and Command System
BEAR	Beam Experiment Aboard Rocket
BIS	Bank for International Settlements
BOI	Board of Investments
CAMPFIRE	Command Areas Management Programme for Indigenous Resources
CC	Central Committee
CDU	Christian Democratic Union (of Germany)
CEO	Chief Executive Officer
CFC	Chlorofluorocarbons
CITES	Convention on International Trade in Endangered Species of Wild Fauna and Flora
CND	Campaign for Nuclear Disarmament
CoCom	Coordination Committee (on Export Controls)
CODENE	Comité pour le désarmement nucléaire en Europe (Committee for European Nuclear Disarmament)
CPSU	Communist Party of the Soviet Union
CRS	Congressional Research Service
CS	Civil society
CSCD	Center for the Storage of Contemporary Documentation
CSCE	Conference on Security and Cooperation in Europe
CSS	Committee of Soviet Scientists for Peace, against the Nuclear Threat
CSU	Christian Social Union (of Bavaria)
DFI	Direct foreign investment
DM	Deutsche Mark

EC	European Community
ECB	European Central Bank
Ecofin	Council of Economics and Finance Ministers
EEC	European Economic Community
EMI	European Monetary Institute
EMS	European Monetary System
EMU	(European) Economic and Monetary Union
END	European Nuclear Disarmament
ESCB	European System of Central Banks
ETC	Environmental transnational coalition
EU	European Union
FAS	Federation of American Scientists
FERA	Foreign Exchange Regulation Act
FDP	Free Democratic Party (of Germany)
FIDESZ	Fiatal Demokraták Szövetsége (Federation of Young Democrats: of Hungary)
FSX	Fighter Support Experimental
GATT	General Agreement on Tariffs and Trade
GDCT	Gross domestic capital formation
GDP	Gross domestic product
GDR	German Democratic Republic
GEMU	German Economic and Monetary Union
GM	General Motors Corporation
GNP	Gross national product
IBM	International Business Machines Corporation
IGC	Inter-governmental conference
IKV	Interkerkelijk Vredesberaad (Dutch Inter-Church Peace Council)
IMF	International Monetary Fund
INF	Intermediate-range Nuclear Forces
INGO	International non-governmental organization
IO	International organization
IPCC	International Peace Communication and Coordination Centre
IPPNW	International Physicians for the Prevention of Nuclear War
IPW	Institut für Internationale Politik und Wirtschaft der DDR (East German Institute for Politics and Economy)
IUCN	International Union for the Conservation of Nature and Natural Resources

JETRO	Japan External Trade Research Organization
KGB	Komitat gosudarstvennyi bezopasnosti (Committee of State Security: Soviet Union)
KOR	Komitat Obrony Robotników (Committee for the Defense of the Workers: Poland)
KWS	Kenya Wildlife Service
LDP	Liberal Democratic Party (of Japan)
MITI	Ministry of International Trade and Industry (of Japan)
MNC	Multinational corporation
MSDF	Maritime self-defense forces
NATO	North Atlantic Treaty Organization
NGO	Non-governmental organization
NPT	(Nuclear) Non-Proliferation Treaty
NRDC	Natural Resources Defense Council
OECD	Organization for Economic Cooperation and Development
OM	Ost Mark (currency of former East Germany)
pc	per capita
PCMP	Progressive Car Manufacturing Project
PHR-TNC	Peace and human rights trans-national coalition
Pop	Population
PRC	People's Republic of China
PVS	Politische Vierteljahresschrift
SADS	Soviet-American Defense Study
SALT	Strategic Arms Limitation Treaty
SAS	Soviet Academy of Sciences
SDF	Self Defense Forces
SDI	Strategic Defense Initiative
SDIO	Strategic Defense Initiative Organization
SEA	Single European Act
SED	Sozialistische Einheitspartei Deutschlands (Socialist Unity Party of [Eastern] Germany)
SII	Structural impediment initiatives
SPFE	Society for the Preservation of the Fauna of the Empire
START	Strategic Arms Reduction Talks
TI	Texas Instruments
TNA	Transnational actor
TNC	Transnational coalition
TRAFFIC	Trade Records Analysis of Flora and Fauna in Commerce
UCS	Union of Concerned Scientists

UK	United Kingdom
UN	United Nations (Organization)
UNEP	United Nations Environment Programme
UNESCO	United Nations Educational, Scientific, and Cultural Organization
US	United States (of America)
USSR	Union of Soviet Socialist Republics
USTR	United States Trade Representative
WiP	Wolnose i Pokoj (Freedom and Peace branch of Solidarnosc Polish)
WWF	World Wildlife Fund

Setting the agenda

1 Bringing transnational relations back in: introduction

Thomas Risse-Kappen

Introduction

Transnational relations, i.e., *regular interactions across national boundaries when at least one actor is a non-state agent or does not operate on behalf of a national government or an intergovernmental organization,*[1] permeate world politics in almost every issue-area. About 5,000 international non-governmental organizations (INGOs) – from Amnesty International and Greenpeace to the International Political Science Association – lobby international regimes and inter-state organizations for their purposes.[2] Some promote international cooperation, while others try to prevent regulatory regimes which would interfere with the activities of private citizens. Some of the approximately 7,000 multinational corporations (MNCs) with subsidiaries in other countries have gross sales larger than the gross national product (GNP) of even major countries and, thus, create adaptation problems for the foreign economic policies of many states. More loosely organized transnational alliances appear to be everywhere, too. Transnational dis-

---

[1] This definition builds upon, but slightly modifies the original definition of transnational relations by encompassing both trans-societal and trans-governmental relations. I will later address the concept of transnational relations in more detail. For the original definitions see Karl Kaiser, "Transnationale Politik," in Ernst-Otto Czempiel, ed., *Die anachronistische Souveränität* (Cologne-Opladen: Westdeutscher Verlag, 1969), pp. 80–109; Robert O. Keohane and Joseph S. Nye, Jr., "Introduction," in Keohane and Nye, eds., *Transnational Relations and World Politics* (Cambridge, MA: Harvard University Press, 1971), pp. xii–xvi.

[2] For a discussion see Young Kim, John Boli and George M. Thomas, "World Culture and International Nongovernmental Organizations," paper presented at the Annual Meetings of the American Sociological Association, Miami Beach, 1993. See also Jackie Smith, "The Globalization of Social Movements: The Transnational Social Movement Sector, 1983–1993," paper presented at the Annual Meetings of the American Sociological Association, Los Angeles, August 5–9, 1994.

sident movements in Eastern Europe helped to topple the Communist regimes in 1989. Western social movements set the public agenda on peace and environmental questions in many countries during the 1980s. Transnational groups of scientists – "epistemic communities"[3] – contributed to a growing global awareness about various environmental issues. Trans*governmental* networks among state officials in sub-units of national governments, international organizations, and regimes frequently pursue their own agenda, independently from and sometimes even contrary to the declared policies of their national governments. Such knowledge-based or normative principle-based transnational and transgovernmental issue networks seem to have a major impact on the global diffusion of values, norms, and ideas in such diverse issue-areas as human rights, international security, or the global environment. But there is no reason to assume that transnational relations regularly promote "good" causes. Transnational terrorism poses a serious threat to internal stability in many countries, while some scholars have identified Islamic fundamentalism – another transnational social movement – as a major source of future inter-state conflicts.[4]

Almost nobody denies that transnational relations exist; their presence is well established. But despite more than twenty years of controversy about the subject, we still have a poor understanding of their impact on state policies and international relations. Transnational relations do not seem to have the same effects across cases. How is it to be explained, for example, that the spread of democratic values and human rights toward the end of this century, promoted by various INGOs and transnational alliances,[5] has affected some countries more than others – the former Soviet Union as compared to China, former Czechoslovakia as compared to Romania, and South Korea as compared to North Korea? Why have "epistemic communities" and INGOs been able to set the agenda on global warming in Japan and in many European Union (EU) countries, but apparently less so in the United States? How do we explain that the transnational peace move-

---

3 See Peter Haas, ed., *Knowledge, Power, and International Policy Coordination*, special issue of *International Organization*, 46, 1 (Winter 1992).
4 See, for example, Beau Grosscup, "Global Terrorism in the Post-Iran-Contra Era: Debunking Myths and Facing Realities," *International Studies*, 29, 1 (1992), pp. 55–78; Samuel Huntington, "The Clash of Civilizations?," *Foreign Affairs*, 79 (1993), pp. 22–49.
5 On this aspect see Kathryn Sikkink, "Human Rights, Principled Issue-Networks, and Sovereignty in Latin America," *International Organization*, 47, 3 (Summer 1993), pp. 411–41.

4

ments of the early 1980s in Western Europe and North America had a
lasting impact on German security policy, made a significant short-
term difference in the US, but had almost no influence on French
foreign policy?[6]

This study suggests that the debate of the 1970s on transnational
relations closed the book on the subject prematurely and that it is
worthwhile to revive it. The earlier arguments set up the controversy
in terms of a "state-centered" versus a "society-dominated" view of
world politics. We claim instead that it is more fruitful to examine how
the inter-state world interacts with the "society world" of transnational relations. If the conditions under which transnational actors
matter are clearly specified, the claim that "the reciprocal effects
between transnational relations and the interstate system" are "centrally important to the understanding of contemporary world
politics"[7] can be made with greater confidence.

The main question to be asked in this volume is therefore: *under what
domestic and international circumstances do transnational coalitions and
actors who attempt to change policy outcomes in a specific issue-area succeed
or fail to achieve their goals?*

Our question is *not* what difference transnational relations make in
international politics in general. This would require one to vary empirical case studies with regard to the existence or non-existence of
non-state actors. The methodological difficulties of such an approach
seem to be almost insurmountable, since we do not know enough
about the universe of cases to be able to specify whether our case
selection constitutes a reasonably representative sample. Rather, we
will take a more modest and feasible approach by comparing cases in
which transnational coalitions and actors consciously sought to influence policies, mainly state behavior in the foreign policy arena. We
take the existence of transnational coalitions and actors who aim to
change policies in various issue-areas as the point of departure. The
issue-areas investigated include the international economy (chapters
by David Cameron, Peter Katzenstein and Yutaka Tsujinaka, Cal Clark
and Steve Chan), the environment (chapter by Thomas Princen),
international security (chapters by Katzenstein and Tsujinaka,

---

[6] See David Meyer, *A Winter of Discontent. The Freeze and American Politics* (New York: Praeger, 1990); Thomas Rochon, *Mobilizing for Peace: The Anti-Nuclear Movement in Western Europe* (Princeton, NJ: Princeton University Press, 1988).
[7] Keohane and Nye, "Introduction," p. xi. For a discussion see also M.J. Peterson, "Transnational Activity, International Society, and World Politics," *Millennium*, 21, 3 (Winter 1992), pp. 371–88.

Matthew Evangelista), and human rights (chapter by Patricia Chilton). We look at the policy impact of transnational actors such as MNCs (Katzenstein and Tsujinaka, Clark and Chan), INGOs (Princen), transnational and transgovernmental actors within international institutions (Cameron, Katzenstein and Tsujinaka), as well as loose alliances among societal groups (Evangelista, Chilton). We look at the differential impact of these actors on highly industrialized states (Cameron, Katzenstein and Tsujinaka), on former Communist countries (Evangelista, Chilton), and on industrializing as well as less developed states (Clark and Chan, Princen). Finally, the transnational relations investigated here vary with regard to their embeddedness in bilateral and/or multilateral institutions – from the EU (Cameron) and the US–Japanese alliance (Katzenstein and Tsujinaka) to the East–West détente of the Cold War (Evangelista, Chilton), and North–South relations (Clark and Chan, Princen).

The volume builds upon and integrates two theoretical approaches which have been developed independently from each other and have rarely been brought together – the concepts of *domestic structures* and of *international institutions*. They both deal with structures of governance, they both have generated fruitful empirical research, and, thus, together enlighten this inquiry.

This book argues, in short, that the impact of transnational actors and coalitions on state policies is likely to vary according to:

1 differences in *domestic structures*, i.e., the normative and organizational arrangements which form the "state," structure society, and link the two in the polity; and
2 degrees of *international institutionalization*, i.e., the extent to which the specific issue-area is regulated by bilateral agreements, multilateral regimes, and/or international organizations.

Domestic structures are likely to determine both the availability of channels for transnational actors into the political systems and the requirements for "winning coalitions" to change policies. On the one hand, the more the state dominates the domestic structure, the more difficult it should be for transnational actors to penetrate the social and political systems of the "target" country. Once they overcome this hurdle in state-dominated systems, though, their policy impact might be profound, since coalition-building with rather small groups of governmental actors appears to be comparatively straightforward. On the other hand, the more fragmented the state and the better organized civil society, the easier should be the access for transnational actors. But the requirements for successful coalition-building are likely to be quite staggering in such systems.

Domestic structures and international institutionalization are likely to interact in determining the ability of transnational actors to bring about policy changes. The more the respective issue-area is regulated by international norms of cooperation, the more permeable should state boundaries become for transnational activities. Highly regulated and cooperative structures of international governance tend to legitimize transnational activities and to increase their access to the national polities as well as their ability to form "winning coalitions" for policy change. Transnational relations acting in a highly institutionalized international environment are, therefore, likely to overcome hurdles otherwise posed by state-dominated domestic structures more easily.

Refining the concept of transnational relations

An effort at renewing the debate about transnational relations has to overcome conceptual and empirical hurdles. The odds are against such an enterprise, since the earlier debate on the subject failed to clarify the concept which then did not generate much empirical research – except for the study of MNCs – and withered away.[8] The first debate essentially resulted in confirming the state-centered view of world politics. There are several reasons for this outcome.

The original concept of "transnational relations" was ill-defined. It encompassed everything in world politics except state-to-state rela-

---

[8] Among the most important works of the earlier debate are Walter Bühl, *Transnationale Politik* (Stuttgart: Klett-Cotta, 1978); Czempiel, *Die anachronistische Souveränität*; Annette Baker Fox, Alfred O. Hero Jr., and Joseph S. Nye, Jr., *et al.*, eds., *Canada and the United States: Transnational and Transgovernmental Relations* (New York: Columbia University Press, 1976); Harold Jacobson, *Networks of Interdependence. International Organizations and the Global Political System* (New York: Knopf, 1979); Keohane and Nye, eds., *Transnational Relations and World Politics*; Robert O. Keohane and Joseph S. Nye, Jr., *Power and Interdependence* (Boston: Little, Brown, and Co., 1977); Werner Link, *Deutsche und amerikanische Gewerkschaften und Geschäftsleute 1945–75: Eine Studie über transnationale Beziehungen* (Düsseldorf: Droste, 1978); Richard W. Mansbach, Yale H. Ferguson, and Donald E. Lampert, *The Web of World Politics. Non-State Actors in the Global System* (Englewood Cliffs, NJ: Prentice Hall, 1976); Edward L. Morse, *Modernization and the Transformation of International Relations* (New York: Free Press, 1976); James N. Rosenau, *Linkage Politics* (New York: Free Press, 1969); James N. Rosenau, *The Study of Global Interdependence. Essays on the Transnationalization of World Affairs* (London: Frances Pinter, 1980); Peter Willets, ed., *Pressure Groups in the Global System. The Transnational Relations of Issue-Oriented Non-Governmental Organizations* (New York: St. Martin's Press, 1982).

tions. But transnational capital flows, international trade, foreign media broadcasts, the transnational diffusion of values, coalitions of peace movements, transgovernmental alliances of state bureaucrats, INGOs, and MNCs are quite different phenomena. To study the policy impact of transnational relations becomes virtually impossible if the concept is used in such a broad way.

This volume does not deal with transnational relations in an all-encompassing sense. It is not about *interdependence*, defined as patterns of interactions which are mutually costly to disrupt or break.[9] The volume also does not consider *transnational diffusion effects* of cultural values and norms or the impact of international communication networks on public attitudes and national societies. It is hard to develop propositions about these effects that can be measured empirically.[10]

This volume focuses on the policy impact of transnational relations maintained by clearly identifiable actors or groups of actors and linking at least two societies or sub-units of national governments (in the case of transgovernmental relations). Moreover, the transnational coalitions and actors considered are purposeful in the sense that they attempt to achieve specific political goals in the "target" state of their activities.

This sub-set of transnational relations still leaves a whole range of different actors. With regard to purpose, the volume concentrates on two types of actors – those motivated primarily by instrumental, mainly economic, gains and those promoting principled ideas as well as knowledge.[11] The former include multinational corporations

[9] See Keohane and Nye, *Power and Interdependence*. For a review of the "interdependence" literature concluding that there was no "integrated theoretical model" and that the concept only generated "impressionistic descriptions" rather than rigorous empirical research see Beate Kohler-Koch, "Interdependenz," in Volker Rittberger, ed., *Theorien der internationalen Beziehungen* (Opladen: Westdeutscher Verlag, 1990), pp. 110–29, 125. See, however, James Rosenau and Hylke Tromp, eds., *Interdependence and Conflict in World Politics* (Aldershot: Avebury, 1989); James Rosenau, *Turbulence in World Politics. A Theory of Change and Continuity* (Princeton, NJ: Princeton University Press, 1990); Ernst-Otto Czempiel, *Weltpolitik im Umbruch. Das internationale System nach dem Ende des Ost–West-Konflikts* (Munich: Beck, 1991).

[10] For pioneering work in this direction see the studies on the "world polity" initiated by John W. Meyer and other sociologists, for example, George M. Thomas, John W. Meyer, Francisco O. Ramirez, and John Boli, ed., *Institutional Structure. Constituting State, Society, and the Individual* (Beverly Hills, CA: Sage, 1987); John Meyer, "The World Polity and the Authority of the Nation-State," *ibid.*, pp. 41–70; John Meyer and Brian Rowen, "Institutionalized Organizations: Formal Structures in Myth and Ceremony," in Paul J. DiMaggio and Walter Powell, eds., *The New Institutionalism in Organizational Analysis* (Chicago: University of Chicago Press, 1991).

[11] I owe these categories to suggestions by Kathryn Sikkink; see her "Human Rights, Principled Issue-networks, and Sovereignty." On knowledge-based networks see

(chapters by Katzenstein and Tsujinaka, Clark and Chan), while the latter range from INGOs (chapter by Princen), transnational coalitions among human rights groups, peace movements, arms control experts, and central bankers (chapters by Chilton, Evangelista, Cameron) to transgovernmental networks among state officials (chapters by Cameron, Katzenstein and Tsujinaka).

The notion of *transgovernmental coalitions*[12] raises additional conceptual problems. Transgovernmental relations could be regarded as the transnational equivalent of bureaucratic politics.[13] They are all-pervasive in world politics, since interactions among heads of states and governments only form a very small portion of inter-state relations. But conceptualized in this way, transgovernmental relations would become virtually indistinguishable from inter-state relations so that the notion loses any analytical strength. To put it differently, the parsimonious "government-as-unitary-actor" model should not be abandoned in the international realm too easily. Only those networks among governmental actors which cannot be captured in the framework of inter-state relations will be considered here. Sub-units of national governments have to act on their own in the absence of national decisions, not just on behalf of their heads of state implementing agreed-upon policies. Transgovernmental coalitions are then defined as networks of government officials which include at least one actor pursuing her own agenda independent of national decisions. The European Committee of Central Bank Governors monitoring the European Monetary System (EMS), for example, represents a transgovernmental institution given the independent status of some of its powerful members (e.g., the German Bundesbank; see Cameron's chapter). Transgovernmental coalitions among senior officials of various North Atlantic Treaty Organization (NATO) governments

---

Peter Haas, *Knowledge, Power, and International Policy Coordination*; Peter Haas, *Saving the Mediterranean* (New York: Columbia University Press, 1990); Ernst Haas, *When Knowledge Is Power* (Berkeley, CA: University of California Press, 1990).

[12] See Robert O. Keohane and Joseph S. Nye, Jr., "Transgovernmental Relations and International Organizations," *World Politics*, 27 (1974), pp. 39–62.

[13] The classic studies are Graham Allison, *Essence of Decision. Explaining the Cuban Missile Crisis* (Boston: Little, Brown, and Co., 1972); Morton Halperin, *Bureaucratic Politics and Foreign Policy* (Washington, DC: The Brookings Institution, 1974). There is one important conceptual difference between Allison's original concept and the notion of transgovernmental relations as used in this volume. Allison's bureaucratic actors are primarily motivated by instrumental goals, i.e., they want to increase their turf, their budget, and the like. But bureaucratic and transgovernmental coalitions might as well be motivated by principled ideas.

have been found to shape the transatlantic relationship significantly.[14] When Chancellor Kohl reaches an agreement with President Mitterrand on EU matters, however, such interaction can be conceptualized as inter-state relations and the concept of transgovernmental relations is unnecessary.

The transnational coalitions and actors investigated in this volume can be distinguished according to the degree of their institutionalization.[15] In order to qualify as a transnational *coalition*, the interaction has to occur with regularity over time. A merely "tacit alliance" across national boundaries would not be considered a transnational coalition.[16] Transnational alliances operate on the basis of both implicit and explicit rules based on informal understandings as well as formal agreements. Examples of informal networks include most transnational "epistemic communities" and transgovernmental coalitions. In this volume, two chapters examine the policy impact of rather loose transnational alliances formed across the East–West divide during the Cold War (Evangelista, Chilton).

The most highly institutionalized forms of transnational relations are INGOs and MNCs. They consist of bureaucratic structures with explicit rules and specific role assignments to individuals or groups working inside the organization. The policy impact of INGOs and MNCs will be examined in the chapters by Katzenstein and Tsujinaka, Clark and Chan, and Princen.

Two trends can be observed with regard to the institutionalization of transnational relations over time. First, the number of INGOs has exploded throughout this century, particularly during the 1970s and 1980s – from 176 in 1909 to 832 in 1951, 1,255 in 1960, 2,173 in 1972, and 4,518 in 1988.[17] This is particularly true for INGOs representing trans-

---

14 See Thomas Risse-Kappen, *Cooperation among Democracies. The European Influence on US Foreign Policy* (Princeton, NJ: Princeton University Press, 1995); also Helga Haftendorn, *Kernwaffen und die Glaubwürdigkeit der Allianz* (Baden-Baden: Nomos, 1994).

15 I follow Keohane's definition of institutions as sets of rules which shape expectations, prescribe roles, and constrain activities. See Robert O. Keohane, *International Institutions and State Power* (Boulder, CO: Westview, 1989), pp. 3/4.

16 For example, "hawks" in both the US and the former USSR frequently played into each other's hands during the Cold War. Implicit transnational alliances can be analyzed in the framework of "two-level games" and are not part of this project. On "two-level games" see Robert Putnam, "Diplomacy and Domestic Politics: The Logic of Two-Level Games," *International Organization*, 42, 3 (Summer 1988), pp. 427–60; Peter B. Evans, Harold K. Jacobson, Robert D. Putnam, eds., *Double-Edged Diplomacy. An Interactive Approach to International Politics* (Berkeley, CA: University of California Press, 1993).

17 Data in Jaap de Wilde, *Saved from Oblivion: Interdependence Theory in the First Half of the 20th Century* (Aldershot: Dartmouth, 1991), p. 36; Rosenau, *Turbulence in World Politics*,

national social movements. Their number has increased from 1983 to 1993 by 73 per cent, from 319 to 533.[18] This trend helps to clarify the debate about whether or not transnational relations have increased over time. With the exceptions of capital mobility and of direct foreign investments, it is hard to sustain the thesis that transnational relations as such have multiplied. However, as others have noted before,[19] the data show that the institutionalization of transnational relations has definitely increased.

Second, this institutionalization took place in parallel to, but recently surpassed the creation of inter-state institutions. In 1909, there were on average less than 5 INGOs per International Governmental Organization (IO). From the 1950s to the early 1970s this ratio increased to about 7–9 INGOs per IO. From the late 1970s throughout the 1980s, the growth rate of INGOs surpassed the increase in inter-state organizations. In 1988, the UN counted 4,518 INGOs and 309 IOs, i.e., a ratio of more than 14:1.[20]

Even if we can observe a trend toward the institutionalization of transnational relations, it is not clear that, therefore, they should affect state practices. Various examples suggest that neither institutionalization nor economic power alone are decisive for the policy impact of transnational actors:

> In the *environmental issue-area*, "epistemic communities" – i.e., networks of professionals with an authoritative claim to policy-relevant knowledge[21] – and INGOs are often pitched against economically powerful MNCs. In the case of the ban

p. 409. For a discussion of INGOs and transnational social movements before 1945 see Charles Chatfield, "Networks and Junctures: International Nongovernmental Organizations and Transnational Social Movements to 1945," paper presented to the Workshop on International Institutions and Transnational Social Movement Organizations, University of Notre Dame, April 21–23, 1994.

18 For details see Smith, "The Globalization of Social Movements."

19 See, for example, Samuel Huntington, "Transnational Organizations in World Politics," *World Politics*, 25 (April 1973), pp. 333–68; Joseph Nye, "Transnational Relations and Interstate Conflicts: An Empirical Analysis," in Fox *et al.*, *Canada and the United States*, pp. 367–402, 383/384. For a more recent analysis see Kim *et al.*, "World Culture and Nongovernmental Organizations." For arguments disputing the increase in transnational interactions see, for example, Janice E. Thomson and Stephen Krasner, "Global Transactions and the Consolidation of Sovereignty," in Ernst-Otto Czempiel and James N. Rosenau, eds., *Global Changes and Theoretical Challenges* (Lexington, MA: Lexington Books, 1989), pp. 195–219; Kenneth Waltz, *Theory of International Politics* (Reading, MA: Addison-Wesley, 1979).

20 Calculated from data in de Wilde, *Saved from Oblivion*, p. 36, and Rosenau, *Turbulence in World Politics*, p. 409.

21 See Peter Haas, *Knowledge, Power, and International Policy Coordination*.

against whaling, the epistemic community was initially unable to prevail over the whaling industry. When environmental INGOs adopted the cause, states moved to impose a ban on whaling. In the ozone-depletion case, an epistemic community set the international agenda on the issue and formed an alliance with INGOs against powerful MNCs. When a major US MNC – DuPont – defected from the united front of chlorofluorocarbon (CFC) producers, the Montreal protocol to protect the ozone layer became possible.[22]

In the *international economic realm,* a recent example includes the European Community (EC)'s approach to the Uruguay Round of the General Agreement on Tariffs and Trade (GATT) negotiations. Economically almost irrelevant but politically powerful transnational farmers' associations were pitched against the entire European business community, which supported cutting agricultural subsidies in order to preserve the international free trade order. Nevertheless, the farmers' associations blocked an EC–US agreement for several years.[23]

In the *human rights area,* loose coalitions of anti-apartheid activists in various countries and human rights INGOs prevailed over MNCs in convincing powerful Western states

---

[22] On the whaling case see M.J. Peterson, "Whalers, Cetologists, Environmentalists, and the International Management of Whaling," in Peter Haas, *Knowledge, Power, and International Policy Coordination,* pp. 147–86. For the ozone depletion case see Peter Haas, "Banning Chlorofluorocarbons: Epistemic Community Efforts to Protect Stratospheric Ozone," ibid. pp. 187–224. For a discussion of transnational issue networks in the environment and human rights areas see Margaret Keck and Kathryn Sikkink, "International Issue Networks in the Environment and Human Rights," paper for the Workshop on International Institutions and Transnational Social Movement Organizations, University of Notre Dame, April 21–23, 1994. See also Thomas Princen and Matthias Finger, *Environmental NGOs in World Politics: Linking the Local and the Global* (London: Routledge, 1994).

[23] On transnational interest groups in the EC see Beate Kohler-Koch, "Interessen und Integration. Die Rolle organisierter Interessen im westeuropäischen Integrationsprozeß," in Michael Kreile, ed., *Die Integration Europas* (Opladen: Westdeutscher Verlag, 1992), pp. 81–119; Beate Kohler-Koch, "The Evolution of Organized Interests in the EC: Driving Forces, Co-Evolution, or New Type of Governance," paper prepared for the XVIth World Congress of the International Political Science Association, August 21–25, 1994, Berlin. On the EC's role during the GATT negotiations see Stephen Woolcock, *Trading Partners or Trading Blows?* (New York: Council of Foreign Relations Press, 1992).

to institute economic sanctions against South Africa which substantially contributed to bringing down the apartheid regime.[24] As Patricia Chilton argues in this volume, extremely fragile alliances among Western European peace and human rights activists, on the one hand, and dissident groups in Eastern Europe, on the other, nevertheless affected the evolution of civil societies in these countries in a crucial way.[25]

Examples concerning *international security* include the formulation of a joint European policy toward the nuclear non-proliferation regime. An epistemic community aligned with a transgovernmental coalition of foreign ministry officials against the European nuclear industry and economic ministries in various countries. In the end, the former coalition prevailed over the latter in convincing states to join the Nuclear Non-Proliferation Treaty (NPT) (France) or to strengthen its export controls (Germany).[26]

These examples do not suggest that epistemic communities, transnational coalitions, or INGOs always succeed over economically powerful MNCs. But they challenge the proposition that the degree to which transnational relations are institutionalized or the economic clout of transnational actors alone determine their political impact on state practices. The examples suggest that a more fruitful approach would be to analyze how transnational actors interact with the domestic and/or bureaucratic politics in the "target countries." Success or failure of transnational coalitions, INGOs, or MNCs to achieve their goals would then depend on their ability to persuade or line up with domestic and/or governmental actors. The above-mentioned examples also suggest that it might be fruitful to explore how international norms and institutions mediate the policy impact of transnational actors.

---

24 See Audie Klotz, *Protesting Prejudice: Apartheid and the Politics of Norms in International Relations* (Ithaca, NY: Cornell University Press, 1995).
25 On this case see also Daniel Thomas, "When Norms and Movements Matter: Helsinki, Human Rights, and Political Change in Eastern Europe, 1970–1990," PhD dissertation, Cornell University, 1994.
26 See Harald Müller, ed., *A European Non-Proliferation Policy* (Oxford: Clarendon Press, 1987); Harald Müller, ed., *How Western European Nuclear Policy is Made. Deciding on the Atom* (London: Macmillan, 1991).

Mediating the impact of transnational relations: domestic structures and international institutions

Deficiencies of existing theories

The earlier debate on the subject did not only lack a precise notion of transnational relations. Some contributions claimed to replace the state-centered paradigm of world politics by a society-dominated perspective.[27] More recently, some authors distinguish between "two worlds" of international relations, i.e., a realm in which states dominate and a domain in which societal actors and transnational relations prevail.[28] According to Ernst-Otto Czempiel, for example, the "society world" dominates non-security issues in the Organization for Economic Cooperation and Development (OECD)-region of highly industrialized countries. If outcomes are emphasized, however, proponents of the state-centered paradigm can easily refute the proposition by pointing out that states created the international economic regimes such as GATT and set the parameters in which international trade, direct foreign investments, etc., take place (see chapter by Stephen Krasner). In the environmental area, MNCs might affect outcomes directly through pollution if left to their own devices; but INGOs such as Greenpeace are powerless unless they convince national governments to agree upon regulatory regimes. Are environmental regimes triumphs of the "state world" over the "society world" (MNCs) or do they constitute the victory of one transnational actor over another with states being the pawns of the latter?

To establish that transnational relations matter in world politics, the interesting question is not whether international relations are dominated by states or by societies. As the earlier debate on the subject shows, posing the question in such a way leads to an easy triumph of the "state-centered" paradigm. To set the debate in terms of a "state-centered" versus a "society-dominated" view of world politics misses

---

[27] For example Mansbach *et al.*, *The Web of World Politics*; Rosenau, *Study of Global Interdependence*. Note, however, that the original Keohane and Nye volume (*Transnational Relations and World Politics*) pursued a far more moderate goal by investigating the "contamination of interstate relations by transnational relations" (Peter Evans quoted in Keohane and Nye, "Transnational Relations and World Politics: An Introduction," p. xxiv). The problem with the original *Transnational Relations and World Politics* volume was not that it did not pose the right set of questions. Rather, it lacked a theory to answer them.

[28] See, for example, Czempiel, *Weltpolitik im Umbruch*; Rosenau, *Turbulence in World Politics*.

14

the mark. There is no logical connection between the argument that states remain dominant actors in international politics and the conclusion that societal actors and transnational relations should, therefore, be irrelevant. One can subscribe to the proposition that national governments are extremely significant in international relations and still claim that transnational actors crucially affect state interests, policies, and inter-state relations. Confusing the impact of transnational relations on world politics with a "society-dominated" view of international relations leads one to overlook the more interesting question of how inter-state and transnational relations interact. One does not have to do away with the "state" to establish the influence of transnational relations in world politics.

But there is not much guidance in the international relations literature if one wants to show how transnational relations affect the inter-state world. The study of international institutions, which has generated a lot of empirical research during the past fifteen years and was partly an outgrowth of the literature on interdependence and transnational relations,[29] did not challenge the assumption that states can be treated as unitary actors. Until quite recently, regime analysis was confined to the study of inter-state relations, took state preferences and interests as given, and largely ignored the role of non-state actors in the processes of international institution-building.[30]

Empirical research in comparative foreign policy has established that domestic politics accounts alone are as insufficient as international level explanations and that they have to be complemented by "second-

---

[29] See, for example, Keohane and Nye, *Power and Interdependence*. The classical text on regime analysis is Stephen Krasner, ed., *International Regimes* (Ithaca, NY: Cornell University Press, 1983). On the state of the art see Volker Rittberger, ed., *Regime Theory and International Relations* (Oxford: Oxford University Press, 1993).

[30] For recent work on non-state actors and international institutions see Martha Finnemore, "Restraining State Violence: The International Red Cross as a Teacher of Humanitarian Norms," Paper presented at the Annual Meeting of the American Political Science Association, Chicago, September 1992; Martha Finnemore, *Defining National Interest in International Society*, forthcoming; Peter Haas, *Knowledge, Power and International Policy Coordination*; Klotz, *Protesting Prejudice*; Harald Müller, "The Internalization of Principles, Norms, and Rules by Governments: The Case of Security Regimes," in Rittberger, *Regime Theory and International Relations*, pp. 361–88; Ethan Nadelmann, "Global Prohibition Regimes: The Evolution of Norms in International Society," *International Organization*, 44, 4 (Autumn 1990), pp. 479–526; Sikkink, "Human Rights, Principled Issue-Networks, and Sovereignty"; Oran Young, "Political Leadership and Regime Formation: On the Development of Institutions in International Society," *International Organization*, 45, 3 (Summer 1991), pp. 281–308; Michael Zürn, "Bringing the Second Image (Back) In. About the Domestic Sources of Regime Formation," in Rittberger, *Regime Theory and International Relations*, pp. 282–311.

image reversed" concepts. A growing consensus in the field maintains that *interactive approaches* integrating external and internal factors offer a better and richer understanding of foreign policy than accounts exclusively relying on one aspect.[31] But most conceptualizations ignore transnational activities. Putnam's "two-level game" model,[32] for example, links international relations and domestic politics, but accepts the state-centered paradigm. The international and the domestic realms are connected through the actions of national governments and state negotiators. Transnational relations, the links between the "domestic games," remain outside the framework.[33]

In contrast, the recent literature on epistemic communities explicitly theorizes about one specific group of transnational actors.[34] But the emerging literature on the subject shares some of the shortcomings of the earlier debate on transnational relations insofar as it lacks a theory of domestic politics and the state. The debate so far has not specified sufficiently under what conditions epistemic communities have a policy impact.

In sum, there is a bifurcation in the international relations literature. Those who theorize about international relations and about domestic politics tend to ignore the linkages between societies and societal actors across national boundaries. Those who study transnational relations mostly neglect structures of governance, in particular the state. An effort to renew the concept of transnational relations must try to bridge this gap.

---

[31] See the literature reviews in Andrew Moravscik, "Introduction: Integrating International and Domestic Explanations of International Bargaining," in Evans *et al.*, *Double-Edged Diplomacy*, pp. 3–42; Harald Müller and Thomas Risse-Kappen, "From the Outside In and From the Inside Out. International Relations, Domestic Politics, and Foreign Policy," in Valerie Hudson and David Skidmore, eds., *The Limits of State Autonomy: Societal Groups and Foreign Policy Formulation* (Boulder, CO: Westview, 1993), pp. 25–48. See also Peter Gourevitch, "The Second Image Reversed: The International Sources of Domestic Politics," *International Organization*, 32, 4 (1978), pp. 881–911.

[32] Putnam, "Diplomacy and Domestic Politics." See also Michael Mastanduno, David A. Lake, G. John Ikenberry *et al.*, "Toward a Realist Theory of State Action," *International Studies Quarterly*, 33, 4 (December 1989), pp. 457–74.

[33] On this point see also Jeffrey Knopf, "Beyond Two-Level Games: Domestic-International Interaction in the Intermediate-Nuclear Forces Negotiations," *International Organization*, 47, 3 (Autumn 1993), pp. 599–628.

[34] See Peter Haas, *Knowledge, Power, and International Policy Coordination*; Peter Haas, *Saving the Mediterranean*; Ernst Haas, *When Knowledge Is Power*.

Debates about the state

The attack on the state-dominated view of international relations during the 1960s and 1970s coincided with a broader critique of the concept of the state in political theory and comparative politics from both liberal and Marxist perspectives. First, *liberal pluralist* theories in the tradition of Robert Dahl defined political systems functionally in terms of the authoritative allocation of values in a given society.[35] Political actors were seen as substantially constrained by societal pressures and the political process itself was conceptualized as perpetual bargaining among societal interest groups and organizations. Political decisions were analyzed predominantly in terms of the preferences and the strength of societal actors. Second, *"power elite"* theories in the tradition of C. Wright Mills attacked the pluralist model and argued that the political process in Western countries was dominated by concurring interests of business and political elites. This concept found one of its most prominent expressions in the non-Marxist versions of the "Military-Industrial-Complex" model.[36] Third, *instrumental Marxism* and the theory of state-monopolistic capitalism conceptualized the state as essentially representing the "executive committee of the ruling class."

The three approaches have in common that the state is more or less theorized away. Governmental actors become the transmission belts of societal interest groups, elites, or ruling classes. To understand and analyze politics, one has to look at the coalition-building processes within society. Politics becomes "society-centered."

But efforts to theorize the state away did not last long. In parallel to the revival of the state against the transnationalism and interdependence literature in international relations, scholars brought "the state back in" to comparative politics, too, during the late 1970s and early 1980s. States "conceived as organizations claiming control over territories and people may formulate and pursue goals that are not simply reflective of the demands or interests of social groups, classes,

---

[35] For this definition see, among others, David Easton, *A Systems Analysis of Political Life* (New York: Wiley & Sons, 1965). See also Robert Dahl, *Who Governs: Democracy and Power in an American City* (New Haven, CT: Yale University Press, 1961). For a discussion see Stephen Krasner, "Approaches to the State: Alternative Conceptions and Historical Dynamics," *Comparative Politics*, 16 (1984), pp. 223–46.

[36] See, for example, C. Wright Mills, *The Power Elite* (New York: Oxford University Press, 1956). For a critical discussion of the "military-industrial-complex" model see Steven Rosen, ed., *Testing the Theory of the Military-Industrial-Complex* (Lexington, MA: Heath, 1973).

or society" and, thus, enjoy a certain degree of autonomy.[37] The state was conceptualized as an actor in its own right pursuing its own goals in the absence of and even against strong societal forces. First, "*statists*" claimed that the domestic power of states over society stemmed largely from the need to preserve the survival of the nation in an anarchic international system. They emphasized the coercive rather than the distributive role of the state in its relation to society. The emergence of modern nation-states was not so much the result of original social contracts but of internal coercion and extraction of resources as well as external war-fighting against rivals. "Statists" also maintained that state actors have considerably more leeway from societal constraints in the foreign policy arena than in other issue-areas.[38]

Second, *structural Marxism*, in particular the theory of late capitalism, also ascribed a certain degree of autonomy to the state. It was no longer conceptualized as the agent of the ruling class, but as primarily concerned with the long-term maintenance of the capitalist order, including its political and cultural components.[39]

The attempts to do away with the state in the earlier debate and to bring it "back in" during the more recent discussion, share two theoretical problems. First, they do not differentiate between agents and structures. The "statist" as well as the structural Marxist state is sometimes treated like an individual actor maximizing expected utilities, in particular power and wealth. The extreme pluralist view of the state as well as the instrumental Marxist conceptualization avoid talking about structures of authoritative decision-making altogether. But, states do not act, governments do. "The state, as structure, constitutes and shapes the interests and powers of the government, as agent,

---

[37] Theda Skocpol, "Bringing the State Back In: Strategies of Analysis in Current Research," in Peter B. Evans, Dietrich Rueschemeyer, and Theda Skocpol, eds., *Bringing the State Back In* (Cambridge: Cambridge University Press, 1985), pp. 3–37, 9.

[38] See, for example, Evans *et al.*, eds., *Bringing the State Back In*; Stephen Krasner, *Defending the National Interest: Raw Materials Investment and US Foreign Policy* (Princeton, NJ: Princeton University Press, 1978); Eric A. Nordlinger, *On the Autonomy of the Democratic State* (Cambridge: Cambridge University Press, 1981); Theda Skocpol, *States and Social Revolutions* (Cambridge: Cambridge University Press, 1979); Charles Tilly, *The Formation of National States in Europe* (Princeton, NJ: Princeton University Press, 1975). For a critical discussion see Michael Banks and Martin Shaw, eds., *State and Society in International Relations* (New York: Harvester, Wheatsheaf, 1991).

[39] See, for example, Paul Cammack, "Review Article: Bringing the State Back In?," *British Journal of Political Science*, 19 (1989), pp. 261–90; Bob Jessop, *The Capitalist State: Marxist Theories and Methods* (New York: New York University Press, 1982); Claus Offe, *Strukturprobleme des kapitalistischen Staates* (Frankfurt/M.: Suhrkamp, 1972); Nicos Poulantzas, *Political Power and Social Classes* (London: New Left Books, 1973).

while the state only exists insofar as it is instantiated and reproduced by the practices of governmental and other agents that are embedded in the structure of governance and rule in society."[40] The state as a structure of authority encompassing political institutions, organizational routines, legal procedures, and norms prescribing appropriate behavior, should be distinguished from governments and governmental actors taking decisions, negotiating treaties, and interacting with society and other governments (see also Krasner's chapter in this volume).

Second, the debate on "state autonomy" sometimes treated states as if they were identical across time and space. But, the American, French, Japanese, Brazilian, Kenyan, or Russian states are quite different from each other. "State autonomy" depends internationally on the state's position in the distribution of power and its embeddedness in international regimes and organizations. Domestically, "state autonomy" is a function of variation in domestic structures, in particular state–society relations, and in socio-economic development.[41]

Domestic structure approaches allow differentiation between various degrees of state strength and autonomy *vis-à-vis* society and go beyond the generalities of "statist" versus "pluralist" approaches to the state. Originally developed in the field of comparative foreign economic policy, they have generated empirical research across issue-areas to explain variations in state responses to similar international pressures, constraints, and opportunities.[42] Domestic structure

---

[40] Raymond Duvall and Alexander Wendt, "The International Capital Regime and the Internationalization of the State," unpublished manuscript, University of Minnesota/ Yale University, June 1987, pp. 49/50. On the "agent-structure" debate see Alexander Wendt, "The Agent-Structure Problem in International Relations Theory," *International Organization*, 41, 3 (Summer 1987), pp. 335–70.

[41] On the international and domestic dimensions of state autonomy see particularly G. John Ikenberry, *Reasons of State: Oil Politics and the Capacities of American Government* (Ithaca, NY: Cornell University Press, 1988).

[42] See, for example, Peter Katzenstein, "International Relations and Domestic Structures: Foreign Economic Policies of Advanced Industrial States," *International Organization*, 30, 1 (Winter 1976); Peter Katzenstein, ed., *Between Power and Plenty* (Madison, WI: University of Wisconsin Press, 1978); Peter Katzenstein, *Small States in World Markets* (Ithaca, NY: Cornell University Press, 1984); Peter Gourevitch, *Politics in Hard Times* (Ithaca, NY: Cornell University Press, 1986). See also Michael Barnett, "High Politics is Low Politics. The Domestic and Systemic Sources of Israeli Security Policy, 1967–1977," *World Politics*, 42, 4 (1990), pp. 529–62; Matthew Evangelista, *Arms and Innovation* (Ithaca, NY: Cornell University Press, 1988); Matthew Evangelista, "Domestic Structure and International Change," in Michael Doyle and G. John Ikenberry, eds., *New Thinking in International Relations* (forthcoming); Ikenberry, *Reasons of State;* G. John Ikenberry, David A. Lake, Michael Mastanduno *et al.*, eds., *The State and American Foreign Economic Policy* (Ithaca, NY: Cornell University Press, 1988); G. John

approaches should be well suited to account for the variation in the impact of transnational actors on state policies.

The concept of domestic structures

The notion of domestic structures refers to the political institutions of the state, to societal structures, and to the policy networks linking the two. Domestic structures encompass the organizational apparatus of political and societal institutions, their routines, the decision-making rules and procedures incorporated in law and custom, as well as the values and norms embedded in the political culture.

The concept, as used here, goes beyond earlier definitions in, for example, Katzenstein's *Between Power and Plenty*. These conceptualizations concentrated on organizational features of state and society, especially on the degree of their centralization. This led to the rather simplistic distinction between "weak" and "strong" states.[43] State strength was sometimes defined in terms of state capacity to extract resources from society or to achieve goals in the international environment. Such a conceptualization confuses structures and outcomes, leading to tautological propositions. The debate on the strength of the American state suffered from this confusion. It was argued that the US state is more autonomous from society in national security affairs than in economic questions, because government officials were able to overcome Congressional opposition in various defense-related questions.[44] But to infer institutional strength from individual policies obscures the problem that we need measurements of institutional strength independently of policy outcomes. The notion of "domestic structures" as used in this volume refers strictly to institutional features of the state, of society, and of state–society relations established separately from specific policies.

The second major difference from earlier conceptualizations of the domestic structure concept concerns the incorporation of political culture. Insights from the "new institutionalism" are included, in

Ikenberry, "Conclusion: An Institutional Approach to American Foreign Economic Policy," ibid., pp. 219–43; Thomas Risse-Kappen, "Public Opinion, Domestic Structure, and Foreign Policy in Liberal Democracies," *World Politics*, 43, 4 (July 1991), pp. 479–512.

43 See Katzenstein, "International Relations and Domestic Structures;" Krasner, *Defending the National Interest*; Mastundano et al., "Toward a Realist Theory of State Action."

44 Cf. Ikenberry et al., *State and American Foreign Economic Policy*, particularly the essay by Michael Mastundano, "Trade as a Strategic Weapon: American and Alliance Export Control Policy in the Early Postwar Period," ibid., pp. 121–50.

particular the emphasis on communicative action, duties, social obligations, and norms of appropriate behavior.[45] To incorporate values and norms and, thus, informal understandings and rules into a concept emphasizing "structure" only seems odd if one has a rather mechanical understanding of domestic structure. But political culture includes the collective self-understandings of actors in a given society that are stable over time. It defines their collective identity as a nation and, thus, provides them with a repertoire of interpretations of reality as well as of appropriate behavior.

As a result, the normative structure of state–society relations is not fully captured if one only focuses on organizational and legal characteristics of political and social institutions. For example, the Japanese decision-making norm of "reciprocal consent," the German understanding of "social partnership," and the American notion of "liberal pluralism" are only partly embodied in explicit regulations, but constitute nevertheless powerful cultural norms which define appropriateness with regard to the way decisions should be made in the political system.

Three tiers of domestic structures can be distinguished.[46] First, the structure of the *political institutions* – the state – can be analyzed in terms of its centralization or fragmentation. To what extent is executive power concentrated in the hands of small groups of decision-makers? To what degree is bureaucratic infighting considered as normal and expected behavior (US) or as inappropriate (Japan)? How do institutional features which regulate the relationship between the executive and the legislative constrain the national government's ability to control the parliamentary process (parliamentary democracies versus presidential systems)? How far does the domestic authority of the national government reach into the administration of regions

---

[45] See, for example, DiMaggio and Powell, *The New Institutionalism in Organizational Analysis*; James G. March and Johan P. Olsen, *Rediscovering Institutions. The Organizational Basis of Politics* (New York: The Free Press, 1989); Ikenberry, "Conclusion: An Institutional Approach"; Friedrich Kratochwil, *Rules, Norms, and Decisions* (Cambridge: Cambridge University Press, 1989); Sven Steinmo, Kathleen Thelen, and Frank Longstreth, eds., *Structuring Politics. Historical Institutionalism in Comparative Analysis* (Cambridge: Cambridge University Press, 1992); Thomas *et al.*, *Institutional Structure*.

[46] The following builds upon and modifies Risse-Kappen, "Public Opinion, Domestic Structures, and Foreign Policy," p. 486. See also Katzenstein, "Introduction" and "Conclusion," in *Between Power and Plenty*; Evangelista, "Domestic Structure and International Change"; Gourevitch, *Politics in Hard Times*; Ikenberry, "Conclusion: An Institutional Approach."

and local communities (central or federal structures)? Does the political culture emphasize the state as a "benign" institution taking care of its citizens (France) or rather as a threat to individual liberties (US)? "Centralized states" would then be characterized by political institutions and cultures which concentrate executive power at the top of the political system, in which national governments enjoy considerable independence from legislatures (if they exist at all), and which emphasize the state as caretaker of the needs of the citizens.

Second, the *structure of demand-formation in civil society* can be examined with regard to the internal polarization in terms of ideological and/or class cleavages. Do political attitudes and beliefs about social and political life correlate with religious, ideological, or class cleavages, and how far are these beliefs apart from each other? To what extent can societal demands be mobilized for political causes, and how centralized is the structure of interest groups, societal coalitions, and social organizations? "Strong societies" are then characterized by a comparative lack of ideological and class cleavages, by rather "politicized" civil societies which can be easily mobilized for political causes, and by centralized social organizations such as business, labor, or churches.

Third, the institutions of the *policy networks* linking state and society and the norms regulating the coalition-building processes in these networks have to be investigated. To what degree do intermediate organizations such as political parties aggregate societal demands and channel them into the political process? Does the political culture emphasize consensual decision-making or rather distributive bargaining and dissent in the policy networks? Consensual polities would then be characterized by strong intermediate organizations operating in a compromise-oriented decision-making culture, while polarized polities would emphasize distributive bargaining, often leading to decision blockades.

These three components of domestic structures form a three-dimensional space with the axes defined as

1   the *state structure* (centralization versus fragmentation);
2   the *societal structure* (weak versus strong);
3   the *policy networks* (consensual versus polarized).

This framework should allow one to locate the domestic structures of specific countries. To reduce complexity, each of the three components of domestic structures can be dichotomized, as a result of

Table 1.1 *Types of domestic structures and countries investigated in this study*

		Society			
		Strong		Weak	
		Policy networks		*Policy networks*	
		Consensual	Polarized	Consensual	Polarized
Political institutions	Centralized	Corporatist (Japan)	Stalemate (India; pre-1989 Hungary)	State-dominated (Singapore; South Korea; Zimbabwe)	State-controlled (USSR; East Germany; Romania)
	Fragmented	Society-dominated (Hong Kong, Philippines, USA)		Fragile (Kenya; Russia)	

which six distinct types of domestic structures emerge (see table 1.1).[47] These ideal types are then linked to specific propositions on the policy impact of transnational coalitions and actors (see below, pp. 25–8).

State-controlled domestic structures encompass highly centralized political institutions with strong executive governments and a rather weak level of societal organization. In the absence of strong intermediate organizations in the policy networks and/or a consensus-oriented political culture, civil society is too weak to balance the power of the state. Many of the former Communist systems with centrally planned economies and various authoritarian Third World states (less developed countries – LDCs) seem to fit the description. The countries represented in this volume which seem to match the state-controlled structure, are the former USSR, the former East Germany, and – as an extreme example – Communist Romania (chapters by Clark and Chan, Evangelista, and Chilton).

State-dominated domestic structures can be distinguished from the

---

[47] In the case of a fragmented state faced with either strong or weak societies, the nature of the policy network seems to matter less. I have, therefore, summarized these types into one category each. I am fully aware of the fact that the following is simplistic and that the empirical reality of specific countries is more complex than suggested.

state-controlled category because of the different nature of the policy networks. There are stronger intermediate organizations channeling societal demands into the political system and/or more consensus-oriented decision-making norms. The political culture of such systems often emphasizes the state as caretaker of the needs of its citizens. In other words, the political culture and/or intermediate organizations counterbalance the power of the state as compared to the state-controlled case. Countries in this volume which seem to approximate to this type are Singapore, South Korea, and Zimbabwe (chapters by Clark and Chan, and Princen).

"Stalemate" domestic structures are characterized by comparatively strong states facing strong social organizations in a highly polarized polity and a political culture emphasizing distributional bargaining. Social and political conflicts among the major players are unlikely to be resolved in this type of system; decision blockades are expected to occur frequently. Among the countries investigated in this volume, India and pre-1989 Hungary appear to resemble this domestic structure (chapters by Clark and Chan, and Chilton).

Corporatist domestic structures are likely in cases in which powerful intermediate organizations such as political parties operate in a consensus-oriented political culture resulting in continuous bargaining processes geared toward political compromises.[48] The domestic structures of many of the smaller European states come close to this model. Among the countries investigated in this volume, Japan seems to fit the description to some degree (chapter by Katzenstein and Tsujinaka).

Society-dominated domestic structures are to be expected in countries with comparatively strong social interest pressure, but decentralized and fragmented political institutions. Among the countries investigated in this volume, the US and – to some degree – Hong Kong seem to represent this category (chapters by Katzenstein and Tsujinaka, and Clark and Chan). The Philippines appear to represent a case of an even more fragmented state faced with strong social interest pressure in an extremely polarized political culture (chapter by Clark and Chan).

Finally, *"fragile"* domestic structures combine fragmented state institutions, a low degree of societal mobilization, and weak social organizations. Many African states seem to resemble this type including

---

[48] This description is broader than the original concept of "corporatism." See, for example, Philippe Schmitter and Gerhard Lehmbruch, eds., *Trends Towards Corporatist Intermediation* (London: Sage, 1979); Peter Katzenstein, *Corporatism and Change* (Ithaca, NY: Cornell University Press, 1984).

Kenya (chapter by Princen). The same appears to hold true for post-Soviet Russia (chapter by Evangelista).

Transnational relations and domestic structures

The main proposition investigated in this volume claims that, under similar international conditions, *differences in domestic structures determine the variation in the policy impact of transnational actors.* Domestic structures mediate, filter, and refract the efforts by transnational actors and alliances to influence policies in the various issue-areas. In order to affect policies, transnational actors have to overcome two hurdles. First, they have to gain access to the political system of their "target state." Second, they must generate and/or contribute to "winning" policy coalitions in order to change decisions in the desired direction. Their ability to influence policy changes then depends on the domestic coalition-building processes in the policy networks and on the degree to which stable coalitions form sharing the transnational actors' causes. Domestic structures are likely to determine both the availability of access points into the political systems and the size of and requirements for "winning coalitions."

The extent to which transnational actors gain *access* to the political systems seems to be primarily a function of the state structure. National governments ultimately determine whether foreign societal actors are allowed to enter the country and to pursue their goals in conjunction with national actors. Governments have considerable leeway to enable or constrain transnational activities (Krasner's chapter). They distribute visas, issue export licenses, and guarantee property rights.[49] The capacity of governments to prohibit transnational activities is itself a function of the state structure. The assumption advanced here is rather straightforward. The more centralized the political system, the less access points should transnational actors have to penetrate the institutions of the "target state." In other words, access should be most difficult in state-controlled domestic structures, while it is expected to be easiest in countries with "weak" political institutions. In countries with state-controlled domestic structures,

---

[49] The centrality of governments in allowing or prohibiting transnational interactions was one of the reasons why the "state-centered" paradigm prevailed in the earlier debate. Again, framing the issue in such a way misses the mark. First, the capacity of governments to control transnational activities is itself a function of domestic structures. Second, even if governments are crucial in enabling transnational activities, the effects of these activities can still be significant.

governments should have the most leeway to restrict transnational access. Examples include the enormous difficulties which Western peace and human rights groups encountered in establishing contact with dissident movements in Communist Eastern Europe (Chilton's chapter). The more fragmented the state structure, however, the less capable should national governments be to prevent transnational activities. In the case of society-dominated domestic structures, trans-national actors and coalitions should have no trouble in penetrating the societal and political systems, since they provide multiple channels to influence policies. In some extreme cases of Third World countries, even the issuing of visas seems to be irrelevant with regard to trans-national activities.

But easy access does not guarantee policy impact. As stated above, the ultimate success of transnational actors to induce policy change depends on their ability to form "winning coalitions" in the target country the size of which is again a function of domestic structures. While the first hurdle – access – can only be influenced in a very limited way by conscious strategies of the transnational coalitions, the second hurdle – building "winning coalitions" – depends to a large degree on their ability to adjust to the domestic structure of the "target country."[50] "Clever" transnational actors adapt to the domestic struc-ture to achieve their goals; a prime example discussed in this volume is the success of Japanese lobbying in the US (chapter by Katzenstein and Tsujinaka). Some transnational coalitions, however, adopt strategies which might be suitable in the domestic structures of their home countries without acknowledging the differences encountered in the "target state." A good example is the ivory trade ban promoted by "public opinion" INGOs which proved counterproductive in a country like Zimbabwe with a self-sustaining conservation policy to preserve the elephant (Princen's chapter).

If we assume that transnational actors normally tend to adjust their policy strategies to the specific situation of the target country, some domestic structures should make their task easier than others. First, while *state-controlled or state-dominated domestic structures* (see table 1.1) make it difficult for transnational actors to overcome the initial hurdle of gaining access, their policy impact might be profound, once this barrier is mastered. If powerful state actors are pre-disposed toward their goals, they can directly influence policies (chapters by Clark and

---

50 I owe this point to Robert Keohane. See also the chapter by Krasner.

Chan, and Evangelista). Alternatively, transnational contacts might serve to empower and legitimize the demands of otherwise weak social groups (Chilton's chapter).

In domestic structures characterized by *stalemate*, access of transnational actors might be a little easier than in the state-dominated case. However, one would expect the policy impact to be rather limited, given the structural disfunctionality of the societal and political institutions to produce policy changes. If change occurs, it is to be expected to come primarily from within the domestic polity, altering the domestic structure during the process (see particularly Chilton's chapter).

This is very different from what is to be expected in consensus-oriented *corporatist structures*. If transnational actors succeed in penetrating the powerful societal and political organizations in such countries, their policy impact can be as significant as in the state-dominated case. Given the slow and compromise-oriented decision-making processes in such systems, one would expect that transnational actors achieve their goals in a more incremental way than in the case of state-dominated systems. Since corporatist structures tend to institutionalize social and political compromises, the policy impact of transnational actors could last for a long time (chapter by Katzenstein and Tsujinaka).

Concerning the cases represented in the bottom row of table 1.1, governments are likely to have less control over the access of transnational actors into the societal and political institutions. But it is less clear whether easy access guarantees policy impact. Given the fragmented nature of the political institutions, the requirements for putting together "winning coalitions" are likely to demand much greater efforts by the transnational actors. Particularly in countries with a high degree of political mobilization and strong social organizations, there is always the possibility that transnational activities provoke countervailing coalitions which have to be dealt with. Policy impact requires quite elaborate efforts by transnational actors in coalition-building and nurturing different players in the political system. Moreover, the effect on policies might not last very long, given the fragmented structure of the state which prevents the institutionalization of domestic consensus. The chapters by Katzenstein and Tsujinaka, and Clark and Chan explore these assumptions with regard to the US and the Philippines.

Finally, in the case of *"fragile"* domestic structures, there is not much that transnational actors can do to achieve their goals, even though

Table 1.2 *Propositions about the policy impact of transnational actors as mediated by domestic structures*

Domestic structure	Access to domestic institutions	Policy impact in case of access
State-controlled	Most difficult	Profound if coalition with state actors predisposed toward TNA goals or empowerment of social actors
State-dominated	Difficult	Ditto
Stalemate	Less difficult	Impact unlikely
Corporatist	Less easy	Incremental but long-lasting if coalition with powerful societal and/or political organizations
Society-dominated	Easy	Difficult coalition-building with powerful societal organizations
Fragile	Easiest	Impact unlikely

they should have no trouble in penetrating the political institutions. Coalition-building with societal actors is next to impossible and bound to fail given their organizational weakness. Aligning with governmental actors does not help, either, given the fragmented nature of the state. Even if transnational actors do achieve their goals in changing policies, the state is expected to be too weak to implement decisions. Thomas Princen looks at this proposition with regard to Kenya and the ivory ban, while Matthew Evangelista explores it concerning post-Soviet Russia.

Table 1.2 summarizes how the ideal-types of domestic structures are expected to mediate the policy impact of transnational coalitions and actors.

International institutions and transnational actors

So far, the argument has exclusively focused on domestic structures. But state autonomy and state control over outcomes is not just a function of domestic structures, but also of the state's position in the international distribution of power. It is obvious that transnational coalitions which manage to influence great powers in a major international policy area have accomplished more than those who successfully affect the policies of a small state. This point is straightforward and reconcilable with the theoretical framework sketched out above.

It could be argued, though, that foreign policy changes can be explained as state responses to the conditions and constraints of the international environment. If so, transnational actors become epiphenomenal. But the structure of the international system does not simply determine state policies. Not even hard-headed structural realists claim that the foreign policy of states is solely a function of the international distribution of power.[51] If governments do have choices to respond to international pressures and opportunities, there is no a priori reason for excluding transnational actors from the consideration of agents who might influence such decisions.

But international structures do not just consist of power hierarchies. International relations are regulated by institutions defined as "persistent and connected sets of rules (formal and informal) that prescribe behavioral roles, constrain activity, and shape expectations."[52] After more than ten years of empirical research, regime analysis has established that international institutions have substantial effects on government practices, both on policies and definitions of interests and preferences. State autonomy and governmental control over policies are affected by the degree of the state's embeddedness in international structures of governance. While differences in domestic structures affect state autonomy "from below," variations in international institutions should equally influence state capacities "from above," since both represent structures of governance.

If we assume that domestic structures mediate the policy impact of transnational coalitions, we can equally suppose that international structures of governance should filter such policy influence in a similar

---

51 Cf. Kenneth Waltz, "Anarchic Orders and Balances of Power," in Robert O. Keohane, ed., *Neorealism and Its Critics* (New York: Columbia University Press, 1986), pp. 98–130, 122: "Balance-of-power theory is a theory about the results produced by the uncoordinated actions of states . . . What it does explain are the constraints that confine all states. The clear perception of constraints provides many clues to the expected reactions, but by itself the theory cannot explain those reactions." For a discussion see Robert Keohane, "Theory of World Politics: Structural Realism and Beyond," ibid., pp. 158–203.

52 Keohane, *International Institutions and State Power*, p. 3. See also Ernst-Otto Czempiel and James N. Rosenau, eds., *Governance Without Government: Order and Change in World Politics* (Cambridge: Cambridge University Press, 1992); Krasner, *International Regimes*; Kratochwil, *Rules, Norms, and Decisions*; Harald Müller, *Die Chance der Kooperation* (Darmstadt: Wissenschaftliche Buchgesellschaft, 1993); Rittberger, *Regime Theory and International Relations*; Young, *International Cooperation*.

fashion.[53] It should make a difference whether transnational coalitions act in a heavily institutionalized environment such as the EU (Cameron's chapter) or in a milieu unregulated by international agreements (chapter by Clark and Chan). In the latter case, the variation in domestic structures should account for the difference in policy impact almost exclusively. In the former case, things should become more complicated.

The more regulated the inter-state relationship by cooperative international institutions in the particular issue-area, the more are transnational activities expected to flourish and the less should national governments be able to constrain them. Examples include, again, the EU (Cameron's chapter), the transatlantic relationship,[54] and the American–Japanese security relationship (chapter by Katzenstein and Tsujinaka). The relationship does not have to be governed by formal institutions such as regimes and organizations. In the case of the Anglo-American "special relationship," for example, informal norms and tacit rules enable transnational activities to an extent unsurpassed by almost any other bilateral relationship. In the case of hostile inter-state relationships, however, which are less regulated by cooperative regimes and institutions, governments are expected to put strong controls on transnational activities (from visas to export controls).

The emergence of trans*governmental* coalitions seems to be almost entirely a function of highly cooperative and institutionalized inter-state relationships. Transgovernmental network-building involves behavior of bureaucratic actors which could be regarded as disloyal by their home governments. In the framework of international regimes and institutions, however, such practices become more legitimized,

---

[53] Note that this volume – except for Cameron's chapter – does not investigate how transnational actors affect international institution-building and/or state compliance with international regimes. This would be an entirely different project following the line of reasoning developed by Keohane and Nye (in *Power and Interdependence*) that states form international regimes to cope with the effects of transnational interdependence. This volume, however, treats international institutions as intervening variables between transnational activities and state policies in an analogous way as domestic structures. For studies investigating how specific transnational actors affect international regimes see, for example, Alison Brysk, "Social Movements, the International System, and Human Rights in Argentina," *Comparative Political Studies*, 26, 3 (1993), pp. 259–85; Brysk, "Lost in the Palace of Nations? Latin American Indian Rights Movements at the United Nations," paper presented to the Workshop on International Institutions and Transnational Social Movement Organizations, University of Notre Dame, April 21–23, 1994; Finnemore, "Restraining State Violence"; Peter Haas, *Knowledge, Power, and International Policy Coordination*; Klotz, *Protesting Prejudice*; Nadelmann, "Global Prohibition Regimes."

[54] See Risse-Kappen, *Cooperation Among Democracies*.

since most regimes and international organizations include frequent meetings and inter-governmental forums which permit transgovernmental activities. Such informal networks can then generate the high-quality information which international institutions provide for the participants.[55]

International institutions are then expected to facilitate the *access* of transnational actors to the national policy-making processes. International regimes and organizations are likely to increase the availability of channels which transnational actors can use to target national governments in order to influence policies. INGOs and transgovernmental networks lobbying governments can do so more easily in the framework of international institutions. To a certain degree, international regimes and organizations are likely to reduce the differences in filtering effects of the various types of domestic structures. Even countries with state-dominated domestic structures such as France are probably unable to cut themselves off from demands of transnational actors when dealing with international institutions. International regimes and organizations would then provide channels into the national political systems which domestic structures might otherwise limit.

But access does not guarantee influence. How do international institutions affect the policy impact of transnational actors on state policies, particularly the requirements for "winning coalitions?" Unfortunately, the interaction between international norms and institutions, on the one hand, and domestic politics, on the other, is not yet fully understood; work in this area has just begun.[56] Harald Müller has shown in an analysis of security regimes how international regime norms change the parameters of the domestic discourses in the respective issue-area. Concerning nuclear non-proliferation, for example, there is no longer a serious debate about whether proliferation should be allowed or not. Rather, the discourse shifts to the question whether specific practices are in compliance with the regime forcing opponents to make their cause within the framework of the institutional rules. Regime norms tend to strengthen those domestic coalitions advocating compliance.

Following this line of reasoning, one can then assume that inter-

---

[55] See Robert Keohane, "The Demand for International Regimes," in Krasner, ed., *International Regimes*, pp. 141–71, 162–66.
[56] See, for example, Zürn, "Bringing the Second Image (Back) In." For the following see Müller, "The Internalization of Principles, Norms, and Rules by Governments."

national institutions have two effects on the policy impact of transnational actors. First, the demands of transnational coalitions for changes in national policies may be legitimized and strengthened by the respective regime norms, in which case such alliances would work as "transnational moral entrepreneurs."[57] When the domestic discourse is framed by the norms of the international regime, it should be easier for compliance-promoting transnational actors to find domestic coalition partners. Transnational actors opposing the respective norms and rules, however, are expected to be at a disadvantage in their attempts to form "winning" domestic coalitions.

Second, as argued above, cooperative and highly institutionalized inter-state relations tend to lower state boundaries thereby allowing for flourishing transnational relations. At the same time, these institutions also legitimize transnational activities in the "target state"; actors are less and less treated as "foreigners," but as almost indistinguishable from other domestic players. The collective identity of a pluralistic security community such as the transatlantic alliance enables transnational actors to influence policy decisions directly.[58] Such effects should also lower the requirements for building domestic "winning coalitions."

In sum, the degree to which the inter-state relationship in the respective issue-area is regulated by cooperative international institutions should have two effects on the ability of transnational actors to influence policies. First, international institutions are likely to facilitate access to the national political processes and, in particular, to enable the emergence of transgovernmental networks. Second, international institutions in the respective issue-area are expected to reduce the coalition-building requirements for transnational coalitions, particularly those advocating norm compliance.

Conclusion

A renewed attempt at theorizing about transnational relations requires, first, to specify the concept more clearly than the earlier debate did, and, second, to differentiate the international and dom-

---

[57] See Nadelmann, "Global Prohibition Regimes."

[58] For details see Risse-Kappen, *Cooperation among Democracies*. On pluralistic security communities see Karl W. Deutsch, *et al.*, *Political Community and the North Atlantic Area* (Princeton, NJ: Princeton University Press, 1957). See also David Cameron's chapter on transnational and transgovernmental actors within the European Community.

estic conditions under which transnational coalitions and actors are able to influence state policies. The major proposition put forward in this volume is that variation in domestic structures accounts for differences in the policy impact of transnational coalitions and actors. Moreover, the more cooperative international institutions regulate the inter-state relationship in the particular issue-area, the more channels should transnational coalitions have available to penetrate the political systems and the more should they be able to use international norms to legitimate their demands. Structures of governance – both domestic and international – interact in determining the policy impact of transnational actors.

Reviving the subject of transnational relations and linking it systematically to the concepts of domestic structures and international institutions does not re-invent the wheel in international relations theory. This volume does not develop a new theoretical approach but tries to promote theoretical and empirical progress by integrating various theories which have been developed separately from each other, and by evaluating the resulting propositions through a set of comparative case studies. The attempt to combine the literature on domestic structures with that on international institutions promises fresh insights with regard to the subject of transnational relations. As a result, it is likely to overcome the shortcomings of the earlier debate.

Case studies

2 Transnational relations and the development of European economic and monetary union

David R. Cameron

On February 7, 1992, in the Dutch city of Maastricht, the foreign and finance ministers of the twelve member states of the European Community signed the Treaty on European Union.[1] The most ambitious effort ever undertaken in the Community to create new supranational institutions, and to transfer authority from the member states to those institutions, the Treaty committed the member states, among other things, to moving to full Economic and Monetary Union (EMU) by 1999 at the latest.[2] By that date, if not before, some, if not all, of the members will move to the third and final stage of EMU, and the exchange rates between their currencies will be irrevocably locked, a single currency instituted, and a single central bank created that is charged with conducting monetary policy among the participating states.[3]

Those who study policymaking and politics within the European Community (EC) – since November 1993, Union – typically conceive of them as the product, in varying degrees, of two forces – *intergovern-*

[1] The Treaty had been approved by the European Council, the recurring summit conference of heads of state and government of EC member states, at its meeting in Maastricht in December 1991.

[2] Two states negotiated "opt-outs" from the third and final stage of EMU. Britain negotiated an "opt-out" Protocol in the Treaty that allowed it to reserve for a future Parliament the right to decide whether to participate in stage three. At the Edinburgh meeting of the European Council in December 1992, Denmark was exempted from moving to stage three (as well as from certain other provisions of the Treaty) as a condition for calling a second referendum to approve the Treaty. (The first, on June 2, 1992, had produced a defeat; the second, on May 18, 1993, approved the Treaty.)

[3] The first stage of EMU had begun on July 1, 1990. The Treaty stipulated that the second stage would begin on January 1, 1994, and during that stage the member states would pursue fiscal and monetary targets – the so-called "convergence criteria" pertaining to the rate of inflation, the magnitude of the public deficit and debt, interest rates, and exchange rates – that must be satisfied as a condition for moving to the third and final stage.

mentalism and *supranationalism.*[4] Some accord primacy to the member states and view the policy choices of the Community as manifestations of the continuing domination of the states, acting to achieve their national interests through such institutions as the Council of Ministers and the European Council. From that perspective, Community politics and policy-making largely consist of the formation of coalitions and alliances among states, and the attainment and defeat of the interests and preferences of the states. In contrast, others accord primacy to the supranational institutions and actors within the Community, such as the Commission and the Court of Justice, and perceive its politics and policymaking as manifestations of the influence of those institutions and actors.

The development of the EMU initiative in the late 1980s and early 1990s suggests that the dichotomization between intergovernmentalism and supranationalism oversimplifies reality. That development – especially in its most formative period, from 1988 through 1990 – demonstrates the presence and importance of a *third* distinctive type of politics – one that involves *transnational* actors, institutions, and politics.[5] Relative to the attention given the other types, transnational politics have been neglected in the study of the EC.[6] Yet if Keohane and Nye are correct that "the nearer a situation is to complex interdependence, the more we expect the outcomes of political bargaining to be affected by transnational relations,"[7] the impact of such relations should be evident in abundance in the EC, for it is hard to think of a group of states more "complexly interdependent" than that consisting of the member states of the Community. Their high degree of inter-

---

[4] On this point, see the discussion in David R. Cameron, "The 1992 Initiative: Causes and Consequences," in Alberta M. Sbragia, ed., *Euro-politics: Institutions and Policymaking in the "New" European Community* (Washington, DC: The Brookings Institution, 1992).

[5] On transnational relations, see Robert O. Keohane and Joseph S. Nye, Jr., eds., *Transnational Relations and World Politics* (Cambridge, MA: Harvard University Press, 1971). The editors extend their analysis of transnational relations in Robert O. Keohane and Joseph S. Nye, Jr., *Power and Interdependence: World Politics in Transition* (Boston: Little, Brown, and Co., 1977). See also James N. Rosenau, *The Study of Global Interdependence: Essays on the Transnationalization of World Affairs* (London: Frances Pinter, 1980). For more recent analyses, see Ernst-Otto Czempiel and James N. Rosenau, eds., *Global Changes and Theoretical Challenges: Approaches to World Politics for the 1990s* (Lexington, MA: Lexington Books, 1989); and Thomas Risse-Kappen, "Ideas Do Not Float Freely: Transnational Coalitions, Domestic Structures, and the End of the Cold War," *International Organization* 48 (Spring 1994), pp. 185–214.

[6] For an exception, see Wayne Sandholtz and John Zysman, "1992: Recasting the European Bargain," *World Politics*, 42 (October 1989), pp. 95–128.

[7] Keohane and Nye, *Power and Interdependence*, p. 34.

dependence – exemplified by the high and increasing trade dependence among them, the dense network of institutions that have developed over the past forty years, and the complicated intertwining of national and supranational policy-making – could be expected to have facilitated and encouraged the appearance and even proliferation of transnational relations among actors within the Community, and it would not be surprising if such actors were involved and influential in the development of an initiative as consequential as EMU.

This chapter examines how and why transnational actors influenced the development of the EMU initiative, especially in its formative period, prior to the start of the Intergovernmental Conference in late 1990. In so doing, we shall consider certain institutional features of the Community that enhanced the role of transnational actors in the domain of economic and monetary policy. We shall also consider why transnational actors located in certain countries were more influential than those located in other countries. That will lead us, in turn, to consider how the institutional context of domestic politics within member states affects the bargaining power and influence of such actors.

The idea of EMU

EMU is an old idea in the EC. It first appeared in January 1968, when Pierre Werner, the prime minister and minister of finance of Luxemburg, proposed that the six member states of the Community irrevocably lock the exchange rates among their currencies and create a European Fund that could intervene in exchange markets in order to maintain the locked rates. Formulated in anticipation of the removal of the last remaining internal tariffs within the European Economic Community in July, as well as the inauguration of the Common Agricultural Policy, under which producers would be paid identical prices, Werner's proposals provoked several memoranda to the Council of Ministers from Raymond Barre, the Vice President of the Commission in charge of monetary affairs. Barre did not fully endorse Werner's proposals; nevertheless, he did call for elimination of margins of fluctuation between currencies, institution of multilateral negotiation of currency realignments, a fund and mechanism for joint invention in currency markets, and a joint exchange rate *vis-à-vis* non-EC currencies.[8]

[8] For discussions of these early proposals, see D. C. Kruse, *Monetary Integration in Western Europe: EMU, EMS and Beyond* (London: Butterworth, 1980); Giovanni Magni-

In July 1969, the Council approved Barre's recommendation that some form of joint consultative and decision-making mechanism be established in the domains of monetary and exchange rate policy, including a facility to support joint interventions in currency markets. At their summit meeting in The Hague in December of that year, the six national leaders endorsed the concept of EMU and recommended that the Council accept Barre's proposal that the Community move to EMU in three stages – stage one in January 1971, stage two in January 1974, and the third and final stage by December 1980. The Council approved the plan in March 1970 and established a working group, chaired by Werner, to specify the details.

The Werner Committee reported in October 1970.[9] Representing something of a compromise between the views of the German and Dutch governments, which emphasized the need for economic policies to be coordinated and harmonized prior to the creation of Community-wide monetary institutions, and those of France, Italy, and Belgium, which gave priority to the immediate establishment of supranational monetary institutions and rapid movement toward monetary union, the Committee proposed a sequence that meshed the two objectives, although it adopted, in essence, the German and Dutch position. During the first stage (the only one it described in detail), the fiscal and monetary policies of the member states would be coordinated and harmonized, regulatory restrictions in financial markets eliminated, and the range of fluctuation among exchange rates narrowed. Only in the later stages would the new monetary institutions come into being.

At its meeting in February 1971, the Council of Ministers accepted the Werner Committee's Report and its program for EMU, and the Community embarked on stage one. However, its ambition to achieve EMU by 1980 was not, of course, realized; it foundered in the wake of the collapse of the Bretton Woods exchange rate regime in 1971–73 and the inflationary effects of the Yom Kippur War-induced increase in oil

fico, *European Monetary Integration* (New York: John Wiley, 1973); and Loukas Tsoukalis, *The Politics and Economics of European Economic Integration* (London: George Allen & Unwin, 1977).

[9] See *Report to the Council and the Commission on the Realization by Stages of Economic and Monetary Union in the Community* (Brussels: EEC, 1970). Werner's committee included the chair of the Monetary Committee (which consists of the deputy governors of the central banks and the most senior deputies of the finance ministries of the member states), the chair of the Committee of Central Bank Governors, and other economic and financial officials of the Commission.

prices soon thereafter.[10] Confronting greater volatility among exchange rates after the International Monetary Fund's December 1971, decision to widen the fluctuation range of currencies against the dollar from ± 1 percent to ± 4.5 percent, in April 1972, the leaders of the Community introduced a mechanism – the "snake" – to limit the magnitude of the fluctuations in exchange rates among the currencies of the member states.[11] They reaffirmed their objective of achieving EMU in summit conferences in October 1972 and December 1974. But by 1976, when the leaders met in The Hague to consider a report on "union" prepared by Prime Minister Leo Tindemans of Belgium,[12] it was obvious that the opportunity to institute EMU by 1980 had long since slipped away, and they turned their attention to more pressing matters.

The European Monetary System and the Balladur initiative: the resurrection of EMU

The broad contours of EMU, established by Werner and Barre and their colleagues in the late 1960s, were resuscitated by a new generation of advocates in the late 1980s. But in one important respect, the later EMU initiative differed from the earlier one. Whereas the first was very largely the combined product of *supranational* and *governmental* actors in the EC – in particular, one Commissioner and several national leaders and ministers – the later one involved not only those actors but *transnational* actors as well. In particular, the initiative that culminated in the treaty signed at Maastricht involved *institutionalized* transnational actors – specifically, the Committee of Governors of the Central Banks of the Member States of the European Economic Community,[13] the Monetary Committee, and certain central bankers acting independently of national governments – that were largely absent in the first elaboration of EMU.

---

[10] On the collapse of the Bretton Woods regime, see, among many, Joanne Gowa, *Closing the Gold Window: Domestic Politics and the End of Bretton Woods* (Ithaca, NY: Cornell University Press, 1983); and John S. Odell, *US International Monetary Policy: Markets, Power, and Ideas as Sources of Change* (Princeton, NJ: Princeton University Press, 1982).

[11] The "snake" consisted of a parity grid among European currencies. Each was to fluctuate against each other currency within a range of ± 2.25 percent – half the width of the band instituted by the IMF in December 1971.

[12] See *Report on European Union* (Brussels: European Communities, 1975).

[13] Henceforth, for convenience, we shall speak of the "Committee of Central Bank Governors."

The return of EMU: Delors and the Single European Act preamble

For a decade after the Tindemans report, the idea of EMU remained dormant, and the Community turned its attention to other, more immediate problems. The "snake" was replaced in March 1979 by the European Monetary System (EMS),[14] and soon thereafter the Community undertook an effort to remove the barriers to an internal market that culminated in the Single European Act of 1986.[15] However, the Single European Act (SEA) put EMU back on the agenda of the Community, for its Preamble claimed as one of the Act's objectives the "progressive realization of economic and monetary union." The Act itself contained a chapter with the somewhat ambiguous title of "Co-operation in Economic and Monetary Policy (Economic and Monetary Union)."

The references to EMU in the SEA were apparently the work of Jacques Delors, the Commission President (who also held the Commission portfolio for monetary policy). According to Nigel Lawson, at the time the British Chancellor of the Exchequer and as close to the SEA negotiations as any observer, Delors "put up" the Luxemburg presidency to include language pertaining to EMU in its final draft of the Act just prior to the European Council meeting that approved it. Alerted by Lawson and supported by the Germans, Margaret Thatcher was able to get the language watered down; nevertheless, the references remained, and, with the ratification of the SEA, EMU was enshrined once more as a policy objective. With that, Lawson says, the Community began to slide down "a dangerous slippery slope towards EMU."[16]

Soon after the formal signing of the SEA, Delors sought to marshall support for monetary reform by commissioning a group of economists

[14] The "snake" lacked a mechanism by which joint interventions in markets could be undertaken in support of weak currencies as well as a mechanism for negotiating realignments when weak currencies fell through their floors against stronger ones. As a result, when a currency went through its floor it simply dropped out of the "snake." The British pound and the Irish punt dropped out in June 1972, the Italian lira in February 1973, and the French franc in January 1974 and again in March 1976. By then, the "snake" included only Germany and four of its smaller neighbors (as well as Norway and Sweden, which were not in the EC but participated in the "snake"). Efforts begun shortly thereafter to improve it culminated in the EMS. See, among many, Peter Ludlow, *The Making of the European Monetary System: A Case Study of the Politics of the European Community* (London: Butterworth, 1982).

[15] See Cameron, "The 1992 Initiative."

[16] See Nigel Lawson, *The View from 11* (New York: Doubleday, 1993), pp. 890–94.

and other experts, headed by Tommaso Padoa-Schioppa, to investigate the economic consequences of the 1986 enlargement of the Community and the decision to create a single internal market by 1992. In their report, Padoa-Schioppa and his colleagues foresaw the need for greater monetary cooperation in the wake of those developments. Although they did not explicitly call for a new variant of EMU, they did note the incompatibility of nationally determined monetary policies with EC-wide free trade, free movement of capital, and fixed exchange rates, and they urged greater coordination of monetary policy and a strengthening of the EMS.[17]

EMS asymmetry and the Balladur initiative

In putting EMU back on the agenda of the Community, Jacques Delors acted as a supranational policy entrepreneur, in much the same way Raymond Barre had nearly two decades earlier. As important as Delors' initiatives were, however, the resurrection of EMU owes much more to *another* actor, one who represented not a supranational institution in the Community but, rather, a government of one of the member states. For Edouard Balladur, the minister of the economy, finance, and privatization in the French *co-habitation* government headed since March 1986 by Jacques Chirac, EMU was espoused not to further European integration but, rather, to alleviate a perceived asymmetry of influence and benefit that existed in the EMS.

Over the course of the 1980s, as the EMS evolved into an increasingly stable exchange rate regime,[18] inflation rates in the Community dropped sharply. As prices and exchange rates became increasingly stable, a normative convergence developed in the Community regarding the wisdom of the macroeconomic policy objectives pursued, above all, in Germany and the Netherlands – the countries with the lowest rates of inflation and the only ones never to devalue their currencies within the EMS.[19] The German mark came to be

---

[17] See Tommaso Padoa-Schioppa with Michael Emerson, Mervyn King, Jean-Claude Mitteron, *Efficiency, Stability, and Equity: A Strategy for the Evolution of the Economic System of the European Community* (New York: Oxford University Press, 1987).

[18] One manifestation of that evolution was the decreasing frequency over time in the number of realignments within the EMS – seven in its first four years, five in its second four years, and only one in the more than five and a half years from January 1987 to September 1992. See Cameron, "The 1992 Initiative."

[19] The decisions of the French government from 1981 to 1983 to keep the franc in the EMS and negotiate modest devaluations that were accompanied by fiscal and monetary restraint played a major role in the development of this consensus. See David R.

regarded as the "anchor" currency of the EMS, and the German Bundesbank was widely perceived as having the power to shape monetary policy throughout the Community by, in effect, setting the floor for interest rates in all the countries that were in the EMS.[20] In the words of two knowledgeable observers, "The Bundesbank in Frankfurt has become Europe's de facto central bank. Other EMS participants have to ape a German monetary policy in which they have no formal say."[21]

When the EMS was founded, it was assumed that the burdens of adjustment would be distributed symmetrically between both the strong-currency and weak-currency countries. As the system evolved, however, that presumption was displaced by an emerging reality – that adjustment was ultimately the responsibility of the weak-currency countries, whose policy diverged from that of Germany (and its close associate, the Netherlands) and, therefore, had to be changed. So too, the distribution of material benefits in the EMS – also assumed, initially, to be symmetric among the participants – came to be seen as distinctly *asymmetric*. For example, because the greater stabilization and less frequent realignment of exchange rates caused strong currencies to become increasingly undervalued over time, the countries with strong currencies tended to earn increasingly large surpluses in their international transactions. Conversely, the countries with weak currencies – which typically were in deficit to begin with – found their currencies becoming increasingly *over*valued and their *deficits* increasing over time. Thus, during the first decade of the EMS, Germany earned a cumulative surplus of more than $200 billion in its trade with other EC member states, and the Netherlands earned a cumulative surplus of more than $100 billion. In contrast, France, Britain, and Italy experienced large cumulative *deficits* – more than $40 billion for Italy, more than $75 billion for France, and more than $100 billion for Britain![22]

In July 1987, Balladur called upon the Community to strengthen the

Cameron, "Exchange Rate Politics in France, 1981–83: The Regime-Defining Choices of the Mitterrand Presidency," in Anthony Daley, ed., *The Mitterrand Era* (New York: Macmillan, forthcoming).

20 On the mark as an "anchor" in the EMS, see, among many, Heinz-Dieter Smeets, "Does Germany Dominate the EMS?" *Journal of Common Market Studies*, 29 (September 1990), pp. 37–52; and Axel A. Weber, "Reputation and Credibility in the European Monetary System," *Economic Policy*, 12 (April 1991), pp. 588–602.

21 Nicholas Colchester and David Buchan, *Europower: The Essential Guide to Europe's Economic Transformation in 1992* (London: The Economist Books, 1990), pp. 160–61.

22 See Cameron, "The 1992 Initiative," p. 69.

EMS and alleviate the asymmetry that existed between Germany and its partners. Prompted by a dispute in January, in which the French government deliberately let the franc fall through its floor against the mark in order to force the Bundesbank to intervene in support of the franc and the German government to revalue its currency, Balladur's call, reiterated in August, led to the Basle–Nyborg Agreements of September 1987, in which the Committee of Central Bank Governors and the ministers of finance agreed to create a credit facility to support intramarginal interventions in currency markets.[23]

Balladur continued to call for alterations in the EMS. In December 1987, he publicly called for reform of the EMS and prepared a set of proposals for his colleagues in the finance ministries of the Community designed to improve the functioning of the EMS and promote greater exchange rate stability. Prepared in the wake of renewed attacks on the franc – prompted by a rise in the mark as the American dollar dropped in value – that had forced several increases in French interest rates, just as the French presidential campaign was getting under way, Balladur's proposals sought to introduce a greater degree of symmetry in the operation of the EMS – especially in the obligation to defend currencies under attack.[24] Among other things, he called for a strengthening of the European Monetary Cooperation Fund to assist central bank intervention in markets. He proposed that, in order to present a common European posture *vis-à-vis* the dollar and the yen, a common currency be created that would be managed by a single central bank. In short, he called for EMU.

Several of Balladur's colleagues – for the most part, ministers in weak-currency countries – endorsed his proposals. Giuliano Amato, the Italian minister of finance and an economist (and, like Balladur, subsequently a prime minister), was the first to do so publicly. In a paper circulated to his Community colleagues, Amato criticized the EMS for enabling Germany to systematically undervalue the mark –

---

[23] On the Basle–Nyborg agreements, see Colchester and Buchan, *Europower*, p. 163.

[24] On the Balladur proposals, see Colchester and Buchan, *Europower*, p. 166; George Graham, "French Finance Chief Suggests Setting Up an EC Central Bank," *Financial Times*, January 7, 1988, p. 2; Ian Davidson, "Chirac Endorses Call to Set Up EC Central Bank," *Financial Times*, January 8, 1988, p. 2; and George Graham, "Balladur Spares the Fine Print," *Financial Times*, January 25, 1988, p. 3. Balladur first made the proposals in a speech in December 1987 and discussed them in detail in a television interview on January 6, 1988. Jacques Chirac publicly endorsed them the next day and the memorandum containing them was circulated to the finance ministers shortly thereafter. We might note that by then Chirac had announced his candidacy for president in the election that would occur in April and May 1988.

and thereby accumulate huge trade surpluses at the expense of its partners in the Community – while generating a deflationary bias throughout the Community through its tight money policy. For Amato, the political cost of an "agreed loss of autonomy" through the creation of a European central bank was preferable to the unilateral loss of autonomy to Germany that existed in the EMS and the economic costs suffered in that system.[25]

Not surprisingly, the Balladur initiative was criticized by German leaders and officials. Helmut Kohl registered his "coolness" toward the plan almost immediately,[26] and Gerhard Stoltenberg, the minister of finance, and Karl Otto Pöhl, the president of the Bundesbank, voiced their skepticism as well.[27] They disputed France's claim that it was disadvantaged by the operation of the EMS, urged Britain to enter the EMS as a first step in a process that might eventually lead to a single central bank and common currency, and called for the elimination of all capital controls in the Community. The Balladur proposals *did*, however, receive the endorsement of one important German official – Hans-Dietrich Genscher, the foreign minister;[28] and because Germany held the Council presidency in the first half of 1988, it fell to Genscher, as chair of the Council of Ministers, to prepare the agenda for the forthcoming meeting of the European Council in Hanover in June.[29]

Designing EMU: Hanover, 1988 and the Delors Committee

Perhaps the greatest irony about the initiative that culminated in the Treaty signed at Maastricht is the fact that, although the old idea of EMU was resurrected by France – with the support of such allies as Italy – in order to correct what it perceived as asymmetries of influence

[25] See Colchester and Buchan, *Europower*, p. 167.

[26] See David Marsh, "Kohl Rejects Plan to Move towards EC Central Bank," *Financial Times*, January 15, 1988, p. 2, which reports Kohl's comments at a press luncheon.

[27] See David Marsh, "Bonn Sees Monetary Union as Distant Goal," *Financial Times*, January 25, 1988, p. 3. Stoltenberg became minister of finance when the CDU-led government came to power in October, 1982. Helmut Schmidt appointed Pöhl vice president of the Bundesbank in 1977 and President in 1979, and Kohl reappointed him to a second eight-year term in 1987.

[28] Genscher, a member of the Free Democrats, had been foreign minister since 1974 and retained that position when the CDU and Christian Social Union (CSU) replaced the Social Democrats as the Free Democratic party (FDP)'s coalition partners in October 1982.

[29] See Colchester and Buchan, *Europower*, pp. 167–68; Marsh, "Bonn Sees Monetary Union"; and Tim Dickson, "Genscher Calls for Closer European Monetary Links," *Financial Times*, January 21, 1988, p. 2. Genscher made his comments in a speech to the European Parliament.

and benefit in the EMS that favored Germany and its Bundesbank, the negotiations resulted in an agreement that "reflects most fully the position of Germany."[30] To understand how a set of proposals that had been put forward to reduce the power of the Bundesbank and German monetary policy resulted in an agreement that created a "super Bundesbank"[31] – a European central bank that incorporated, and in some aspects improved upon, the essential institutional and normative characteristics of the German bank – one must understand the role of certain institutionally-defined transnational actors – most notably, the central bankers of the Community – in the elaboration of the Balladur initiative.

At the Hanover meeting of the European Council in June 1988, the leaders discussed the various ideas of several of the member states for strengthening the EMS and increasing the coordination of monetary policy, as well as more general ideas pertaining to the creation of a single central bank, a common currency, and EMU. Much of the discussion apparently concentrated on the central bank, with President Mitterrand of France, supported by the Italian Prime Minister Ciriaco De Mita, making the case for a bank and Britain's Margaret Thatcher attacking the idea. Among the German participants at the two-day meeting, Genscher supported the French proposal of a central bank while Kohl – as would be characteristic of the chancellor throughout the EMU negotiation – took a middle position between that of Mitterrand, Delors, and Genscher, on one hand, and the well-known positions of the head of the Bundesbank and the German ministry of finance, on the other.[32] Thus, while supporting EMU, the chancellor reiterated the Bundesbank's view that a European central bank would have to be as independent of political authority as the German central bank.

Mrs. Thatcher dismissed the idea of a European central bank as "airy-fairy," and in deference to her, the European Council made no mention of a bank in its closing communiqué. But it did agree to create a committee, chaired by Jacques Delors, that would "study and propose concrete stages leading to the progressive realization of

---

[30] "A Sensible Draft on Emu," *Financial Times*, October 30, 1991, p. 22, describing the draft Treaty prepared by the Dutch presidency in late 1991, just prior to the Maastricht meeting.

[31] "A Sensible Draft."

[32] Because foreign ministers attend the meetings of the European Council but finance ministers (and central bank governors) do not, Genscher was at the Hanover meeting while Stoltenberg and Pöhl were not.

economic and monetary union." The so-called Delors Committee – formally the Committee for the Study of Economic and Monetary Union – included, in addition to its chair, the twelve members of the Committee of Central Bank Governors, as well as three "non-official" experts and another member of the Commission (Frans Andriessen of the Netherlands, the Commissioner in charge of external relations).

Over the ten months following the Hanover meeting, the Delors Committee met on a monthly basis in Basle, in conjunction with the monthly meetings of the central bankers of the Group of 10 and the Committee of Central Bank Governors at the Bank for International Settlements (BIS).[33] Although the Committee deliberated behind closed doors, a good deal is known about the debates and divisions within it. At its March 1989 meeting in Basle, as it prepared the final text of its report, for example, a "furious argument" pitted Pöhl, Wim Duisenberg of De Nederlandsche Bank, Robin Leigh-Pemberton of the Bank of England, and Pierre Jaans of the Luxemburg Monetary Institute against Jacques de Larosière of the Banque de France, the governors of the banks of Italy and Spain, and Delors, over the pace and preconditions for transition from one stage to another as they were described in a draft of the Committee's proposals prepared by the Commission.[34] The former group, accompanied by the governors of the banks of Ireland and Denmark, preferred a slower pace of transition and the achievement of greater convergence in economic and monetary policy prior to the creation of new monetary institutions, while the latter group preferred a faster timetable, an earlier creation of such institutions as a Reserve Fund, and less restrictive criteria for policy convergence and harmonization.

After the March meeting, a new draft of the Committee report was prepared that took into account the amendments proposed by Pöhl, Duisenberg, Leigh-Pemberton, and Jaans. It stipulated that a greater degree of policy convergence was a necessary precondition for the development of new monetary institutions such as a central bank and the institution of a single currency, and for the transition from one stage to another. It also removed specific deadlines and end-dates for

---

[33] Indicative of the transnational, rather than EC-based supranational, character of the Committee of Central Bank Governors was the fact that it met in Basle at the BIS, in conjunction with the monthly meetings of the central bankers of the Group of 10. The Commission was not represented on the Committee, the Committee elected its own chairman for a three-year term, and it could even co-opt non-EC governors into its deliberations as it saw fit.

[34] See *Financial Times*, April 13, 1989, pp. 1, 30.

the achievement of those transitions. In so doing, the draft moved away from positions advocated by Delors and the Commission and the two governments that had been most responsible for resurrecting EMU – France and Italy.[35] After a two-day meeting in Basle in mid-April, the Committee unanimously approved the report. Nevertheless, as a sign of the continuing disagreement over the timing, transitional criteria, and institutional structures of the various stages, six of the governors – among them Pöhl, de Larosière, Jaans, and Duisenberg – submitted separate papers that were published with the report.[36]

Like the Werner Committee some two decades earlier, the Delors Committee proposed a three-stage process of transition to economic and monetary union. In the first stage, which it said should begin no later than July 1, 1990, it called for complete removal of all barriers to the free flow of goods and services and, in particular, the creation of a single EC-wide financial system without any national capital controls. It also called for increased coordination among the member states in fiscal, economic, and monetary policy, an expanded role for the Committee of Central Bank Governors in coordinating monetary and exchange rate policy, the inclusion of the currencies of all member states in the Exchange Rate Mechanism (ERM), and reform and expansion of the structural funds available to the poorest member states.[37]

The second stage of EMU, described in less detail than the first, was to be primarily transitional and concerned with the preparation for the third and final stage. The basic structures and institutions of EMU would be set up, the most important of which would be the European System of Central Banks (ESCB), consisting of the national central banks and a new central institution that would absorb the Committee of Central Bank Governors.[38] The ESCB would continue the coordination of monetary policy begun in stage one, monitor and analyze macroeconomic developments, establish general monetary orientations for the Community and an operational framework for a common monetary policy, and promote a process of common decision-making in preparation for its responsibilities in stage three. The second stage

---

[35] See *Financial Times*, April 8–9, 1989, p. 22.
[36] See Committee for the Study of Economic and Monetary Union, *Report on Economic and Monetary Union in the European Community* (Luxemburg: European Communities, 1989), including *Collection of Papers Submitted to the Committee for the Study of Economic and Monetary Union*. We might note that although Pöhl submitted a paper to the Committee that was published with the Report, he announced he was "quite happy" with the report. See *Financial Times*, April 13, 1989, p. 1.
[37] See Committee for the Study of Economic and Monetary Union, *Report*, pp. 34–37.
[38] Ibid. pp. 37–39.

would also witness the strengthening of procedures for convergence in macroeconomic policy through the creation of a medium-term framework for economic objectives and precise – albeit non-binding – rules relating to the size and financing of budget deficits.

In the third and final stage of EMU, exchange rates would be irrevocably fixed and the fluctuation margins among currencies in the EMS eliminated. As that happened, the ESCB would assume responsibility for the formulation and implementation of a common monetary policy within the Community. It would manage the pooled reserves of the member states and would have exclusive control over decisions to intervene in exchange markets. The irrevocably locked exchange rates would be replaced with a single currency, not out of necessity but in order to demonstrate the irreversibility of the transition to EMU. Coordination among national budgetary policies would be improved, in order to maintain monetary and exchange rate stability, and macroeconomic and budgetary rules and procedures would become binding.[39]

As this brief summary suggests, the Delors Committee's report established the broad parameters of EMU as it eventually appeared in the Treaty on European Union – three stages, a transitional second stage, creation of a System of Central Banks and a European Central Bank, irrevocably locked exchange rates in the third and final stage, etc. The Committee's role in structuring the subsequent debate about EMU within the Community is typically taken – in part, no doubt, because of the name with which it is most frequently associated – as a measure of the primacy of a *supra*national actor – the Commission – in the gestation of EMU. However, notwithstanding the important role played by Delors and the Commission in the preparation of the report, the influence of the report is a measure of the importance of *transnational actors – in particular, the twelve members of the Committee of Central Bank Governors – in the development of EMU*. If nothing else, the composition of the Delors Committee – in particular, the inclusion of the twelve central bank governors among the seventeen members – suggests that it was, first and foremost, a committee of the *central bankers* of the Community. Indeed, Nigel Lawson indicates that one of Margaret Thatcher's objectives at the Hanover meeting that created the Committee was to insure that it *not* be a committee of experts, which was what France and Genscher wanted (or even worse, from

---

[39] Ibid. pp. 17–30 and 39–41.

her perspective, a committee of Commission officials), but, rather, a committee of central bank governors. The former, she felt, would produce "airy-fairy ideas unrelated to political realities," whereas a committee of bank governors "not only possessed the expertise required but could be relied upon to keep their feet on the ground."[40] Thatcher herself refers to the Delors Committee as "a Committee of European Community central bank heads – serving in a personal capacity."[41]

Perceiving the Delors Committee's report as a product of the transnational community of European central bankers, rather than simply the articulation of the preferences of a supranational actor (the Commission), allows one to understand better one of the most consequential decisions made in designing the new EMU. One of the most contentious issues involved the timing of the creation of the proposed central bank – in particular, whether it should be created quickly or not until the economies had converged in both policy and performance. As they had in the 1960s, France and Italy, as well as Delors and the Commission, espoused the "monetarist," or "institutions-first," position. In contrast, the strong-currency countries – most notably, Germany and the Netherlands – espoused, as they also had in the late 1960s, the "economist" position that new institutions with control over monetary policy in the member states should be created only after their economies had converged in both policy and performance.

Despite the fact that France and the Commission President had initiated the resurrection of EMU, it was the "economist" vision of EMU that ultimately triumphed in the negotiations that produced the Maastricht Treaty. That victory may appear to have been simply the product of German and Dutch bargaining power in the negotiations in

---

[40] Lawson, *The View from 11*, pp. 902–03. It wasn't just a matter of keeping their feet on the ground; Thatcher notes that "Nigel and I hoped together Robin Leigh-Pemberton, governor of the Bank of England, and Karl Otto Pöhl, president of the Bundesbank, would prevent the emergence of a report which would give momentum to EMU. Herr Pöhl was considered strongly hostile to any serious loss of monetary autonomy for the Bundesbank and Robin Leigh-Pemberton was in no doubt about the strength of our views ... I hoped [they] would manage to put a spoke in the wheel of this particular vehicle of European integration." Margaret Thatcher, *The Downing Street Years* (New York: Harper Collins, 1993), pp. 740–41. What she (and Lawson) did not count on was the fact that Delors would chair the group – something that, according to Lawson, was never canvassed prior to the meeting and that "may have been a Franco-German plot of which the Foreign Office had failed to get wind."
[41] Thatcher, *The Downing Street Years*, p. 708. Thatcher attributes the idea of forming the EMU study group from the central bank governors plus a few others to Helmut Kohl, supported by the German finance ministry and the Bundesbank.

the Intergovernmental Conference (IGC) in 1991. But in fact, it was, to a large extent, the result of *earlier* battles, the first of which occurred in the Delors Committee as Pöhl, Duisenberg, and the governors from Luxemburg and England responded to the Commission's initial draft. Although the Committee's report was, in nearly every respect, sketchy, ambiguous, and imprecise, it did not simply articulate a "monetarist" design of EMU of the sort envisioned by Delors and his Commission officials. Thus, for example, while it proposed that a European System of Central Banks be created in stage two, the Delors Committee stated that monetary policy would remain in the hands of national authorities in that stage, and that a common monetary policy, conducted by the ESCB, would only come into being in the third stage.[42] In a real sense, then, the Committee's report represented the first significant modification of the design of EMU favored by France, Italy, and the Commission.

The Councils respond: S'Agaro and Madrid

Of all the member states, the United Kingdom was least enthralled by the report of the Delors Committee,[43] and the report immediately provoked yet another confrontation between the British government of Margaret Thatcher and those she believed were intent upon enhancing the supranational authority of the Community to the point of transforming the Community into a federal system. Prior to its completion, a draft of the report had circulated among the governments in February 1989, and soon thereafter Lawson, the British chancellor, arranged to give a speech in which he asserted that EMU:

> is incompatible with independent sovereign states with control over their own fiscal and monetary policies . . . It is clear that EMU implies nothing less than a European Government – albeit a federal one – and political union: the United States of Europe. That is simply not on the agenda now, nor will it be for the forseeable future.[44]

---

42 See Committee for the Study of Economic and Monetary Union, *Report*, pp. 38–40.
43 Lawson, we might note, takes a very negative view of the Delors Committee's report – largely because of what he sees as Pöhl's equivocation in its deliberations. "Pöhl," he says, "was the key. He was known to have doubts about EMU, nor did the Bundesbank relish its own extinction . . . But Pöhl proved a broken reed . . . he did not stand firm. He made a number of sceptical interventions in the Committee's deliberations, but he never really engaged himself; at the end of the day shrugging his shoulders and going along with Delors and de Larosière." Lawson, *The View from 11*, p. 908.
44 At Chatham House, January 25, 1989, quoted in Lawson, *The View from 11*, p. 909. In accusing the Delors Committee of proposing a transfer of sovereignty, Lawson was

At the informal meeting of finance ministers and central bank governors at S'Agaro (Spain then holding the presidency) in May 1989,[45] Lawson did, however, agree with his colleagues that the Community should start preparing for stage one and should define the operational elements of stages two and three so that a decision could be taken in regard to convening an Intergovernmental Conference to make the necessary treaty revisions.

The European Council was to meet in Madrid at the end of June 1989. Its primary task would be to consider the Delors Committee's report. Before the meeting, Margaret Thatcher received a lengthy official minute from Lawson and Sir Geoffrey Howe, the foreign secretary, and heard their arguments that, to be taken seriously within the EC, Britain would have to commit itself to joining the Exchange Rate Mechanism of EMS and to accepting the first stage of EMU.[46] Although Howe's words and actions before Madrid were to cost him his job,[47] Thatcher appeared to have been at least partially persuaded by her ministers, and she surprised her European colleagues by announcing that Britain would join the ERM when the time was right (defined in terms of five conditions, of which the most important was a drop in the inflation rate in Britain).

In spite of the apparent moderation in the British position on the ERM issue, Thatcher and Mitterrand found themselves, characteristically, on opposite poles on EMU – specifically, in regard to whether EMU represented a *single* process and thus whether a commitment to stage one meant a commitment to stages two and three as elaborated by the Delors Committee and, secondly, whether a date for the IGC

alluding, in particular, to paragraph 19 of the *Report*, p. 18, in which it speaks of "the need for a transfer of decision-making power from Member states to the Community." See, also, Lawson's comments when the *Report* was issued, in *Financial Times*, April 18, 1989, p. 24.

[45] The finance ministers gather for a one-day meeting each month in either Brussels or Luxemburg. In addition, they meet with the central bank governors for a longer (i.e., weekend) "informal" meeting every spring and autumn in the country then holding the six-month rotating Council presidency.

[46] On the discussions at this time between Thatcher, Howe, and Lawson, see Thatcher, *The Downing Street Years*, pp. 709–13, and Lawson, *The View from 11*, especially chapter 74, pp. 927–36. In describing the meetings, Thatcher speaks at p. 709 of "the ambush before Madrid." In the second meeting between Howe, Lawson, and Thatcher, the day before Howe and Thatcher were to travel to Madrid, Howe told Thatcher that if she was unwilling to take his advice and to make some accommodating move at Madrid he would have to resign. Lawson said if that happened, he too would resign.

[47] In July, Howe was removed as foreign secretary and became deputy prime minister and leader of the House of Commons, a major demotion. (Lawson resigned as chancellor of the exchequer in October 1989, over an unrelated dispute.) As noted later, Howe was to have his revenge in November 1990.

should be set immediately. Mitterrand, along with De Mita of Italy, Felipe Gonzalez of Spain, and Wilfried Martens of Belgium (and Genscher of Germany) said yes on both, Thatcher, supported only by Denmark,[48] said no on both, and, characteristically, Kohl found himself between the two poles. Also characteristically, it was he who found a middle ground for compromise between the French (and Genscher) position and the one advocated by Thatcher (and the German finance ministry and the Bundesbank). Having reservations about both issues, he proposed that the leaders agree that the Delors Committee's report be taken to define "a" process (not *the* process) leading to EMU and that an IGC be convened sometime after the first stage had begun on July 1, 1990, after "full and adequate" preparations for stages two and three were "sufficiently far advanced" so as to make negotiations worthwhile.[49] All twelve leaders, including Thatcher, agreed.

Convening the IGC: autumn 1989 and Strasbourg

After Madrid, the finance ministers concentrated on such stage-one issues as improving coordination between the Council and the Committee of Central Bank Governors. Meanwhile, there was continued activity among both supranational and transnational actors. In September, Delors presented a paper to the Council which outlined the critical issues that would confront an IGC on EMU. In it, he proposed that at its December meeting in Strasbourg, the European Council set a date for the IGC that would be early enough to allow ratification of the Treaty amendments by the end of 1992 and commencement of stage two in January 1993. Meanwhile, behind the scenes, the Monetary Committee, composed of the chief deputies of the finance ministries and the central banks of the EC, proposed a number of changes in the Commission's latest draft pertaining to relations between finance ministers and bank governors, aimed largely at enhancing the independence of the latter.[50]

---

[48] See Thatcher, *The Downing Street Years*, p. 741.

[49] See *Financial Times*, June 28, 1989, p. 2. The Kohl compromise had the virtue for Germany, of course, of starting the first stage – devoted largely to achieving greater economic convergence – soon while delaying the preparation and implementation of the later stages. It had the additional virtue of eliminating the possibility that the French, through their control of the council presidency in the second half of 1989, could accelerate the movement toward the later stages.

[50] See *Financial Times*, November 2, 1989, p. 3.

In November, the Councils of both the foreign ministers and finance ministers received a brief report from a committee of senior officials of the two ministries in the twelve member states that had been created by the French presidency. Chaired by Elisabeth Guigou, an aide to President Mitterrand, the committee was designed to set the stage for a decision at Strasbourg to convene the IGC in the second half of 1990. But as it consisted only of ten pages of questions and answers about the second and third stages of EMU, the Guigou Committee's report did not appear, to some, to satisfy the conditions for preparation of the IGC stipulated at Madrid. The Dutch and Danish ministers, among others, expressed their doubts about whether the report represented a "full and adequate" preparation of the IGC, and at their November meeting the Foreign Ministers "took note" of the report – a euphemism for putting it aside.[51] A week later, the Council of Finance Ministers also agreed to set the report aside and leave the issue to the European Council. As it did, several ministers – most notably, those of Germany, Britain, Denmark, and the Netherlands – expressed their misgivings about convening an IGC dealing with the later stages of EMU when the first had not even begun; as Theo Waigel, the German minister, put it, "one cannot build a roof without being sure of the foundation."[52]

Despite the ambivalence expressed by several member states in the European Council, the Strasbourg meeting of heads of state or government in December 1989 voted, by an 11 to 1 margin, in favor of Mitterrand's proposal to convene the IGC one year hence. Mrs. Thatcher's lone vote against was entirely predictable, as were those in favor by France, Italy, Spain, Belgium, and most of the others. However, it is less obvious why *all* the other member states voted in favor of the proposal – in particular, why Germany and the Netherlands, the two leading proponents of a lengthy transition to EMU preceded by policy convergence, voted in favor.

The German and Dutch willingness to support Mitterrand's accelerated timetable for the IGC may, of course, have reflected only the absence at Strasbourg of the officials who were most ambivalent about EMU – the heads of the central banks and the finance ministers – and the greater likelihood, in their absence, that Helmut Kohl and

---

[51] See *Financial Times*, November 7, 1989, p. 2.

[52] *Financial Times*, November 14, 1989, p. 28. Waigel replaced Stoltenberg as German minister of finance in April 1989. He had served as the leader of the Bavaria-based CSU's parliamentary group until October 1988, when he was elected chair of the CSU after the death of Franz-Josef Strauss.

Ruud Lubbers would accommodate the wishes of a majority of their colleagues. But it may have reflected, also, the institutional context of German and Dutch domestic politics, on one hand, and the external context within which the European Community existed, on the other. The domestic context of German and Dutch politics caused there to be a dispersion of views about EMU within each government that, paradoxically, created a relatively wide range within which the German chancellor and Dutch prime minister could take positions in European Council discussions. For example, the German government consisted, as it had since 1982, of a coalition of *three* parties – the Christian Democrats, the Bavaria-based Christian Social Union, and the Free Democrats. Each party leader – Kohl, Waigel, and Genscher – was deeply involved in the EMU negotiations, but they did not share a common position toward EMU. As a result, Germany's position varied widely across the Councils in which each participated – respectively, the European Council, the Council of Economics and Finance Ministers, and the Council of Ministers. This dispersion in German positions – for example, between Genscher and officials of the foreign ministry, on the one hand, and Waigel and officials of the finance ministry, on the other[53] – provided Kohl with considerable latitude for position-taking in *his* negotiations within the European Council; which, in turn, enhanced his ability to broker agreements within the Council. Likewise, while it was quite implausible, given their subordination to government, that the central banks of such countries as France, Italy, Belgium, and Spain would articulate views about EMU that were distinctive from those of the government, it was not only possible but quite likely, in view of their constitutional independence, that the German and Dutch central banks would articulate such views. Conversely, it was quite possible that a German chancellor or Dutch prime minister would endorse a position distinctive from that espoused by the central bank, simply because in those countries (but not the others) the banks were able to articulate views that could (and often did) differ from those of the government.[54]

---

[53] The fact that Genscher had been foreign minister since 1974 – including more than eight years *before* Kohl became chancellor – and the fact that the FDP was the pivotal party in the coalition undoubtedly enhanced his, and the ministry's, autonomy from the chancellor and the other coalition parties.

[54] On the independence of the German and Dutch central banks, see John B. Goodman, *Monetary Sovereignty: The Politics of Central Banking in Western Europe* (Ithaca, NY: Cornell University Press, 1992); and Paulette Kurzer, *Business and Banking: Political Change and Economic Integration in Western Europe* (Ithaca, NY: Cornell University Press, 1993), chapter 6.

The German willingness to support France in regard to the date for the IGC on EMU may have derived, also, from the external European context of late 1989. In all likelihood, Kohl's vote at Strasbourg reflected a concern that would remain paramount throughout the EMU negotiations and that would cause him, at several later points as well, to deviate from the bargaining positions articulated by Waigel and Pöhl. That involved, of course, the emerging issue of German unification. On November 28, 1989, three weeks after the Berlin Wall had come down, Kohl had proposed (without consulting with Genscher, Mitterrand, or the other Allies) a "ten-point program" for German reunification. He sought Community approval at Strasbourg for a declaration supporting German "unity through free self-determination."[55] In what appears to have been a tacit bargain, after receiving the Council's endorsement of a slightly modified version of his declaration – modified to include a reference to existing treaties and the Helsinki principles as well as to the fact that unification would occur "in a context of European integration" – (and after being assured that the IGC would not start until after the German elections scheduled for the autumn of 1990), Kohl agreed to support Mitterrand's proposal to convene the IGC in December 1990, with an eye to its conclusion one year later.[56] For the first time in the negotiations over EMU – but not the last time – the emerging issue of German unification, coupled with a concern about electoral consequences, caused Kohl to distance himself from the positions advocated by the German Finance Ministry and the Bundesbank.

The monetary committee and Ashford Castle: the serious work begins

After the Strasbourg meeting, the Council of Economics and Finance Ministers (Ecofin) assigned the task of preparing for the IGC to the Monetary Committee. A far cry from the *ad hoc* Guigou Committee, the Monetary Committee consisted of the deputy ministers of finance and deputy governors of the central banks of the member states and represented a unique amalgamation of governmental and transnational actors – the term "transgovernmental" seems especially

[55] On the events of late 1989 – early 1990 in Germany, and Kohl's unification initiative, see Timothy Garton Ash, *In Europe's Name: Germany and the Divided Continent* (New York: Doubleday, 1993), pp. 343–56 and 384–98.

[56] See David Marsh, "Bonn and Paris Disagree over EMU Pace," *Financial Times*, November 3, 1989, p. 22.

appropriate in this case – with an institutional history dating back a quarter of a century.[57] The Committee was charged with preparing a report for the next meeting of finance ministers and central bank governors, scheduled for Ashford Castle in Ireland in March, regarding the institutions and practices of the new European Central Bank and its relationship with the national central banks.

At the Ashford Castle informal meeting, the finance ministers and central bank governors had before them the preliminary report of the Monetary Committee, as well as a plan for EMU prepared by the Commission. The latter adhered closely to the Delors Committee's report, although it did relax the Committee's recommendations in several respects – as in its proposal that there should be only "binding procedures" for reporting and monitoring fiscal policy, rather than "binding rules." The Monetary Committee's report, concentrating on the design of the European System of Central Banks, recommended that the new European Central Bank should be politically independent and committed to the objective of price stability, that it should have exclusive responsibility for establishing and implementing monetary policy in the member states, that it be responsible for managing foreign exchange reserves and day-to-day exchange rate policy, including interventions in currency markets, and that it not be responsible for bank supervision within the member states.[58]

The conclusions of the Monetary Committee were largely congruent with German and Dutch preferences on most issues – for example, in regard to independence, price stability, and separation of monetary policy from bank supervision. However, while the German and Dutch governments wanted the *national* central banks, as well as the European bank, to be independent and wanted virtually all exchange rate policy and currency intervention to be conducted by the new central Bank, the Monetary Committee struck a compromise between those views and the position of the French and British representatives, who wanted the national central banks to remain subordinate to the national governments and responsibility for exchange rate policy to remain in the hands of the finance ministers. Thus, while reserving for the new Bank the right to conduct day-to-day exchange rate policy, including managing foreign exchange reserves and intervening in

---

57 Among other things, since March 1979 the Monetary Committee had been charged with monitoring the EMS and, if necessary, negotiating realignments of currencies in the EMS. See Ludlow, *The Making of the European Monetary System*.
58 See *Financial Times*, March 31, 1990.

currency markets, the Committee proposed that the finance ministers be given the authority for exchange rate policy *vis-à-vis* external currencies.

At Ashford Castle, the finance ministers and bank governors agreed on the essential features of the European Central Bank and the ESCB as described by the Monetary Committee. However, they were unable to agree on the guidelines regarding budget deficits – whether, as the Commission proposed, there should be "binding procedures" or, as the Monetary Committee proposed, "binding rules." Waigel of Germany, as well as the finance ministers of the Netherlands, Belgium, and Italy, supported the latter. But Pierre Bérégovoy, the French finance minister, endorsed the Commission position, and John Major, the British chancellor of the exchequer, supported only "binding surveillance." Nor were the ministers and governors able to agree on the creation of a single currency rather than the retention of national currencies in stage three. They *did*, however, agree on one matter that was to prove consequential later on in the negotiations: at the insistence of Germany and the Netherlands – and contrary to the wishes of Spain, Greece, Portugal, and Ireland – after noting that regional aid for the poorer countries of the Community was scheduled to double between 1987 and 1992, they agreed that EMU should entail no additional regional aid for the poorer countries.

During the next several months, as the Committee of Central Bank Governors gathered in Basle for its normal monthly meetings, it discussed the statutes of the new bank and made plans to draft them, drawing on proposals submitted by both the Commission and the Monetary Committee. Pöhl, who had succeeded Demetrius Chalikias of Greece as the Chairman of the Committee at the end of 1989, met with the finance ministers to discuss issues of transition to later stages of EMU – in particular, whether it was desirable and feasible for all member states to transit from one stage to the next at the same time.

EMU, political union, and unification: the German quid pro quo

In April 1990, Kohl and Mitterrand proposed a second IGC to run concurrently with the one on EMU. Meeting soon after the March elections in the GDR that gave the Christian Democratic Union (CDU) a landslide victory and, in so doing, accelerated the timetable for

David R. Cameron

unification,[59] the two leaders proposed that a second IGC be convened to deal with "political union," including within that rubric such issues as the democratic legitimacy of the Community and the definition and implementation of a "common foreign and security policy." Their colleagues endorsed the idea at a special meeting of the European Council in Dublin one week later and instructed the foreign ministers to prepare to commence the second IGC in December.

The initiative for this second IGC apparently came from the German chancellery.[60] Kohl understood that any acceleration in the pace of unification would require the acquiescence of the Community – especially France. The desire for acceptance of an accelerated timetable for unification appears to have generated an important concession by the German chancellor that ran contrary to the position of the Bundesbank and the ministry of finance in regard to the timing of EMU. Specifically, as part of their joint declaration announcing the proposal for a second IGC devoted to political union, in exchange for French acceptance of the pace of unification and the program of German economic and monetary union, and as evidence of Germany's commitment to the Community, Kohl agreed to the French president's long-standing proposal that the ratification of an EMU agreement be accelerated so that it could be put into effect by January 1, 1993.[61]

Establishing the *ex ante* position: Pöhl and the Bundesbank

In the months preceding the start of the IGC on EMU in December 1990, no one did more to establish his *ex ante* bargaining position than Karl Otto Pöhl. Over a period of several months in the summer and early

59 In the election for the Volkskammer on March 18, 1990, the Alliance for Germany won 48 percent of the vote compared to 22 percent for the Social Democrats, 16 percent for the Socialists (ex-SED), and 5 percent for the Free Democrats. Of the Alliance vote, 41 percent was won by the Christian Democrats, 6 percent by the German Social Union, and 1 percent by Democratic Awakening. Before the election, Kohl called for quick unification under Article 23 of the Basic Law and opened negotiations with the GDR for German Economic and Monetary Union (GEMU) – apparently without consulting Pöhl beforehand.

60 See George Graham, David Marsh, and Philip Stephens, "France and W. Germany Launch New Drive for European Union," *Financial Times*, April 20, 1990, p. 1; and David Marsh, "Bonn Initiative Behind Ambitious Target," *Financial Times*, April 20, 1990, p. 2. We should note that Delors, among others, had proposed a second IGC involving political reform in December 1989.

61 The portion of the quid pro quo pertaining to unification was delivered at Dublin. In its final statement, the European Council stated that "the Community warmly welcomes German unification. It looks forward to the positive and fruitful contribution that all Germans can make, following the forthcoming integration of the territory of

autumn of 1990, Pöhl, acting both as president of the Bundesbank and chairman of the Committee of Central Bank Governors, articulated, both to the government and in public, his views regarding EMU, and he did so in a manner that was unmatched by any other official in the Community.

Pöhl launched his offensive at the June 1990 meeting of finance and foreign ministers in Luxemburg. Speaking as Chairman of the Committee of Central Bank Governors, he raised for the first time the possibility of a two-speed EMU – a theme that was to recur throughout the negotiations and later ratification process. He suggested that some countries – Germany, the Netherlands, and perhaps France, Luxemburg, and Belgium – would probably satisfy the still-to-be-defined convergence criteria, then being discussed by the Committee of Central Bank Governors and the Monetary Committee, that would determine whether states were prepared to move to later stages of EMU. But others would not, and thus some states would be able to move to the third and final stage of EMU while the others remained behind in stage two. Needless to say, several of the countries that, by the criteria being discussed (e.g., size of the budget deficit of government, the size of government debt, the rate of inflation, etc.), would most probably be late in qualifying for stage three were less than enthusiastic about the suggestion.[62]

In July 1990, in an address at the Institute of Economic Affairs in London, speaking this time as President of the Bundesbank, Pöhl restated his support for an ESCB and a common monetary policy.[63] But he emphasized that the bank would have to be fully independent of political instruction, have exclusive control of monetary policy, and be committed to price stability. He argued there was no need for the new bank to be accountable; it would, he said, be accountable by its performance! Holding out as models his own bank and the American Federal Reserve, he argued that the national central banks themselves would also have to be independent of political instruction. The next day, addressing the House of Lords, Pöhl again made the case for a strong, independent, federal European Central Bank with sole control over monetary policy, and for a single currency.[64]

the German Democratic Republic into the Community. We are confident that German unification . . . will be a positive factor in the development of Europe as a whole and of the Community in particular . . . We are pleased that German unification is taking place under a European roof." Quoted in "German Unity Welcomed," *Financial Times*, April 30, 1990, p. 2.

[62] See *Financial Times*, June 12, 1990, p. 1.   [63] See *Financial Times*, July 3, 1990, p. 1.
[64] See *Financial Times*, July 4, 1990, p. 9.

By early September, Germany had two months of experience with German Economic and Monetary Union (GEMU). Already, Pöhl saw a "visual lesson" in that experience for the Community. In a speech in Munich, he argued that the German experience demonstrated the problematic consequences of moving to a single currency and a single central bank when the inflation rates and other aspects of economic performance of national states were widely divergent.[65] Eliminating the exchange rate as an instrument of adjustment would place the burden of adjustment on production, employment, and income, and significant drops in those would eventually require significant increases in transfer payments and heighten the risk of budget deficits. Applied to EMU, Pöhl suggested that the German experience demonstrated how problematic a rapid transition to the third stage could be; once in that stage, with exchange rates irrevocably locked, countries with inflation rates several times that of Germany (then around 3 percent) would inevitably suffer economic contraction and mass unemployment when forced to adjust without recourse to devaluation.[66]

Pöhl and the Bundesbank also developed the "visual lesson" of GEMU for EMU in documents and letters that were sent to Kohl, Waigel, Genscher, and other ministers in the autumn of 1990. In September, the Bundesbank circulated within the government a "Statement on the Establishment of an Economic and Monetary Union in Europe."[67] In it, the bank reiterated its opposition to any timetables or deadlines for transitions to the later stages of EMU, as well as its opposition to a short first stage and to vague and imprecise con-

[65] Katherine Campbell, "Pöhl Warns of Danger in Rapid Moves to EMU," *Financial Times*, September 4, 1990, p. 1.
[66] As he was to do on several occasions, Pöhl reminded his audience that the Bundesbank had favored a lower exchange rate for the Ost Mark (OM) and a considerably longer transition period for GEMU than the government had promised in the run-up to the March 1990 election in the GDR. In the campaign, Kohl had implied a 1:1 exchange rate between the Deutsche Mark (DM) and the OM and endorsed an acceleration of the timetable for unification. The Bundesbank warned that an exchange rate of 1:1 not only risked inflation through a consumption binge in the GDR, but risked enormous losses in production, income, and employment in the wake of what would be, in effect, a fivefold *re*valuation of the OM. That, in turn, would drive up public expenditures and – unless taxes were also increased, which seemed unlikely in an election year – deficits, forcing the Bank to raise interest rates. In late April, the government decided on a 1:1 exchange for cash, wages, pensions, and savings up to 4,000 OM per person, with a 2:1 rate for everything over 4,000 OM. The 1:1 ceiling was 6,000 OM for persons over 60 and 2,000 OM for persons under 14. All company debts were converted at the 2:1 rate. The Bank's prophecy proved accurate in every respect.
[67] Deutsche Bundesbank, "Statement on the Establishment of an Economic and Monetary Union in Europe," Frankfurt, September 1990.

vergence criteria for the transition to later stages. Drafted largely by Hans Tietmeyer, the director for international monetary policy (and, subsequently, vice president and then, in 1993, president), the statement noted the marked divergence in the Community between the inflation rates, levels of budget deficit, and trade balances of Germany and Greece, Portugal, Spain, Italy, and Britain. It warned that once the option of adjusting exchange rates had been eliminated, as would be the case in the third stage of EMU, adjustment for economic divergence, as in rates of inflation, would inevitably occur through increased unemployment and rising public sector transfer payments and deficits in the high-inflation countries and increased inflation in the low-inflation countries. As a result, unless the divergence among economies was eliminated prior to the locking of exchange rates, Germany would suffer monetary instability and increasing inflation, while the high-inflation countries would suffer economic contraction, high interest rates, and losses of production, employment, and income.[68] Therefore, it was necessary for the Community to attain much greater convergence of policy than existed at the moment before embarking on the transition to the later stages of EMU. And that being the case, it was too soon to set a date for the transition to stage two.

Regarding the transition to the third and final stage of EMU, the Bundesbank argued that it should occur only when anti-inflation policy had so converged that there were no significant differences in rates of inflation in the member states, budget deficits had been reduced to tolerable levels, capital markets had been harmonized and capital flowed freely among the member states, and all of the members had their currencies in the Exchange Rate Mechanism of the EMS. In addition, the statutes of the national central banks would have to have been harmonized to insure their independence and the member states would have to have adopted contractual arrangements on budget discipline – including binding rules and sanctions – to reflect their "adequate commitment" to a "lasting anti-inflationary stance." EMU also required, it said, that the ESCB give priority to monetary stability, be politically independent, have a Council to set monetary targets and an executive board to implement them, control all aspects of monetary policy, have sole responsibility for foreign exchange market intervention, and not be obliged to lend to public authorities. To underscore

[68] For discussions of this paper, see Andrew Fisher, "Bundesbank Battles to bring Bonn into Line on 'Go-Slow' EMU," *Financial Times*, September 10, 1990, p. 10; and David Marsh, "A War of Monetary Nerves," *Financial Times*, October 29, 1990, p. XII.

the importance of these conditions, the bank argued, in concluding, that these features were not optional but indispensable, and that if an agreement on EMU did not follow these guidelines, the bank would not give up the mark and transfer its rights to the new European central bank system.

The Rome Councils: the emergence of a "go-slow" coalition

During the autumn of 1990, the finance ministers, central bank governors, and heads of government met on several occasions to prepare for the forthcoming IGC on EMU. While they discussed many issues, debate concentrated on the timing of the transitions to the second and third stages of EMU. It pitted the proponents of the "go-slow" perspective articulated by the Bundesbank against the advocates of a "fast track" to EMU – most notably, the Commission and its French, Italian, and Belgian allies. With a few exceptions, those meetings resulted in the triumph of the "go-slow" supporters and the defeat of the "fast-trackers." As in earlier moments in the development of the initiative, transnational actors operating within the institutions of the Community played a decisive role in the emergence of a "go-slow" majority.

In September, the finance ministers and central bank governors met in Rome in one of their semi-annual informal meetings. Two reports were presented, one from the Commission and one from the Committee of Central Bank Governors. The Commission's memorandum reiterated its position that the second stage of EMU should commence on January 1, 1993 (as France, Italy, Belgium, and Genscher, the German foreign minister, preferred), that it should be a short one, that the new monetary institution should come into being during the second stage, and that the third and final stage should begin "soon thereafter."[69] Pöhl presented an interim report of the deliberations of the Committee regarding the statutes of the proposed European Central Bank and then the discussion turned to the Commission's proposed timetable. John Major, the British chancellor, opposed the timetable and argued that no dates be set for subsequent stages of EMU without having first attained much more convergence in rates of inflation and budget deficits. Waigel and Pöhl supported the British position, and Pöhl also reiterated the Bundesbank's view that specific

[69] See Commission of the European Communities, "Economic and Monetary Union" (Brussels: European Communities, August 21, 1990).

quantitative convergence targets were required for the transition to the third and final stage of EMU and should be developed by the Council. Waigel endorsed the bank's position and the finance ministers of the Netherlands and Luxemburg agreed with the Germans that there should be no transition timetable, the transition to the second stage should be delayed, and the transition to the third stage should be preceded by a convergence of member states in certain indicators and targets of fiscal and monetary performance.[70]

The most important result of the Rome meeting was the addition of several nations to the German–Dutch core of the "go-slow" approach.[71] The most important of these were Britain and Spain. Prior to the meeting, Britain (and Denmark) had been opposed in principle to EMU while Spain had supported the French–Italian–Commission "fast-track" approach. The British chancellor's concern with convergence as a necessary pre-condition was not simply yet another reiteration of the intransigent position of his prime minister. Rather, it signaled a potentially important basis for agreement within the Council between Britain and Germany. The Spanish movement toward the "go-slow" position, represented by Carlos Solchaga's proposal to delay the transition to the second stage from 1993 to 1994 and to stretch it out until 2000,[72] constituted an important potential defection from the "fast-track" pole. Moreover, it brought in its wake several other member states – in particular, Ireland, Greece, and Portugal, the other three of the "poor four" – closer to the "go-slow" position. For the first time, the proponents of that approach outnumbered the "fast-trackers" in the Council.

The roots of the Solchaga proposal lay in the agreement of the finance ministers at Ashford Castle some months earlier that no additional regional aid would accompany EMU. In the wake of that decision, Greece, Portugal, Ireland, and Spain – all of which had previously supported some variant of the "fast-track" position put

[70] For discussions of the meeting, see David Buchan and John Wyles, "EC Ministers Fall Out over Speed of Monetary Union," *Financial Times*, September 10, 1990, p. 2; and "Not So Fast, Jacques," *The Economist*, September 15, 1990, p. 61.

[71] Luxemburg also supported the approach, although with some ambiguity because of its monetary union with Belgium. (In 1922, Belgium and Luxemburg had formed the Belgium–Luxemburg Economic Union, and, since that date, had agreed to lock their currencies at a 1:1 rate without a margin of fluctuation.)

[72] Solchaga's proposal was formulated after a visit by John Major to Madrid immediately before the Rome ministerial meeting. In addition to proposing that the transitions to stages two and three be delayed, Solchaga also provided a qualified endorsement of Major's scheme for a "hard ecu" by suggesting that the ecu be "hardened" in the second stage.

forward by France, Italy, and Belgium – began to lose enthusiasm for that position. As they contemplated the fiscal and monetary adjustment that would be required to enter EMU – and the economic contraction that might be required in stage three, when devaluation was excluded as a means of adjustment – in light of the Ashford Castle decision, it became increasingly apparent they would either be left behind in Pöhl's "two-speed" EMU or would be forced to implement a severe program of austerity that would exact a high price in terms of growth, income, employment – and electoral support. Given that choice between unattractive alternatives, the four nations began to align with the "go-slow" coalition as a means of delaying the transition to EMU, dampening the magnitude of economic adjustment required during that transition, and delaying the day when they would almost certainly be left behind by those moving ahead to the third and last stage.

The Rome meeting in September 1990 broke up with no agreement on the timetable for the later stages of EMU. But the ministers had rejected the Commission's timetable, and Delors found that he had the support of only three countries – France, Italy, and Belgium – for his proposal of an early transition to a brief second stage of EMU. A new majority coalition had formed within the Council around the slow-transition, convergence-first position espoused by Germany, the Netherlands, and the central bankers (of whom the most vocal was Pöhl, the Committee's chair). Not surprisingly, Delors reacted with some bitterness; appearing before the European Parliament after the meeting, he spoke of the emergence of "a sort of rejection front . . . those who want an economic and monetary union so beautiful, so perfect, that it will never get started, it will never be born."[73]

Soon after the Rome meeting, the Committee of Central Bank Governors completed most of the work drafting the statutes of the new European central bank. Pöhl indicated that the governors had agreed on almost all of the basis issues – for example, that price stability was the bank's first priority, that it would be independent of governments and political instruction, that the monetary financing of deficits would be prohibited, that the bank would be called the European Central Bank (ECB) (not "Eurofed," as the Commission preferred), and that it would copy the Bundesbank in its organization of a board and council. Only relatively technical issues, such as the pooling

---

[73] Alan Riding, "Hesitation Now Greets Europe's Unity Plans," *The New York Times*, September 30, 1990, p. D1.

of reserves and allocation of its capital, remained – as well, of course, as the issues pertaining to criteria and timing of transitions that required Council, and ultimately European Council, decision.[74]

The finance ministers met again in October, in Luxembourg. The "go-slow" majority that formed in the Council at Rome remained intact. John Major brought the pound sterling into the ERM on the day of the meeting.[75] Despite the somewhat equivocal endorsement of the Monetary Committee – Britain having unilaterally set the rate for the pound at 2.95 marks, rather than negotiating a central rate in the Committee, as was the normal procedure – Major's colleagues praised the decision, and Solchaga of Spain again spoke in support of the British chancellor's scheme for a "hard ecu." More important, Solchaga and Wim Kok, the Dutch minister, offered similar proposals regarding the timing and conditions for transition to the later stages of EMU. Both called for delaying the transition to the second stage by one year beyond the date proposed by the Commission – that is, to January 1, 1994 (as Solchaga had proposed in Rome). They proposed that that transition be conditional on all states participating in the ERM, public sector deficits having been curbed and their monetization eliminated, and national central banks having been made independent. In addition, the Dutch proposed that the European Central Bank not be created until the third and final stage and that, in the second stage, a Council of Central Bank Governors be created out of the present Committee of Governors to monitor monetary and exchange rate policy and prepare the way for stage three.[76]

As the finance ministers met, the Bundesbank issued its own proposal for the second stage, entitled "Compromise Proposal for the Second Stage of EMU." Largely the work of Tietmeyer, the Bank's proposal endorsed and elaborated upon the Dutch and Spanish proposals regarding the conditions that would have to be satisfied in order to move to the second stage of EMU on January 1, 1994.[77] It stipulated that the single market would have to have been fully implemented, all currencies would have to be within the ERM and its

---

[74] See *Financial Times*, September 10, 1990, p. 4
[75] In May, Margaret Thatcher had told the Scottish Conference of the Conservative Party that the conditions she had stipulated the year before had been met and that the decision was therefore in the chancellor's hands. See *Financial Times*, May 14, 1990, p. 1.
[76] See David Buchan, "EC Members Move Closer to Agreement on Monetary Union," *Financial Times*, October 9, 1990, p. 2.
[77] See Peter Norman, "Stiff Conditions for Next Move to Monetary Union," *Financial Times*, October 8, 1990, p. 5.

David R. Cameron

narrow band, central banks would, where necessary, have to have been made fully independent, substantial progress would have to have been made in obtaining convergence in anti-inflation policy, and the monetization and compulsory financing of deficits would have to have been prohibited. It also proposed, as had the Dutch at Luxemburg, that the ECB come into being at the start of stage three, rather than early in stage two as the "fast-track" proponents desired. For stage two, it proposed, instead, that the Committee of Central Bank Governors be transformed into a Council of Governors. The Bank also outlined a set of criteria – the so-called "convergence criteria" – that would have to be satisfied during the second stage in order to move to the third and final stage: inflation would have largely to be eliminated, budget deficits reduced to "unproblematic" levels, and capital markets harmonized (as reflected in convergent long-term interest rates). Finally, it proposed that the statutes of the new European Central Bank be accepted as drafted by the Committee of Governors and be included in the Treaty.[78]

With the Bundesbank's acceptance, for the first time, of a specific (albeit conditional) date for transition to the second stage of EMU and its elaboration of preconditions for stage three that were nearly identical to those developed by Spain and the Netherlands, the ministers had before them the basis for an agreement that was acceptable to most, if not all, of the member states.[79] When Kohl announced (despite Waigel and Pöhl's continued opposition to unconditional transition dates, on one hand, and Genscher's continued advocacy of a 1993 starting date, on the other) that the Spanish proposal to begin stage two in 1994 was "sensible," Delors congratulated the German leader on a "reasonable compromise" and agreement on the date and terms of stage two was imminent. Indeed, only Britain continued to oppose setting a specific date.[80]

Italy convened a special meeting of the European Council in Rome in late October 1990. The meeting's major accomplishment was agree-

[78] This last point, we might note, would in effect give the Committee – a transnational actor – a formal role in a process – treaty-making – that was reserved for *governmental* actors.

[79] This is not to say the debate was not heated and even acrimonious at times; see David Buchan, "Battle Rages on Speed of EC Monetary Union," *Financial Times*, October 12, 1990, p. 2.

[80] See Philip Stephens, Peter Norman, and David Marsh, "Pöhl warns UK to adopt tough anti-inflation policy," *Financial Times*, October 16, 1990, p. 1; and David Buchan and David Goodhart, "Delors and Kohl Agree Emu Date," *Financial Times*, October 19, 1990, p. 2.

68

ment by all of the leaders except Mrs. Thatcher on the terms of reference of the IGC on EMU that would begin in December. All but the British prime minister agreed that the second stage would begin on January 1, 1994.[81] All but Mrs. Thatcher agreed, also, to a set of conditions for moving to stage two that represented a somewhat modified and softened amalgamation of proposals made by the German, Dutch, and Spanish finance ministers – that the single market program be fully implemented, the EMU treaty ratified, a process begun to make the national central banks independent of political instruction, the greatest possible number of states be in the ERM, and "further satisfactory and lasting progress toward real and monetary convergence . . . especially as regards price stability and the restoration of sound public finances" be achieved.[82] Following the Dutch and Bundesbank proposals, the leaders also agreed that a new institution – not the European bank itself but a more institutionalized form of the Committee of Central Bank Governors – would be established at the start of stage two to facilitate cooperation among the national central banks and coordination of the member states' monetary policies, as well as prepare the institutions and policies necessary for the third and final stage. Finally, as the Bundesbank and the Dutch had proposed, they agreed that the transitional second stage be of relatively short duration but that a precise date for moving to stage three not be set. They did, however, agree that within three years of the start of stage

[81] On Thatcher's refusal to accept the January 1, 1994, starting date, see Thatcher, *The Downing Street Years*, p. 767. Immediately upon her return from Rome, Thatcher made a statement in the House of Commons about the meeting that provoked Sir Geoffrey Howe to resign as leader of the House and deputy prime minister. Two weeks later, Howe delivered a resignation speech that was, in the words of Nigel Lawson, "quite simply, the most devastating speech I, or I suspect anyone else in the House that afternoon, had heard uttered in the House of Commons." The next day, Michael Heseltine challenged Thatcher in the annual Conservative Party leadership contest. One week later, although having won well over 50 percent of the vote in the leadership contest, Mrs. Thatcher received 4 votes less than the number necessary for the required 15 percent margin between the leading and second candidates. Two days later, she resigned as leader and prime minister. One week later, John Major – who had replaced Howe as foreign secretary in July 1989, and then Lawson as chancellor in October 1989 – defeated Heseltine and Douglas Hurd and became prime minister. See Lawson, *The View from 11*, p. 1000, and Thatcher, *The Downing Street Years*, pp. 832–62.

[82] See the excerpts from the Council's "Final Statement" in "Pointing Path to Second Phase of Economic and Monetary Union," *Financial Times*, October 29, 1990, p. 4. Britain stated that it was "unable to accept the approach set out above . . . [W]hile ready to move beyond stage one through the creation of a new monetary institution and a common community currency, [it] believes that decisions on the substance of that move should precede decisions on its timing."

two – that is, by January 1, 1997, at the latest – the Commission and the Council of the new monetary institution would report on the functioning of the second stage and whether "real convergence" had been attained, and that a decision to move to the third and final stage would be made within a "reasonable time" thereafter.

The Intergovernmental Conference and Maastricht

The IGC on EMU met for the first time in Rome in December 1990. Involving as it did a treaty-writing negotiation among the member states, the IGC was, by definition, an exercise in intergovernmental politics, and the primary actors were the representatives of the national governments – first and foremost, the ministers of finance and their subordinates, but also, on occasion, the heads of government.[83] Transnational actors such as the central bankers, as well as supranational actors such as Delors and the Commission, quite naturally receded in importance. Nevertheless, both transnational and supranational actors were influential over the course of the year-long IGC. Thus, for example, the IGC began by considering a draft Treaty prepared by the Commission that combined the 42 articles in nine chapters pertaining to the European Central Bank that had been prepared by the Committee of Central Bank Governors with articles pertaining to the other issues involving EMU that had been prepared by the Commission.[84] To cite another example, in the spring of 1991, the Committee of Central Bank Governors oversaw the preparation of the final statutes of the European System of Central Banks, including those of the new European Central Bank, that were then submitted to the IGC. The IGC itself consisted of monthly meetings of the finance

[83] In regard to the latter, we might note the important series of bilateral summits between Major and Kohl in 1991 that, in addition to repairing the damage to the relationship done by the personal friction between Thatcher and Kohl, furthered the convergence of German and British views regarding the length of stage two, the timing of the creation of the new monetary institution, and the issue of a British "opt-out" from stage three. They met in Bonn in February, March, and November, and in England in June. See, for example, *Financial Times*, February 12, 1991, and *Financial Times*, March 12, 1991, p. 1.

[84] On the Commission draft, see *Financial Times*, December 15–16, 1990, p. 3. The Commission's proposals were greeted with considerable hostility. Delors later described Waigel as having been "very tough" and said the German minister "violently attacked" portions of the Commission draft. Moreover, according to Delors, the Dutch, Spanish, and even French finance ministers appeared to renege on earlier commitments to EMU and the agreements reached at Rome. See *Financial Times*, December 17, 1990, pp. 1, 2; December 18, 1990, p. 1.

ministers. But those meetings were prepared by senior officials of the finance ministries who operated within the framework of the "transgovernmental" Monetary Committee and met biweekly. Finally, the central bankers who enjoyed some autonomy from national governments continued to express their views about EMU. In March 1991, for example, Pöhl called again for a two-tier EMU in which some states would move to the third stage before others; indeed, he said, to insist that all twelve countries enter the final stage of EMU at the same time in the face of economic divergence would have the same "disastrous" consequences as GEMU![85]

Perhaps the most consequential role played by the transnational actors in the IGC involved the preparation of draft treaties. During the first half of 1991, when Luxembourg held the Council presidency, several countries submitted drafts. In late February, Germany submitted a draft of a complete EMU treaty that presaged many of the features of EMU that were subsequently adopted – most notably, delaying the start of the ECB until the third stage, stipulating stringent quantitative conditions pertaining to inflation, deficits, and debt that would have to be met prior to moving to stage three, allowing states that satisfied the conditions to move to the third stage while the others remained behind, and making the second stage little more than an extension of the first coupled with an upgrading of the Committee of Central Bank Governors.[86] It was not only the German draft's completeness and detail that made it unusually authoritative in the IGC; it was authoritative, also, because, although formally submitted by the government, it had been prepared in close consultation with the Bundesbank and embodied the Bank's well-known and frequently articulated views.

After the "stock-taking" meeting of the European Council in Luxemburg in June 1991, the Council presidency passed to the Netherlands. As in the first half of the IGC, governmental actors – in particular, finance ministers and heads of government – dominated the negotiations. But again, transnational actors were influential. For example, in early September, the Dutch presidency put forward a set of proposals it intended to include in its draft treaty. Echoing the earlier German draft treaty, the Netherlands proposed that stage two

[85] See *Financial Times*, March 10, 1991, pp. 3, 22. Needless to say, Kohl and Waigel reacted angrily to Pöhl's characterization of GEMU as a "disaster." Two months later, Pöhl announced his intention to resign as president of the Bundesbank at the end of the summer, four years before the end of his term.
[86] See *Financial Times*, February 27, 1991, p. 7.

be transitional, that the ECB be created only in stage three, that a "European Monetary Institute" (not bank) be created in stage two on the foundation of the Committee of Central Bank Governors, that strict quantitative "convergence criteria" pertaining to inflation, deficits, and debt be satisfied as a necessary condition for moving to stage three – thereby assuring a "two-speed" or multi-speed EMU – and that Britain have the option of deciding later not to enter stage three. At about that time, Tietmeyer, who had been elevated to Vice President and designated as Helmut Schlesinger's successor as President upon Pöhl's resignation, appeared before a Bundestag committee. He unambiguously supported the Dutch proposals, which were then under assault by Belgium, Italy, Greece, and the Commission, emphasizing that much more convergence was required before exchange rates could be locked, that specific, quantitative convergence criteria were required as conditions for transition to stage three, that stage two must be short and transitional, that national central banks must retain full authority over monetary policy during the second stage, and that the creation of the new monetary institution must be delayed until stage three.[87] Although addressing a Bundestag committee, Tietmeyer was not speaking solely to a German audience; the finance ministers and central bank governors were to gather for their semi-annual "informal" weekend at Apeldoorn in the Netherlands in only three days. Not surprisingly, they endorsed the Dutch proposals.[88]

Even at the very last stages of the Intergovernmental Conference, the central bankers of the Community – preeminently transnational – remained influential in a process that was, in formal terms, intergovernmental. In October, the Dutch presidency presented its draft of the treaty provisions pertaining to EMU. With few alterations,[89] it became the basis of the EMU provisions in the Treaty on European Union. As with the German draft treaty some months before, what

[87] See *Financial Times*, September 19, 1991, p. 3.
[88] See *Financial Times*, September 23, 1991, p. 4.
[89] Perhaps the most significant alteration was the one concocted by Mitterrand and Andreotti of Italy over dinner on the eve of the December meeting of the European Council in Maastricht. To avoid EMU remaining forever in stage two, for lack of a majority of member states which satisfied the "convergence criteria," and to make EMU "irreversible," they devised a clause for the Treaty (embodied in Article 109j.4 and Protocol 10) that stipulated that the third stage would begin no later than January 1, 1999, even if the number of qualifying states did not constitute a majority. On this, see David Marsh, "Bonn Agrees to Surrender the D-Mark," *Financial Times*, December 12, 1991, p. 2. David Buchan reports, in *Financial Times*, December 11, 1991, p. 2, that this commitment to the "irreversibility" of EMU was orchestrated by Pierre Bérégovoy, the French minister of finance.

made the Dutch draft especially authoritative, in addition to its completeness (and the fact that it had been prepared by the presidency) was the fact that, although formally presented by the government, it had been prepared in close consultation with the Dutch Central Bank and incorporated the bank's views about EMU. Moreover, prior to submission to the IGC it had been presented to the Committee of Central Bank Governors at its monthly meeting in Basle for its approval, as well as the addition of the last relevant details pertaining to the European Monetary Institute and the statutes of the ECB.[90]

Conclusion

At their meeting in Maastricht in December 1991, the twelve leaders of the Community negotiated and agreed to the last details of the Treaty on European Union. As they did so, they brought to a conclusion a process that had started nearly five years earlier, with Edouard Balladur's proposals to reform the EMS. They also began another process, one that, if completed, will transform the Community more profoundly than any other innovation in its history.

This chapter has examined in detail the development of the EMU initiative in the late 1980s and early 1990s. That examination suggests that while both intergovernmental and supranational politics were influential, the EMU initiative also witnessed a *third* type of politics that involved *neither* the national governments of the member states *nor* actors embedded in the supranational institutions of the Community but, rather, *transnational* actors. Indeed, our account suggests that transnational actors and their politics were present and influential *throughout* the development of the EMU initiative, from the first meetings of the Delors Committee in 1988 to the last meetings of the IGC nearly four years later, and in some respects and at some moments,

---

[90] See *Financial Times*, October 29, 1991, pp. 1, 2, 22. This is not to say that *all* issues were resolved by the time the Dutch draft was tabled. A number – the location of the EMI and ECB, the amount of capital to be paid in, the voting system within the EMI and ECB, how to choose the President and Vice President of the EMI, how to define the role of the governors of member states that were unable or unwilling to join stage three and the ECB, etc. – remained, most of which were resolved in four ministerial meetings in Brussels, Scheveningen, and Maastricht in late November and early December. Resolution of the issues pertaining to the selection of the EMI's officers, its reserves, the composition of the ECB's boards, etc., was achieved in the second Brussels meeting on December 4, 1991. The last matter – whether to accept the Franco-Italian "irreversibility" proviso concocted the night before the European Council meeting in Maastricht – was agreed by the ministers the next day, a few hours before the meeting began!

they were *more* influential than *either* governmental or supranational actors.

Transnational actors and their politics were present and influential throughout the development of the EMU initiative for several reasons. First, of course, the very existence of the Community itself encourages and facilitates the activity of transnational actors to a far greater extent than might exist among a random collection of sovereign states. The unusually high degree of economic interdependence among the member states – itself the product of the Community's past efforts to eliminate trade barriers and create a single "common" market – coupled with the dense network of Community institutions, and the accumulation over decades of a long history of interaction within those institutions, provides both a *rationale* and an *opportunity* for non-state actors to come into contact and to pursue common interests. Second, as one aspect of this institutionalization, forums exist either within the Community or coterminous with it not only for *governmental* actors, such as the leaders and ministers of the governments of the member states, but for *transnational* actors as well. Most notably – and of most relevance for the EMU initiative – interaction among the central bankers, as well as collective action *by* them, was facilitated by the long-standing existence of the Committee of Central Bank Governors and the Monetary Committee. In addition to facilitating their interaction and enhancing their capacity for collective action, the institutionalization of these transnational actors enhanced their ability to influence policy in the Community. To note but two examples, the chair of the Committee of Central Bank Governors participated frequently in meetings of the Council of finance ministers, and the Committee as a whole participated in the semi-annual "informal" deliberations of finance ministers.

The presence and influence of transnational actors in the development of the EMU initiative was facilitated not only by the existence of the Community as a highly interdependent, densely institutionalized organization of states but by the existence, as well, of a monetary regime, the EMS, the management of which was delegated by the member states to these *institutionalized transnational* actors. Their responsibility for the EMS – as, for example, in changing interest rates or intervening in currency markets to keep currencies within their fluctuation ranges (the responsibility of the national central banks) and in monitoring the EMS and, if necessary, negotiating realignments (the responsibility of the Monetary Committee) – insured their presence

74

and influence in any initiative that involved monetary policy and exchange rate policy – especially one designed to repair alleged defects in the EMS.

The influence of the central bankers in the EMU initiative derived not only from their formal responsibility for EMS but also, we suspect, from the way in which the EMS evolved over time. As noted above, the EMS evolved, in its first decade, into a highly stable exchange rate regime. That stability, accompanied as it was by a growing convergence of inflation rates at historically low levels in the mid-to-late 1980s, was widely perceived as a measure of success. To the extent that it *was* perceived to have been successful in stabilizing prices and exchange rates, the performance of the EMS over its first decade may have enhanced the aura of competence and authority of the transnational actors who managed and directed the system. That, in turn, may have enhanced their capacity to influence monetary and exchange rate policy in the Community.

If the evolution of the EMS over its first decade enhanced the authority of the European central bankers, and their potential capacity to influence monetary and exchange rate policy, the aura of competence and authority deriving from its success may have accrued more to some central bankers than others. In particular, however much it may have enhanced the authority of European central bankers in general, the success of the EMS may have enhanced most the authority of those located in the countries that were most successful in achieving a low rate of inflation and a strong currency and were most closely identified with it. Throughout our discussion of the EMU initiative, we noted the active and influential role of Karl Otto Pöhl and Hans Tietmeyer, leading officials of the German Bundesbank. Their vocal presence, and influence, may have reflected not simply the power of Germany in the Community, conceived in conventional "structural realist" terms but, rather, the enhanced authority of the German central bank and its top officials in the wake of the evolution within the Community of the EMS into a highly stable exchange rate regime that accorded the Bundesbank a leading role in the formulation of monetary policy.

The most important conclusion to be drawn from this case study undoubtedly involves the impact of international institutions on the activity and influence of transnational actors. The facilitating effect of European Community institutions on the activity and influence of transnational actors can not be exaggerated. The development of the

EMS as a monetary regime, superimposed as it was upon an existing organization of interdependent states that was already densely populated with institutions – including institutions representing transnational actors – undoubtedly enhanced the authority and influence of the transnational actors charged with its management, especially those perceived to be most influential in it.

Important as the multiplicity of European institutions – the Community itself, such bodies as the Committee of Central Bank Governors, the Monetary Committee, the ministerial "informals," the EMS, etc. – was in facilitating the activity and influence of transnational actors in the EMU initiative, it is important not to lose sight of the impact on those actors of *domestic structures* as well, for those structures affected not only the degree of activity and influence of transnational actors but even their *identity* as transnational actors. While many aspects of the domestic political context of states could, in principle, affect the degree of activity and influence of transnational actors, one appears especially important in the story we have told about the EMU initiative. That involves the *institutional context* within which *domestic* politics and policy occurs within the member states of the Community.

Germany has figured prominently in our account of the EMU initiative, and no country better illustrates how the institutional context of domestic politics can affect the activity, influence, and even identity of transnational actors. At several points in the discussion, for example, we noted the highly pluralist – even fragmented – character of the German polity. Compared with most other member states in the Community, Germany is fragmented in regard to *both* the composition of the government (having a three-party coalition in which the views of the leaders of the coalition parties about EMU were widely dispersed) *and* control over economic and monetary policy (having a central bank that is constitutionally independent of the government). (It is also, of course, fragmented by federalism into separate levels of government.) Generalizing from the German experience, it would appear that fragmentation, decentralization, and a dispersion of policy preferences among political leaders not only create a multiplicity of access points for transnational (and other) actors seeking to influence policy *within* it but, *also*, are conducive to the appearance of transgovernmental and transnational actors *within* a polity and to their activity *outside* that polity.[91] Thus, for example, we observe at several instances during the development of the EMU initiative a trans-governmental coalition, between the German and French foreign ministers, that articulates positions quite distinctive from those espoused by other German ministers and the Chancellor. To take another example, we noted at various points in the development of the initiative the vocal role of leading officials of the German central bank – most notably, Herren Pöhl and Tietmeyer. Their active effort to influence the elaboration of EMU obviously reflected all the institutional features of the Community described above. But it also reflected certain institutional characteristics of *Germany* as well – in particular, the fact that the German central bank, like the Dutch bank (but unlike the other national central banks), enjoyed a considerable degree of independence and autonomy from the government. That independence created the possibility that the German (and Dutch) central bank officials could articulate positions distinctive from those taken by the ministries of finance and the government – a possibility that was, in a sense, institutionally precluded for central bankers in countries in which the central banks were subordinated to the ministries of finance.

This last point is intriguing, for it suggests not only that the institutional context of domestic politics within the member states can affect the ability of transnational actors to act, and thus influence policy, but that it may define the extent to which actors *are* in fact truly transnational, as opposed to agents of the national governments. We have, for convenience sake, treated all central bankers as transnational – i.e., non-state – actors. But some, in fact, are much more transnational than others. There can be little doubt that the German and Dutch central bank officials, exercising their constitutional independence and autonomy, were not simply agents of their governments. But can the same be said of the other central bankers – for example, those of France, Spain, Italy, Belgium, Britain? To a much greater extent than is

[91] For a suggestive discussion of the ways in which the centralization (or fragmentation) of states may hinder (or facilitate) the access to policy-making of external trans-national actors and enhance (or diminish) the capacity of states to act coherently in manipulating interdependence, see Keohane and Nye, *Power and Interdependence*, pp. 34–35.

the case with the central bankers of the Netherlands and Germany, the central bankers of the latter countries were simply agents of the national governments – in particular, the ministries of finance. This, we suspect, may have had the paradoxical effect of *diminishing* their influence, relative to that of the German and Dutch bankers, in the various forums where the central bankers gathered, by diminishing their capacity to speak independently and authoritatively with their colleagues *as bankers*, rather than subordinates of government ministers.

The story of EMU is complex, and full of twists and turns and unachieved ambitions. That EMU came to resemble, as it evolved and took shape prior to Maastricht, less the original French–Italian vision and more the vision articulated by German and Dutch central bankers and finance officials is indicative of the importance of institutionalized transnational actors in the Community – in particular, actors such as the central bankers of Germany and the Netherlands, whose activity and influence was enhanced *both* by international institutions that provided forums for their activity and enhanced their authority *and* by domestic political-institutional structures that empowered them to articulate their preferences and exert influence. Relative to their colleagues, the central bankers who happened to be German or Dutch were able to combine advantages deriving from *domestic structure* (independence and autonomy) with advantages deriving from the *international context* within which they operated (the existence of Community institutions that provided forums for activity and that enhanced their authority). Taken together, those advantages enabled them not only to influence the development of EMU but to shape it as well. For that reason, EMU, as it came to be defined in the Treaty on European Union, corresponds more closely to *their* preferences than to those of Delors, Balladur, Genscher, Mitterrand, and the others who resurrected the old idea in 1987 and 1988.

3 "Bullying," "buying," and "binding": US–Japanese transnational relations and domestic structures

Peter J. Katzenstein and Yutaka Tsujinaka

The problem addressed by this chapter is illustrated by the difference in the political strategy and tactics adopted by the American automobile and the Japanese electronics industries. Confronted by growing American protectionism in the 1970s and 1980s, Japanese corporations increasingly invested in American plants and produced in North America. But in some situations Japanese corporations also acted politically. When it became clear in 1987 that one of the Toshiba Group Corporations had sold to the Soviet Union sensitive technologies, it confronted a possible economic boycott in Congress. The Toshiba Group waged a sophisticated public relations campaign that succeeded brilliantly in undercutting the political forces in Congress favoring the embargo. The American automobile industry, on the other hand, in a period of deep recession, plunging sales, and mounting losses relied on its political connections with Congress and the White House to initiate negotiations over voluntary export restraints with Japan in 1981. These restraints have been periodically renewed throughout the 1980s, first in bilateral negotiations between the United States and Japan and, since 1985, unilaterally by Japan. When the automobile industry faced again economic hardship in 1991, the heads of the three major automobile corporations, blaming Japan for "unfair competition," joined the President of the United States in an ill-fated mission to Tokyo. The President returned with an empty stomach, the industry with empty hands.

There exists then a very great difference in how Americans typically

For comments on earlier drafts of this paper we would like to thank Ethan Nadelmann, James Goldgeier, Judith Goldstein, Ikuo Kume, T.J. Pempel, Judith Reppy, Thomas Risse-Kappen, Robert Smith, Takao Takahara, and Shibley Telhami as well as the participants in the two workshops on transnational relations.

pursue their political objectives in Tokyo and how the Japanese typically proceed in the United States. For reasons of convenience this is
referred to here as the difference between "bullying," "buying," and
"binding." Some American corporations operating in Japan try to
cooperate with the bureaucracy and trade associations ("binding").
But they also rely on top-level, direct and explicit political pressures by
the US government, often articulating new rules in support of
American liberal ideology ("bullying"). The Japanese favor private
corporations exerting indirect influence, normally abiding by and
exploiting existing rules in support of some concrete economic interests ("buying").

In the light of this characteristic difference in political behavior and
the conflicts to which it gives rise, it is striking that the security
relations between the United States and Japan have grown increasingly intimate in the last two decades. Few of the frictions that have
marked the economic relations between the two countries can be
found in their security arrangements. "Bullying" and "buying" have
been conspicuously absent; instead, the security relationship between
the United States and Japan is best described by "binding,"[1] with the
United States doing most of the "advising" and Japan most of the
"accepting." By and large since the mid-1970s defense cooperation
has increased smoothly and apparently to the satisfaction of both
militaries. Since that cooperation involved primarily governments and
sub-units of governments implementing policy, "binding" results primarily from transgovernmental relations. Since it offers a sharp contrast to the troubled economic relations between the two countries,
this cooperative extension of the security arrangements between the
United States and Japan should also be explainable by distinctive
features of the US and Japanese domestic structures.

On one central point the first generation of transnational scholarship agreed with the realist doctrines that it sought to enrich. Realism
stipulates states as central, unified, and rational actors in world politics
and thus assumes a pervasive similarity in the domestic politics that is
relevant for an understanding of international relations. Analogously,
the first generation of transnational scholarship relied on categories of
structural–functional theory and an implicit liberal convergence
theory, and applied them to domestic structures that were presumed
to be essentially similar. It erroneously abstracted from the specific

[1] Joseph Grieco, "The Renaissance of the European Community and the Crisis of Realist
International Theory," unpublished paper, 1992.

historical experiences that had shaped domestic structures differently in different countries. Focusing on these differences permits us to gain analytical leverage to explain different kinds of transnational relations. Central to this chapter's analysis are the differences in the domestic structures and states that are both capitalist and democratic. States are neither immutable actors embodying the principles of rational action nor parts of templates transformed similarly by a brave new world of transnational relations. Instead, shaped by different historical experiences, states refract differently the transnational relations (defined here as involving at least one set of non-governmental actors in the process of international politics) and transgovernmental relations (defined here as governments or sub-units of governments acting on their behalf in a process of transgovernmental coalition politics) through which they are partly constituted and to which they are exposed.[2]

Social and economic changes over the last several decades have created favorable conditions for rapid growth in the transnational ties in what former Ambassador Mansfield used to refer to as the most important bilateral relationship in the world. Trade relations between the United States and Japan exceeded 160 billion dollars in 1993.[3] Between 1951 and 1989 41 percent of Japan's total direct foreign investment, or 100 billion dollars, was invested in the US market. Between 1990 and 1993 Japan invested an additional 77 billion dollars; it now ranks first among foreign investors in the United States, with 22 percent of the cumulative total.[4] The increase of Japan's direct foreign investment in the United States has been striking, especially in the second half of the 1980s, even though it has been exceeded by either British or French acquisitions in 1987, 1989 and 1990.[5] The cumulative total of American direct foreign investment in Japan came to 31 billion dollars in 1993, and US corporations account for about half of the total

[2] Gregory P. Nowell, *Mercantile States and the World Oil Cartel, 1900–1939* (Ithaca, NY: Cornell University Press, 1994).

[3] International Monetary Fund, *Direction of Trade Statistics* (Washington, DC: International Monetary Fund, June 1994), p. 158.

[4] Okurasho (kokusaikinyukyoku kokusaisihonka taigai chokusetsu tosi gakari) [Ministry of Finance, International Finance Bureau, International Capital Division, Foreign Direct Investment Section], *Taigai chokusetsu tosi todokede jisseki [Japanese Direct Foreign Investment]*. (Tokyo: Okurasho, 1991); US Bureau of Economic Analysis, *Survey of Current Business* 74, 8 (Washington, DC: Bureau of Economic Analysis, August 1994), p. 137; Japan's Ministry of Finance, Institute of Fiscal and Monetary Policy, *Monthly Finance Review*, 252 (June 1994), p. 18.

[5] Randall Smith, "French Firms Pass British, Japanese as Leading Acquirers of US Concerns," *The Wall Street Journal*, April 24, 1991, p. A4.

direct foreign investment in Japan. The definition of what counts as
foreign ownership is complex and differs somewhat in the two countries. In 1989–90 there were 507 Japanese companies, with 114,000
employees in which US investors were holding more than 50 percent
of equity, compared to 1,777 Japanese companies with 218,000 employees in the United States.[6] While more than 3 million Japanese tourists
visited the United States in 1990, 244,000 American tourists traveled to
Japan.[7] Twenty-four thousand Japanese were studying at American
universities in 1988, and their number had increased to 40,000 by 1992;
in 1988 961 Americans were studying in Japan.[8] At the end of 1990
38,000 Americans were living in Japan, compared to 236,000 Japanese
living in the United States.[9] Thirty-nine American states maintain
offices in Japan, while twelve Japanese prefectures have offices in the
United States.[10] In most instances the Japanese entanglement with the
United States is greater than the reverse. This asymmetry is particularly evident in language instruction. Despite the explosion of
interest in Japan and skyrocketing enrollments in Japanese language
courses in the United States only 45,000 Americans were studying
Japanese in the early 1990s. But virtually all Japanese with a university
education had learned English, for at least a decade. These social and

6   Tsusansho (sangyo seisakukyoku) [Ministry of International Trade and Industry,
    Industrial Policy Bureau], *Dai 18, 19 kai wagakuni kigyo no kaigai jigyo katsudo* [*Activities of
    Japanese Companies Abroad*], 18th and 19th edns. (Tokyo: Okurasho [Ministry of
    Finance], 1990); Tsusansho (seisakukyoku) [Ministry of International Trade and Indus-
    try, Policy Bureau]. *Dai 24 kai gaishikei kigyo no doko* [*Conditions of Foreign Companies in
    Japan*], 24th edition (Tokyo: Okurasho [Ministry of Finance], 1991); Dennis J. Encar-
    nation, *Rivals beyond Trade: America versus Japan in Global Competition* (Ithaca, NY:
    Cornell University Press, 1992); US Bureau of Economic Analysis, *Survey of Current
    Business*, p. 137.
7   Homusho (homudaijin kanbo siho hosei chosabu) [Ministry of Justice, Secretariat
    Bureau, Judicial System and Research Department], *Dai 30 kai shutsu nyukoku kanri tokei
    nenpo* (30th Annual Immigration Statistics) (Tokyo: Okurasho [Ministry of Finance],
    1991), pp. 98–99, 150–52.
8   Monbusho [Ministry of Education, Science, and Culture] *Wagakunino bunkyo seisaku*
    [*Japan's Education Policy*] (Tokyo: Okurasho [Ministry of Finance], 1990), pp. 356, 553;
    Ezra Vogel, "Japanese–American Relations after the Cold War," *Daedalus* (Fall 1992),
    p. 47.
9   Homusho, *30th Annual Immigration Statistics*; Gaimusho (gaimudaijin kanbo ryoji
    ijyubu) [Ministry of Foreign Affairs, Secretariat Bureau, Immigration and Consular
    Affairs Department], *Kaigai zairyu hojinsu chosa tokei* [*Statistical Survey of Overseas
    Japanese*] (Tokyo: Okurasho [Ministry of Finance], 1991).
10 "Japan: What Kind of Power to Be," *World Press Review* (1989), p. 13; Toshio Obi,
    Nichibei Kanryo Masatsu [*US–Japan Bureaucratic Frictions*] (Tokyo: Kodansha, 1992),
    p. 184; Richard C. Sachs, "Lobbying by Foreign Interests: Japan," *CRS Report for
    Congress* (Washington, DC: The Library of Congress, Congressional Research Service,
    April 5, 1991), p. 7.

economic contacts find expression in a number of public–private contacts such as semigovernmental organizations, including the Japan–United States Economic Relations Group and the United States–Japan Advisory Commission, the "wise men's group" and "new wise men's group" created, respectively, in 1979 and 1983.[11]

This chapter briefly summarizes first some central aspects of the domestic structures of the United States and Japan which filter the effects transnational relations have on policy. It then argues that these differences in domestic structures account for the difference between "binding," "bullying," and "buying." American actors tend both to cooperate and to put pressure on the Japanese state bureaucracy, and its ancillary political and social interests, to gain access to Japanese markets and concessions. Japanese actors tend to exert influence indirectly by creating political leverage through investing in American plants, political influence and a favorable social climate. The analysis is then extended to security issues and the transgovernmental relations between the United States and Japan. "Binding" describes here the cooperative extension of security arrangements between the United States and Japan. It is explained here by the different role that the American state and the Japanese state play on military security issues. The chapter concludes with a brief summary.

Different domestic structures

The domestic structure of the United States is characterized by both distinctive organizational and normative features. A pervasive pluralism within society goes hand in hand with a national state with limited capacities in most fields. The normative context for politics is defined by a strong liberal ideology which defines the United States as the champion of unfettered market competition within and between national economies.

Successive waves of immigration in the nineteenth century and the migration from the rural south to the urban north in the first half of the twentieth century established the pluralism of American society. The rapid growth of the Hispanic and Asian-American populations in the last three decades thus reinforces a long-standing pattern that sets American society apart from much of the rest of the industrial world.

At its center, in Washington, the American state has very limited

---

[11] Hiroshi Masuda, "The Roles of Semigovernmental Organizations in Japanese–American Relations," *Journal of Northeast Asian Studies*, 6,1 (Spring 1987), pp. 76–83.

capacities to affect directly the evolution of society and economy. Federalism, the separation of power, and judicial review – as well as the weakening of some important institutions, such as the American party system, and the strengthening of others, such as the litigation system – impose severe limitations on the institutional capacities of those holding public office. Specifically, government officials have been consumed, especially during the last two decades, by fierce battles over jurisdictional issues that tend to push to the margins policy problems of increasing urgency.

The combination of social pluralism and limited state capacities enjoys the support of a strong norm of the United States as a champion of free markets. This norm is diffused throughout state and society, and it enjoys very strong support in virtually all political quarters. The political contest over values – what kind of liberalism, what kind of pluralism, what kind of past, and what kind of future – is of great importance because of the central political role that norms play in holding state and society together.

The behavioral consequences of the domestic structure of the American state and society as well as their normative foundations are political stalemate on central policy issues and political conflict over norms. The history of American energy policy in the 1970s and the American budget deficit in the 1980s illustrate well how institutional stalemate translated into policy stalemate regardless of the international consequences it had for the long-term position of the United States. Deregulation in energy and a growing dependence of the US treasury on Japanese and German investors in the 1980s – that is, a politically conditioned recourse to market solutions – became the preferred policy which sidestepped problems, such as increasing energy conservation and decreasing social consumption, that proved to be simply too intractable for American politics.

Power in Japan is organized in a system that Richard Samuels has aptly called a system of "reciprocal consent."[12] This consent balances the autonomy of the state against its embeddedness in civil society. It generates very different capacities for political action than does the combination of social pluralism and limited government in the United States. The normative context for politics is less explicit than in the United States. It rests rather on the implicit understanding that national policy is to serve Japan's long-term interests.

[12] Richard J. Samuels, *The Business of the Japanese State: Energy Markets in Comparative and Historical Perspective* (Ithaca, NY: Cornell University Press, 1987).

Although it should not be overestimated, the homogeneity of Japanese society offers a striking contrast to the United States. While Japanese society is sometimes marked by a social movement politics, the space for autonomous social action is more constrained than in the United States. Many social sectors are penetrated and organized indirectly as a whole by the government. Only a failure of political leadership and a serious erosion of state legitimacy will generate large-scale violence indicating a breakdown in political bargaining rather than the conflicts that inhere in social diversity.

The importance of social homogeneity, however, does not mean that Japan is ruled by a monolithic coalition of business and government, a "Japan Inc."[13] Nor does Japan feature a system of unfettered market competition. During the last decade various general interpretations which Japan specialists have advanced stress instead the interaction between state and market, politicians and bureaucrats, as well as social movements and political organizations, in creating a complex political system that combines factional and bureaucratic rivalries and political immobilism with political planning and flexible adjustments to external constraints. The close interaction between state and society endows Japan's developmental state with institutional capacities, such as its national bureaucracy with its advisory commissions, that give it formidable institutional capacities, especially when compared to those of the American state.

As is true of the United States, Japanese politics is based on strong normative foundations, but in contrast to the United States these norms are expressed less explicitly especially on economic issues. It is widely assumed that public policy should serve the long-term interests of Japan to enhance its economic prosperity and social stability through growing technological autonomy and the pursuit of a policy of international cooperation. The concepts of *Wa* (harmony) or *Kyoei* (co-prosperity) traditionally have expressed this norm. Recently a growing number of business and political leaders and some legal scholars have referred to a new concept, *Kyosei* (symbiosis or con-viviality).[14] However, appeals to the benefits of free market com-

---

[13] T.J. Pempel, "The Unbundling of 'Japan Inc.': The Changing Dynamics of Japanese Policy Formation," *Journal of Japanese Studies*, 13, 2 (Summer 1987), pp. 271–306.

[14] Tatsuo Inoue, Toshihiko Nawada, and Takao Katsuragi, *Kyosei eno Boken [In Search of Conviviality]* (Tokyo: Mainichi Shinbunsha, 1992). *Kyosei* generally means that there should exist mutually prosperous and harmonious relations, for example, between private and public, between Japan and other countries (especially the US), and between humans and nature. The concept of *Kyosei* appeared first in the mid-1980s

petition as a panacea are rare, except in meetings with high-level delegations visiting from Washington.

The behavioral consequences of the interaction between state and society in Japanese politics is to encourage adaptable public policies. Energy, the restructuring of industries, the reorganization of industrial relations and public spending are good examples. These issues posed enormous challenges in the 1970s and 1980s. The Japanese government, business and labor succeeded in the 1970s and 1980s in changing their policies to establish the foundations for future economic growth without increasing energy consumption, with adapatable industries and a reorganized, functionally more centralized industrial relations system, and dramatically curtailed public deficits.

These domestic structures in the United States and Japan evolve over time, in part because of changes in transnational relations. In the United States, for example, the end of the Cold War has shifted political priorities toward a greater concern with the revitalization of American society and its economy. This is bound to affect domestic structures. While it is too early to assess the extent of this change in the United States, in Japan policy reform efforts of the 1980s – including tax reform, the attempted liberalization of agriculture, electoral reform initiatives, and efforts to spur consumption and leisure over investment and work – all illustrate the political effort to reshape Japan's domestic structure and the difficulty of accomplishing this task. Granting that domestic structures evolve over time, we can still stipulate that these structures provide incentives and constraints which shape the behavior of political actors and thus transnational and transgovernmental relations.

Transnational economic relations

Internationalization

The growth of transnational economic relations has affected the United States and Japan differently. In the case of the United States it has occurred through market pressures that have opened an increas-

and has been used with increasing frequency in the early 1990s – 279 times between 1986 and 1991, and 294 times in 1992, for example – in four Nikkei Shinbun papers (data from Nikkei Needs Data Bank). Some legal philosophers rely on this concept for describing a "new Japan" as a society open to other countries and characterized by diverse social elements.

ing number of sectors of the American economy to foreign competition thus encouraging "buying" strategies. Not so in Japan. Internationalization is one of the most favored descriptions in Japan of the political, economic, and social processes that have made the 1980s a decade most easily compared to the 1860s. "Bullying" strategies by external actors (*gaiatsu*) in the policy process are probably the most notable aspects of transnational relations in Japan. Foreign actors are included either directly or indirectly into domestic policy coalitions in which "nationalists" and "internationalists" seek to find compromises acceptable to each other as well as the Americans who insist on changes in Japanese policies and domestic structures.[15]

Much of the writing on Japan's liberalization policies in trade, finance, and services can be read from this perspective. This literature supports the view that the internationalization of Japan has different dimensions. It describes, first, a change in policies that have abandoned many of the mercantilist practices of the past as Japanese industries have gained positions of strength in global markets. It describes, secondly, the dismantling of the government–business relationship that had grown up during the 1950s and 1960s.[16] Lastly, it describes recent attempts by the United States to target (as in the super 301 trade bill, the 1991 Semiconductor Agreement and the January 1992 auto parts agreement) the system of Japanese corporate alliances (*keiretsu*) and preferential buying practices that make it difficult for foreign companies to gain market share in Japan.[17]

These changes are illustrated, for example, by a reduction in Japanese tariff levels that have, on average, made them lower than those of the United States and the European Community. It is also illustrated by a change in the general approach taken by the revised

---

[15] Leonard J. Schoppa, "Two-Level Games and Bargaining Outcomes: Why *Gaiatsu* Succeeds in Japan in some Cases but not Others," *International Organization*, 47, 3 (Summer 1993), pp. 353–86; Leonard J. Schoppa, Jr., "Comparing the Impact of *Gaiatsu* over Time: Clinton, Bush and the Effort to Pry Open the Japanese Market," paper prepared for delivery at the 1994 Annual Meeting of the American Political Science Association, the New York Hilton, September 1–4, 1994; John C. Campbell, "Iraira gata sessho no kino to koyo" ["The Functions and Benefits of Tough Negotiations"], *Chuo Koron* (December 1989), pp. 112–23; Jiro Yamaguchi, "External Pressure and Policy Making in Japan," unpublished paper (Ithaca, NY: Cornell University, Government Department, 1988).

[16] Chalmers Johnson, "The 'Internationalization' of the Japanese Economy," *California Management Review*, 25, 3 (Spring 1983), p. 14.

[17] Takatoshi Ito, "US Political Pressure and Economic Liberalization in East Asia," in Jeffrey A. Frankel and Miles Kahler, eds., *Regionalism and Rivalry: Japan and the United States in Pacific Asia* (Chicago: The University of Chicago Press, 1993), pp. 391–422.

Peter J. Katzenstein and Yutaka Tsujinaka

Foreign Exchange and Foreign Trade Control Law in 1979 which moved from prohibiting Japan's external transactions in principle to freeing them in principle, subject to some emergency restrictions that the government is authorized to impose.[18] The *de jure* liberalization of the Japanese economy has progressed very rapidly. In the area of finance, for example, James Abegglen and George Stalk concluded that "within only six years, the apparatus of controls had been dismantled, with Japan as open to capital investment as any other of the OECD member countries."[19] In the views of some observers, like Kent Calder, these changes in policies and structural arrangements were forced on a reactive Japanese state by the political pressures of foreign actors, primarily the US government.[20] In the opinion of others, changes in Japan's foreign economic policies occurred when political pressures, especially by foreign multinationals, gained the support of domestic Japanese corporations whose interests had shifted over time to a position better served by a more open Japanese economy.[21]

The numerous *de facto* restrictions that remain in place are the subject of never-ending negotiations especially with the United States as the most forceful source of external pressure or *gaiatsu*. The intensifying American pressure in the 1970s and 1980s evokes memories of Commodore Perry: American pressure is sometimes referred to as a "second coming of the Black Ships."[22] In some of the Japanese media this pressure is now viewed as calling into question the basic nature of Japan, its social and cultural institutions as well as attitudes and traditions.[23] Japan's defense effort and the trade imbalance have been the two interacting issues which have fueled this external pressure. The negotiation of voluntary export restraint agreements since 1955 and the Structural Impediment Initiatives (SII) Talks designed in the

---

[18] Johnson, "The 'Internationalization' of the Japanese Economy," pp. 15–16.
[19] James Abegglen and George Stalk Jr., *Kaisha: The Japanese Corporation* (New York: Basic Books, 1985), p. 223.
[20] Kent E. Calder, "Japanese Foreign Economic Policy Formation: Explaining the Reactive State," *World Politics*, 40, 4 (July 1988), pp. 517–41.
[21] Dennis J. Encarnation and Mark Mason, "Neither MITI nor America: The Political Economy of Capital Liberalization in Japan," *International Organization*, 44, 1 (Winter 1990), pp. 25–54; Yasunori Sone and Masao Kanazashi, *Nihon no Seiji [Japanese Politics]* (Tokyo: Nihon Keizai Shinbunsha, 1989).
[22] Aurelia George, "Japan's America Problem: The Japanese Response to US Pressure," *The Washington Quarterly* (Summer 1991), p. 5.
[23] Ibid. p. 6.

late 1980s to open the Japanese economy are both examples of a repetitive political process that at times takes on ritualistic forms.[24]

John Campbell has argued that the conflict engendered by *gaiatsu* follows six stages: (1) the American government identifies some pattern of Japanese behavior that it finds objectionable; (2) the Japanese government agrees to negotiations even though it sees nothing wrong; (3) the American side legitimizes its demands by calling the Japanese behavior "unfair"; (4) the Japanese government rejects the charge and finds "unfairness" on the American side; (5) the American government threatens Japan with protectionism or some other dire consequence, thus accentuating a sense of crisis; (6) eventually the Japanese government gives in by agreeing to most or all American demands. After a brief period of goodwill the cycle repeats itself. "Negotiations are held repeatedly, on questions which can be settled, between two parties who have real conflicts of interest but who also see themselves in a beneficial long-term relationship."[25] In a similar vein Aurelia George has listed a range of common Japanese responses to American pressure including "package diplomacy," "affirmative action," "incrementalism," "substitution-compensation," "tokenism," "bilateralism," and "culturalism."[26]

This external pressure has to some extent become institutionalized in Japanese decision-making as foreign, and specifically American, interests are activated in the domestic political arena. While other countries exploit foreign pressure to sell unpopular policies to domestic constituencies, the distinctive aspect of *gaiatsu* is to overcome the immobilism that inheres in the Japanese policy system with its bottom-up consensus decision-making style.[27] Because self-persuasion is so difficult, *naiatsu* or internal pressure is a rare commodity in Japan's political system. This is a critical piece of evidence that lays to rest the

---

[24] Mitoji Yabunaka, *Taibei Keizai Kosho* [*In Search of New US–Japan Economic Relations: Views from the Negotiating Table*] (Tokyo: Saimaru shuppankai, 1991); Glen Fukushima, *Nichibei Keizai Masatsu no Seijigaku* [*The Politics of US–Japan Economic Frictions*] (Tokyo: Asahi Shinbun, 1992).

[25] Campbell, "The Functions and Benefits of Tough Negotiations," p. 10.

[26] George, "Japan's America Problem," pp. 7–16.

[27] Schoppa, "Two-Level Games and Bargaining Outcomes"; Schoppa, "Comparing the Impact of *Gaiatsu* over Time"; Yoichi Funabashi, "Structural Impediments of Japan's International Economic Policy Making," paper prepared for the Conference of "The European–Japanese Relations: The Next Phase," Ebenhausen, November 26–28, 1989, p. 7; J.A.A. Stockwin, Alan Rix, Aurelia George, James Horne, Daiichi Ito, and Martin Collick, *Dynamic and Immobilist Politics in Japan* (Honolulu: University of Hawaii Press, 1988); Sone and Kanazashi, *Japanese Politics*, pp. 232–36.

notion of a monolithic Japan Incorporated.[28] In the words of John Dower, *gaiatsu*, or "small violence," is often invited by the government or business "to put pressure on the bureaucracy. Or, in certain circumstances, the bureaucracy itself may desire *gaiatsu* to strengthen its case against recalcitrant politicians or rival ministries. Whatever the case, it is apparent that a complex political dance is taking place."[29] In any case *gaiatsu* has become an integral part of the shifting coalition of political forces that has led to the opening of Japanese markets in the last two decades, particularly when it supported a growing domestic coalition favoring a change in traditional policy.[30]

The transnational politics that is a central feature of *gaiatsu* is creating substantial and probably irreversible changes in Japanese policies and political arrangements. Not known as a proponent of arguments celebrating the early convergence between Japan's developmental state and other forms of capitalism, Chalmers Johnson nonetheless concludes that "young and middle-aged Japanese born in the 1950s and 1960s, are just now achieving responsible positions in government and private industry. They differ from all other Japanese born in this century in their ready familiarity with peace and prosperity . . . They can be expected to persist with the internationalization of the economy since it has become fundamental to Japan's continued prosperity . . . The continuing process of the internationalization of Japan's economic institutions and norms is well started but not yet completed."[31]

Foreign lobbies are an important element in the process of internationalization. Foreign lobbies share some common characteristics that set them apart from domestic lobbies. Except for unusual circumstances they cannot mobilize votes. And foreigners are normally

---

[28] Edward A. Olsen, "Determinants of Strategic Burdensharing in East Asia: The US–Japan Context," *Naval War College Review* (May–June 1986), p. 13; Robert C. Angel, "US–Japan Economic Relations: Lessons from the 1971 Yen Revaluation Crisis," paper prepared at the University Seminar on "Modern East Asia: Japan," New York, Columbia University, April 14, 1978, p. 5.

[29] John Dower, "Psychological Aspects of Contemporary US–Japan Relations," unpublished paper (January 1988), p. 26.

[30] Kent E. Calder, "Opening Japan," *Foreign Policy*, 47 (Summer 1982), pp. 82–97; Shigeko N. Fukai, "The Role of 'Gaiatsu' in Japan's Land Policymaking," paper prepared for delivery at the 1992 Annual Meeting of the American Political Science Association, The Palmer House Hilton, September 3–6, 1992; Brian Woodall, "The Calculus of Collusion: External Pressure and Collusive Action in Japanese Public Works," paper prepared for delivery at the 1992 Annual Meeting of the American Political Science Association, the Palmer House Hilton, September 3–6, 1992.

[31] Johnson, "The 'Internationalization' of the Japanese Economy," p. 24.

prohibited from making direct political contributions. Foreign lobbies thus have a difficult time gaining direct influence in bodies such as the Diet. Instead foreign lobbies tend to concentrate their resources on information gathering and analysis. When foreign lobbies want to exert direct influence they have several alternatives. They can focus on the executive branch of government and the national bureaucracy; activate political actors in their home countries; build alliances with interest groups in the host country; or bypass the formal political process, for example, by investing directly in the economy or by creating a favorable climate of opinion through a variety of economic and social measures.

These similarities, shared by both the American and the Japanese lobby are, however, counteracted by some distinctive differences.[32] The Japanese lobby in the United States is largely private in character with individual corporations, business associations, and Japan External Trade Research Organization (JETRO) as its central actors. The American lobby in Japan has a more public character, with the embassy, the representatives of thirty-nine American states, and the American military complementing the activities of individual American corporations. This difference is the key to an understanding of the "buying" and "bullying" strategies of the two lobbies.

The United States in Japan

The American lobby in Tokyo is large and varied. It consists of the American Embassy, representatives of thirty-nine individual states, the American Chamber of Commerce with 600 corporate affiliates, the International Enterprise Committee of Keidanren (which is chaired by Takeo Shina, President of Japan IBM), and think tanks, as well as consulting and public relations companies.[33] A central staple of American lobbying, lawyers, operate under severe restraints in Tokyo. Under the Foreign Law Attorney System, which became effective in April 1987, as of August 1992, 123 foreign lawyers have been registered, 88 of whom are American. The system permits them to deal only with legal matters of their home countries. They are prohibited by law to address Japanese legal problems; they cannot hire Japanese lawyers; and they are forbidden even to sign partnership contracts with Japanese firms. Although a substantial amount of lobbying takes place

---

[32] Obi, *US–Japan Bureaucratic Frictions*, pp. 249–52.   [33] Ibid. pp. 170–76.

indirectly through what is known as the "old-boy network" and influential middlemen, the system is fundamentally driven by the political pressure that is exerted by the US government on the networks linking Japanese government, bureaucracy, and business.[34] The effort, energy, and resources that American corporations and politicians have invested in mastering the ins and outs of the Japanese political system are of recent origin.

A survey of about 150 foreign lobbies operating in Tokyo in 1987 makes these general impressions more precise.[35] It reported that two-thirds of the respondents felt that Japan's administrative procedures impaired their operations in Japan, and more than half indicated that it is necessary to lobby. But the wielding of influence requires political contacts. By a ratio of 3:1 foreign lobbies trust the bureaucracy more than party politicians (60 versus 20 percent); about half have cooperative relations with administrative agencies; 15 percent (as compared to 66 percent of Japanese interest groups at the national level) send company representatives to advisory committees of the government;[36] about 30 percent hire retired bureaucrats (as compared to only 19 percent of Japanese interest groups at the national level); finally, foreign lobbies put much store in Japanese business associations, particularly as sources of valuable information and as an indispensable and effective lobbying instrument.[37] These data record, therefore, that American corporations are to a substantial degree seeking to play the political game in Tokyo by Japanese rules.

A survey of American corporations conducted in the autumn of 1991 in Tokyo permits us to refine further this general characterization.[38]

[34] Steve Lohr, "American Lobby Gaining in Japan," *The New York Times*, April 9, 1984, p. D10; Yuko Iida, "How to Lobby 'Japan Inc.'," *The Five College International Forum* (Spring 1988), pp. 12–15; Paul Addison, "US Companies Increasingly Tap Japan's Network of Ex-Bureaucrats," *The Japan Economic Journal* (May 26, 1990), p. 7; Clyde McAvoy, "Yankee Traders as 'Agents of Influence' in Japan," *Washington Times*, November 19, 1990; Michael Berger, "Lobbying in Japan," *Journal of the American Chamber of Commerce in Japan* (December 1990), pp. 7–8; Robert Neff, "Wooing Bureaucrats, Winning Business," *Business Week* (January 29, 1990), pp. 74F–74H; Obi, *US–Japan Bureaucratic Frictions*, pp. 155–96; John Fallows, "The Japan-Handlers," *Atlantic Monthly*, 264, 2 (August 1989), pp. 14–23.

[35] Sone Yasunori Kenkyukai [Sone Study Group], *Nihon ni Okeru Gaikoku Robi [The Foreign Lobby in Japan]* (Tokyo: Sone Yasunori Kenkyukai, 1987).

[36] Michio Muramatsu, Mitsutoshi Ito, and Yutaka Tsujinaka, *Sengo Nihon no Atsuryoku Dantai [Japanese Pressure Groups in the Post-War Era]* (Tokyo: Toyo Keizai Shinposha, 1986), p. 204.

[37] Sone Yasunori Kenkyukai, *The Foreign Lobby in Japan*.

[38] The House Wednesday Group, *Insiders and Outsiders: American Firms Tackle The "Tokyo Loop"* (Washington, DC: Congress of the United States, March 1993).

The survey was sent to 284 of the largest US firms operating in Japan. Of the 130 firms which returned the survey most were majority-owned American joint ventures; one-third of them has established representative offices or branches in Japan. One-fourth of them came, respectively, to Japan before 1959, in the 1960s, 1970s, and 1980s. These are then the largest, best established, and most successful American corporations operating in Japan today. They have developed an encompassing political strategy which includes the exertion of direct political pressure by American officials as well as the normal political activities.

Indeed, what is striking is the fact that these corporations appear to have adapted themselves to the political requirements of Japanese politics and seek to follow a strategy of "binding." In their responses they stress the importance of working together with the bureaucracy, Japanese business leaders, and Japanese interest groups. They are aware of the importance of public opinion and the media but attach less importance to politicians (Question 20). This evaluation differs dramatically from the ones American interest groups give in the United States.[39] Generally speaking, American interest groups operating in the United States consider politicians and Congress to be more important than the White House and the federal bureaucracy. In contrast, American corporations in Tokyo have especially good contacts with the national bureaucracy. Forty-five percent exchange information with bureaucratic agencies about business developments (Question 26). Most of them meet periodically with bureaucrats from almost all of the economic ministries. In sharp contrast to the United States, meetings with the Ministry of Justice are rare. The information exchange with the Japanese bureaucracy is more frequent and intense than with the business advisory system that the US government has set up for American corporations operating in Japan (Questions 26 and 47). This is not surprising if one considers that, on average, the ratio between the commercial staff of the US government in Japan and US business executives in Japan is 1:62, compared to a ratio of 1:21 in the case of Britain and 1:9 in the case of Germany.[40] Some of the American corporations are already deeply embedded in the intimate relations between state and society that characterize Japan. Ten percent, for

[39] Kay L. Schlozman and John T. Tierny, *Organized Interests and American Democracy* (New York, Harper and Row, 1986), pp. 272–73; Yutaka Tsujinaka, *Rieki Shudan [Interest Groups]* (Tokyo: Tokyo Daigaku Shuppankai, 1988), pp. 119–21.
[40] Keith Bradsher, "Level of Government Assistance for Exporters is Debated," *The New York Times*, March 4, 1992, p. A20.

example, are currently participating in some government-sponsored research initiative; 12 percent offer positions to retired Japanese bureaucrats; and 30 percent send representatives to government-sponsored advisory committees (Questions 28, 36, and 37). Although these figures are low compared to those for Japanese interest groups and corporations, they point toward a slowly emerging symbiosis between American corporations and the Japanese bureaucracy. But it is noteworthy that the more recent the arrival of an American corporation, the more closed it perceives the Japanese economic and political systems to be (Questions 4, 10 and 18).

The interaction between American corporations and Japanese interest groups points in the same direction. Sixty-one percent of the sampled corporations belong to a Japanese trade association, with the balance not interested in joining. That is, all companies interested in joining can do so. But only 50 percent of these corporations belong to American trade associations operating in Japan (Questions 39 and 41), and American corporations prefer Japanese to American associations. Through Japanese trade associations, 60 percent established important personal contacts, 49 percent received information and advice about marketing, and 37 percent received privileged information reserved for insiders (Question 39). Virtually all of those who belong to Japanese associations consider their membership in trade associations to be important in seeking to influence Japanese policy. The reason lies probably in the fact that "the network of associations in Japan is denser, somewhat more amply endowed with financial resources, and more intimately connected to the state than the corresponding network in the United States."[41] In sharp contrast, 58 percent of the corporate respondents are not satisfied with the performance of American trade associations operating in Japan (Question 42). As is true in their relations with the bureaucracy, American corporations are increasingly linked to the Japanese system of interest groups.

[41] Leonard H. Lynn and Timothy J. McKeown, *Organizing Business: Trade Associations in America and Japan* (Washington, DC: American Enterprise Institute for Public Policy Research, 1988), p. 172. The density of Japanese business associations is at least twice as high as in the US. In 1986 there were 13,386 business associations with 81,831 employees in Japan and 11,637 business associations with 90,159 employees in the US. Per 100,000 population, the Japanese number is 11.0 associations with 67.4 employees. See Yutaka Tsujinaka, "Nihon to Amerika ni okeru tai aitekoku robi no hikakubun-nseki" ["Comparative Analysis of Foreign Lobbies between the USA. and Japan"], in Ikuo Kabashima, ed., *Nihonseiji no Dotai* [*Dynamism of Japanese Politics*] (Tokyo: Tokyo Daigaku Shuppankai, 1993). Data from Somucho Tokeikyoku, *The Establishment Statistics in Japan in 1986* (Tokyo: Nihon Tokeikyokai); Bureau of the Census 1988, *The Country Business Patterns 1986* (Government Priority Office, 1988).

Forty-two percent of these American corporations characterize their approach to public policy matters as active or aggressive and 31 percent feel that they have been able to contribute to the formulation or implementation of policies, regulations, or laws that affect their interests (Questions 21 and 22). Indeed 26 percent of the corporations reported that they have a special department or section in charge of lobbying. They feel that their lobbying efforts have been quite successful. Their success is astonishing considering that 42 percent of the corporations employ no Japanese-speaking Americans and 47 percent employ fewer than five American employees who can speak Japanese.

However, American corporations rely also on "bullying" tactics. For it is heavy pressure, especially heavy political pressure exerted by the government rather than by American business leaders (as T. Boone Pickens and the top leadership of the American automobile industry experienced in recent years), that makes the system of *gaiatsu* function. The American preference for exerting political pressure directly at the top is pronounced. American corporations find most useful their contacts with the United States Office of the US Trade Representative (USTR) (57 percent) and the American embassy (41 percent) which get particularly high marks for the quality of service and information that they provide (Question 46). These corporations would like the American government to keep the pressure on Japan to open up its markets (Question 49). Well behind in their usefulness rank Japanese trade associations (36 percent), Japanese cabinet members (35 percent), and Japanese media (29 percent). Least useful are the American Chamber of Commerce in Japan (24 percent) and American trade associations operating in Japan (20 percent).

Japan in the United States

Japan's lobbying in American politics has received in recent years growing attention and is the subject of a number of different studies by American authors, generally stressing its size, broadly gauged nature, and effectiveness.[42] A knowledgeable and well-known lobbyist

---

[42] Pat Choate, *Agents of Influence: How Japan's Lobbyists in the United States Manipulate America's Political and Economic System* (New York: Knopf, 1990); Pat Choate, "Political Advantage: Japan's Campaign for America," *Harvard Business Review* (September–October 1990), pp. 87–103; Clyde H. Farnsworth, "Japan's Loud Voice in Washington," *The New York Times*, December 10, 1989, pp. F1, F6. Sachs, "Lobbying by Foreign Interests: Japan"; Ronald A. Morse, "The Japan Lobby and American Foreign Policy Interests," paper presented in a slightly different version at the Fourth

Table 3.1 *Foreign lobbies in the USA, 1951–1991*

	1951	1957	1962	1967	1972	1977	1982	1987	1991
Japan	1	17	24	46	54	71	87	123	119
Korea	3	5	0	7	5	23	34	46	33
Taiwan	16	14	15	11	15	19	24	32^a	28
UK	10	6	8	14	17	27	37	81	57
Germany	6	16	18	28	23	26	39	63	20
France	10	18	19	29	21	38	37	38^a	43
Italy	6	6	11	20	13	15	20	13^a	21
Canada	8	6	9	19	19	32	47	98	73
Mexico	14	9	13	22	31	36	43	29	25
Brazil	3	1	6	14	8	9	9	23^a	21
Israel	14	16	12	19	17	21	18	22	24
USSR	23	30	27	43	34	27	24	10	34

^{a} *Washington Representatives*, Columbia Books 1987 (11th edn), 1990 (14th edn)
Source: 1951–91: Department of Justice
    1987 data cited from Richard J. Sachs, "Lobbying by Foreign Interests: Japan," *CRS Report for Congress* (Washington DC: The Library of Congress, Congressional Research Service, April 5, 1991), p. 3

himself, Ira Wolf, argues that: "There is little doubt that the Japan lobby in the United States is the largest and most effective foreign effort to influence legislation, policy making, and public attitudes in this country."[43] In contrast an older Japanese literature has pointed to the weaknesses and failures of the Japanese lobby in American politics.[44] One Japanese electricity industry association, for example, reported that it succeeded in only 20 percent of the issues on which it

Tamkang American Studies Conference, Taipei, November 1984; Ronald A. Morse, "Japanese Lobbynomics: Shaping America's Political Agenda," *Venture Japan* 1, 4 (1989), pp. 29–35; Russell Warren Howe and Sarah Hays Trott, *The Power Peddlers: How Lobbyists Mold America's Foreign Policy* (Garden City, NY: Doubleday 1977).

[43] Aaron Pempel, "From the Bottom Up: Understanding Business–Government Relations from a Corporate Perspective," undergraduate honors thesis (Ithaca: Cornell University Government Department, April 22, 1991), p. 43.

[44] Jiro Tokuyama, *Kigyo no Taiseifu Katsudo* [*The Political Strategies of Corporations in the United States*] (Tokyo: Saimaru shuppankai 1970); Yoshihisa Komori and Toshio Obi, *Japan robi* [*The Japan Lobby*] (Tokyo: Yell shuppansha 1980); Masataka Takahashi, *Za Robiisuto* [*The Lobbyist*] (Tokyo: Daiyamondosha 1977); Masataka Takahashi, *Robiisuto no Uchimaku* [*The Inside Story of Lobbying in America*] (Tokyo: Nihon Keizai Shinbunsha, 1980); Makiko Yamada, *Robiingu: Beikoku Gikai no Pawa Poritikkusu* [*Lobbying: Power Politics in the US Congress*] (Tokyo: Nihon Keizai Shinbunsha, 1982).

lobbied actively in the United States.[45] These contrasting images probably reflect different historical periods as well as different national perspectives.

The first image is one of unobtrusive political activity. The Japanese lobby in the United States has a relatively long history of steady growth. Starting with only one lobbyist in 1951, by 1957 Japan had joined other client states such as West Germany, Taiwan, and Israel, as well as France, in the number of lobbyists it deployed in Washington. By 1962 it had moved into the number one position among the Western powers, a position which it has not relinquished since (table 3.1). For historical reasons the Japanese lobbying maintained a low profile for many years and recorded very few successes in legislative lobbying. In the words of one well-known lobbyist, William Tanaka, "My office does not lobby either for private companies or the Japanese government. For Japanese corporations simply cannot exert any influence on the process of policy formulation in the federal bureaucracy or legislative debate in Congress."[46] Instead Tanaka gathered information and provided legal assistance for his Japanese clients.[47] Shinoda concurs in this assessment. Since the Japanese lobby lacked ideological appeal for members of Congress, and since it did not gain the support of Japanese Americans, its activities aimed at the gathering of information and the giving of advice.[48] It is in keeping with this image that the Japanese lobby has avoided making any substantial contributions to Political Action Committees.[49] It invests instead in "old boys," that is, in well-placed officials, many of them former members of the US government, who enjoy excellent access to key decision-makers. Based on a survey of 41 corporations and associations, one study reports that Japanese companies and associations are more active in lobbying the government in the US (49 percent) than are American companies in Japan (42 percent).[50] But their unobtrusive

---

45 Tsujinaka, *Interest Groups*, p. 17.
46 Atsushi Kusano, *Amerika Gikai to Nichibei Kankei* [*The American Congress and US–Japan Relations*] (Tokyo: Chuo kouron, 1992), p. 123; Christopher Madison, "Is Japan Trying to Buy Washington or Just Do Business Capital Style?" *National Journal* (October 1982), p. 1710.
47 Kusano, *The American Congress and US–Japan Relations*, pp. 123–24.
48 Tomohito Shinoda, *Amerika gikai o robiisuru: wasinton no nakano nichibeikankei* [*Lobbying the American Congress: US–Japan Relations in Washington, DC*] (Tokyo: Japan Times, 1989), p. 142.
49 Sachs, "Lobbying by Foreign Interests: Japan," p. 4.
50 Yutaka Tsujinaka, "Nihon Robi Sobyo" ["A Sketch of the Japanese Lobby"], *UP* (1989), p.15.

style is in line with the networking and buying of access that is also very important in Japanese politics.

This may explain why the Japanese lobby expends very large amounts of resources on a very distinctive and low-profile set of activities. Japanese corporations and, to some extent, the Japanese government spend a great deal of money and effort trying to create a favorable public climate in the United States. The concern which the Japanese government and corporations have with Japan's image in the United States is illustrated by numerous studies.[51] Japan, for example, has the largest number of consulates in the US (fifteen); and these consulates regularly hire local public relations firms to advise them on how to create a favorable public climate for Japan's political objectives on a regional basis.[52] Furthermore, *Business Week* estimates that Japanese corporations spend annually 45 million dollars on public relations, 140 million on corporate philanthropy, and 30 million on academic research grants.[53] At about 300 million dollars Choate's estimate is considerably higher.[54] Suzanne Alexander reports that Japanese philanthropy increased from 30 million dollars in 1986, to 300 million dollars in 1990, and 500 million in 1991.[55] A large portion of these funds is being spent on grass-roots politics. Academic research is particularly vulnerable to a potential overdependence on Japanese funds. According to one recent estimate up to 80 percent of the studies on United States–Japan relations conducted at American universities and research institutes are financed at least partly by Japanese corporations, foundations, or government agencies.[56] "With its American face, the Japanese lobby has become almost integrated into the funda-

---

[51] *Business Week.* "Japan's Clout in the US: It's Translating Economic Might into Influence" (July 11, 1988), pp. 64–75; Choate, *Agents of Influence*; William J. Holstein, *The Japanese Power Game: What It Means for America* (New York: Charles Scribner, 1990), pp. 221–40; John B. Judis, "How the Japanese Are 'Helping' the US Media Understand Japan," *Columbia Journalism Review* (January–February 1990), pp. 42–45; John B. Judis, "The Japanese Megaphone," *The New Republic* (January 22, 1990), pp. 20–25; Suzanne Alexander, "Japanese Firms Embark on a Program of Lavish Giving to American Charities," *The Wall Street Journal*, May 23, 1991, p. B1; Chung Hee Lee, *Foreign Lobbying in American Politics* (Seoul: Seoul National University, 1988); James Fallows, "The Great Japanese Misunderstanding," *New York Review of Books* (November 8, 1990), pp. 36–40; Elaine Sciolino, "Amiable Idea Merchant Who Is Viewed as the Most-Feared Japan-Basher," *The New York Times*, February 8, 1990, p. A24.

[52] Lee, *Foreign Lobbying in American Politics*, p. 142.

[53] Farnsworth, "Japan's Loud Voice in Washington," p. 6.

[54] Choate, *Agents of Influence*, p. xviii.

[55] Alexander, "Japanese Firms Embark on a Program of Lavish Giving to American Charities."

[56] Farnsworth, "Japan's Loud Voice in Washington," p. F6.

mental structure of advice giving, consultation and governance in Washington."[57] The attention to image building and the creation of a favorable public climate in America is a distinctive feature of Japan's transnational relations with the United States which is rooted both in the constraints under which foreign lobbies operate as well as in the political importance of the media and a favorable public climate in Japan's domestic politics.

The second image of the Japanese lobby paints a very different picture. Like other political and ideological lobbies operating on behalf of China, Taiwan, Israel, the Arab states, and South Korea, the Japanese lobby has become conspicuous. The reason lies in the growing economic frictions brought about by America's growing trade deficit with Japan and the increasing role of Japanese capital in the American economy brought about by the appreciation of the yen in the second half of the 1980s. The extreme conflict over textile trade in 1970–71, a series of orderly marketing arrangements and voluntary export restraints negotiated in the 1970s and 1980s for steel, consumer electronics, automobiles, and semiconductors, as well as the negotiations held under the auspices of the SII talks, are only some of the highlights of the growing trade frictions that have mobilized the Japanese lobby. The shift in power from the Presidency to Congress, both as the result of changes in the structure of political parties and in trade legislation, has broadened political opportunities for foreign lobbies. Furthermore, the lack of coherence with which the American government bureaucracy conducts its Japan policy also helps Japanese lobbies exploit the sharp internal conflicts that divide three parts of the American federal bureaucracy: the State Department, Pentagon, and National Security Council on the one hand, the Office of the United States Trade Representative and the Commerce Department, on the other, and, thirdly, the Treasury Department, the Office of Management and Budget and the Council on Economic Advisors.[58] The Japanese lobby has the political skill and resources to exploit these political opportunities.

The image of the Japanese lobby buying American democracy has created a volatile political issue. Estimates of Japanese expenditures seeking to influence American politics vary widely. The recent report of the US Department of Justice estimates the figure to be 76.8 million

---

[57] Ibid. p. F6.
[58] Thomas L. Friedman, "Fractured Vision," *The New York Times Magazine*, section 6, June 28, 1992, pp. 24–25, 47–52.

dollars in 1991.[59] Takahashi gives an estimate of 60 million dollars for 1988.[60] Pat Choate offers a figure of 100 million dollars for 1990.[61] The true figure probably lies somewhere between 70 million and 100 million dollars around 1990. The combined total expenditures of the 1988 House and Senate elections in the United States, for example, amounted to about 400 million dollars.[62] Lobbying expenditures falling in the range of 70 to 100 million dollars thus are a substantial sum in American politics. This has led Choate to write that the "Japanese penetration of the American political system is now so deep that its integrity is threatened. In their own country the Japanese call this sort of money politics 'structural corruption.' In this case, it means that so many advocates of Japan's position are involved in decision-making that the ultimate outcome is structurally biased in Japan's favor."[63]

Japanese politics is extremely expensive as a number of political scandals in the early 1990s have illustrated. For example, Fukui and Fukai[64] estimate that national elections on a per capita basis cost about 0.65 dollars in Britain (1983), 3.50 dollars in Australia (1984), 4.40 dollars in Canada (1984), and 6.00 dollars in Israel (1984). Based on party expenditures Yutaka Tsujinaka estimates for the United States a per capita figure of 2.20 dollars in 1987–88.[65] Pat Choate reports similar figures suggesting, on a per capita basis, that national elections are about ten times as expensive in Japan as in the United States.[66] But since Choate's data, as Tsujinaka notes, exclude other political funding which should be included before one can make reliable estimates, they do not reveal an accurate picture. Nonetheless, Japanese electoral politics are arguably more expensive than the politics of any other democracy. Based on party expenditure data, Tsujinaka calculates a

[59] Calculated by Tsujinaka based on US Department of Justice, *Report of the Attorney General of the Congress of the US on the Administration of the Foreign Agents Registration Act of 1938, as amended for the Calendar Years 1988, 1989, 1990 and 1991* (Washington, DC: Department of Justice, n.d.), pp. 611–744.
[60] Masataka Takahashi, *Seijyoki no robiisuto* [*Lobbyists in the United States*] (Tokyo: Tokuma Shoten, 1988), p. 58.
[61] Choate, *Agents of Influence*, p. xi.
[62] Harold W. Stanley and Richard Niemi, *Vital Statistics on American Politics* (Washington, DC: Congressional Quarterly Press, 4th edn, 1994), p. 209.
[63] Choate, *Agents of Influence*, p. xx; Stephen Engelberg with Martin Tochin, "Foreigners Find New Ally in US Industry," *The New York Times*, November 2, 1993, pp. A1, B5.
[64] Haruhiro Fukui and Shigeko Fukai, "Informal Politics and One-Party Dominance in Japan: A Case Study and a Rudimentary Theory" ["Nihon ni okeru infomaru poritikkusu to ittoyuisei"], *Leviathan*, 9 (1991), pp. 62–63.
[65] Calculated by Tsujinaka using Stanley and Niemi, *Vital Statistics on American Politics* (1994 edn.), p. 209.
[66] Choate, *Agents of Influence*, pp. xi, xviii, 29.

figure of 13.50 dollars. That figure increases to 24.00 dollars if one uses political fund statistics.[67] With total expenditures of about 1.5 billion dollars in 1986, the Japanese figures are substantially higher both on a per capita basis and in absolute terms than are corresponding American figures.

Japan's lobby in American politics reflects the structure of American politics. In times of political need, because of the weakness of the American party system, Japanese lobbies target individuals, Congressional districts and individual states rather than national political institutions. Since the 1950s Japanese institutions and individuals have spent enormous time, energy, and resources in mastering the American political process. The network of institutional and individual contacts they have built is both deep and broad. Typically the Japanese lobby is private and organized by the Japan External Trade Research Organization (JETRO), business associations, and individual corporations. In the terminology of this paper the Japanese lobby focuses on "buying" political influence.

Corporate strategies

In a compelling piece of research Aaron Pempel has argued for the great importance that the foreign political context has on the political strategies of American and Japanese corporations.[68] In an effort to minimize the role of extraneous variables such as differences in markets and industries, Pempel chose four competitors, of roughly equal size, manufacturing high-technology electronic products – personal computers, microchips, and photocopiers – in the US and Japan: Xerox and Motorola from the United States, Matsushita and Toshiba from Japan. Neither the domestic structures of the United States and Japan nor the cultures of the four corporations explain adequately the political strategies these four corporations pursue at home and abroad. What matters instead for the character of corporate strategies is the political setting of the host country.

In their domestic markets Motorola and Toshiba have made aggressive efforts to develop political support for advancing their economic interests. Xerox and Matsushita typically have adopted a more self-reliant market strategy. These differences are quite marked,

---

67 Calculated by Tsujinaka using *The Political Funding Report* by the Ministry of Home Affairs in 1992; data from *Asahi Shinbun*, September 3, 1992.
68 Pempel, "From the Bottom Up."

for example, in the views of two former Chief Executive Officers (CEOs) of Xerox and Motorola. According to Xerox's David Kearns, "American business has got to stop blaming the government for its problems. There are other reasons why we are falling behind."[69] Motorola's Robert Galvin has a different view: "The global economy is not laissez faire . . . There has to be an understanding – and imposition of the rules of the game . . . The rules have not been right for America."[70] Equally striking is the difference between the two Japanese corporations. Toshiba is part of Japan's largest *keiretsu* system, the Mitsui group, and it benefitted from government assistance over many decades. Matsushita, on the other hand, is not a typical Japanese corporation. Pascale and Athos argue, for example, that as a relative upstart Matsushita has "consistently violated the strategic rules by which Japanese business is played."[71] These differences in the strategies which American and Japanese corporations pursue in their home markets are not explainable in terms of the effects of domestic structures.

Nor can they be explained by the organizational culture of these four corporations. For in their foreign operations two of the four corporations reveal preferences that differ substantially from those in their home political environments. To be sure, as in Japan, Matsushita has retained a low political profile in the United States. Its legal department has concentrated on behind-the-scenes lobbying, on public and community affairs, philanthropy, industrial relations, and networking with state and local governments. Matsushita chose not to contest five anti-dumping cases that were filed against it between 1981 and 1989. The one instance when Matsushita assumed a high political profile was in 1988. When the Omnibus Trade Bill threatened to undercut severely its ability to sell its products in the American market, the company targeted specific Congressmen over whom it had some political leverage. Similarly, Motorola's strategy in Japan has also been consistent with its politicized approach to the American market place. Motorola waited until 1980 to enter the Japanese market in earnest. But when it did, it committed significant resources "to develop long-term relations with Japan's ministries and agencies; to

---

[69] Gary Jacobson and John Hillkirk, *Xerox: American Samurai* (New York: Macmillan, 1986).

[70] James Braham, "Robert W. Galvin," *Industry Week* (October 13, 1986), p. 54.

[71] Richard Pascale and Anthony Athos, *The Art of Japanese Management: Applications for American Executives* (New York: Simon & Schuster Publishing, 1981) p. 30.

work with various trade associations; and to help improve community relations."[72]

But the political strategies of Toshiba and Xerox contradict the expectation of one corporate culture, shaping strategies similarly at home and abroad. Toshiba, for example, was very reluctant, except in dire straits, to build close political links with the US government. The issues that have arisen between Toshiba and the US government have been handled instead by American lawyers hired to lobby the US government quietly on Toshiba's behalf. Even though Toshiba had the opportunity to deal directly with the US government at numerous occasions in the 1980s, it chose not do so. When asked about Toshiba's political approach in the United States, its American representative, Joyce Kopidakis, stated that "we have a passive relationship with the US government, which, as you know, is the Japanese way."[73] Only when Congress sought to impose sanctions against Toshiba in 1987, on account of its violation of Coordinating Committee on Export Controls (CoCom) regulations, did the company wage a full-blown and very successful political campaign.[74]

In its Japanese operations Xerox relinquished the strategy of political self-reliance that it had followed in the US market. It linked with Fuji in a joint venture and has dealt with the Japanese government on a sustained and regular basis, thus cutting against the political strategy it has adopted in the American market. In the words of David Kearns "We are fortunate to have Fuji-Xerox working with MITI . . . What Fuji-Xerox basically does, when they need a product from us, is to go to those people and say, 'this is what we need' (pounds fist on the table) and we are a Japanese company."[75] Through close contacts especially with the bureaucracy Fuji-Xerox and Xerox have worked hard to establish, among others, joint ventures with Toshiba, one of Xerox's direct competitors on world markets.[76]

Corporate strategy thus is explained fully neither by domestic structures nor by corporate cultures. Instead it is the political setting of the host country that determines corporate strategy. The two Japanese corporations behave astonishingly similarly in the United States and so do the two American companies in Japan. Japanese corporations

---

[72] Pempel, "From the Bottom Up," p. 35.   [73] Ibid. p. 32.
[74] Ibid. pp. 44–51; Dan Granirer, *Multinational Corporate Power in Inter-State Conflict: The Toshiba Case* (Economics and National Security Program, John M. Olin Institute for Strategic Studies, Harvard University Center for International Affairs, #OIWP-90–003, 1990).
[75] Pempel, "From the Bottom Up," p. 37.   [76] Ibid. p. 38.

adopt a relatively low political profile in the United States; and when they must act politically on crucial issues, they focus their political attention on Congress. Conversely, American corporations tend to develop more intensive, long-term political relations with the Japanese government, bureaucracy, and trade associations than they do in the United States. In sum, Aaron Pempel's more detailed case studies[77] corroborate this chapter's analysis which is based on aggregate survey and financial data. Differences between corporate strategies that are pronounced in the home market tend to narrow or vanish in foreign markets. This is strong evidence for the proposition that domestic structures act as filters for transnational relations.

Transgovernmental security relations

On economic issues the transnational relations between the United States and Japan have been marked by a mixture of "bullying," "buying," and "binding." The security relations between these two states since the mid-1970s have been remarkably free of acrimony. In the terminology of this chapter it approximates "binding" more than "bullying" or "buying," with the United States typically "advising" and Japan "accepting."[78] This outcome results from a mixture of intergovernmental, transgovernmental, and transnational relations. The extension and intensification of US–Japanese security arrangements have involved heads of states and national governments, governments and sub-units of governments, and governments and private corporations. The question arises, which features of the US and Japanese domestic structures account for this striking difference between security issues on the one hand and transnational economic issues on the other?

The answer lies in the fact that, viewed comparatively, the role of the state in the US domestic structure is much stronger and in Japan much weaker on security than on economic issues. On questions of national security the state has sought to protect the United States

---

[77] Ibid. pp. 43–70.

[78] Contacts between the CIA and some senior right-wing LDP politicians appear to have occurred in the 1950s and 1960s. See for example, Tim Weiner, "CIA Spent Millions to Support Japanese Right in 50's and 60's," *The New York Times*, October 9, 1994, pp. 1, 14 and the Foreign Service of the United States of America RM/R.Files, "memorandum of Conversation, by S.S. Carpenter, First Secretary of the Embassy, with Mr. Eisaka Sato, Minister of Finance and Brother of Prime Minister Kishi, American Embassy, Tokyo," July 25, 1958.

against surprise attack. The American military offers the President an opportunity to display his capacity for political leadership, relies on a powerful central bureaucracy, has close connections with Congress, enjoys strong support from the judiciary, and commands a substantial institutional presence in the American economy. Furthermore, on questions of national security the state is supported by the widely shared social norm that the United States must be second to none militarily, should act as the leader of all the democratic nations of the world, and is entitled to take strong unilateral measures when its interests are at stake. In contrast to important economic issues, such as fiscal and industrial policy, national security policy thus is not made by default.

This picture offers a striking contrast to Japan. On military aspects of national security Japan's state is uncharacteristically weak. It can be described as a depoliticized "developmental state"[79] which embeds military concerns in broader economic and political aspects of Japan's "comprehensive security." On military security issues the capacities of the Japanese state are extremely weak compared to those of the American state. As a consequence of deliberate policies adopted after 1945 the position of the Self Defense Forces (SDF) in the Defense Agency and that of the Defense Agency in the government are clearly subordinate to institutions that articulate the economic and political aspects of Japan's security policy.[80] The normative basis of Japan's military security policy has been the source of fundamental political conflicts in the 1950s and 1960s that at times rocked the very foundations of Japan's political system. Historical memories of these deep divisions have faded but not passed away. A more muted tug-of-war in the 1970s and 1980s reveals nonetheless the severe limitations, both in legal and social norms, that constrain the role the Japanese state can play on questions of military security. Military security policy thus is extremely cautious, gradualist and, to some American critics of Japan, timid and selfish.

The mutual "binding" that has emerged from the extension of security cooperation between the United States and Japan reflects these aspects of their domestic structures. This is not to argue that security relations between the United States and Japan have been

---

[79] Chalmers Johnson, *MITI and the Japanese Miracle: The Growth of Industrial Policy* (Stanford: Stanford University Press, 1982).

[80] Peter J. Katzenstein and Nobuo Okawara, *Japan's National Security: Structures, Norms and Policy Responses in a Changing World* (Ithaca, NY: Cornell University East Asia Program, 1993), pp. 21–56.

totally devoid of conflict. The US Congress, for one, has been a persistent critic of the magnitude of Japan's defense effort, while the Department of Defense has been a strong supporter of the very considerable increases in Japanese defense expenditures in the 1980s. Similarly, in Japan some segments of the SDF and Liberal Democratic Party (LDP) politicians favoring a more autonomous national defense effort have occasionally been in conflict with the government's policies. By and large, though, security relations have been unproblematic. The United States has led (in asking Japan to play a larger role in containing the Soviet navy and to assume a larger role in Asian security) while Japan has followed (in expanding and modernizing the SDF and integrating their operations and weapons systems more closely with the US armed forces). Significantly, the relationship has involved the growth of transgovernmental relations not only between the two militaries but to some extent also between different units of the executive and legislative branches of government.

The Mutual Security Treaty and the American security guarantee have tied Japan very closely to the United States. Indeed, one would be overstating the case only slightly if one called Japan an "incomplete" state, with the defense function largely filled by its American ally. Transgovernmental ties between the two militaries have increased greatly since the late 1970s. Transgovernmental relations have been quietly effective in gradually enhancing Japan's profile on questions of national defense. This is illustrated by the absolute and relative growth of defense expenditures culminating in a scrapping of the 1 percent ceiling in 1987; the extension of the notion of Japanese defense in terms of mission and new weapon systems, for example in the Ground Self-Defense Forces' adoption of a seashore defense posture which seeks to block the strategic straits around Japan through which the Russian navy must break; the Maritime Self-Defense Forces' decision to acquire several Aegis destroyers and to alter its mission to protect sea-lanes 1,000 miles away from the home islands; and the Air Self-Defense Forces' acquisition of the Airborne Warning and Command System (AWACS) and the creation of a 100-mile defensive air space around Japan. Although there exist institutionalized links between the two governments – the Security Consultative Committee, the Subcommittee for Defense Cooperation, the Security Subcommittee and the Japan–US Joint Committee – they are not very well developed. More important has been the smooth cooperation between services (in particular between the US Navy and the MSDF). Informal, plural channels of communication and coordination between the different military services have been built up during the 1980s which provide numerous opportunities for a broadening of contacts down to the middle-level of government bureaucracies.[81] In virtually all instances it has been the direct or indirect weight of the American senior partner in the security relationship that has tilted the scale in Japan's domestic political battles that have been fought over the issue of a higher defense profile.[82]

On one important issue, weapons procurement, the broadening and deepening of defense cooperation has at times resembled "bullying" and "buying" more than "binding." The acquisition process of military aircraft, for example, such as the decision in favor of Lockheed's P-3C antisubmarine patrol airplane in 1977, the highly controversial decision in favor of the joint development of the Fighter Support Experimental (FSX) in the late 1980s, and the prolonged conflict over Japan's purchase of a number of AWACS from Boeing illustrate the process by which the US government, in the attempt to diminish the trade imbalance between the two countries and on behalf of the American defense industry, became an active participant in the Japanese policy process through contacts at all levels, including the highest political level (the Ron–Yasu relationship during much of the 1980s). Policy conflicts in Japan typically pit Japan's defense officials and contractors as well as technical experts who favor indigeneous weapons programs against the ministries of finance and foreign affairs who favor American weapons because they tend to be cheaper and improve the political relations between the two states.[83] The American government, or various units of the government, have attempted at various times to influence this balance of power in Japanese domestic politics. The story is often complicated by the fact that the US government is itself often divided internally on what it should do.

Economic aspects of the security relationship thus have a political dynamic that differs from that of the transgovernmental relations between the two militaries. Since governments and the large defense

---

[81] Katzenstein and Okawara, *Japan's National Security*, pp. 139–202.
[82] For an analysis of why realists' arguments are inadequate for an analysis of US–Japan security relations see Peter J. Katzenstein, *Norms and National Security: Japan's Police and Military as Agents of Nonviolence* (unpublished book manuscript, 1994), chapters 1 and 2.
[83] Sangjoo Han, "Japan's 'PXL' Decision: The Politics of Weapons Procurment," *Asian Survey*, 18, 8 (August 1978), pp. 769–84; Masaru Kohno, "Japanese Defense Policy Making: The FSX Selection, 1985–87," *Asian Survey*, 29, 5 (May 1989), pp. 457–79.

contractors in both countries are deeply involved in major procurement contracts, future transnational politics on issues such as technology transfer is likely to be conflictual. On the issue of technology the Japanese government acceded to American pressure when it made a one-time exception to the prohibition of the export of weapons and weapons related technologies in 1983. But the Joint Military Technology Commission which was set up to administer the flow especially of dual-use technology from Japan to the United States was as ineffective as a number of subsequent agreements resulting in the creation of the International High Tech Center in 1989 and a new round of technology negotiations commencing after the visit of Secretary of Defense Cheney in February 1990. In all of these cases one stumbling block is the hesitation of Japanese corporations to part with their proprietary control over technologies that US corporations are increasingly eager to exploit both for military and commercial purposes. Japan has been the largest importer of American defense technology during the post-war era. Japanese firms signed 40,000 separate technology contracts with American firms between 1951 and 1984 and were involved in more than 100 military coproduction agreements.[84] The reluctance of Japanese corporations to provide information about the range of technologies that they are developing as well as their hesitation to make available existing technologies on a preferential basis for US firms is likely to become a source of growing irritation and concern for the Department of Defense and American defense contractors.

On questions of military security there exists then a system of intergovernmental (for example, the Ron–Yasu relationship), transgovernmental (for example, the close contact between the US navy and the Japanese MSDF) and transnational (involving government agencies and defense contractors) relations. In transgovernmental relations the American pressure for an expansion in Japan's military role has strengthened a relatively weak coalition in the Japanese government advocating that Japan assume a higher profile on defense issues. While the formal restraints on the expansion of Japan's security policy have not been lifted, informally policy has moved considerably to accommodate American pressure.

In the future, however, on security issues with economic aspects, such as technology transfer – an emerging second dimension of trans-

---

[84] Katzenstein and Okawara, *Japan's National Security*, pp. 191–94.

national security relations – conflict may grow with Japan's increasing importance as a supplier of components and component technology important in the development and procurement of high-technology weapons for the US Department of Defense and its major weapons contractors. In this instance in fact Japanese corporations are confronting America's "military-industrial complex," a tight web of state–society relations that, at its apex, resembles Japan's system of "reciprocal consent." The frictions that are building along this dimension may eventually rival or exceed in their political salience those in the economic transnational relations.

Conclusion

This chapter argues that a key insight of the older theory of trans-national relations was correct, even though one of its key assumptions was mistaken. Transnational relations matter in contemporary world politics. But modernization does not lead to a far-reaching convergence of domestic structures. This chapter has argued instead that the domestic structures of the United States and Japan act like filters which refract differently the transnational relations between the United States and Japan. Domestic structures create incentives that shape the political behavior of governmental and non-governmental actors. American actors confronted relatively closed markets in Japan and a political system which does not make it easy for outsiders to wield influence. In the name of fair market access the US government exerted massive political pressure on the Japanese government. It targeted in the 1970s protectionist policies of the Japanese government before aiming subsequently in the 1980s at a reorganization of the system of business–government relations. In the 1990s it seeks to affect substantial changes in the way Japanese business is organized and conducts its affairs. Japan's system of "reciprocal consent" in the relations between state and society has made it exceedingly difficult for this political pressure to pry open the doors to create what American business and politicians consider to be a level playing field.

In sharp contrast, Japanese actors have confronted American markets which were quite open to foreign competitors and a political system that was relatively accessible. Japanese corporations, not the Japanese government, have thus reacted to the rise of American protectionism by investing in plants to defend their market share and by seeking to create indirectly a favorable political climate for Japanese business in the United States. They have done so quite effectively. The differences in American and Japanese domestic structures are thus essential to an understanding of how transnational relations affect the policies of governmental and non-governmental actors. In the short-hand of this chapter, on economic issues Americans "bully" or "bind" and Japanese "buy" as they seek to influence policy developments, respectively, in Japan and the United States.

On security issues the transgovernmental relations between the United States and Japan have led to a different outcome, "binding" between a United States that led and a Japan that followed. The reason, this chapter argues, lies in the profound difference in the domestic structures shaping security policy in the United States and Japan. Put succinctly, on questions of military security the American state is strong, not weak, the Japanese state weak, not strong.

The evidence suggests, furthermore, that transgovernmental and transnational relations generate intense conflict in the presence of specific conditions. Transgovernmental relations between the central decision-makers and sub-units of the American and Japanese defense establishments have been relatively uncontroversial, as have been relations linking Japanese corporations primarily to societal actors in the United States. Conversely, conflict has been intense on a broad range of economic issues in the transnational relations linking the US government to the Japanese system of "reciprocal consent" between state and society. Substantial conflict is also likely to occur as Japanese corporations are increasingly forced to deal with America's defense economy on questions of component technologies for advanced weapon systems. In short, transnational relations that activate the full range of state–society relations on either side of the Pacific appear to create more political conflicts than do private sector and transgovern-mental relations that do not.

Transnational relations are both imports and exports. During the last three decades transnationalism as an extension of the *Pax Americana* has been propelled by a revolution in communications and trans-portation that was met in Japan by what is, except for the United States, arguably the most information-intensive of all of the advanced industrial states. As is true of the United States, Japan's approach to transnational relations is an extension of its own domestic experiences. Power is the exploitation of points of leverage carefully built up in a system of mutual vulnerabilities. Personal contacts, superior infor-mation, and quiet middlemen working behind the scenes do not confront issues head-on, but seek to influence them indirectly. This type of politics is embedded in a public climate that needs to be cultivated carefully. For without the support of a favorable public opinion, Japan's subtle game of politics cannot endure. These features of Japanese domestic politics shape the transnational relations that Japanese political actors pursue abroad.

4 MNCs and developmentalism: domestic structure as an explanation for East Asian dynamism

Cal Clark and Steve Chan

Multinational corporations (MNCs) are important transnational agents in the contemporary global political economy. Although they can be viewed as economic actors following the logic of international markets, their activities inevitably arouse questions of national power as well.[1] Not surprisingly, such questions are most pronounced in the study of developing countries, where weak governments and societies potentially give the MNCs a strong bargaining position. Thus, the nature of the relationship between MNCs and developing countries and the implications of this relationship for economic growth remain highly controversial. For several decades, the debate occurred primarily between modernization theory (which saw MNCs as promoting growth in the periphery) and dependency theory (which argued that MNCs prevented or distorted growth). More recently, statist theory has argued that "strong and autonomous" states can regulate MNCs, thereby making them contribute to national development.[2]

We are very grateful for the valuable comments of Peter Katzenstein and Thomas Risse-Kappen upon an earlier draft of this paper.

[1] Robert Gilpin, *The Political Economy of International Relations* (Princeton, NJ: Princeton University Press, 1987); and *US Power and the Multinational Corporation: The Political Economy of Foreign Direct Investment* (New York: Basic Books, 1975).

[2] Peter B. Evans, Dietrich Rueschemeyer, and Theda Skocpol, eds., *Bringing the State Back In* (Cambridge: Cambridge University Press, 1985). For applications to the Asian context discussed in this paper, see Alice H. Amsden, *Asia's Next Giant: South Korea and Late Industrialization* (New York: Oxford University Press, 1989); Steve Chan and Cal Clark, *Flexibility, Foresight, and Fortuna in Taiwan's Development: Navigating between Scylla and Charybdis* (London: Routledge, 1992); Stephan Haggard, *Pathways from the Periphery: The Politics of Growth in the Newly Industrializing Countries* (Ithaca, NY: Cornell University Press, 1990); and Robert Wade, *Governing the Market: Economic Theory and the Role of Government in East Asian Industrialization* (Princeton, NJ: Princeton University Press, 1990).

112

Table 4.1 National profiles, 1989

	Population (millions)	GDP (billion $)	GDP pc[a] ($)	Exports % GDP	GDP growth 1965–80 (%)	GDP Growth 1980–89 (%)	Net DFI[b] % GDCF	Income ratio[c]
Hong Kong	5.7	52.5	10,350	135	8.6	7.1	3.1	8.70
Singapore	2.7	28.4	10,450	191	10.0	6.1	12.7	—
Taiwan	20.4	157.8	7,735	48	9.9	8.0	−37.1	4.69
China	1,113.9	417.8	350	14	6.9	9.7	1.5	—
South Korea	42.4	211.9	4,400	34	9.9	9.7	1.2	7.94
Japan	123.1	28,818.5	23,810	15	6.6	4.0	−2.6	4.31
Malaysia	17.4	37.5	2,160	74	7.4	4.9	8.0	16.02
Philippines	60.6	44.4	710	25	5.9	0.7	3.6	10.10
Thailand	55.4	69.7	1,220	36	7.3	7.0	2.2	8.89
Indonesia	178.2	94.0	500	26	7.0	5.3	0.9	7.48
India	832.5	235.2	340	8	3.6	5.3	0.1	8.72

[a] Gross domestic product per capita
[b] Net direct foreign investment as percentage of gross domestic capital formation, 1987
[c] Ratio of the income share of the richest fifth of the population to that of the poorest fifth, 1908s

Sources: Taiwan Statistical Yearbook, 1991 (Taipei: Council for Economic Planning and Development, 1991); World Bank, World Development Report: 1991 (Washington, DC: Oxford University Press, 1991).

We are interested in this chapter in analyzing the role played by a host country's domestic structures in shaping the access and impact of MNCs. Access in this case is a product of bilateral negotiation between the firms and the host government (which has political jurisdiction to bar entry). The terms and extent of this access reflect the joint interests of these actors and their reciprocal bargaining leverage. Access (even if limited) is a precondition for impact which, in our case, refers to the size (large versus small) and nature (positive versus negative) of the MNCs' influence on their host's economic growth. Therefore, MNC impact is our dependent variable, while MNC access is the intervening variable.

We focus our analysis on several Asian cases (see table 4.1 for the wide cross-national variations in economic performance and MNC presence in Asia). A strong state is able to deny MNC access, even though it may choose not to exercise this ability. Once access is extended to MNCs, whether these firms contribute to or hinder economic growth depends on the nature and capacity of social institutions. A state's ability to regulate MNC access (and to extract MNC concessions as a price for entry), and a society's "absorptive capacity" to take advantage of the MNCs' offerings (e.g., capital, technology, management skills) are part of the domestic structures discussed by Risse-Kappen. To understand their interaction fully, however, we argue that one needs to consider national political culture. The synergistic relation between state and society is embedded in this broader and more basic aspect of domestic structure.

The first section of the chapter constitutes a *theoretical departure*. It offers a simple two-variable model that considers the competing arguments of modernization and dependency theories. However, paired comparisons of the Asian cases fail to provide empirical closure. Several additional factors emphasized by statist theory and Risse-Kappen's "domestic structures" perspective are then added. While they help to elucidate the gross inconsistency in the initial case comparisons, they also indicate that statist variables by themselves raise almost as many questions as they answer. The second section, hence, seeks to extend the statist model by proposing *political culture* as a necessary factor for understanding the relationship between domestic structures and transnational relations in Asia. The third section then illustrates this approach by presenting more detailed *case studies* of the five political economies (Hong Kong, India, the Philippines, Singapore, and South Korea) considered in the initial case comparisons.

MNCs, statism, and the domestic structures approach to transnational relations in Asia: theoretical departures

Both the dependency and modernization paradigms assume that the market dynamics of international capitalism are the prime factor determining developmental outcomes. Both imply that the degree of MNC access to a developing country (as a key indicator of its integration into global markets) should influence its economic growth significantly, even though they expect diametrically opposite effects to result from this access (see table 4.2). Each perspective can seemingly support its case by pointing to a prominent paired comparison of Asian cases. Dependency theory can contrast the poor growth record of the highly accessible Philippines with the "economic miracle" of the largely exclusionary South Korea. In contrast, neoclassicists can compare the prosperity of *laissez-faire* Hong Kong with the poverty of India, which has effectively dislodged large MNCs. The experience of Singapore adds even more variability. This case resembles Hong Kong in its openness to MNCs and in its attainment of a high growth rate. However, the role of the state is exactly the opposite of the Hong Kong case – instead of *laissez-faire*, the government plays a rather intrusive role in the economy. Thus, if one accepts the assumptions of either dependency or modernization theory, the results from these Asian cases would appear quite confusing.

The role of MNCs in developing nations

This stalemate, therefore, implies the need to extend the analysis. Table 4.3 presents summary classifications of the role of foreign capital in our five cases. Its first column concerns MNC access, or the extent to which foreign capital is allowed to enter a host country. Entry in part reflects MNC interest in a local economy, but is also a function of a host state's willingness to admit direct foreign investment (DFI) and its ability to bar it. High levels of DFI in Hong Kong and Singapore underscore their relative attractiveness to MNCs, as do a *laissez-faire* government in the former case and an aggressive policy of recruiting certain foreign enterprises in the latter. Conversely, for South Korea and India, low levels of DFI are indicative of their states' greater skepticism toward DFI *and* their ability to restrict MNC access. Note that simply opening an economy will not necessarily attract foreign

Table 4.2 *Relationship between MNC access and economic growth*

	Closed to MNCs	Open to MNCs
Low growth	Modernization[a] INDIA	Dependency[a] PHILIPPINES
High growth	Dependency SOUTH KOREA	Modernization HONG KONG SINGAPORE

[a] The terms "modernization" and "dependency" denote the cells consistent with the assumptions of these competing theoretical paradigms. The five cases studied are placed in the cells representing their particular combination of growth and MNC access.

Table 4.3 *MNC access and impact in Asian economies*

	MNC access	MNC impact	
		Size	Direction
Hong Kong	High	Moderate	Positive
India	Low	Negligible	Neutral
Philippines	High	Moderate	Negative
Singapore	High	High	Positive
South Korea	Low	Moderate	Positive

capital. MNCs have little interest in investing in many developing countries.[3] This is precisely the situation in the Philippines where a poor "investment climate" has limited DFI despite high accessibility.

The second and third columns in table 4.3 refer to MNC impact on the host's economy. This impact can be direct, such as when the MNCs create new production capacity or when they displace existing indigenous businesses.[4] It can also be indirect, such as when the MNCs become a catalyst for stimulating local entrepreneurial impulses, diffusing technological innovations, and promoting forward and backward industrial linkages. In either case, the determination of impact naturally requires counterfactual judgments about how the host economy

[3] John M. Stopford and Susan Strange, with John S. Henley, *Rival States, Rival Firms: Competition for World Market Shares* (New York: Cambridge University Press, 1991).
[4] Thomas J. Biersteker, *Distortion or Development? Contending Perspectives on the Multinational Corporation* (Cambridge, MA: MIT Press, 1978), especially chapters 1–3.

would have fared differently had MNCs been totally excluded. In this light, we consider MNCs to have had a generally positive impact in Hong Kong, South Korea, and Singapore, although the size of this impact has been more moderate in Hong Kong and South Korea than in Singapore. Given the limited role of MNCs in India's development, their impact has necessarily been negligible. As for the Philippines, the MNCs have had a moderate, negative impact. These firms have tended to reinforce an enclave pattern of development, denationalization of local firms, wide socioeconomic inequities, a form of "crony capitalism," and a persistent dependency on the export of cash crops.

Statist explanations

Can the cross-national variations just noted be adequately explained by the statist perspective? This perspective suggests that strong states – "state dominated" and "state controlled" ones in Risse-Kappen's typology – should be best able to harness the MNCs for the purpose of national economic development. Table 4.4, therefore, summarizes our five cases in terms of the elements emphasized in statist theory (the reasons for the individual ranks are discussed in more detail in the next section on case studies). The first three columns refer to the three components in Risse-Kappen's model (see chapter 1 in this volume); the next one provides summary scores of state capacity and state–society relations; and the final two describe two central state policies toward MNCs.

Our five cases differ greatly in their state–society relations, especially as they relate to the economy. Hong Kong is *society dominated* because the state eschews intervention in the name of the free market, leaving most decisions about economic activities to a myriad of actors in the private sector. Thus, its economic policy can be considered fragmented or decentralized because it is the result of myriad independent decisions made in the private sector. In the Philippines, the state is penetrated by competing economic elites who use their power over government policy to further their own economic interests. The conflict between personalistic factions and class segments reflects long-lasting polarization, thereby creating a *volatile* set of state–society relations. In South Korea, Singapore, and (before the partial liberalization of the 1980s) India, a centralized and unified state plays a major role in organizing the economy – through state enterprises and planning in India, through control of the financial system

Table 4.4 State characteristics of cases

| | Defining components | | | State policy | |
	Fragmented policy-making	Social pressures	Polarized polity	State–society relations	MNC access	State regulates MNCs
Hong Kong	Yes	Yes	No	Society dominated	High	No
India	No	Yes	Yes	Stalemate	Low	Yes
Philippines	Yes	Yes	Yes	Volatile	High	Some
Singapore	No	No	No	State dominated	High	Yes
South Korea	No	No	No	State dominated	Low	Yes

and direct negotiations with the *chaebol* (large conglomerates) in South Korea, and through pervasive policies of economic and social control in Singapore. Thus, until the 1980s, all three could probably best be classified as *state-dominated* political economies according to the Risse-Kappen model (were it not for the strong role of MNCs in Singapore, that society might even have merited the label "state-controlled"). The growing importance of independent and polarized social forces in both India and South Korea have significantly altered their political economies over the last decade, though. In the former, social upheaval has been so great that it now is approaching *stalemate*, while the Korean regime remains strong enough to keep the latter in the *state-dominated* category.

State–society relations are important because of their assumed impact on actual policies. The last two columns of table 4.4, hence, contain rankings of the five cases on two central policies toward foreign capital. The first is the access granted to MNCs (the same variable reported in table 4.3) which is determined by the state's application of its sovereign powers to exclude MNCs or to impose conditions on their entry to the domestic economy. As discussed earlier, Hong Kong, the Philippines, and Singapore permit access to foreign capital, while India and South Korea pursue much more restrictive policies. However, as found in our discussion of the dependency and modernization perspectives, MNC access *per se* has little relationship to the contribution of MNCs to the host economy.

Another dimension of state policy toward MNCs is whether the state attempts to regulate their activity by limiting them to specific sectors, forcing linkages with the domestic economy, and imposing performance standards (e.g., export quotas, domestic-content requirements). As would be expected, there is a stark difference between statist Singapore which regulates foreign capital and the "open" economy of Hong Kong which does not. In the case of the Philippines, the state's attempts at imposing performance standards have often been ineffective. The relatively low levels of DFI in the other two "closed" economies (India and South Korea; see the data in table 4.1) suggest a general goal of "dislodging the multinationals,"[5] while selectively working with certain foreign firms in order to promote specifically targeted industries (see the discussion in the case study on pp. 128–29, 142–43).

[5] Dennis J. Encarnation, *Dislodging Multinationals: India's Strategy in Comparative Perspective* (Ithaca, NY: Cornell University Press, 1989).

If statist theory is correct, "state characteristics" and "state policy" should have a pronounced effect on whether or not MNCs contribute to economic growth. However, the contents of tables 4.3 and 4.4 engender some skepticism about this theory. Concern with possible "idiosyncrasy" is heightened by the fact that generically similar policies to restrict the MNCs by the strong states of South Korea and India have produced rather different developmental outcomes. Conversely, concern with "irrelevance" is aroused when we notice that divergent state–society relations and different openness to DFI have produced, in Hong Kong and Singapore, generally positive MNC contribution to economic growth. Thus, the structural factors that form the basis of statism are not quite adequate for understanding why MNCs have had a positive impact on economic growth in some developing countries but not others. In addition, this perspective fails to consider why countries differ in their state–society relations. The next section, therefore, introduces political culture as a more fundamental "structural" force which may explain the anomalies noted earlier.

Political culture and economic performance

Students of political culture have long argued that a nation's governmental institutions and economic performance are decisively shaped by its underlying political culture. This section, hence, briefly sketches the principal types of Asian political culture according to the pioneering work by Lucian Pye.[6] Based on this discussion, political culture is then introduced in the more detailed case studies of the following section for examining the impact of MNCs in the five Asian cases.

Political culture refers to widely shared social values impinging upon a nation's political economy. Social values concern whether hard work and economic enterprise are stressed, whether social relationships are seen as hierarchic or egalitarian, whether political office primarily involves power or status, how (or if) an individual can achieve socioeconomic mobility, and to which social or political institutions loyalty is owed. Such beliefs permeate the political economy, setting norms of expectation and behavior for both the elite and the masses. They form broad patterns of what Pye terms the "cultural dimensions of authority," which, he argues, are more or less functional

[6] Lucian W. Pye, with Mary W. Pye, *Asian Power and Politics: The Cultural Dimensions of Authority* (Cambridge, MA: Harvard University Press, 1985).

for various tasks, such as for promoting industrialization, fighting wars, or maintaining the status quo in a primitive society.

In Pye's typology, our five cases come from three cultural traditions. The Northeast Asian countries (China, Hong Kong, Japan, South Korea, Taiwan, and Singapore despite its location) all have Confucian cultures. Clientelistic relationships, in contrast, predominate in the Southeast Asian nations, even though they have quite different religious traditions (Buddhism, Catholicism, and Islam). Finally, India has what might be called a caste-bureaucratic political culture. Clearly, as the data on economic performance in table 4.1 showed, the Confucian cases have scored impressive economic growth, while the economies of India and most of Southeast Asia have been more stagnant. Thus, political culture and economic performance seem to have had some relationship. However, as will be seen, it turns out to be far more complex than simply linking cultural patterns or religious values to economic motivations.

Confucian cultures

Confucianism is in essence a secular philosophy aimed at creating the good society through the leadership of a benevolent state staffed by the most educated and moral people. In theory, this ethos creates a social and political hierarchy, but one based on merit and on reciprocal obligations between those in authority and those below them. The historical practice, however, was far different, representing what Pye calls "sweet and sour Confucianism" (benevolent theory versus malevolent practice).[7]

Despite tendencies toward "sour Confucianism," several aspects of Chinese Confucian culture are strongly supportive of developmental activities. The government is exhorted to protect and promote the public good; respect for authority provides more maneuverability for officials; a high premium is placed upon education; an individual's fate is linked to his or her own talents and efforts; strong kinship ties create incentives for family-based entrepreneurship; and, in historical reality, the entrepreneurial vitality of Chinese emigrants in Southeast Asia stood in stark contrast to the economic failure of nineteenth-century China.

In all countries with a strong Confucian influence, hence, there is a

[7] Lucian W. Pye, *China: An Introduction*, 4th edn (New York: HarperCollins, 1991), pp. 73–76.

widespread social consensus about the importance of effort mobilization, deferred gratification, meritocratic competition, economic frugality, deference to authority, and knowledge and education. Concomitantly, cultural norms emphasize the virtues of group conformity, interpersonal collaboration, collective responsibility, and social integration at the expense of personal liberty. These values can be quite conducive to commercial entrepreneurship and industrial development.[8] Thus, the Confucian background enhances the absorptive capacity by both the public and private sectors to apply the MNCs' assets (e.g., capital, technology, overseas market) to economic growth. There is also a stronger social "safety net" to cushion the inevitable socioeconomic dislocations stemming from rapid growth.

These cultural norms are operationalized somewhat differently in the three Confucian cases analyzed here. Hong Kong and Singapore show two opposite paths to economic dynamism in a patriarchal Chinese culture that is marked by strong leadership but also by rather limited loyalties outside of close circles of kinship and friendship. In Hong Kong, the absence of state controls allowed commercial entrepreneurship and a skilled labor force to produce a highly dynamic economy, thus demonstrating the often hypothesized linkage between Confucian culture and an aptitude for small-scale business.[9] Conversely, Singapore offers an example of state-guided development effort under an able political leadership and bureaucracy.[10] In sum, the

---

[8] Peter Berger and Hsin-huang Michael Hsiao, eds., *In Search of an East Asian Development Model* (New Brunswick, NJ: Transaction Books, 1988); Roy Hofheinz, Jr., and Kent E. Calder, *The Eastasia Edge* (New York: Basic Books, 1982); Herman Kahn, "The Confucian Ethic and Economic Growth," pp. 78–80 in Mitchell A. Seligson, ed., *The Gap Between the Rich and Poor* (Boulder, CO.: Westview, 1984); Pye with Pye, *Asian Power and Politics*, chapters 3, 11 and 12; and Hung-chao Tai, "The Oriental Alternative: A Hypothesis on East Asian Culture and Economy," *Issues and Studies*, 25 (March 1989), pp 10–36.

[9] Susan Greenhalgh, "Families and Networks in Taiwan's Economic Development," pp. 224–45 in Edwin A. Winckler and Susan Greenhalgh, eds., *Contending Approaches to the Political Economy of Taiwan* (Armonk, NY: M.E. Sharpe, 1988); Hofheinz and Calder, *The Eastasia Edge*; Danny Kin-Kong Lam and Ian Lee, "Guerrilla Capitalism and the Limits of Statist Theory," pp. 107–24 in Cal Clark and Steve Chan, eds., *The Evolving Pacific Basin in the Global Political Economy: Domestic and International Linkages* (Boulder, CO: Lynne Rienner, 1992); Pye with Pye, *Asian Power and Politics*, chapter 3; and Siu-lin Wong, *Emigrant Entrepreneurs: Shanghai Industrialists in Hong Kong* (Hong Kong: Oxford University Press, 1988); and "Modernization and Chinese Culture in Hong Kong," *China Quarterly*, 106 (June 1986), pp. 306–25.

[10] Hafiz Mirza, *Multinationals and the Growth of the Singapore Economy* (New York: St. Martin's, 1986); and Gary Rodan, *The Political Economy of Singapore's Industrialization: National, State, and International Capital* (New York: St. Martin's, 1989).

Confucian patriarchal culture molds the "strong state" in Singapore and the "strong society" in Hong Kong.

The feudal tradition in Korea (as well as Japan) has produced a variant of Confucianism, which is distinct from the Chinese "patriarchal Confucianism." Japan and Korea share many of the central values of Chinese Confucianism, such as strong group loyalties, respect for authority, concern with achievement, and a high premium placed on education. However, feudalism forced Japanese and Koreans to work and fight together in large groups that extended beyond kinship lines. It made these feudal Confucians much more practical and down to earth than aspiring Chinese Mandarins. Today, it promotes cooperation in the large corporate structures that distinguish the Korean and Japanese economies from the Chinese ones where small firms are much more prominent.[11]

The feudal Confucianism in South Korea and Japan was quite conducive to the formation of a strong state, a tendency that they share with Singapore. However, their political economies have been much more nationalistic toward foreign capital than Singapore and the other Chinese societies (post-Mao China, Hong Kong, and Taiwan). The Japanese industrial drive excluded foreign capital so that native conglomerates could attain the experience necessary to reach international competitiveness, while the Koreans (reflecting their later industrialization) were more likely to invite MNCs into specific sectors in order to help the Korean *chaebol* first to acquire the necessary knowhow and then to assert operational control.[12] In any event, the two feudal Confucian nations relied much more on large *national* enterprises and moved up the product cycle more quickly than the Chinese systems with their somewhat different cultures.

Political cultures in South and Southeast Asia

The Southeast Asian countries have much more clientelistic cultures (akin to the more "sour" type of Chinese factionalism and *guanxi* or personal relations). There tends to be more stress on "dividing the

---

11 Pye with Pye, *Asian Power and Politics*, chapters 6 and 8; and Edwin O. Reischauer, *The Japanese Today: Change and Continuity* (Cambridge, MA: Harvard University Press, 1988).
12 Amsden, *Asia's Next Giant*; Russell Mardon, "The State and Effective Control of Foreign Capital: The Case of South Korea," *World Politics*, 43 (October 1990), pp. 111–38; and Russell Mardon and Won K. Paik, "The State, Foreign Investment, and Sustaining Industrial Growth in South Korea and Thailand," pp. 147–68 in Cal

spoils" than on working to "increase the pie." Most of these cultures view events as beyond human control and authority as status rather than the power or obligation to get things done. Pye also argues that a fundamental difference exists between the "paternalistic clientelism" of normal patronage relationships and a much more "pathological clientelism" where almost all relationships are strained by distrust and potential treachery.

Consequently, compared to the Confucian cultures, less effort is expended on pursuing pragmatic goals; there is less willingness to accept sacrifice and deferred gratification for long-term objectives; and feelings of social solidarity are weaker. These countries are less able to regulate and control the MNCs for two interrelated reasons. First, their states are considerably weaker and less capable than the Northeast Asian ones; second, elite groups in society (especially in business) are often willing to take on subordinate roles in alliances with trans-national capital.[13]

The Philippines certainly appears to be suffering from the counter-productive legacies of "pathological clientelism." First, the political culture creates extreme personal insecurity that carries over into the patronage networks dominating the government. Thus, political groupings are constantly fighting and rearranging themselves.[14] Second, the long heritage of Spanish colonial rule created the same institutions (e.g., grossly unequal land tenure) that are central to dependency conditions in Latin America. Finally, the twentieth-century tutelage of the United States cast doubts on the legitimacy of a developmental state. Taken together, these legacies fostered a doleful political economy. The combination of a plantation agriculture and a patronage-based polity creates "crony capitalism," and leaves the country ripe for exploitation by MNCs.

India's political culture is quite distinctive from both the Confucianism of East Asia and the clientelism of Southeast Asia. Unfortu-

Clark and Steve Chan, eds., *The Evolving Pacific Basin in the Global Political Economy: Domestic and International Linkages* (Boulder, CO: Lynne Rienner, 1992).

[13] Pye with Pye, *Asian Power and Politics*, chapter 4.

[14] Harold Crouch, *Economic Change, Social Structure, and the Political System in Southeast Asia: Philippine Development Compared with the Other ASEAN Countries* (Singapore: Institute of Southeast Asian Studies, 1985); Richard F. Doner, *Driving a Bargain: Automobile Industrialization and Japanese Firms in Southeast Asia* (Berkeley, CA: University of California Press, 1991); Fernando Fajnzylber, "The United States and Japan as Models of Industrialization," pp. 323–52 in Gary Gereffi and Donald Wyman, eds., *Manufacturing Miracles: Paths of Industrialization in East Asia* (Princeton, NJ: Princeton University Press, 1990); and Gary Hawes, *The Philippine State and the Marcos Regime: The Politics of Export* (Ithaca, NY: Cornell University Press, 1987).

nately, this political culture appears rather dysfunctional for development. The central elements of India's Hindu culture create dynamics that, on the one hand, bolster a strong state stifling individual initiatives but, on the other, also prevent state power from being used effectively. The caste system smothers the need for individual achievement and goal-seeking, and separates political and religious leadership with the former being quite amoral and "pragmatic." Yet, the emphasis on the "inner world of the self" leads to moralistic posturing. This dichotomy has created an ineffectual leadership style which combines grand "plans" for national development that are not seriously meant to be carried out (the moral dimension) with an extensive patronage system for distributing political spoil (the amoral one). In India, therefore, the "caste-bureaucratic" culture stresses status rather than performance in both economic and political activities, as well as legitimating considerable inequality (despite India's ostensibly Gandhian philosophy) and the neglect of rural areas.[15]

Case studies

This section discusses in more detail how political culture can shape a state's capabilities. It also shows the importance of political culture in determining a society's absorptive capacity to take advantage of the MNCs' contributions to national development and its ability to resist these firms' economic and political domination. In effect, we argue that in discussing a country's domestic structures, we should not be satisfied with just studying the role and strength of its state. The nature of its society is important in determining whether or not state policies are effective; and both are embedded in and therefore have to be understood from the broader context of political culture.

South Korea

In Korea, the feudal Confucian culture helped to engender a popular ethic stressing competition and achievement, and to create a strong state devoted to promoting economic development and welfare. The nature of both state and society, in turn, interacted positively to promote a vibrant economy. Conversely, this culture also engendered

---

[15] Cal Clark and Kartik C. Roy, *Comparing Development Patterns in South and East Asia: Challenge to Neoclassical Economics* (Boulder, CO: Lynne Rienner, 1995); and Pye with Pye, *Asian Power and Politics*, chapter 5.

social and political polarization which has occasionally erupted in violent confrontations and regime changes. Given such instability, South Korea's economic dynamism appears all the more remarkable.

To promote rapid industrialization, the government resorted to a battery of policy instruments, including the allocation of financial credit, production subsidies, tariff protection, export quotas, and tax rebates to influence entrepreneurial incentives. Its control over the financial system has been very important, permitting it to decide specific firms' participation in any project by starting or stopping the cash flow. It would support individual companies in specific projects – but only for a limited time. If the private corporations could not meet specific performance targets, they were simply dropped. Thus, while both the South Korean and Philippine (see below) governments have practiced patronage politics in undertaking national development projects, the former's actions have generally stimulated corporate competitiveness and industrial upgrading, rather than the inefficiency and rent extraction associated with "crony capitalism" in the latter. There is an irony in state–business relations, however. Until the early 1980s, the state clearly dominated its relations with the business community, even the large *chaebol*. However, the success of state-led development ultimately made the *chaebol* so strong that the balance of power has recently begun to tip in their direction.

Given its fairly large domestic market, South Korea has also been able to pursue industrial deepening with an emphasis on the heavy and chemical industries to a much greater extent than the smaller East Asian nations. This emphasis has fostered economic concentration in the form of the *chaebol*, and a "top-down" approach to industrial management that gives government bureaucrats a powerful role. There is in this approach a strong "bias for action" in the sense that the Koreans are often willing to initiate large projects without detailed long-range analysis. Instead, they seek to gain experience and modify plans on the basis of "learning by doing." Although this approach has the advantage of promoting concerted public–private efforts and a rapidly rising "learning curve," it can also result in expensive errors, given its attempt at "big spurt" industrialization. For example, some of Seoul's most assertive strategies – such as debt financing and the drive for heavy industries in the late 1970s and early 1980s – encountered occasional setbacks that were quite severe. In both instances, however, "failure" was only temporary – by the late 1980s accelerating growth was producing more than enough resources to pay down South

Korea's debt (unlike most other developing countries which were mired down in escalating debt);[16] and Korea had successfully made the transition to heavy and high-tech production.[17]

These examples of (at least temporary) policy failure also point to a far less laudatory aspect of South Korea's post-war political economy – the polarization that has often led to repressive government and violent regime change. Since the Second World War, South Korea has been marked by periods of strongman rule under Syngman Rhee in the 1950s, Park Chung Hee in the 1960s and 1970s, and Chun Doo Hwan in the 1980s, whose reigns were ended by protest or coup and separated by brief, fruitless attempts to create more democratic governments. However, a more fundamental transformation may have occurred in 1987 when growing popular opposition, particularly from students and the middle class, forced Chun's retirement; and a more institutionalized democracy appears to be emerging, despite the continuing personalistic and fractious nature of Korean politics.[18]

South Korea also stands out in its practice of "sovereignty en garde," in that it has imposed some of the most stringent conditions on MNC access in Asia. It has one of the lowest net DFI to total investment ratios among Asia's developing countries in table 4.1 (a negative sign means net capital outflow), and has preferred to rely more on foreign debt as a source of external finance. This has the twin benefit, at least from the

16 Jeff Frieden, "Third World Indebted Industrialization: International Finance and State Capital in Mexico, Brazil, Algeria, and South Korea," *International Organization*, 35 (Summer 1981), pp. 407–31.
17 For general treatments of the South Korean development model, see Amsden, *Asia's Next Giant*; Mun Boo Cho and Chung-in Moon, "State Structure and Policy Choice: Japan and South Korea in Comparative Perspective," paper presented at the annual meeting of the International Studies Association, Vancouver, 1991; Yun-han Chu, "State Structure and Economic Adjustment of the East Asian Newly Industrializing Countries," *International Organization*, 43 (Autumn 1989), pp. 647–72; Stephan Haggard and Chung-in Moon, "Institutions and Economic Policy: Theory and a Korean Case Study," *World Politics*, 42 (January 1990), pp. 210–37; Stephan Haggard and Chung-in Moon, "The South Korean State in the International Economy: Liberal, Dependent, or Mercantile?" pp. 131–89 in John Gerard Ruggie, ed., *The Antinomies of Interdependence: National Welfare and the International Division of Labor* (New York: Columbia University Press, 1983); Sung Gul Hong, "Paths of Glory: Semiconductor Leapfrogging in Taiwan and South Korea," *Pacific Focus*, 7 (Spring 1992): pp. 59–88; Leroy Jones and Il Sakong, *Government, Business, and Entrepreneurship in Economic Development: The Korean Case* (Cambridge, MA: Harvard University Press, 1980); T. W. Kang, *Is Korea the Next Japan? Understanding the Structure, Strategy, and Tactics of America's Next Competitor* (New York: Free Press, 1989); and Chung-in Moon, "The Demise of a Developmentalist State? Neoconservative Reforms and Political Consequences in South Korea," *Journal of Developing Societies*, 4 (Spring 1988), pp. 67–84.
18 Steve Chan and Cal Clark, "The Price of Economic Success," *Harvard International Review*, 15 (Winter 1992/93), pp. 24–26 and 64.

regime's perspective, of minimizing the dangers of "denationalization" in the domestic economy and of giving the state added leverage over national development because it controls the distribution of this investment capital.

Thus, the government has acted to limit the entry of MNCs into South Korea fairly severely. For example, DFI was never more than 1 percent of GNP and very rarely exceeded 5 percent of total capital inflows.[19] Although other governments also often stipulate technology transfer, domestic content, export quotas, and majority ownership as a price for MNCs to enter their countries, Seoul tends to drive a harder bargain. However, the restrictions on foreign capital were not aimed at simple exclusion. Rather, the regime acted to channel MNCs into a few priority sectors and to regulate them in order to maximize their contribution to national development. South Korea's policies have aimed at building up "national champions" among the *chaebol*, first by forcing MNCs into joint ventures with them and then by forcing the foreign corporations to divest once the Korean enterprises "learned the business and technology." Thus bolstered, the latter conglomerates have spearheaded South Korea's assault to move into increasingly sophisticated and higher value-added production and exports. For example, South Korea has been the only developing nation since the Second World War whose automobile industry has become a major player on world markets.[20]

South Korea's utilization of foreign capital in its developmental strategy is well illustrated by its efforts to create a petroleum-refining industry, first through joint ventures and then by promoting divestitures. This process started in the early 1960s when the government convinced Gulf Oil to enter into a joint venture (about which Gulf was none too enthusiastic) with the Korean Oil Company by offering it a lucrative package, including a guaranteed profit of 15 percent, a monopoly for providing crude oil, and various tax concessions. As the demand for refined petroleum escalated, the regime negotiated similar joint ventures with Caltex, Union Oil, and the National Iran Oil Company between 1965 and 1976, each with a corporate member of a different *chaebol*. By the late 1970s, the Korean partners had gained the know how, technical sophistication, and financial resources to take

[19] Amsden, *Asia's Next Giant*, pp. 72–77.
[20] Ibid.; Frieden, "Third World Indebted Industrialization"; Haggard and Moon, "The South Korean State"; Mardon, "The State and Effective Control of Foreign Capital"; and Mardon and Paik, "The State, Foreign Investment, and Sustaining Industrial Growth in South Korea and Thailand."

over these projects; and the government provided subsidized credit for most of them to buy out their foreign partners when international instability (e.g., the Iranian Revolution and the second oil shock) made this possible.[21] As Mardon and Paik conclude:

> Today, South Korea refines 100 percent of its domestic oil requirements, ... hauls the bulk of it on its own ships, and holds total financial and operational control ... All these refining operations are owned by large and diversified domestic corporations. The capital earned and the technical knowledge gained ... are applied to the expansion of these firms in other sectors. Such policies and actions led to the establishment of Korean-owned and Korean-controlled production in a wide range of heavy and chemical industry sectors.[22]

South Korea's political culture of feudal Confucianism, therefore, has played a central role in structuring its successful political economy through its impact on both the state and society. As discussed in the second section, this culture is conducive to the formation of effective large organizations. In fact, Korea has extremely competitive large corporations (*chaebol*) and a strong developmental state which used its considerable powers to foster these conglomerates. The strong state and the *chaebol* then interacted to ensure foreign capital's positive impact on Korean economic development. State policy forced MNCs to transfer technology, but this policy could only be effective because the *chaebol* were able to absorb the technology and become internationally competitive rapidly.

Hong Kong

In Hong Kong, the Chinese patriarchal Confucian culture generates a somewhat different set of dynamics. In this political culture, building large-scale organizations is difficult because of the lack of trust outside kinship groups. Not so coincidentally, the backbone of Hong Kong's dynamic export economy has been a myriad of small enterprises, many of them family owned and operated. Furthermore, the British colonial regime prevents the degeneration into the "sour Confucianism" of a government (and economy) based on *guanxi* (personal favors), thereby allowing the Confucian virtues of entrepreneurship and education to come to the fore. As a tiny city whose entrepôt trade was destroyed by

---

21 This case study is taken from Mardon and Paik, "The State, Foreign Investment, and Sustaining Industrial Growth in South Korea and Thailand."
22 *Ibid.*, pp. 158–59.

the communist victory in 1949, Hong Kong had little choice but to adopt an export-oriented strategy of growth. Its abundant and cheap but skilled labor force was, in addition, a major comparative advantage. Thus, labor-intensive light industry has formed the most dynamic core of its rapid growth for most of the post-war period. For example, textiles, electronics, and plastics have dominated the manufacturing sector with shipbuilding being the only notable heavy industry.

Hong Kong is generally perceived (with more than a little but not total justification) to represent the neoclassical vision of a *laissez-faire* economy. The British administration has traditionally refrained from active economic intervention. However, contrary to the popular view of a minimalist government, it has always underwritten a large public-housing sector and has recently adopted more stringent regulations of the stock market, banking, real estate, and medical practice. Interestingly, Hong Kong's large investment in public housing is usually viewed, not as an "unproductive" social expenditure, but as an indirect subsidy to business which can pay lower wages because of the artificially low housing costs in the colony.[23]

Although the major banks have played an active role in ensuring financial stability, the key source of entrepreneurial élan has come from the numerous small and medium-size firms. These firms are the backbone of the Colony's dynamic export sector. They tend to be owned and operated as family enterprises with relatively low capitalization. They are highly adaptable to changing market conditions, and excel in the flexible manufacturing of small batches of "faddish" consumer goods – such as digital watches, transistor radios, mobile telephones – with short product cycles. Because they are able to redeploy resources quickly from one product line to another, these firms practice what Danny Lam has called "guerrilla capitalism."[24] They present a moving target to competitors (e.g., those in the US) with far greater capital and technology assets to take advantage of economies of scale. Although Hong Kong's entrepreneurs have been

---

[23] Manuel Castells, Lee Goh, and R. Yin Wang Kwok, *The Shek Kip Mei Syndrome: Economic Development and Public Housing in Hong Kong and Singapore* (London: Pion, 1990); and Jonathan R. Schiffer, "State Policy and Economic Growth: A Note on the Hong Kong Model," *International Journal of Urban and Regional Research*, 15, 2 (1991), pp. 180–96.

[24] Danny K.K. Lam, *Explaining Economic Development: A Case Study of State Policies Towards the Computer and Electronics Industry in Taiwan (1960–80)* (Ottawa: PhD dissertation, Carleton University, 1992); and Lam and Lee, "Guerrilla Capitalism."

very adept in seizing business opportunities and in exploiting temporary market niches, they typically have a short commercial time horizon and a low capacity for long-range planning.[25]

Hong Kong's actual developmental trajectory represents a fortuitous sequence of interweaving external and internal factors. In particular, the evolving political economy of China first stimulated and then depressed manufacturing "on the rock" in an ironic reversal. The communist victory both forced Hong Kong to reorient its entrepôt economy and provided the entrepreneurial talent to start an industrial drive in the form of refugee textile manufacturers from Shanghai who combined their knowledge of the industry with the marketing power of what were then the colony's dominant MNCs – British trading companies (or *hong*).

The next upgrading of Hong Kong's economy also involved foreign corporations, both directly and indirectly. In the late 1950s, US retailers (e.g., Sears, Penney, Ward) came to Hong Kong when the relevant Western patents expired; they helped to start a local electronics industry by showing domestic firms how to assemble final products from components made elsewhere, particularly in Japan. This, in turn, stimulated American producers to move their production offshore to places such as Hong Kong in order to meet competitive pricing. Over time, Hong Kong's manufacturers (both domestic and foreign) moved into more sophisticated production, but industry in Hong Kong remained essentially labor-intensive because of the continuing large pool of workers that migration from China produced.[26]

Ultimately, however, Hong Kong's basic assembly operations began to be priced out of international competition in the late 1970s. In the 1980s, then, many Hong Kong entrepreneurs saved their businesses by moving production to the newly opened People's Republic of China – more than half of Hong Kong's manufactures are now actually made in China. Thus, Chinese entrepreneurs in Hong Kong became transnational actors in their own right. Together with similar entrepreneurs from Taiwan, who also began investing in China in the late 1980s, they

---

[25] Lawrence B. Krause, "Hong Kong and Singapore: Twins or Kissing Cousins?" *Economic Development and Cultural Change*, 36 (April 1988), pp. S11–S43; Lam and Lee, "Guerrilla Capitalism"; Alvin Rabushka, *Hong Kong: A Study in Economic Freedom* (Chicago: University of Chicago Press, 1979); and Wong, *Emigrant Entrepreneurs*.

[26] Bela Balassa, *Economic Policies in the Pacific Asian Developing Countries* (New York: New York University Press, 1991); Krause, "Hong Kong and Singapore"; and Rabushka, *Hong Kong*.

account for a considerable share of China's burgeoning trade surplus with the United States.[27]

The policy of *laissez-faire* has been applied to MNCs as well as to the domestic economy. Hong Kong's government does not as a matter of policy treat local and foreign investors by different standards. It has not sought to erect entry or exit barriers that discriminate against foreign businesses. As noted in the foregoing description of Hong Kong's economic evolution, MNCs have played important roles at several key junctures of economic transition. Today, foreign corporations are important in plastics and, to a lesser extent, electronics; and, increasingly, Hong Kong has also become a financial center, thus opening another avenue for foreign capital.

What is perhaps more striking than the important contributions to Hong Kong's growth that can be attributed to the attractiveness for MNCs of the colony's *laissez-faire* policies, however, is the surprisingly small role of foreign capital in Hong Kong's overall economy. For example, in the late 1980s MNCs accounted for only 12 percent of Hong Kong's exports; and most of Hong Kong's trade is now handled by small import–export firms rather than the large (and foreign) British *hong*. The principal reason for this is the tremendous dynamism of the local small firms whose "guerrilla capitalism" has allowed them to outcompete MNCs, rather than being displaced by them. Especially in electronics, many entrepreneurs learned the business by working for MNCs and then set up their own firms. Thus, MNC involvement in Hong Kong led to a substantial transfer of technology and skills. Unlike South Korea, though, government policy was not involved. Rather, "society" was so strong (in terms of education, skills, and abilities) and motivated that it was able to benefit from the MNC presence without the assistance of state regulation.[28]

More recently, there has been a new surge of DFI in Hong Kong, albeit for political reasons and in a somewhat ironic counterpoint to the stereotypes of capitalist and socialist economies. As Hong Kong's incorporation into the People's Republic of China in 1997 nears, Beijing has assumed increasing political and economic power (the Bank of China is now the largest financial center in the colony); and China's international prestige and ability to continue its economic

27 Lowell Dittmer, "Hong Kong and China's Modernization," *Orbis*, 30 (Fall 1986), pp. 525–42; and Yu-shan Wu, "The Political Economy of Taiwan-Mainland Economic Relations," paper presented at the Conference on Permutations Across the Taiwan Strait, Texas A&M University, 1991.
28 Lam and Lee, "Guerrilla Capitalism."

reforms are tied to the bottom not falling out in Hong Kong. Thus, the PRC has been forced to pour money into Hong Kong to keep the stock market and real estate prices stable. London responded to this indication of Chinese vulnerability by trying to increase the scope of local democracy before 1997 which caused Beijing to retaliate by threatening not to guarantee the loans for Hong Kong's international airport. Thus, "socialist" China is investing considerable amounts of money to prop up capitalism in Hong Kong; and "capitalist" Britain is trying to use economic leverage for political purposes.[29]

In summary, the Confucian patriarchal culture has sustained in Hong Kong norms supporting family entrepreneurship and upward mobility through education. Because of a colonial government committed to a *laissez-faire* philosophy, a "society-dominated" political economy has emerged in which the dynamics emanating from the culture have been allowed to play out, unfettered by the strong government that is normally engendered by patriarchal Confucianism. The result has been a vibrant economy based on guerrilla capitalism and an ability to capture technology and skills from the MNC presence. What is central to the Hong Kong "economic miracle," therefore, is the strength of "society."

Singapore

The political economy of Singapore represents a combination of some of the disparate elements found in Hong Kong and South Korea. It has a patriarchal Confucian culture, like Hong Kong's. Yet, it has a state-led economy, like South Korea's, despite the problems that the culture creates for large organizations. State leadership in Singapore depends upon two factors, one geographic and one idiosyncratic. Because of the small size of the city state, exercising command and control is much easier than in larger countries; and Singapore has benefitted from a strong and effective leader in the person of Lee Kuan Yew.

While Singapore's statist economy is in many ways the polar opposite of Hong Kong's *laissez-faire*, its general strategy was similar to Hong Kong's in the sense that it derived from a "big bang" in the external environment. Initially, Singapore planned to follow a path of import-substitution industrialization primarily aimed at markets in the

[29] John P. Burns, "Hong Kong in 1992: Struggle for Authority," *Asian Survey*, 33 (January 1993), pp. 22–31.

Cal Clark and Steve Chan

much less developed Malayan states. However, when Singapore's union with Malaysia proved abortive, this strategy became unworkable. Thus, the government switched gears radically and began to create an export-based economy by recruiting foreign MNCs to bring their internationally competitive industries to Singapore and by using state corporations to develop or maintain shipbuilding and, in joint ventures with MNCs, petrochemicals. In addition to the latter sectors, the electronics industry became a leader in the first phase of Singapore's export drive. Due to the MNCs, Singapore started significantly higher up the international product cycle than the other Little Dragons. Still, the Lee government felt the need to adopt a specific program for industrial upgrading in 1979 called the "Second Industrial Revolution" which included an emphasis on high-tech production, a state commitment to increased education and training and to several large infrastructure projects, and a "corrective wage policy" that tried to force salary increases of 50 percent over a three-year period. The program was successful in attracting substantial new investment in the computer, chemicals, and petroleum industries. However, it fell short of many of the more ambitious goals for sophisticated manufacturing and was supplemented by an increased emphasis on services, especially banking, in the late 1980s.

The nature of the state's role in the economy is significantly different from both of the other Little Dragons discussed above. Although Singapore and Hong Kong have had similar British colonial traditions and historically entrepôt economies in addition to their common small populations and national products noted above, their political economies have now diverged markedly. In contrast to Hong Kong with its decentralized and *laissez-faire* system, the state assumes a dominant position in Singapore's economy. Whereas Hong Kong practices a sort of "market rationality" that promotes individual entrepreneurial initiatives, diffused technical learning and market adaptation, and opportunistic or even speculative commercial ventures, Singapore provides an example of "plan rationality," whereby government agencies and public enterprises play an active role in developing infrastructure, mobilizing resources, and especially making long-range preparations for orderly transitions to higher stages of the international product cycle. Government bureaucrats engage in thorough analysis of socioeconomic conditions and plot various courses for economic development; they plan with a view of "getting things done right the first time." This attitude stands in sharp contrast, incidentally,

134

to the typical South Korean posture of "let us get the ball rolling and then figure out what to do next."

The institutional basis for Singapore's strong state resides in several specific programs which the regime has used to great advantage. In the economic realm, the Pioneer Industries Ordinance which is administered by the Economic Development Board allows the technocratic bureaucracy to channel investment capital into desired sectors primarily through the provision of incentives (e.g., tax breaks, subsidized financing) rather than through restrictions. For example, when Singapore decided to transform the economy into more sophisticated and higher value-added production at the end of the 1970s, it simply withdrew previous tariff breaks for automobile assembly and tire production which, in effect, closed down these less sophisticated industries. State power over the economy is also exercised through large public enterprises. State corporations, public utilities, and other governmental bodies constitute 50 percent of GNP and 20 percent of employment (mostly in the finance rather than the manufacturing sector).[30]

In addition, the Singapore case (as well as Hong Kong) raises the interesting point that government spending for subsidized housing, education, and other aspects of popular welfare actually constitutes a "subsidy" for businesses which can pay lower wages for fairly skilled labor, rather than a "drag" which diverts resources from "more productive" private investment. In particular, the Central Provident Fund (which is created by payroll deductions of about 25 percent that are matched by additional employer contributions) – equal to slightly over 10 percent of GNP – is an ingenuous invention that ensures a high investment rate, finances subsidized housing and human capital that make Singapore more attractive to MNCs, and creates a welfare dependency (e.g., withdrawals are used to purchase apartments) that controls labor without resort to direct repression.[31]

The role of MNCs and their relationship with the host government are also very different in Singapore from elsewhere in Asia. In terms of a comparison with the equally statist South Korea, Singapore with its explicit strategy of growth through invitations-to-MNCs defines the

[30] Frederic C. Deyo, *Dependent Development and Industrial Order: An Asian Case Study* (New York: Praeger, 1981); Krause, "Hong Kong and Singapore"; Mirza, *Multinationals and the Growth of the Singapore Economy*; and Rodan, *The Political Economy of Singapore's Industrialization*.
[31] Castells *et al.*, *Public Housing in Hong Kong and Singapore*; and Rodan, *The Political Economy of Singapore's Industrialization*.

Table 4.5 *MNC share of the Singapore economy*

	1966	1972	1975	1980	1982
Foreign share of GDP	9%	18%[a]	23%	28%	26%
Foreign investment share of GDCF	—	16%	28%	33%	41%
Foreign investment and foreign borrowing share of GDCF	—	54%	54%	67%	50%
Foreign share of manufacturing investment commitments	—	80%	81%	86%	69%
Foreign share of paid-up capital in commercial banks	—	—	—	—	76%

[a] 1970

Source: Hafiz Mirza, *Multinationals and the Growth of the Singapore Economy* (New York: St. Martin's, 1986). pp. 5, 7, 9 and 130.

other end of the spectrum of MNC access. Moreover, although both Hong Kong and Singapore welcome MNCs, the state plays a much more active and direct role in recruiting and screening these companies in the latter. Consequently, DFI plays a much larger role in Singapore than in any of our other cases (as shown in table 4.1). MNC production, for instance, constitutes about 70 percent of Singapore's exports (compared to 10 to 15 percent for Hong Kong); and foreign capital dominates such leading sectors as electronics and petrochemicals. Tables 4.5 and 4.6 provide a summary overview of foreign capital's dominant role in Singapore's economy. MNCs have provided most of the investment in manufacturing and a sizeable share of total investment as well. Compared to local firms, foreign manufacturers are larger, more capital-intensive, more export-oriented, and more profitable (but surprisingly equal in wage levels and productivity). Clearly, the impact of MNCs on Singapore's economy has been far greater than in the other Asian countries studied.

The state in Singapore plays a subtle role of both recruiting and regulating the multinationals. On the one hand, the government has explicitly sought MNCs as allies in national development, and has provided generous incentives for investing in Singapore. The state also underwrites popular welfare, human capital development, and physical infrastructure to increase its already considerable attraction due to geographic position as a site for MNC location. On the other hand, the state manipulates incentives to channel foreign (and domestic) capital into desired sectors; and the large role of state

Table 4.6 *Role of foreign capital in Singapore's manufacturing, 1982*

	MNC share
Number of firms	25%
Number of employees	55%
Total employee pay	57%
Capital expenditures	63%
Output	63%
Value added	65%
Exports	72%
Pre-tax profits	70%

Source: Hafiz Mirza, *Multinationals and the Growth of the Singapore Economy* (New York: St. Martin's, 1986), p. 105.

corporations restricts the space for MNC penetration. We see in Singapore, hence, a limited partnership between the state and MNCs, with private domestic capital assuming a minor role. In fact, the primarily Chinese small businessmen often claim that they have been largely excluded from the fruits of Singapore's "economic miracle."[32]

To summarize, rather than family entrepreneurialism, the policies of a paternalistic state provide the key explanation for Singapore's economic success. Paternalistic support for society created a highly productive work force satisfied with its quality of life. The strategy of growth by invitation-to-MNCs then permitted a leapfrogging up the international product cycle. Presumably, the state turned to foreign capital as the best (and perhaps only) means for financing rapid industrialization. However, the nature of Singapore's political economy also prevented either of the different types of technology transfer that occurred in South Korea and Hong Kong, since there were neither large domestic firms acting as national champions nor many small "guerrilla capitalists."

The Philippines

In contrast to the success stories of the three Little Dragons sketched above, the Philippines has had a rather disappointing economic history recently. It has been dubbed the most "Latin" of the Asian

[32] Donald K. Crone, *The ASEAN States: Coping with Dependence* (New York: Praeger, 1983); Chi Huang, "The State and Foreign Investment: The Cases of Taiwan and Singapore," *Comparative Political Studies*, 22 (April 1989), pp. 93–121; Deyo, *Dependent*

states because of its history of Spanish colonialism, its Catholic culture, and its poor economic performance in the 1980s. Indeed, many of the conditions stressed by dependency theory on the basis of the Latin American experience are easy to find. Due to the imposition of Spanish colonial rule in the late 1500s, this country had the longest history in Asia of being integrated into the global economic system. Agricultural commercialization (sugar, hemp, tobacco) has been the central feature of its political economy, whereby large landowning families have dominated provincial politics in the fashion of powerful political dynasties up to this day. The power of these political barons has been based on an extensive patronage system, and this power has always been a source of centrifugal force challenging the authority of the state. These oligarchs, with extensive entrenched interests in agricultural exports and import substitution, have led blocking coalitions that have effectively prevented socioeconomic reforms. In particular, the traditional plantation mode of production has created a highly inegalitarian system of income and land distribution, and efforts to bring about greater equality have been stymied by the oligarchs.[33]

Unlike most other Asian countries, the Philippines did not have an indigenous aristocratic-bureaucratic class, or a tradition of a central bureaucracy prior to the establishment of colonial rule. These legacies left the country very vulnerable to external domination. Even after political independence, Americans still maintained "parity rights" in the commercial sector, enjoying the same economic freedom as Philippine citizens. This humiliating condition understandably stimulated periodic surges of economic nationalism, such as the "Filipino First" program in the late 1950s and early 1960s and the restrictions placed on the ownership ratios and sectoral location of foreign capital by the Marcos regime in the 1970s. Yet, these regulatory regimes, especially the Marcos one, were not very effective.[34] Thus, the Philippines has been left with a relatively low ability to buffer external influences.

The pressure exerted by foreign (primarily American) economic influence has also been greater in the Philippines than elsewhere in

Development; Krause, "Hong Kong and Singapore"; Mirza, *Multinationals and the Growth of the Singapore Economy*; and Rodan, *The Political Economy of Singapore's Industrialization*.

33 Crouch, *Philippine Development*; and David G. Timberman, *A Changeless Land: Continuity and Change in Philippine Politics* (Singapore: Institute of Southeast Asian Studies, 1991).

34 Crone, *The ASEAN States*; and Kunio Yoshihara, *Philippine Industrialization: Foreign and Domestic Capital* (Singapore: Oxford University Press, 1985).

Asia. Whereas the United States was primarily motivated to defend South Korea, Taiwan, and Thailand for political and strategic reasons during the Cold War, its interests in the Philippines have been driven more by commercial concerns. This US influence fostered a more autonomous business class than elsewhere in Southeast Asia. This business class – as well as the political oligarchs, as noted earlier – have been in a better position to lobby the state for favorable policies, although these interests have themselves been sharply divided among those favoring agricultural exports, import substitution, and sub-contracting for multinationals interested in using the Philippines as an export platform.[35]

Instead of being attracted by the weakness of the state and the openness of the economy, MNCs have been repelled by the recent instability in the Philippines. Although this country could in the 1960s boast of richer human resources and a longer history of import substitution than its Southeast Asian neighbors, it has been mired in economic stagnation in the recent years. Despite the notoriety of the Marcos regime, its problems almost certainly stemmed from the broader socioeconomic forces sketched above, rather than from the personal idiosyncracies of a dictator tied to his wife's "shoe-fetish" greed. The political economy has been gripped by a stalemate among competing elite groups which attempt to use public policies to promote their particularistic interests in the style of what Mancur Olson has called "distributional coalitions."[36]

The failure of the Progressive Car Manufacturing Project (PCMP) initiated by the Board of Investments (BOI) illustrates the various internal and external problems facing the Philippines. The PCMP was an ambitious plan to increase greatly the local content of automobile manufacturing (from 10 percent to 60 percent), to rationalize the market structure by reducing the huge number of competing producers, and to promote exports. Although some gains were realized (an initial spate of MNC investment occurred and local content rose to about 30 percent), the program ultimately made little progress toward upgrading the Philippine automobile industry and, in particular,

---

[35] Crouch, *Philippine Development*; Doner, *Driving a Bargain*; Hawes, *The Philippine State and the Marcos Regime*; Timberman, *A Changeless Land*; David Wurfel, *Filipino Politics: Development and Decay* (Quezon City: Ateneo de Manila University Press, 1988); and Kunio Yoshihara, *The Rise of Ersatz Capitalism in South-East Asia* (Singapore: Oxford University Press, 1988), and *Philippine Industrialization*.

[36] Mancur Olson, *The Rise and Fall of Nations: Economic Growth, Stagflation, and Social Rigidities* (New Haven, CT: Yale University Press, 1982).

toward improving the capabilities of domestic firms. Richard Doner traces this failure to a variety of reasons: the bureaucratic isolation of BOI, the ability of inefficient firms with political contacts to manipulate the patronage system, the economic problems of local assemblers, and the strong foothold that MNCs had established in the country – in short, a soft and fragmented state *and* a weak and contentious business sector.[37]

This dour political economy and its disadvantages *vis-à-vis* the three Confucian ones that were just discussed can be directly related to its underlying political culture. The "pathological clientelist" culture produces great personal insecurity which, in turn, engenders patronage politics and "rent seeking" in both economic and political activities. Consequently, the state is weak and unable to regulate and control foreign capital; businessmen try to gain profits through using political contacts to secure opportunities for high-profit monopolies rather than engaging in productive activities or "learning from" the MNCs that do set up shop in the Philippines; and there is little support for "social investment." The result is a "volatile" type of state–society relations in which neither state nor society is capable of contributing much to national development, leading to the deleterious results of "crony capitalism" – low growth and high inequality.

India

India has had a generally poor economic record, similar to the Philippines. However, the dynamics of the relationships between traditional culture, colonial legacies, economic strategy, political evolution, and ultimate growth performance are quite different. Instead of being victimized, like the Philippines, by the ongoing legacies of the colonial (and precolonial) period, India decisively rejected them; instead of a weak state, India developed a strong state; instead of a fairly supine posture before MNCs, India aimed at (and succeeded in) dislodging them. Yet, India's economic performance has been much closer to that of the Philippines than to that of the Little Dragons. The answer to the puzzling question of why this is so is that India's "caste-bureaucratic" political culture almost inevitably produces massive political corruption and economic inefficiency.

At independence, India was ready to reject all vestiges of British

---

[37] Doner, *Driving a Bargain.*

imperial rule and economic domination as an affront to Indian dignity and as a potentially dangerous mechanism for continuing unequal and exploitative relationships. This economic nationalism was summed up well in the slogan "Be Indian! Buy Indian!" As a result of this orientation, India embarked upon a strategy of rapid industrialization, technological independence, and (hopefully) rapid progress toward greater social equity. Any loss of pure economic efficiency from opting out of the international division of labor that this strategy of self-reliant import substitution entailed (e.g., higher prices, lower-quality goods, shortages) in the short run was considered worthwhile to avoid the long-term implications of continued foreign domination of the economy. In addition, geography was favorable for such a strategy because the subcontinent's huge population made import substitution much more viable than in small nations, such as the four Little Dragons (they include Taiwan in addition to South Korea, Hong Kong, and Singapore) in East Asia. Strong state leadership was almost certainly necessary for such a strategy; and India's traditional culture and the legacy of British colonialism both supported large bureaucracies. The result was a commitment to central planning which, while well short of a full command economy, gave the state extensive powers over licensing new enterprises and expansions in the capacity of existing enterprises. For the first decade, this system worked fairly well, at least from the perspective of the Indian government. The presence of foreign corporations was held to a minimum, both because of the government's policies and the general unattractiveness of India's unstable economy. Moreover, the private business sector, especially the leading large "business houses" (e.g., Birla, Tata), remained strong advocates of economic nationalism because they profited greatly from the monopoly position that India's protectionist walls and regulation of the domestic market provided.

The foreign exchange crisis of 1957 made the continuation of this political economy untenable by confronting the regime with the difficult choice of either opening the economy to MNCs or forgoing the foreign technology that appeared necessary to maintain the pace of industrialization. The government decided that opening the economy was the lesser of the two evils and, therefore, became much more permissive in allowing DFI with majority or sole ownership when the equity was tied to desired technology. Private businesses, as well, began to license more foreign technology and engage in some joint ventures in production. Consequently, a huge inflow of DFI occurred

141

over the next decade as the share of assets controlled by DFI doubled from one-tenth to one-fifth of India's corporate assets. The changed policy toward MNCs did not mean that India had adopted *laissez-faire* policies, however. In fact, one of the major attractions for MNCs was the potential for substantial monopoly rents that the closed and uncompetitive Indian market created.

These concessions to foreign capital were not particularly popular in India. Thus, the government moved to increase its own economic and political capabilities, so that it could exert more leverage *vis-à-vis* the MNCs. In terms of the internal economy, the 1960s witnessed two critical trends in state power over the economy. First, through several nationalizations in the financial sector, the state came to control industrial finance in the manner of South Korea. Second, in part because of its financial powers and in part to preempt MNCs from moving into the more advanced sectors, a tremendous growth in state corporations commenced. For example, in just the two decades between 1962 and 1982, the proportion of corporate assets controlled by the public sector more than doubled from about a fifth to slightly under a half.[38] This internal augmentation of state power was complemented by changes in the international economy which produced greater competition among MNCs and speeded up the processes of technological diffusion around the globe, thereby undercutting the monopoly control that any given MNC could exercise over a specific technology or industrial process.

India then began to apply this power to "dislodge multinationals" in the late 1960s. This occurred along two lines. First, there was an increasing separation or "unbundling" of technology from equity in the sense that state corporations and private businesses in India were able to get the desired foreign technology by other market routes. Second, the government greatly increased its regulatory power over foreign capital with the Foreign Exchange Regulation Act (FERA) of 1973 which limited MNCs to 40 percent minority ownership in their Indian subsidiaries unless they were in a priority industry, introducing critical new technologies, or exporting most of their products. Given the lucrative Indian market that government protectionism and regulation had created, most MNCs in India reluctantly negotiated with the government which, in return, made such deals more palatable by allowing the foreign corporations to "dilute their equity" through

---

[38] Encarnation, *Dislodging Multinationals*, p. 35.

issuing stocks rather than forming joint partnerships (a far greater threat to their managerial autonomy). Thus, by the early 1980s, the share of foreign capital in India's total corporate assets had been cut to about a third of what it had been at its high-water mark in the 1960s.[39]

India's economic nationalism, therefore, can be judged quite successful in restricting the MNCs. However, the data in table 4.1 certainly show that this was not translated into economic success in the usual sense of rapid growth and an increasing quality of life. This overall failure points to a bitter paradox in India's political economy – the principal method necessary for "dislodging multinationals" (i.e., vastly expanding the state's economic role) made economic stagnation almost inevitable because of India's political culture. As discussed in the previous section, India's "caste-bureaucratic" culture stimulates a type of politics in which leaders articulate "grand moral visions" in which, in reality, they have little interest. Rather, the "reality" of politics is focused on patronage and the "amoral" pursuit of self-interest.[40] Indian development, self-reliance, and socialism have constituted such grand visions during the post-war era. However, the ever more powerful state has been primarily concerned with distributing patronage. Thus, economic regulation became simply the distribution of state-guaranteed monopoly rents; and, in particular, state corporations were quite inefficient. For example, in the late 1980s, India's state corporations had about two-thirds of the fixed capital in industry but produced only one-third of the value added.[41]

Two different interactions between India's caste-bureaucratic culture and the legacies of British colonialism underlie this paradox. On the one hand, reaction against colonial domination produced a strong nationalist state. On the other, the British legacy reinforced the culture's acceptance of a status emphasis and arbitrary power in both the public and private sectors. Thus, while the state was strong enough to dislodge the MNCs, its inefficient bureaucracy exacerbated, rather than attenuated, the domestic inefficiencies and rent-seeking behaviors that distorted and retarded national development. Metaphori-

[39] Jagdish N. Bagwati and Padma Desai, *India: Planning for Industrialization* (London: Oxford University Press, 1970); Clark and Roy, *South and East Asia*; Encarnation, *Dislodging Multinationals*; Joseph M. Grieco, *Between Dependency and Autonomy: India's Experience with the International Computer Industry* (Berkeley, CA: University of California Press, 1984); and F. Tomasson Jannuzi, *India in Transition: Issues of Political Economy in a Planned Society* (Boulder, CO: Westview, 1989).

[40] Pye with Pye, *Asian Power and Politics*, chapter 5.

[41] Sajal Brahmachari, *Impact of Incentives on Productivity in Public Enterprises: An Economic Analysis of Case Studies* (Calcutta: PhD Dissertation, University of Calcutta, 1992).

Cal Clark and Steve Chan

cally, the Indians displaced the East Indian Company but caught the British disease.

Domestic structures and the role of MNCs in Asian political economies

This chapter has examined the role of MNCs in five Asian political economies as a test of Risse-Kappen's framework (see chapter 1) about how transnational relations in a given country are shaped by its domestic structures, in particular the nature of its state–society relations. As a first step, we demonstrated that neither of the conventional approaches to the study of development (the dependency and modernization approaches) could explain the relationship between MNC access to and MNC impact on a host economy. We then invoked the statist formulation, which is concerned with state–society relations as in Risse-Kappen's framework. Although this formulation helps to illuminate some empirical patterns, it still leaves several important anomalies unexplained.

Thus, the principal focus of our analysis turned to political culture as a deeper structural force that shapes the nature of both the state and society. Applying Lucian Pye's typology of Asian cultures provides a new perspective on the nexus between state–society relations and the impact of MNCs on a host economy. This perspective offered greater explanatory power, suggesting that certain *types of states* and certain *types of society* are more adept than others at dealing with MNCs and at promoting autonomous development. Thus, recourse to the underlying political cultures provides explanations for both of the principal anomalies that resulted from applying the "strong state" hypothesis to our cases. The political culture of Hong Kong created a strong society which garnered the potential benefits of MNC presence even in the absence of state regulatory policy, while regulatory policy in India was ineffective because of the way in which both state and society had been shaped by the traditional political culture.

Our primary conclusion, therefore, is that a country's political culture and its state–society relations exercise a decisive influence in regulating MNC access and in orchestrating MNC contributions to national growth. Both political culture and state–society relations are important aspects of domestic structure. They *interact* in significant ways to facilitate certain policy options and block others. Most particularly, societies are not blank sheets on which a strong state can

144

impose its script at will. Instead, pre-existing cultural dispositions can facilitate (or obstruct) state domination by granting (or denying) *legitimacy* for government intervention. Legitimacy facilitates the implementation of state policies and thus their *effectiveness*, thereby creating a positive feedback loop that reinforces state domination. Societies, in addition, possess different proclivities and capacities for economic activities. Thus, one is led to ask which factors shape the basic structure of states and societies, making some functional and some dysfunctional for economic growth. It is here that Pye's model of political culture apparently correlates well with the political and economic world in Asia. According to this logic, political culture is a first-order variable, whereas state–society relations have a secondary influence.

The evidence also supports several of Risse-Kappen's hypotheses about the relationship between state power and transnational access. In general, his framework expects MNCs to have more limited access in state-dominated systems. This is certainly true for a comparison of India and South Korea, on the one hand, with Hong Kong and the Philippines, on the other. However, if a strong state is willing to permit access voluntarily, Risse-Kappen predicts that the impact of transnational actors can be quite large. This, in fact, describes the situation in Singapore where MNCs play a far larger role than anywhere else in Asia.

Finally, our analysis makes a strong case for *bringing society back in*. Countries endowed with stronger and more coherent states have been better able to regulate MNC access, but neither MNC access nor state power always corresponds with higher (or for that matter, lower) contributions of MNCs to economic growth. It thus appears that national autonomy over the MNCs is in itself neither a sufficient condition (witness the case of India) nor a necessary condition (witness the case of Hong Kong) for superior economic performance. *The nature of society must be added to the equation as well*. Thus, MNC activities in a host country are not just affected by the capacity of the state. Rather, how well a state and society work together in a synergistic fashion and the society's capacity to absorb, take advantage of, and complement the MNCs' contributions are vital as well. Almost needless to say, these factors are primarily a function of the embedded political culture.

5 Transnational relations, domestic structures, and security policy in the USSR and Russia

Matthew Evangelista

> We tried to create a new reality by the old methods, sending out directives from above. Well, directives, whether statutes or decrees, are accepted for implementation only by a community that is connected with the command center either by a unity of interests or by bonds of obedience and fear. When these are absent, the directive does not work.
>
> Former Soviet Foreign Minister Eduard Shevardnadze[1]

This study of the effect of transnational actors on Soviet security policy addresses a country and an issue-area that were left out of the original theorizing about transnational relations in the 1970s. That literature, and the related work on interdependence, assumed that transnational relations would predominate in issue-areas outside the realm of "high politics," and in countries where democratic polities would permit penetration of government policy-making by transnational as well as domestic actors.[2] According to this perspective, the centralized,

A previous version of this article appeared in *International Organization*, 49, 1 (Winter 1995). Research was supported by grants from the Michigan Memorial-Phoenix Project at the University of Michigan, the National Council for Soviet and East European Research and the United States Institute of Peace and completed under the auspices of Harvard University's Center for Science and International Affairs. I am grateful to all four institutions. For research assistance I thank Marc Bennett and Sharon Werning. My greatest intellectual debt is to Thomas Risse-Kappen for collaboration over several years in working out the theoretical basis for understanding the impact of transnational relations on security policy. Peter Katzenstein, Robert Keohane, Stephen Krasner, James Goldgeier, and the other participants in the workshops provided valuable comments, as did Michael Desch, Peter Hall, Christopher Paine, and Joanna Spear. Correspondence with Emanuel Adler and Jeff Checkel was particularly helpful.

1 Eduard Shevardnadze, *Moi vybor: v zashchitu demokratii i svobody* [*My choice: in defense of democracy and freedom*], (Moscow: Novosti, 1991), p. 316.
2 Robert O. Keohane and Joseph S. Nye, Jr., eds., *Transnational Relations and World Politics* (Cambridge, MA: Harvard University Press, 1971). Keohane and Nye, "Transgovernmental Relations and International Organizations," *World Politics*, 27, 1 (October 1974), pp. 39–62.

secretive, and authoritarian regime that prevailed in the Soviet Union until the end of the 1980s was one of the least likely candidates for transnational influence. By the same token, we would expect Soviet security policy to have been the most immune to such influence.

This chapter has two main aims. The first is to present a theoretical rationale for understanding why the Soviet Union should have been open to the influence of transnational actors – in this case, organizations of Soviet and US scientists pursuing arms control initiatives – even in the high politics of security policy. My argument is consistent with the theoretical framework that Risse-Kappen develops in the introduction to this volume: Certain aspects of the domestic structure of the Soviet Union – in particular the domination of a weak, fragmented society by a strong, hierarchical party-state apparatus – made it difficult for new ideas to find their way to the top of the policy process. Once a window of opportunity provided policy entrepreneurs with access to the leadership, however, they were often able to see their ideas implemented quickly. In the security field, such policy entrepreneurs were typically members of transnational organizations – most notably the Pugwash conference of scientists and its offshoots – and many of their ideas came from international discussions. Moreover, given the relationship between security policy and the economic crisis that preoccupied Soviet leaders in the late 1980s, that particular issue-area was ripe for new initiatives generated through transnational coalitions.

The second aim of the chapter is to evaluate an important implication of the generalization linking domestic structure to transnational activities. If, as I argue, domestic structure affected the nature and degree of transnational influence on Soviet policy, then a change in that structure should be associated with changes in the behavior and influence of transnational actors. Changes in the domestic structure in the Soviet Union during the late 1980s were dramatic. They entailed the transformation from a secretive, authoritarian, one-party state with a command economy to an incipient democracy with an elected parliament possessing real legislative authority, an increasingly active civil society, the proliferation of informal political organizations and new political parties, and the breakdown of central economic planning and the introduction of some elements of a market economy. The hypothesis I examine is that these changes in domestic structure should have had the paradoxical effect of making transnational actors simultaneously less constrained in promoting their policies and less effective in getting them implemented. Moreover, the actors who had enjoyed good access to the leadership in the centralized system would be expected, under the new circumstances, to face competition from other groups with divergent policy goals and their own transnational allies.

In evaluating the effect of domestic structure on the success of transnational lobbying efforts, I focus on two cases: the effort to defend the Antiballistic Missile Treaty of 1972 and to prevent the development of new strategic defense systems; and the effort to achieve a comprehensive nuclear test ban. The revival of transnational activity in pursuit of disarmament dates to the early 1980s, when the deterioration in East–West relations threatened to halt any further progress on arms control and to undermine what had already been achieved. This chapter covers the period from approximately 1982 to 1994.

Before the end of 1989, when most of the major changes in Soviet domestic structure had been accomplished, a transnational community of US and Soviet supporters of arms control influenced Soviet security policy in broad conceptual terms, and on several specific issues, including the two I examine here – halting nuclear testing and limiting strategic defenses.[3] After 1989 the traditional institutions of the Soviet military-industrial sector came close to reversing many of the prior achievements: they sought to revive interest in developing strategic-defense weapons and to secure the government's commitment to a renewal of nuclear testing. Only major changes in US policy, initiated under the Clinton administration, prevented the pro-military forces from gaining the upper hand on these issues of Russian security policy. My general proposition about the impact of domestic structure does not necessarily predict policy reversals after 1989, but it would anticipate a loss of the transnational actors' privileged position *vis-à-vis* the top leadership and a new opportunity for US policy to weigh into the balance.

Transformation of the Soviet domestic structure

During the decade of the 1980s the domestic structure of the Soviet Union changed dramatically – thanks mainly to the reforms initiated

---

[3] These cases are not limited to ones with a substantial technical component, for which scientists would appear to have an advantage, but include, for example, debates on reducing and restructuring conventional forces as well as broader conceptions such as

by Mikhail Gorbachev. Although the changes were momentous, many of them unfolded gradually. Consider, for example, such key dimensions of the old Soviet structure as secrecy, Communist Party domination, and centralization. *Glasnost'* gradually diminished the degree of secrecy enshrouding all aspects of Soviet life, including security policy – as, indeed, its architects intended.[4] The Communist Party's monopoly on political power was undermined bit by bit, with the flourishing of "informal" political groups in 1987, the introduction in 1989 of an elected parliament, the transfer of ultimate power from the Party's general secretary to the country's president, the founding of alternative political parties, the constitutional amendment revoking the Party's monopoly position, and, finally, the banning of the Party in the wake of the failed coup of August 1991. The centralized aspect of the Soviet domestic structure changed both gradually – with the growing fissiparous tendencies in the independence-minded republics – and dramatically, with the breakup of the Union at the end of 1991.

The purpose of this section is not simply to enumerate the various events that constituted the Soviet transformation. Rather, I seek to put those events in the context of a specific definition of domestic structure, in order to further the goal of making domestic structure a useful variable for comparative political inquiry.

We can summarize the changes in Soviet domestic structure in terms of the three components of Risse-Kappen's definition – political institutions, society, and policy networks – by contrasting the structure of the pre-1989 period with the one that replaced it. Although the changes were less abrupt than such a dichotomization suggests, a comparison of Soviet policy-making in, for example, 1986 as against 1990 reveals dramatic differences which underscore the magnitude of the transformation that had occurred. I associate the changes primarily

---

"common security." I discuss them in my forthcoming book, *Taming the Bear: Transnational Relations and the Demise of the Soviet Threat*. I thank Valerie Bunce for bringing this point to my attention.

[4] Aleksandr N. Iakovlev, "Dostizhenie kachestvenno novogo sostoianiia Sovetskogo obshchestva i obshchestvennye nauki" [The attainment of a qualitatively new state of Soviet society and the social sciences"], *Kommunist*, 8 (1987), pp. 3–22; Eduard Shevardnadze, "Doklad E.A. Shevardnadze" ["The report of E.A. Shevardnadze"], *Vestnik Ministerstva Inostrannykh Del SSSR* [*The Herald of the USSR Foreign Ministry*], 15 (15 August, 1988), pp. 27–44); Eduard Shevardnadze, *The Future Belongs to Freedom*, trans. by Catherine Fitzpatrick (New York: Free Press, 1991).

with the election of a functioning parliament in 1989 and the steady weakening of the Communist Party from that point on.

Political institutions

The old Soviet system was highly centralized, with power concentrated in the hands of the Communist Party, and in particular its Politburo and General Secretary. Legislation was mainly enacted by decree – typically joint decrees of the Council of Ministers and the Party's Central Committee.[5]

In 1989 competitive elections were held to fill a majority of the seats in a new Congress of People's Deputies (although some were reserved for Party-controlled organizations).[6] The Congress was enjoined to elect a Supreme Soviet to function as a genuine legislature. During the same time, Gorbachev managed to remove most of his conservative opponents from the Politburo, while simultaneously reducing the role of that body and its leader, the General Secretary (himself). He introduced the role of president and was elected to that office by more than 95 percent of the delegates to the Congress of People's Deputies. Over the course of the next year, the Congress and the Supreme Soviet came to eclipse the Communist Party Central Committee as the country's most important deliberative and legislative bodies. Meanwhile Gorbachev succeeded in shifting policy-making authority from the Party to the new government, establishing a Presidential Council to fulfill many of the policy-making functions previously reserved for the Politburo. Gorbachev's desire for a strong presidency in the French mold often conflicted with the preference on the part of many Supreme Soviet deputies for a strong parliamentary system with reliable checks and balances. The new competition between the executive and legislative branches fatally weakened the centralized, Party-dominated state and left a legacy of policy fragmentation and incoherence that outlived the USSR itself.

A key turning point in the transition from the old domestic structure

---

5 For a thorough discussion of the old system, see Jerry Hough and Merle Fainsod, *How the Soviet Union is Governed* (Cambridge, MA: Harvard University Press, 1979).

6 The events discussed in this section are summarized in a useful "Chronology of Noteworthy Events, March 11, 1985 – July 11, 1991," in Ed. A. Hewett and Victor H. Winston, eds., *Milestones in Glasnost and Perestroyka: Politics and People* (Washington, DC: The Brookings Institution, 1991), pp. 499–536. For a valuable insider account, see the memoir of Gorbachev's top foreign policy aide, A.S. Cherniaev, *Shest' let s Gorbachevym: po dnevnikovym zapisiam* [Six Years with Gorbachev: from Diary Entries] (Moscow: Progress, 1993).

to the new one came with the repeal of Article 6 of the Soviet Constitution in February 1990. That article had provided the legal guarantee for the Communist Party's monopoly on political power. Although the Party remained a powerful institution, it now had to face increasingly organized opposition and eventually alternative political parties. The Party was discredited by the failed coup of August 1991 and outlawed shortly thereafter – leaving, as Georgii Arbatov points out, "a power vacuum and a completely disorganized political process."[7] With the disintegration of the Soviet Union, the emerging political system in Russia was characterized by chaos and uncertainty. Some of its elements resembled systems of interest-group pluralism, others suggested a variant of corporatism, and dominating all aspects of politics was the legacy of Soviet bureaucratic inertia.

Structure of Society

Under the old Soviet system, society played a limited and indirect role in policy-making. Censorship, control of information, and the repressive apparatus of the security agencies ensured passivity and conformity, even though beneath the surface Soviet society reflected the widest possible divergence of views. One might even describe Soviet society as "polarized," in Risse-Kappen's terms, say between the "friends and foes of change," as a prominent Sovietologist put it.[8] It probably makes more sense, however, to retain the old terminology of Soviet studies and consider Soviet society, at the risk of some exaggeration, as "atomized" and passive. Certainly independent social organizations were weak or nonexistent.

The re-emergence of Soviet civil society became evident already in the first year of Gorbachev's tenure in office (he was elected General Secretary in March 1985) and a growing movement of "informal" groups was quite active by 1987.[9] By the end of the decade hundreds of

7 Georgii Arbatov, *The System: An Insider's Life in Soviet Politics* (New York: Random House, 1992), p. 351.
8 Stephen Cohen, "The Friends and Foes of Change," reprinted as chapter 6 in Alexander Dallin and Gail Lapidus, eds., *The Soviet System in Crisis* (Boulder, CO: Westview, 1991).
9 A.V. Gromov and O.S. Kuzin, *Neformaly: Kto est' kto?* [*Informals: Who's Who?*] (Moscow: Mysl', 1990); Vyacheslav Igrunov, "Public Movements: From Protest to Political Self-Consciousness," and Andrei Fadin, "Emerging Political Institutions: From Informals to Multiparty Democracy," both in Brad Roberts and Nina Belyaeva, eds., *After Perestroika: Democracy in the Soviet Union* (Washington, DC: Center for Strategic and International Studies, 1991); Vera Tolz, *The USSR's Emerging Multiparty System* (New York: Praeger, 1990).

Matthew Evangelista

self-defined political parties were in existence competing for influence in a functioning legislature.[10] Vibrant print and broadcast media raised the quality and diversity of political discourse and contributed to an informed and attentive citizenry.[11] All of these developments stemmed from Gorbachev's policy of *glasnost'* which gave voice to the range of political views encompassed by Soviet society and allowed groups access to information as a tool for organizing their political activity.

Policy networks

The correspondence that Risse-Kappen identified between weak social organizations and state-dominated policy networks fits the Soviet case, although here one should speak of *Party*–state domination rather than simply state domination. Under the old Soviet system coalition building by and large excluded societal actors and was influenced only indirectly and weakly by public opinion.

Characterizing the post-reform policy networks in the Soviet Union and post-Soviet Russia is somewhat difficult. The Party–state-dominated policy network is certainly a thing of the past, but it is not clear what has replaced it. The Communist Party was abolished, but many state institutions remained strong, including several economic ministries, the defense and foreign ministries, and the KGB. At the same time social organizations remained active and some of them acquired considerable political influence. At first it was not easy to identify the various organizations' political constituencies. As the Russian neofascist politician Vladimir Zhirinovskii (head of the mis-named Liberal Democratic Party) put it, "My program? It is like everybody else's: *perestroika*, free market, and democracy!"[12] Gradually, however, somewhat distinct political programs emerged so that in some cases – most notably the military-industrial and energy lobbies – one could begin to identify genuine constituencies.[13] These organizations have been engaged in a bargaining process with state institu-

---

10 Vladimir Pribylovsii, *Dictionary of Political Parties and Organizations in Russia* (Washington, DC: Center for Strategic and International Studies, 1992); Tolz, *The USSR's Emerging Multiparty System*.
11 For a useful overview, see Jamey Gambrell, "Moscow: The Front Page," *New York Review of Books*, October 8, 1992.
12 Pribylovsii, *Dictionary of Political Parties*, p. ix.
13 Maria Podzorova, "A New Party Has Been Created in Moscow," *Moscow News*, 24 (June 14–21, 1992), p. 6; David Filipov, "Opposition Mounts Challenge to Gaidar," *Moscow Times*, July 21, 1992, p. 2; David Filipov, "Yeltsin, Volsky Edge Closer," *Moscow Times*, July 24, 1992, p. 1.

Table 5.1 *Changes in Soviet domestic structure*

	Pre-1989	Post-1989
Political institutions	Centralized	Incipient separation of powers
Society	Weak, passive	Strong, assertive
Policy networks	Party–state dominated	Quasi-corporatist

tions, such that one can probably speak of the post-Soviet system of policy networks as it evolved already in the last years of Gorbachev's tenure as a form of corporatism. One must qualify such a characterization, however, in two respects: first, by acknowledging that most "corporate" entities are still in the process of trying to determine where their interests lie and are far from homogeneous; and second, by recognizing the presence of grassroots social movements – active especially on nationalist and ecological issues – that resist corporatist forms of representation in favor of direct appeals to the government.

Theoretical framework

Transnational actors as a policy community

Given the lack of attention of the original transnationalism literature to security policy in a strong state, we must look elsewhere for theoretical justification for expecting to find such states responsive to transnational activity. Here I rely on two sources: Risse-Kappen's generalizations, derived from the work on domestic structure;[14] and the literature on "policy communities," developed mainly by specialists in American politics, but receiving increasing attention in comparative politics as well.[15]

Risse-Kappen's argument about the potential influence of trans-

---

[14] Thomas Risse-Kappen, "Bringing Transnational Relations Back In: Introduction," in this volume.

[15] John W. Kingdon, *Agendas, Alternatives, and Public Policies* (Boston: Little, Brown, and Co., 1984); Jack L. Walker, "The Diffusion of Knowledge, Policy Communities, and Agenda Setting: The Relationship of Knowledge and Power," in John E. Tropman, Milan J. Dluhy, and Roger M. Lind, eds., *New Strategic Perspectives on Social Policy* (New York: Pergamon, 1981); and for comparative perspectives, the special issue of *Governance*, 2, 1 (January 1989), edited by John Creighton Campbell. For a valuable application of this literature to Soviet foreign policy, see Jeff Checkel, "Ideas, Institutions, and the Gorbachev Foreign Policy Revolution," *World Politics*, 45, 2 (January 1993), pp. 271–300, and his forthcoming book.

national actors on a strong state's decision process is consistent with the findings about policy communities in highly centralized, Leninist states. The role of the top leadership in such a hierarchical state is crucial,[16] whether we speak of domestic policy experts trying to promote their pet proposals or transnational actors trying to influence foreign policy with ideas, information, and arguments produced abroad.

Expectations about the impact of domestic structure

When the USSR functions as a strong, hierarchical, centralized state, and the issues for which they propose solutions are on the agenda, transnational actors may have direct access to the top – to the General Secretary of the Communist Party. As the Party–state apparatus weakens, as it did during 1989–90, we should expect a decentralization and fragmentation of the policy process. With the removal of the Communist Party's political monopoly, more actors will participate in policy-making, including in the security sphere. The USSR Supreme Soviet's Committee on Defense and State Security is a case in point.[17] We should also expect the military and the weapons laboratories to have more possibilities to express their views and potentially to influence policy once Gorbachev is no longer able to implement Party discipline and once more societal resources become available to groups espousing views contrary to the government's policy. The transnational coalition will remain active but it will no longer have the preferential access to the top, mainly because the system is no longer as centralized and hierarchical as it was. My expectation for the post-Soviet period is that transnational relations will flourish but their impact will be diffuse and uncertain. As Risse-Kappen hypothesizes, transnational actors will have multiple channels to raise their demands, but given the fragmentation of the process and frequently

16 Nina P. Halpern, "Policy Communities in a Leninist State: The Case of the Chinese Economic Policy Community," *Governance*, 2, 1 (January 1989), pp. 23–41. Mark A. Baskin, "The Evolution of Policy Communities in Socialist Yugoslavia: The Case of Worker Migration Abroad," *Governance*, 2, 1 (January 1989), pp. 67–85. France as a "strong state" is also relevant here; see Frank R. Baumgartner, "Independent and Politicized Policy Communities: Education and Nuclear Energy in France and in the United States," *Governance*, 2, 1 (January 1989), pp. 42–66.

17 G. Sturua, "Komitet po voprosam oborony i gosudarstvennoi bezopasnosti: pervye mesiatsy raboty" ["The Committee on Questions of Defense and State Security"], *Mirovaia ekonomika i mezhdunarodnye otnosheniia* [*The World Economy and International Relations*], 1 (January 1990), pp. 79–85.

shifting policy coalitions, their impact on policies might be short-lived. Societal organizations will be too weak to serve as reliable allies for transnational groups and sympathetic government agencies will face opponents within the bureaucracy.[18]

Case selection

Choosing the debates on ballistic-missile defense and nuclear testing as cases for comparison provides some degree of control, despite the major structural changes in the international system which coincided with the domestic structural changes in the USSR. In particular, as late as January 1993, the objectives of the US government and the transnational groups remained the same *vis-à-vis* the antiballistic missile (ABM) and nuclear testing issues, even as the Soviet Union changed dramatically and then disintegrated: the US government wanted to abolish or at least to amend the ABM treaty and to pursue a new generation of ballistic-missile defenses. The transnational organizations wanted to preserve and strengthen the treaty and prevent the development of new weapons. The US rejected any halt in nuclear testing, even though both Russia and France had ceased their tests by the spring of 1992 and called on other countries to join their moratoriums. The transnational groups continued to pursue a comprehensive test ban treaty and supported unilateral moratoriums as well. US policy finally changed, although sometimes in fits and starts, under the Clinton administration. The new administration's skepticism about strategic defenses and its agreement to abide by Congress's demand for a halt in nuclear testing appear to have helped tip the balance in Russia in favor of the transnational opponents of ballistic-missile defense and new nuclear weapons.

The transnational arms control coalition

The transnational coalition that sought to influence Soviet and American military policy in the 1980s had its origins in the 1950s. At that time, scientists concerned with the danger of a nuclear arms race sought to organize at the international level to persuade their governments to pursue disarmament negotiations and restraint. A manifesto drafted by Albert Einstein and Bertrand Russell in 1955 led to the

[18] Risse-Kappen, "Bringing Transnational Relations Back In."

founding of the Pugwash conferences in 1957. From then on scientists from all over the world met regularly to devise solutions to the arms race and other pressing international problems. In the 1960s, offshoots of Pugwash, such as the Dartmouth Conference and the Soviet–American Defense Study (SADS) group brought Soviet and US scientists into direct, bilateral discussions.[19]

Transnational efforts to promote disarmament slackened in the 1970s as the US and USSR pursued formal negotiations on arms control. At the same time, however, many US scientists maintained contacts with Soviet counterparts both professionally in pursuit of their scholarly research and politically as they supported colleagues, such as Andrei Sakharov, Iurii Orlov, and others, who had become persecuted as dissidents.[20] The deterioration of East–West relations in the late 1970s and especially the bellicose policies of the Reagan administration in the early 1980s revived the transnational linkages of the past and created new ones.

The main actors on the Soviet side were scientists affiliated with various institutes of the USSR Academy of Sciences who formally organized themselves into the Committee of Soviet Scientists for Peace, Against the Nuclear Threat (hereafter the Committee of Soviet Scientists or CSS) in 1983, and members of the Soviet chapter of the International Physicians for the Prevention of Nuclear War (IPPNW), founded in 1980. Among the many Western organizations active in transnational efforts, the most important for our cases were IPPNW, the Federation of American Scientists, the Union of Concerned Scientists, the Natural Resources Defense Council, and the National Academy of Sciences Committee on International Security and Arms Control.

---

[19] Interview with Paul Doty of Harvard University, September 23, 1993; with Jack Ruina of MIT, October 29, 1988; with Joseph Rotblat of Pugwash, May 27, 1990; and with Jeremy Stone, Federation of American Scientists, Washington, DC, June 10, 1991. For a summary of Pugwash's history, see the *FAS Public Interest Report*, 40, 8 (October 1987); and, for a more comprehensive account of the early period, J. Rotblat, *Scientists in the Quest for Peace: A History of the Pugwash Conferences* (Cambridge, MA: The MIT Press, 1972). For a theoretically sophisticated discussion of the scientists' accomplishments, see Emanuel Adler, "The Emergence of Cooperation: National Epistemic Communities and the International Evolution of the Idea of Nuclear Arms Control," *International Organization*, 46, 1 (Winter 1992), pp. 101–145.

[20] Sakharov discusses the efforts of Sidney Drell, Kurt Gottfried, Jeremy Stone, and others in his *Memoirs*, trans. by Richard Lourie (New York: Knopf, 1990) and *Moscow and Beyond, 1986 to 1989*, trans. by Antonina Bouis (New York: Knopf, 1991).

Transnational efforts under the old structure

The Soviet domestic structure and transnational contacts

Ever since the first East–West transnational discussions of arms control in the 1950s, the Communist Party of the Soviet Union (CPSU) has played a central role in approving and sometimes instructing the Soviet delegations. Documents from the CPSU Central Committee archives in Moscow provide considerable detail about how the process worked. Western organizers typically sent their invitations to or proposals for conferences directly to officials of the Academy of Sciences.[21] These officials passed on the letters to a department of the Central Committee Secretariat (usually the international department) along with their recommendations – including, for example, which Soviet scientists should partcipate, and which should not.[22] The decisions would usually be made by the Central Committee secretaries (these were among the most powerful officials in the Soviet system – not the clerical staff!) or passed on to the full Politburo for a decision.[23] This was essentially the system that prevailed until virtually the end of the Soviet Union. Scientists seeking to travel abroad to attend conferences (not only political ones, but purely academic ones as well), were obliged to obtain high-level permission before doing so. Thus, the Communist Party could influence to a considerable degree which transnational contacts Soviet citizens could pursue.[24]

[21] E.g., letter from Joseph Rotblat to A.N. Topchiev, proposing a Pugwash meeting in Geneva to help resolve technical disagreements in the official three-power discussions on a test ban, January 5, 1960; letter from Eugene Rabinowitch, editor of the *Bulletin of the Atomic Scientists*, requesting to publish a statement from Soviet scientists at the official conference on nuclear testing, January 12, 1960, both in the 20th convocation of the Central Committee of the Communist Party of the Soviet Union (CC CPSU), from protocol 138, Secretariat session, February 23, 1960, documents located at the Center for the Storage of Contemporary Documentation (CSCD), former Central Committee archive, Moscow.

[22] Letter to Central Committee from A.N. Nesmeianov, President of the USSR Academy of Sciences, and E.K. Fedorov, proposing to send a delegation to the Geneva Pugwash meeting, January 26, 1960, 20th Convocation of the CC CPSU, from protocol 138, Secretariat session, February 23, 1960, item 16, CSCD, Moscow.

[23] "On the calling of an international conference of scientists on the cessation of nuclear tests," from protocol no. 45, Secretariat session, August 2, 1957, item 24, CSCD, Moscow; "On the participation of Soviet scientists in the International Pugwash conference on the question of the cessation of nuclear tests," 20th Convocation of the CC CPSU, from protocol 138, Secretariat session, February 23, 1960, item 16, CSCD, Moscow.

[24] Information on procedures in the 1980s comes from a conversation with Roald Sagdeev, College Park, MD, April 1994.

The other side of Communist Party supervision of transnational contacts was access to the top Soviet leadership by the Soviet participants in international meetings. Because the number of contacts with Americans, for example, was limited, those who were allowed to pursue them were naturally more knowledgeable than most about the United States and became a valuable resource for the Soviet leaders. This was particularly true of such figures as Georgii Arbatov, director of the Institute of the USA and Canada; Evgenii Velikhov, head of the Committee of Soviet Scientists; and Evgenii Chazov, the "Kremlin doctor," and co-president of the International Physicians.[25] They, in turn, could make use of their access to press for policies they favored.[26]

Transnational policy entrepreneurs

The story of Soviet–American transnational collaboration is as much a story of individuals as of organizations. Among the key figures on the Soviet side, four stand out. Evgenii Chazov of the International Physicians' movement was the personal physician to Leonid Brezhnev, Iurii Andropov, and Konstantin Chernenko. Andrei Kokoshin trained as an engineer at the Bauman Institute in Moscow before pursuing a career in politics and history. He became deputy director of Arbatov's Institute. Much of his collaborative work with Western colleagues has focused on strategic defenses and conventional-force restructuring. Academicians Evgenii Velikhov and Roald Sagdeev were prominent physicists, both students of Lev Artsimovich, a leading figure in the Soviet Academy of Sciences and a long-standing Pugwash participant.

---

25 G.A. Arbatov, *Zatianuvsheesia vyzdorovlenie (1953–1985 gg.): Svidetel'stvo sovremennika* [*Extended Recovery (1953–1985): Witness of a Contemporary*] (Moscow: Mezhdunarodnye otnosheniia, 1991); interview with Evgenii Velikhov, Moscow, July 29, 1992. Chazov was the personal doctor to Leonid Brezhnev, Iurii Andropov, and Konstantin Chernenko, and later became Soviet minister of health. Evgenii Chazov, *Zdorov'e i vlast': Vospominaniia "kremlevskogo vracha"* [*Health and Power: Memoirs of the "Kremlin Doctor"*] (Moscow: Novosti, 1992), esp. pp. 90–96.

26 Arbatov, for example, upon returning from a session of the Dartmouth Conference in 1980 was able to arrange a meeting with Leonid Brezhnev to convey to him the extent to which the Soviet invasion of Afghanistan had damaged détente. Arbatov, *Zatianuvsheesia vyzdorovlenie*, p. 231, footnote. Chazov, by his account, discussed questions of nuclear war and IPPNW's efforts to prevent it with a sometimes skeptical Brezhnev and Andropov. But he did manage to convince the leaders to allow uncensored broadcast of IPPNW conferences on the consequences of nuclear war on Soviet television. *Zdorov'e i vlast'*, pp. 90–96. According to interviews with Soviet foreign policy elites, the IPPNW TV broadcasts influenced their own thinking about nuclear war; see Steven Kull, *Burying Lenin: The Revolution in Soviet Ideology and Foreign Policy* (Boulder, CO: Westview, 1992), p. 18.

Sagdeev served as director of the USSR's Space Research Institute and Velikhov headed the Kurchatov Institute of Atomic Energy.

Velikhov, who was elected as vice president of the Academy of Sciences in 1977, began his involvement in international arms control discussions in 1982 when Soviet leader Brezhnev decided to send him to Rome to represent the USSR at a meeting called by the Papal Academy of Sciences to discuss the threat of nuclear war.[27] In early 1983 Velikhov and Sagdeev went to Washington as members of a Soviet delegation meeting with the US National Academy of Sciences Committee on International Security and Arms Control. Their discussions produced three main policy goals: (1) to defend the ABM treaty; (2) to prevent deployment of weapons in space, including antisatellite weapons (ASAT); and (3) to negotiate a comprehensive nuclear test ban.[28] These became high-priority objectives of the Committee of Soviet Scientists, when Velikhov founded it that same year, with Sagdeev and Kokoshin as his deputies.[29]

The Soviet response to "Star Wars"

The main achievement of the transnational disarmament community in the realm of antiballistic missile systems was to shape the Soviet Union's response to the US Strategic Defense Initiative (SDI) and to strengthen the ABM Treaty by making the Soviet government more forthcoming on questions of its own adherence to the treaty. To argue that the transnational community influenced Soviet policies, one must argue counterfactually that the decisions of the policymakers would have been different were it not for its activities.

The position adopted by the Soviet government – not to respond "in kind" to Star Wars, but to develop relatively inexpensive counter-measures – cannot be understood without considering the role of transnational actors. Their advocacy of an "asymmetric response" was a genuinely new policy idea. The Soviet reaction to the US pursuit of strategic defenses should, by historical precedent, have included an attempt to develop *analogous* systems, and most Western observers

---

[27] Evgenii Velikhov, "Chernobyl Remains on Our Mind," in Stephen F. Cohen and Katrina vanden Heuvel, eds., *Voices of Glasnost: Interviews with Gorbachev's Reformers* (New York: Norton, 1989), p. 160; Velikhov interview, July 29, 1992.

[28] Velikhov interview, July 29, 1992; Jeremy Stone, "FAS Visit to Moscow Initiates Star Wars Dialogue," *FAS Public Interest Report*, 36, 10 (December 1983), p. 1.

[29] Frank von Hippel, "The Committee of Soviet Scientists against the Nuclear Threat," *FAS Public Interest Report*, 37, 1 (January 1984).

anticipated that response.[30] Andropov, the Soviet leader at the time of Reagan's Star Wars speech in March 1983, had argued precisely in those terms just a few months earlier. He maintained that the Reagan administration's arms build-up would not force the Soviet Union to make "unilateral concessions" and that the USSR would match every US development.[31] His first reaction to Reagan's speech was consistent with the longstanding Soviet approach: "Should this conception be converted into reality, this would actually open the floodgates of a runaway arms race of all types of strategic arms, both offensive and defensive."[32]

The ASAT moratorium

Despite Andropov's commitment not to make unilateral concessions, the USSR did precisely that within months of Reagan's Star Wars speech. On August 18, 1983, Andropov met with nine US senators in the Kremlin and pledged a unilateral Soviet moratorium on the testing of antisatellite (ASAT) weapons. Members of the Senate and the House of Representatives had been working on legislation calling for a joint US–Soviet moratorium, so Andropov's action strengthened their case considerably.[33]

Evgenii Velikhov and his transnational allies in the United States deserve credit for persuading the Soviet leadership to impose the unilateral ASAT moratorium. In March 1983, upon his return from the National Academy meeting in Washington, Velikhov proposed the idea to Marshal Sergei Akhromeev, then deputy chief of the general staff, and later to defense minister Dmitrii Ustinov.[34] In May 1983, the Union of Concerned Scientists (UCS) presented a draft treaty limiting

---

[30] Stephen M. Meyer, "Soviet Strategic Programmes and the US SDI," *Survival*, 27, 6 (November–December 1985), pp. 274–92; David Holloway, "The Strategic Defense Initiative and the Soviet Union," *Daedalus*, 114, 3 (Summer 1985), pp. 257–78; Evangelista, *Innovation and the Arms Race*, pp. 258–61.

[31] "Doklad tovarishcha Iu.V. Andropova" ["Report of Comrade Iu.V. Andropov"], *Pravda*, December 22, 1982.

[32] Andropov interview, *Pravda*, March 26, 1983.

[33] *The Arms Control Reporter* (Cambridge, MA: Institute for Defense and Disarmament Studies, monthly compendium, 1982–92), pp. 573.B.15–18.

[34] Velikhov interview, July 29, 1992; E.P. Velikhov, "Science and Scientists for a Nuclear-Weapon-Free World," *Physics Today* (November 1989), pp. 32–36. This article is an expanded version of a speech Velikhov delivered at a "Scientific–Practical Conference" of the Soviet Foreign Ministry, the original of which was published as "Nauka rabotaet na bez''iadernyi mir," *Mezhdunarodnaia zhizn'*, 10 (1988), pp. 49–53. See also Marshal Akhromeev's discussion of Ustinov's reaction to SDI, in (Marshall) S.F. Akhromeev and G.M. Kornienko, *Glazami marshala i diplomata* [*Through the Eyes of a Marshal and a Diplomat*] (Moscow: Mezhdunarodnye otnosheniia, 1992), pp. 19–20.

antisatellite weapons – the work mainly of Kurt Gottfried of Cornell University and Richard Garwin of the IBM corporation.[35] Velikhov had met Garwin at the Washington meeting and had discussed proposals for ASAT limitations with him. He supported the UCS proposals, many of which ultimately became incorporated in a draft treaty submitted by the USSR to the United Nations in early 1984.[36]

A Soviet "Star Wars?"

Despite the restraint that the USSR exercised in the related field of antisatellite weapons, the initial Soviet response to the Reagan Strategic Defense Initiative was of a very different character. It suggested that the USSR would respond vigorously with development of defensive as well as offensive systems, including space-based defenses. Senior military leaders made numerous warnings along those lines.[37] Moreover, there was a constituency within the scientific-military-industrial sector that favored pursuit of strategic defenses and that had promoted such programs at various points – notably in the mid-1970s and again in the early 1980s, before Reagan's Star Wars speech.[38]

Velikhov and Sagdeev were the first to argue against copying the US initiative, just months after Reagan's speech – and they did so in direct contradiction to the impression that top Soviet military and political officials were trying to convey. The scientists argued on the basis of their understanding of the dangerous implications of mutual strategic defense as they were worked out by a transnational community of Soviet and Western scientists during the 1960s;[39] and they did so well

---

[35] *Arms Control Reporter*, pp. 573.C.3–6.
[36] Excerpts of statement by Igor Iakovlev at the UN Symposium on Preventing the Arms Race in Outer Space, January 26, 1984, quoted in the *Arms Control Reporter*, p. 574.D.5. For the text of the Soviet draft treaty, see pp. 574.D.1–3.
[37] See, for example, the remarks by the chief of the general staff, Marshal Sergei Akhromeev, "Dogovor po PRO – pregrada na puti ronki strategicheskikh vooruzhenii" ("The ABM Treaty – a barrier on the path to an arms race in strategic weapons"), *Pravda*, June 4, 1985; and the discussion in Mary C. Fitzgerald, *Soviet Views on SDI*, Carl Beck Papers 601, Center for Russian and East European Studies, University of Pittsburgh, May 1987, pp. 39–40. See also Don Oberdorfer, "Military Response Planned to 'Star Wars,' Soviet Says," *Washington Post*, March 8, 1985.
[38] Roald Sagdeev, *The Making of a Soviet Scientist* (New York: John Wiley, 1994); Bruce Parrott, *The Soviet Union and Ballistic Missile Defense* (Boulder, CO: Westview Press, 1987), pp. 28–35; Velikhov, "Science and Scientists for a Nuclear-Weapon-Free World."
[39] Matthew Evangelista, "Soviet Scientists as Arms Control Advisers: The Case of ABM," paper prepared for the Fourth World Congress for Soviet and East European Studies, Harrogate, England, July 21–26, 1990; Evangelista, *Taming the Bear*; and Adler, "Emergence of Cooperation."

before Mikhail Gorbachev came into office and began articulating his "new thinking" in foreign policy. In 1983 Velikhov, Sagdeev, and Kokoshin were already presenting some of the key ideas to Soviet and Western audiences – not to copy Star Wars, but to pursue arms control, and, if necessary, build cheap countermeasures to SDI.[40] These recommendations were incorporated in a report issued by the newly created Committee of Soviet Scientists and distributed internally and abroad.[41]

At the time, the writings of Velikhov and his colleagues were interpreted by some in the West as part of a government-orchestrated propaganda campaign to defeat the American SDI program while the USSR continued its own military programs unhindered.[42] The Soviet scientists' campaign was, however, directed primarily at the Soviet military and political leaders, to persuade them not to fall for American attempts to undermine the Soviet economy through an expensive and counterproductive arms race.[43] That goal would be served by bolstering the efforts of American opponents of Star Wars, but that was not an end in itself. In addition to reducing the risk of nuclear war, the Soviet

---

[40] See, e.g., the following interviews: with Velikhov, *Los Angeles Times*, July 24, 1983, reprinted in Robert Scheer, *With Enough Shovels: Reagan, Bush, and Nuclear War*, paperback edition (New York: Vintage, 1983), pp. 298–304; with Velikhov, *Sovetskaia Rossiia*, April 21, 1985; with Sagdeev, *Sotsialisticheskaia industriia*, February 9, 1986. Also Stone, "FAS Visit to Moscow Initiates Star Wars Dialogue," p. 3; and Frank von Hippel, "Arms Control Physics: The New Soviet Connection," *Physics Today* (November 1989), pp. 39–46, at p. 40.

[41] *Strategicheskie i mezhdunarodno-politicheskie posledstviia sozdaniia kosmicheckoi protivo-raketnoi sistemy s ispol'zovaniem oruzhiia napravlennoi peredachi energii* [*Strategic and International-Political Consequences of the Creation of a Space Anti-Missile System using Directed-Energy Weaponry*] (Moscow: Institut kosmicheskikh issledovanii AN SSSR, 1984). In 1986 a revised version of the report was published in several languages and attracted considerable attention abroad: E.P. Velikhov, R.Z. Sagdeev, and A.A. Kokoshin, eds., *Kosmicheskoe oruzhie: dilemma bezopasnotsti*, English translation published as *Weaponry in Space: The Dilemma of Security* (Moscow: Mir, 1986).

[42] E.g., Benjamin S. Lambeth, "Soviet Perspectives on the SDI," in Samuel F. Wells, Jr. and Robert S. Litwak, eds., *Strategic Defenses and Soviet-American Relations* (Cambridge, MA: Ballinger, 1987). For a similar interpretation of another initiative of the transnational scientists' organizations, see Leon Gouré, "Nuclear Winter in Soviet Mirrors," *Strategic Review* (Summer 1985), esp. pp. 35–36.

[43] This is also a point that Georgii Arbatov emphasized. He criticized the Soviet propaganda campaign against SDI – after the fact – as having played into the Americans' hands by encouraging the Soviet side to develop costly and unnecessary responses. See *Zatianuvsheesia vyzdorovlenie*, pp. 206, 348. Sagdeev's views were similar: author's interviews with Roald Sagdeev, Moscow, November 1990; Ann Arbor, May 1991; and College Park, April 1994; and Sagdeev, *The Making of a Soviet Scientist*. See also Strobe Talbott, *The Master of the Game: Paul Nitze and the Nuclear Peace* (New York: Knopf, 1988), pp. 360–61.

scientists were keenly interested in the demilitarization and democratization of their own society – goals they saw as closely linked.[44]

Krasnoiarsk

The second major achievement of the transnational coalition regarding the ABM treaty was in getting the Soviet leadership to acknowledge that the giant phased-array radar near Krasnoiarsk in Siberia constituted a treaty violation. The US government had accused the USSR of violating the terms of the ABM treaty, even while the US itself sought to weaken or do away with it altogether. But calling attention to US hypocrisy rarely gained the Soviets much in the US domestic debate on arms control, and in this case the accusation of a treaty violation was correct. The Krasnoiarsk radar constituted a violation because of its location. By the terms of the treaty it could only be constructed on the periphery of the country and facing outwards.

Evidently, the Soviet military had developed plans to build the radar to comply with the treaty but found that it would cost several times as much money to do so as to build it further inland.[45] Knowing that the radar would be in technical violation of the treaty, the defense ministry, foreign ministry, KGB, and ultimately the Politburo, nevertheless advocated building it near Krasnoiarsk.[46] When the US first noticed construction of the complex in 1983 it accused the Soviets not only of violating the treaty, but of planning to break out of the treaty's restraints and deploy a fully-fledged strategic defense system with the Krasnoiarsk radar as part of a "battle management" system.[47] Perhaps influenced by the spuriousness of the latter claim, the Soviet leadership decided to reject all of the US criticisms. Rather than admit that the radar was intended to provide early warning of possible launches

---

44 Andrei Sakharov is, of course, the most famous proponent of these views, but they were evident in the statements and actions of other Soviet scientists, including prominent members of the Committee on Soviet Scientists, such as Roald Sagdeev. See, e.g., Irwin Goodwin, "Soviet Scientists Tell It Like It Is, Urging Reforms of Research Institutes," *Physics Today* (September 1988), pp. 97–98: "Perestroika and the Scientific Intelligentsia," summary of talk by Roald Sagdeev, Kennan Institute for Advanced Russian Studies, Washington, DC, November 16, 1988; Roald Sagdeev, "Science is a Party to Political Decisions," transcript of a speech delivered at a conference of the Soviet foreign ministry, published in *International Affairs* (Moscow), 11 (November 1988), pp. 26–28.

45 Raymond L. Garthoff, "Case of the Wandering Radar," *Bulletin of the Atomic Scientists*, 47, 6 (July/August 1991), pp. 7–9. Interviews with former first deputy foreign minister Georgii Kornienko, Moscow, July 28, 1992; and with Aleksei Arbatov, Cambridge, MA, August 18, 1993.

46 Kornienko interview, July 28, 1992.   47 *Arms Control Reporter*, p. 603.B.17.

of new US Trident missiles, they claimed that it was intended for the purely civilian purpose of tracking objects in space.

The contribution of the Soviet scientists to resolving the Krasnoiarsk issue entailed lifting the veil of secrecy on the complex itself. Velikhov was persuaded of the deleterious effects of Soviet secrecy mainly by his American colleague Bernard Lown, co-chair of the International Physicians for the Prevention of Nuclear War. Lown, said Velikhov, used to speak of the US military buildup and Russian secrecy as "two sides of the same coin," and eventually Velikhov came to agree.[48] When a US congressional delegation visited the Soviet Union in September 1987, Velikhov managed to convince Gorbachev to let the group visit the Krasnoiarsk site (and also the site of laser research at Sary Shagan). The Americans were allowed to photograph the complex extensively. Experts in the delegation dismissed the Pentagon's claim that the system would be useful for "battle management" as part of a nationwide ballistic-missile defense system but they also found Soviet claims of a space-tracking role for the radar implausible. In their view the radar was best suited for early warning of a missile attack – which, as we now know, was its original intention – although they were not particularly impressed with its capabilities even in this area.[49]

Not until October 1989 did the Soviet Union, at foreign minister Eduard Shevardnadze's insistence, admit that construction of the Krasnoiarsk radar violated the ABM treaty.[50] Eventually the Soviets agreed to dismantle the facility. The work of the US–Soviet disarmament coalition contributed to this important turning point in US perceptions of Soviet intentions. Moreover, it set a precedent for considering inspections of suspected treaty violations as an acceptable means of resolving disputes, rather than an infringement on national sovereignty, as the previous Soviet view held.

Unlinking Star Wars

The ultimate accomplishment of the transnational actors consisted of "unlinking" the Strategic Defense Initiative from arms control. Previously the Soviet government had tenaciously insisted that no arms treaties could be signed without a US commitment to abide by its

[48] Interview with Bernard Lown, April 6, 1994, Brookline, MA; Velikhov interview, July 29, 1992.
[49] William J. Broad, "Inside a Key Russian Radar Site: Tour Raises Questions on Treaty," *New York Times*, September 7, 1987, p. 1.
[50] *Arms Control Reporter*, p. 603.B.182.

existing treaty obligations, maintain limitations on ABM systems, and forswear SDI. Gorbachev put forward this position most forcefully at the Reykjavik summit in October 1986, when he presented a "package" of arms control concessions, all contingent on US restraint on Star Wars.[51] The intercession of prominent Soviet scientists such as Sagdeev, Velikhov, and Andrei Sakharov, working with their American colleagues and sympathetic aides to Gorbachev and Shevardnadze, helped to convince the Soviet leadership to sign two major arms accords, without insisting on any US commitments regarding the ABM treaty or SDI. The timing of the transnational actors' policy advocacy, and the fact that major figures in the Soviet security establishment opposed any Soviet concessions on SDI, suggest an important role for the transnational efforts.

Andrei Sakharov was the first and most outspoken internal Soviet critic of the linkage between SDI and arms control. He addressed the issue at his first impromptu press conference at the Iaroslavl train station, on his return to Moscow from internal exile in Gorky in December 1986. He repeated his argument at an international disarmament forum in Moscow in mid-February 1987, to which Velikhov had invited him, and which Gorbachev also attended. Before the opening of the forum, Sakharov met with Frank von Hippel and Jeremy Stone from the Federation of American Scientists, who shared his critique of the SDI linkage. All three spoke at the forum and their speeches were widely disseminated in the Soviet media. Moreover, Stone and von Hippel sat at Gorbachev's table at the forum's concluding banquet, where they had further opportunity to advocate their positions.[52]

Less than two weeks after the Moscow forum, Gorbachev announced the unlinking of Star Wars from the negotiations on Intermediate-Range Nuclear Forces (INF) in Europe, and the INF Treaty was signed by the end of the year.[53] As he later explained, his discussions with foreign and Soviet intellectuals at the forum "made a big impression. I discussed the results of the congress with my colleagues in the Politburo. And we decided to make a major new compromise – to untie the Reykjavik package, detaching from it the problem of

[51] Michael Mandelbaum and Strobe Talbott, *Reagan and Gorbachev* (New York: Vintage, 1987), chapter 5.
[52] Sakharov, *Moscow and Beyond*, pp. 21–24; Talbott, *Master of the Game*, pp. 360–61.
[53] *Arms Control Reporter*, p. 403.B.426.

intermediate-range missiles in Europe."[54] Even as he paved the way for an INF treaty Gorbachev reiterated Soviet opposition to unlinking SDI from the Strategic Arms Reduction Talks (START).[55] Finally, after a vigorous campaign by the Soviet scientists and their US counterparts, working in tandem with foreign minister Shevardnadze, Gorbachev relented in late 1989. As Beschloss and Talbott describe, now "the Soviet Union would be willing to sign and implement a START treaty without a separate accord limiting space-based defenses."[56] The details of the treaty took another year and a half to negotiate, but the main stumbling block was removed by December 1989, in accordance with the prescription of the transnational disarmament community.

Alternative explanations

There are several explanations typically offered to counter arguments about the influence of transnational actors on Soviet security policy.[57] They tend to rely on the notion that the Soviet government, primarily for military or economic reasons, already intended to pursue the policies advocated by transnational actors; therefore transnational relations were irrelevant or transnational actors merely served as instruments of Soviet policy.

There is no denying that economic concerns motivated much of the change in Soviet security policy, including Soviet opposition to SDI, especially after Gorbachev came into office.[58] As theorists of policy change would term it, the Soviet economic crisis constituted a "policy window" through which transnational policy entrepreneurs could promote their solutions. But the content of those solutions depended on the transnational actors themselves. Even if Gorbachev and his predecessors were convinced of the economic necessity of avoiding an arms race in "Star Wars" defenses, they needed the arguments and

---

54 M.S. Gorbachev, *Perestroika i novoe myshlenie dlia nashei strany i dlia vsego mira* [*Perestroika and New Thinking for our Country and the World*] (Moscow: Politizdat, 1987), pp. 157–58.
55 *Arms Control Reporter*, p. 403.B.434.
56 Michael Beschloss and Strobe Talbott, *At the Highest Levels: The Inside Story of the End of the Cold War* (Boston: Little, Brown, and Co., 1993), pp. 117–19. Sagdeev at this point served as an informal adviser reporting directly to Shevardnadze (interview with Sagdeev, College Park, April 1994).
57 For a review, see Matthew Evangelista, "Sources of Moderation in Soviet Security Policy," in P. Tetlock *et al.*, eds., *Behavior, Society, and Nuclear War*, vol. II (New York: Oxford University Press, 1991), pp. 254–354.
58 For an early assessment, see Matthew Evangelista, "The New Soviet Approach to Security," *World Policy Journal*, 3, 1 (Autumn 1986), pp. 561–99.

expertise of the transnational scientists. In private conversations with the military high command, Gorbachev stressed both the economic constraints on Soviet security policy and the need for military officials to take into account the views of the scientists.[59]

The argument that the Soviet armed forces, for their own military reasons, supported an asymmetric or even no response to SDI is less persuasive. Even during Gorbachev's tenure, while the Soviet leader was arguing against imitating SDI, his top military leaders were threatening "to adopt retaliatory measures in both offensive and other spheres, not excluding defensive arms, and including space-based ones."[60] Certainly many Soviet military leaders appreciated the strategic benefits of constraining a race in defensive systems and therefore supported the ABM Treaty. Yet the military leadership – as well as high-ranking foreign ministry officials – were adamantly opposed to concluding arms agreements with the United States in the absence of a US commitment not to go forward with SDI.[61] The intercession of prominent Soviet scientists such as Sagdeev, Sakharov, and Velikhov, working with their American colleagues, helped to convince the Soviet leadership that they should sign major arms accords limiting intermediate-range forces (INF Treaty, 1987) and strategic weapons (START I Treaty, 1991).[62]

The role of transnational actors in opening up Soviet military facilities (Krasnoiarsk, the laser-research laboratories) to inspection is fairly apparent from the public activities of members of the international physicians movement, the Natural Resources Defense Council, the Federation of American Scientists, and the Soviet Committee of Scientists. Certainly the goal of fostering trust in order to broaden the possibilities for arms control was not held exclusively by the transnational disarmament coalition – but its members were the ones who promoted concrete initiatives within the Soviet government which would make the biggest impression on the United States.

[59] Akhromeev and Kornienko, *Glazami marshala i diplomata*, esp. pp. 71–73.
[60] Marshal Sergei Akhromeev, chief of the general staff, in *Pravda*, October 19, 1985. See also the remarks of defense minister Marshal Sergei Sokolov in *Krasnaia zvezda*, May 5, 1985, and numerous other quotations cited in FitzGerald, *Soviet Views on SDI*.
[61] Marshal Akhromeev claimed that foreign minister Shevardnadze was prepared to "delink" START from SDI as early as December 1987, whereas he and first deputy foreign minister Georgii Kornienko insisted that the US forswear pursuit of defenses. See Akhromeev and Kornienko, *Glazami*, pp. 142, 192.
[62] Strobe Talbott, *The Master of the Game: Paul Nitze and the Nuclear Peace* (New York: Knopf, 1988), pp. 360–61; Sakharov, *Moscow and Beyond*, pp. 21–24; Michael Beschloss and Strobe Talbott, *At the Highest Levels: The Inside Story of the End of the Cold War* (Boston: Little, Brown, and Co., 1993), pp. 117–19.

Matthew Evangelista

The only alternative explanation for Soviet behavior of which I am aware is Paul Nitze's argument that the change in Soviet policy came about because the "Soviet Union apparently had decided it had more to learn from on-site inspection than we did."[63] His only "evidence" for this argument is his observation that US military officials evinced considerable reluctance to allow Soviet inspectors into US facilities once the Soviets had accepted the principle of on-site inspection. In fact, Soviet military officials – and, indeed, members of the public at large – remained extremely wary of allowing the West access to Soviet military sites even as part of agreed measures for implementing arms accords such as the INF treaty, regardless of what Soviet inspectors got to see on the other side.[64] But in the most significant initiatives – the inspection of Krasnoiarsk and the laser-research facilities – Nitze's argument does not even apply. The Soviet concessions were unilateral and unconditional. They entailed no Soviet inspection of US facilities.

Soviet policy on nuclear testing

The main achievement of the transnational actors in the realm of nuclear testing was to eliminate the central US objection to a comprehensive nuclear test ban – namely, that it could not be reliably verified – and to promote unilateral restraint as a means of arms control.

The test ban

One of the first foreign-policy initiatives that Mikhail Gorbachev undertook when he became General Secretary in 1985 was to announce a unilateral moratorium on Soviet nuclear testing to take effect on August 6, 1985, the fortieth anniversary of the US atomic bombing of Hiroshima. A number of US arms control groups – including the Washington-based Center for Defense Information and the US chapter of IPPNW – sought to convince the Soviet Union to take the initiative in achieving a comprehensive test ban in the early 1980s.[65]

[63] Paul N. Nitze, *From Hiroshima to Glasnost* (New York: Grove Weidenfeld, 1989), p. 442.
[64] For some evidence, see Matthew Evangelista, "Soviet Policy toward Strategic Arms Control," in Bruce Parrott, ed., *The Dynamics of Soviet Defense Policy* (Washington, DC: Wilson Center Press, 1990), esp. pp. 293–96.
[65] Bernard Lown, "The Urgency of a Unique Initiative," speech to the IVth World Congress of the IPPNW, June 4, 1984; interview with Dr. Lown, April 6, 1994, Brookline, MA; Cortright, *Peace Works*, pp. 209–10; *Defense Monitor*, 13, 5 (1984); *Arms Control Reporter*, pp. 608.B.50–51. This account also draws on Frank M. Castillo, "The International Physicians for the Prevention of Nuclear War: Transnational Midwife of

Their efforts only bore fruit after Gorbachev came into office – reinforcing insights from the theoretical literature on the importance of leadership in highly centralized systems,[66] as well as the role that events such as leadership succession and elections can play in opening windows for policy innovation.[67]

Among the transnational actors who seized the opportunity of a new leader to promote the test ban, the scientists and physicians were probably the most influential. Velikhov, who had been discussing the need for a test ban with American colleagues for over two years, played a key role in convincing Gorbachev to initiate the unilateral moratorium and in organizing an impressive array of international scientists to lobby the Soviet leader on several occasions to extend the ban, despite a consistently negative US response.[68] Gorbachev himself wrote that the many extensions were "the result of a serious study of numerous appeals to the Soviet leadership from various circles of foreign intellectuals," and he called particular attention to a meeting in November 1985, which Velikhov organized, where a delegation of Nobel laureates stressed "the significance of banning nuclear tests and the danger of militarizing space."[69] Internal advocates of the test ban cited the support of Dr. Lown and the International Physicians for extending the moratorium. Using such arguments Gorbachev was able, in the autumn of 1985, to reverse a previous Politburo decision to end it.[70]

The United States ultimately refused to go along with the Soviet moratorium and the USSR resumed nuclear testing in February 1987. Thus, the transnational disarmament coalition failed to achieve its primary goal of a comprehensive test ban treaty. Nevertheless, the

World Peace" (Institute of International Peace Studies, University of Notre Dame, Indiana, unpublished, 1990). I am grateful to Frank Castillo for providing me with a copy.

66 Halpern, "Policy Communities in a Leninist State"; Evangelista, *Innovation and the Arms Race.*

67 Kingdon, *Agendas, Alternatives, and Public Policies*; Valerie Bunce, *Do New Leaders Make a Difference? Executive Succession and Public Policy under Capitalism and Socialism* (Princeton, NJ: Princeton University Press, 1981).

68 "Vstrecha M.S. Gorbacheva s predstaviteliami mezhdunarodnogo foruma uchenykh za prekrashchenie iadernykh ispytanii" ["Meeting of M.S. Gorbachev with Representatives of the International Forum of Scientists for the Cessation of Nuclear Tests"], *Pravda*, July 15, 1986; Velikhov interview, July 29, 1992; Sagdeev interview, April 1994.

69 Gorbachev, *Perestroika*, pp. 157–58.   70 Cherniaev, *Shest' let s Gorbachevym*, p. 62.

group's other accomplishments probably outweigh that failure.[71] In particular, it was the transnational coalition of American and Soviet scientists that successfully conducted the first on-site verification of arms control measures, when the Natural Resources Defense Council (NRDC), in cooperation with the Federation of American Scientists (FAS), pursued a joint project with the Soviet Academy of Sciences (SAS) to install seismic monitoring equipment to verify the unilateral Soviet test moratorium.[72] That effort set a precedent for cooperative verification measures and eliminated the most potent US criticism of a comprehensive test ban – the supposed impossiblity of achieving reliable verification. The US was obliged to fall back on other excuses for continued testing that most analysts found of dubious merit – the need to explode nuclear warheads in order to insure their reliability and safety, and the concern that the Soviets might test new nuclear weapons in outer space, where it would be difficult for the US to monitor them. As one US official argued, "they could go beyond Mars, in which case we'd have to go beyond Mars to measure it."[73]

The seismic verification breakthrough

The success of the transnational actors in obtaining Soviet acceptance of on-site monitoring should be attributed both to the individuals involved and to the structure of the Soviet political system that allowed them access to the top leadership. The collaboration between Velikhov and Frank von Hippel, a Princeton University professor and chair of the Federation of American Scientists, was particularly valuable.[74] In September 1985, Velikhov met von Hippel at a meeting in Copenhagen and suggested that the Soviet Union might be willing to allow an outside group to establish a seismic monitoring system in the country. Although initially skeptical of the merits of such a venture, von Hippel was persuaded by the NRDC's Thomas Cochran – the initiator and most tireless promoter of the seismic monitoring project. In April 1986 von Hippel accompanied a delegation to meet with Soviet foreign minister Shevardnadze in Moscow to urge the Soviet

---

[71] Jeffrey W. Knopf, "Soviet Public Diplomacy and US Policymaking on Arms Control: The Case of Gorbachev's Nuclear Testing Moratorium," paper presented at the International Studies Association annual meeting, London, March 28–April 1, 1989.

[72] *Natural Resources Defense Council Annual Report 1986–87*, pp. 29–30.

[73] Paul Brown of Lawrence Livermore Laboratory, quoted in the *Washington Post*, June 24, 1986, in the *Arms Control Reporter*, p. 608.B.99.2.

[74] The following account draws on von Hippel, "Arms Control Physics," and on discussions with Christopher Paine, April 2, 1994, Arlington, VA.

government to maintain its moratorium on testing in order to give Western activists time to influence their own governments to go along with it. The foreign minister received the delegation politely, but von Hippel was not sure that anything had been accomplished. He proposed meeting with Velikhov. From that point on the seismic monitoring project took off. Velikhov made good use of his personal relationship with Gorbachev, his influential position as vice president of the Academy of Sciences, and his familiarity with the United States to promote the project within the Soviet leadership.[75] The hierarchical, centralized nature of the Soviet system meant that once the top leadership was on board, implementation of the project with all of the necessary resources was pretty well guaranteed.[76]

Alternative explanations

When the Soviet unilateral moratorium was announced in 1985, US government officials argued that it was merely a propaganda ploy, that the USSR had conducted an accelerated number of tests already that year and could refrain from testing without harming its nuclear-weapons modernization. The implication was that the Soviet military authorities were at least neutral but perhaps supported the moratorium in the hope that the United States would follow suit and that a US test moratorium would hinder the development of new US weapons, particularly nuclear-powered lasers related to the Strategic Defense Initiative. In fact, the Soviet military leadership's position ranged from skepticism to outright opposition to the moratorium.

---

[75] The explosion at the Chernobyl' nuclear power plant in April 1986 probably influenced Gorbachev's decision to extend the nuclear testing moratorium and support other efforts, such as the joint seismic experiment, to boost the prospects for a test-ban treaty.

[76] The US case provides a striking contrast. The cooperation required of the US government in the monitoring scheme was fairly modest – the granting of export licenses, visas for visiting Soviet scientists, and permission for setting up seismic stations on US territory. Although at the highest levels most US officials were unenthusiastic about the NRDC–SAS project, their views seemed to have little effect on how the various aspects of the project were handled. The decentralization of the US system meant that many decisions were taken by middle- or low-level bureaucrats following standard operating procedures and adhering to statutory regulations. The result was that some potentially controversial questions – on the export of sensitive technologies needed for seismic monitoring – went rather smoothly, whereas other seemingly routine matters – issuing visas – ran into trouble. The contrast between the domestic structures of the US and USSR seems to account for the differences. See Philip G. Schrag, *Listening for the Bomb: A Study in Nuclear Arms Control Verification Policy* (Boulder, CO: Westview, 1989).

Marshal Akhromeev reports in his memoirs his doubts about Gorbachev's rationale for the unilateral test ban: "It was assumed that a full cessation of nuclear-weapons testing could serve as a powerful impulse to halting the race in nuclear – and indirectly – space weapons. However, this noble intention didn't have a chance of success in view of the simple, firm, negative position of the USA regarding the full cessation of nuclear explosions." The Reagan administration, in Akhromeev's (accurate) view, "considered nuclear tests necessary to improve and create new types of nuclear weaponry and for developing some components of a space-based ABM system."[77] A senior foreign ministry official and close friend of Akhromeev later reported that Soviet military officials had warned the political leaders that a unilateral moratorium would give the US an advantage in SDI-related research, but that their warning came too late to influence the decision.[78] A year into the moratorium Akhromeev publicly complained that the Soviet initiative had harmed the country's security but was nevertheless still "tolerable."[79] Military opposition and US intransigence led Gorbachev reluctantly to end the moratorium.

The seismic monitoring program was clearly a civilian, transnational initiative. No one has credited the armed forces with the idea or offered an alternative account of how the USSR came to accept for the first time on-site verification of an arms-control initiative.

From the new Soviet Union to the ex-Soviet Union

The introduction of a functioning legislature in 1989 provided a new forum for discussion of security issues and legitimated the role of new actors in Soviet foreign policy. The transition to a market economy made enterprises, including those in the military sector, more dependent on their own resources and eager to find international partners and customers. These structural attributes of the new Soviet system which gradually emerged out of Gorbachev's reforms had a noticeable impact on the behavior of transnational coalitions.

---

[77] Akhromeev and Kornienko, *Glazami marshala i diplomata*, p. 56.
[78] Ibid. pp. 95–96.
[79] Press conference broadcast on Moscow television, August 25, 1986, reported in the *Arms Control Reporter*, p. 608.B.107.

The Star-Wars seduction

Soviet Star Warriors

As *glasnost'* flourished and the Communist Party's monopoly on truth diminished, new voices were heard in the Soviet discussions about strategic defenses. Gorbachev was no longer able to impose the "party line" opposing SDI. One of the first to speak out in favor of developing Soviet ballistic missile defenses was not a military official but a senior scientist at the Institute for Space Research. The institute's former director, Roald Sagdeev, was a prominent opponent of Star Wars, yet he was not inclined to impose his views on his subordinates, particularly in the new atmosphere. Viktor Etkin, chief of applied space physics at the institute, argued in *Pravda* in favor of limited defenses against accidental nuclear launches and terrorist attacks: "such a limited system including ground- and space-based positions for combating non-massed missile launches is within the bounds of feasible technical solutions."[80]

Conducted in parallel with, and reinforcing, the efforts of some Soviet scientists to promote strategic defenses was an official US government campaign to sell the Soviets the merits of Star Wars. The US invited Soviet officials to visit the Los Alamos nuclear weapons laboratory to inspect the Beam Experiment Aboard Rocket (BEAR) project intended to demonstrate the feasibility of creating a weapon employing neutral particle beams.[81] Ironically, the BEAR project had evidently benefited considerably from published Soviet research on laser technology in the late 1960s.[82] The US also arranged a visit to a facility of the private military corporation, TRW, in San Juan Capistrano in order to view the company's Alpha laser project. The US government evidently "hoped the visit would lead to Soviet understanding and eventual acceptance of US proposals in the Defense and Space Talks" in Geneva to weaken the ABM Treaty and allow development of space-based defenses.[83]

The US invitations were in some sense offered in reciprocation for the visits of US citizens to secret Soviet military sites to investigate

---

[80] *Pravda*, July 20, 1989, quoted in *Arms Control Reporter*, pp. 575.B.370.
[81] *Arms Control Reporter*, pp. 575.B.375, 392.
[82] Soviet research, according to Colonel Thomas Meyer, head of SDIO's directed energy program, "enabled the US to shrink the machinery enough to loft it into space," *Arms Control Reporter*, p. 575.B.369.
[83] *Arms Control Reporter*, p. 575.B.375.

Soviet progress in laser and particle-beam technology. In August 1989, for example, a US congressional delegation, with Velikhov's assistance, visited a branch of his Kurchatov Institute in Sary Shagan to observe a gas laser project.[84] The initial precedent for such visits, of course, was the NRDC–SAS seismic monitoring project which paved the way for contacts between representatives of the Soviet military-research community and its US counterpart. In effect, these visits by military officers to the research facilities of "the enemy" helped to forge an alternative transnational linkage – one that little by little came to play an active role in thwarting the efforts of the original transnational coalition of disarmament proponents.

US officials and other proponents of SDI took every opportunity to promote the views of Soviet supporters of strategic defenses, often calling attention to articles in the Soviet military press that would otherwise have gone unremarked.[85] The use of US Patriot air defense system against Iraqi SCUD missiles during the war against Iraq in 1990 gave proponents of defenses an opportunity to argue for systems directed not against other major powers but against countries in the Third World. One proposal for a collaborative US–Soviet effort to develop such defenses was put forward publicly in the fall of 1990 by a prominent Soviet *institutchik* and eventually came to influence the official Soviet position.[86]

Gorbachev and Yeltsin on the defensive

In July 1990 Gorbachev cautiously proposed to the Group of Seven industrialized countries the "development of joint ABM early warning systems to prevent unauthorized or terrorist operated launches of ballistic missiles."[87] President George Bush responded in September by agreeing to cooperative efforts on early warning but he also called upon the USSR to permit the limited deployment of non-nuclear defenses. The US Secretary of Defense pursued the matter a few days

---

[84] Michael R. Gordon, "US Visitors See Soviet Laser Firing," *New York Times*, August 17, 1989; Frank von Hippel, "Visit to a Laser Facility at the Soviet ABM Test Site," *Physics Today* (November 1989), pp. 34–35; Frank von Hippel and Thomas B. Cochran, "The Myth of the Soviet 'Killer' Laser," *New York Times*, August 19, 1989; *Arms Control Reporter*, p. 575.B.373.

[85] In November 1990, Keith Payne, of the National Institute for Space Policy, for example, cited an article in the Soviet journal *Voennaia Mysl'* [*Military Thought*] to argue that the USSR was becoming more accepting of strategic defenses. *Arms Control Reporter*, p. 575.B.399.

[86] Sergei Blagovolin, remarks at a conference on economic conversion, Institute of the World Economy and International Relations, Moscow, November 1990.

[87] *Arms Control Reporter*, p. 575.B.403.

later, remarking that in the USSR "there are signs that there are people in positions of responsibility who are willing to entertain the notion of discussing defenses for the first time ... I think there's a growing awareness on the part of the Soviets of their vulnerability to ballistic missile attack from someplace besides the United States."[88] At the same time, an official in the SDI office made clear that Gorbachev's proposal for collaboration on early warning did not go far enough: "If we were to cooperate with them, it would have to be in the context of missile defenses. It wouldn't be early warning for the sake of early warning."[89] White House officials echoed that view.[90] Within a few days Gorbachev had conceded, stating that "we are ready to discuss the US proposals on non-nuclear anti-missile defense systems. We propose to the US side that the possibility of creating joint systems to avert nuclear missile strikes with ground- and space-based elements also be examined."[91]

Russian President Boris Yeltsin and his supporters went further in proposing joint efforts to create defenses. In October 1991, several military officials, who simultaneously served on the Russian republic's State Committee on Defense, attended a meeting in Washington to discuss ballistic missile defense. They argued that, owing to Russia's relatively greater vulnerability to potentially hostile Third World countries, "our interest in joint work on ABM systems is obvious." During the same month several articles in mass-circulation newspapers and specialist journals promoted the idea of ABM defenses for Russia.[92] The new transnational coalition of US and Russian proponents of ballistic-missile defenses was established.[93]

Alternative explanations

Both Gorbachev and Yeltsin had other reasons, besides pressure from transnational actors, for reconsidering the blanket Soviet condemnation of ballistic-missile defense systems that could undermine the ABM Treaty. As the various Soviet republics bordering Russia asserted their claims of sovereignty and independence, they put at risk the integrity of the Soviet early-warning system against missile attack. Thus, one can understand Gorbachev's proposals to cooperate with the United States in developing a joint system of early warning. No

[88] Ibid. p. 575.B.403.   [89] Ibid. p. 575.B.405.
[90] Matthew Bunn, "The ABM Talks: The More Things Change ...," *Arms Control Today*, 22, 7 (September 1992), pp. 15–23, at p. 19.
[91] *Arms Control Reporter*, p. 575.B.405.   [92] Ibid. p. 575.B.405.
[93] Fred C. Iklé, "Comrades in Arms," *New York Times*, December 13, 1991.

doubt there is also some basis to Russian concerns about missile attacks by terrorists or aggressors from the Third World. In a sense though, these rationales mainly provided an opening for policy entrepreneurs – both in Russia and the United States – who wanted to promote the development of major strategic defense systems in any case.[94] Those who have maintained a principled opposition to widespread strategic defenses have no trouble in proposing alternative means to limit the threat of ballistic-missile attacks (e.g., measures to stem the proliferation of missile and nuclear technology) and suggesting collaboration in early warning while maintaining a commitment to the ABM Treaty.[95]

The teeter-totter of nuclear testing

The fate of nuclear testing in the Soviet Union from 1989 to 1993 depended on the relative strengths of the proponents and opponents of a unilateral Soviet moratorium. The transnational coalition of scientists no longer played a key role in influencing Soviet policy. They were eclipsed on the one hand by a mass movement of antinuclear activists who enjoyed considerable success in disrupting the Soviet nuclear test program. On the other hand, the transnational disarmament coalition helped give rise, and then gave way, to a competing transnational group of weapons designers who opposed even a bilateral test ban and who exerted substantial influence on the government of Boris Yeltsin. The politics of the test-ban debate reveals the post-Soviet domestic structure as an unusual mix of societal activism and corporatist bargaining.

The original unilateral nuclear-test moratorium initiated by Gorbachev lasted from August 1985 until February 1987. The resumption of testing should not be understood as the main indication of the weakening of the transnational coalition's influence on Soviet policy. Advocates of the unilateral moratorium had always promoted it as a means of getting the US to stop testing – most likely through the efforts of the

---

[94] An unpublished report by four Russian ABM scientists is particularly revealing in this regard: O.V. Golubev, Ia.A. Kamenskii, M.G. Minasian, B.D. Pupkov, "Proshloe i nastoiashchee Rossiiskikh sistem protivoraketnoi oborony (vzgliad iznutri)" ["The Past and Present of Russian Antimissile Defense Systems (A View from Within)"] (Moscow: Committee of Scientists for Global Security, 1993). I am grateful to David Holloway for providing me a copy of this report. See also Cherniaev, *Shest' let s Gorbachevym*, p. 121; Sagdeev, *Making of a Soviet Scientists*, p. 273.

[95] Aleksei Arbatov, and to some extent Andrei Kokoshin, are good examples. See the *Arms Control Reporter*, pp. 575.B.414–15.

US side of the coalition to convince Congress to legislate a US halt.[96] Those efforts failed and the US continued to pursue a vigorous program of nuclear testing.[97] It was only a matter of time before Gorbachev would have to heed the counsel of his military officials and resume Soviet tests. Given the similarity between Gorbachev's behavior and that of his predecessor Nikita Khrushchev, who also failed in his efforts to use a test moratorium to achieve a comprehensive test ban twenty-five years earlier, we should not look to structural changes as the impetus to the Soviet resumption of tests.[98]

Test-ban opponents speak up

For the most part the structural changes came later. Soviet military objections to the test moratorium in 1985 and 1986 were rather subdued – as one would expect, given the role of Party discipline and restrictions on public discussion of security policy associated with the old domestic structure. What changed with the expansion of *glasnost'* and especially with the transformation of the Supreme Soviet into a medium of public debate was the ability of test-ban opponents to promote their views openly. In July 1989, for example, the Soviet defense minister responded to demands from parliamentary deputies to revive the moratorium by arguing that the "USSR's unilateral suspension of nuclear weapons upgrading could cause the existing parity in this sphere to be upset and lead to catastrophic, unpredictable consequences."[99] Such hyperbolic defense of military prerogatives would have been considered a major breach of Party discipline just a couple of years earlier.[100]

Not only did military officials begin to express their views about nuclear testing in the new conditions of *glasnost'* and parliamentary

96 Interview, Aleksei Arbatov, August 18, 1993.
97 Christopher E. Paine, "Nuclear Test Restriction Fails to Pass Senate: Victim of Weapons Lab Lobbying Campaign; New US–Soviet Agenda for Test Ban Talks," in *FAS Public Interest Report*, 40, 9 (November 1987), p. 1.
98 On the test-ban debate during the Khrushchev period, see Glenn T. Seaborg with Benjamin S. Loeb, *Kennedy, Khrushchev, and the Test Ban* (Berkeley, CA: University of California Press, 1981); and Christer Jönsson, *Soviet Bargaining Behavior: The Nuclear Test Ban Case* (New York: Columbia University Press, 1979).
99 *Krasnaia zvezda* [*Red Star*], July 21, 1989, quoted in the *Arms Control Reporter*, p. 608.B.181.
100 Other deputies, mainly military officers, also supported the continuation of testing, in the absence of US agreement to a mutual ban. See, e.g., the remarks of Col. N.S. Petrushenko in *Krasnaia zvezda*, November 29, 1989, quoted in the *Arms Control Reporter*, p. 608.B.188; and of retired chief of the general staff Marshal Sergei Akhromeev on Moscow television, October 9, 1990, quoted in the *Arms Control Reporter*, pp. 608.B.204–05.

debate. Workers from towns whose very existence had recently been secret – the employees of the Soviet military-industrial complex – began to voice their concerns about imminent unemployment if the nuclear test site were closed.[101] The deputy minister of nuclear power and industry published a long article in *Pravda* in October 1990 making the case for further nuclear tests by warning that "our country's unilateral nuclear disarmament paves the way to a US monopoly."[102] The director of the nuclear weapons laboratory at Arzamas-16 (the previously anonymous "installation," where Andrei Sakharov worked on nuclear weapons from 1950 to 1968),[103] argued that the Soviet nuclear arsenal must be developed "dynamically" in order to keep up with the US: "I recall that when we asked the Japanese how far behind them we were in electronics, the answer was given, 'forever' . . . If we fall behind the Americans it will be simply impossible to catch up."[104]

The Nevada-Semipalatinsk movement

Ranged in opposition to the increasingly outspoken proponents of Soviet nuclear testing was an unprecedented, large, and effective mass movement. The emergence of a popular grassroots movement against nuclear testing was both a consequence of the changing Soviet domestic structure and a catalyst for further change – namely the disintegration of the multi-ethnic state. In 1989, an antinuclear group called "Nevada" was formed in Kazakhstan to protest against nuclear testing at the main Soviet test site near Semipalatinsk.[105] The movement was

---

[101] *Krasnaia zvezda*, January 4, 1990, quoted in the *Arms Control Reporter*, p. 608.B.196.

[102] V. Mikhailov, "Why Should the Country's Nuclear Test Sites Remain Silent?" *Pravda*, October 24, 1990, translation of the Foreign Broadcast Information Service, in *Daily Report: Soviet Union*, FBIS-SOV-90-207, pp. 1–3. Also, V.M. Mikhailov, *Ia – "Iastreb"* [*I am a "Hawk"*] (Moscow: Kron-Press, 1993).

[103] Andrei Sakharov, *Memoirs*; see David Holloway's review in the *Bulletin of the Atomic Scientists*, 47, 6 (July/August 1991), pp. 37–38.

[104] *Krasnaia zvezda*, December 25, 1990, quoted in the *Arms Control Reporter*, p. 608.B.208–09.

[105] My main sources on the Nevada movement include: Peter Zheutlin, "Nevada, USSR," *Bulletin of the Atomic Scientists* (March 1990) pp. 10–12; Ian Mather, "Life and Death under a Cloud in Radiation City," *The European*, weekend edn, June 1–3, 1990; various issues of the movement's newspaper, *Izbiratel'*; S. Erzhanov, "Krepnet golos razuma" ["The voice of reason is becoming stronger"], *Vecherniaia Alma-Ata* [*Evening Alma-Ata*], May 25, 1990; "O Budushchem mira – s trevogoi i bol'iu" ["About the Future of the World – with Worry and Pain"], *Kazakhstanskaia Pravda*, May 26, 1990; "Semipalatinsk-Nevada as Viewed by a People's Deputy of the USSR," interview by Iuri Dmitriev with Olzhas Suleimenov, *Moscow News*, 51 (December 24–31, 1989), p. 15; Daniel Young, "Thousands in Alma-Ata Demand Test Ban," *PSR Reports*, 10, 2 (Summer 1990); *Vital Signs* (IPPNW newsletter), 3, 1 (March 1990) and 3, 2 (August

transnational in its very conception: the name was chosen to attract the attention of grassroots antinuclear activists ("downwinders") working to shut down the US test site in Nevada and links between the two groups were quickly formed.

The Nevada movement was founded by the renowned Kazakh poet Olzhas Suleimenov. In early 1989 Suleimenov was beginning his campaign for a seat in the newly created Congress of People's Deputies. He had scheduled an appearance on local television for 26 February when he learned that two underground nuclear tests at the Semipalatinsk test range earlier in the month had vented radioactive or other toxic materials into the atmosphere. He scrapped his original campaign speech and discussed the accidents instead. He called on all concerned citizens of Kazakhstan to meet at the writers' union hall in Alma Ata two days later. Five thousand people showed up at what turned out to be the founding meeting of the Nevada-Semipalatinsk movement. Among other demands, the movement called for the closing of the Semipalatinsk test site, an environmental clean-up program, and an end to secrecy concerning the fate of Soviet victims of radiation. Eventually over a million signatures were gathered in support of the petition.

Suleimenov handily won election to the Congress of People's Deputies and then to the USSR Supreme Soviet. He became a prominent spokesperson for antinuclear and environmental issues throughout the Soviet Union, but he particularly tapped into the anti-Moscow sentiment of the citizens of his native Kazakhstan (about half of whom are ethnic Russians). As the efforts of the transnational coalition of scientists began to reach the limits of their effectiveness, the volatile mix of environmentalism, antinuclearism, and nationalism propelled the Nevada-Semipalatinsk movement into a central role in the struggle over Soviet nuclear testing. A mass demonstration on August 6, 1989 (Hiroshima Day) drew 50,000 people. Another 20,000 assembled to greet several hundred international delegates to a Congress on Nuclear Testing in Alma Ata in May 1990, and thousands more met the delegates when they visited the city of Semipalatinsk and the village of Karaul near the test site.[106] The movement had such widespread support that Suleimenov could credibly threaten to call the coal miners of Kazakhstan – one of the main coal-producing regions of the USSR –

1990); Peter Zheutlin, "Kazakhstan: Life and Death in the Shadow of the Mushroom Cloud," *Los Angeles Times*, April 1, 1990.
[106] *PSR Reports* (Summer 1990); and personal observation.

out on strike if the movement's demands were not met. In fact, closing the Semipalatinsk test site topped the list of the miners' demands when they threatened strikes in the summer of 1990.[107]

The Nevada movement was a clear example of an effective trans- national coalition – at least in its impact on Soviet policy. It received little attention, however, in the United States and had no impact on US plans for nuclear testing. Members of the transnational test-ban coali- tion tried to come up with ways to tap the power of the grassroots Kazakh movement to influence US policy. Evgenii Velikhov at one point jokingly suggested flying 100,000 Kazakhs to Washington DC on Aeroflot, with or without visas, to demonstrate at the White House.[108]

To influence Soviet policy the Nevada movement required no such fanciful schemes. The impact was direct and powerful. An official in the Soviet foreign ministry admitted in early 1990 that the movement was responsible for forcing the Soviet Defense Military to cancel 11 of its 18 scheduled nuclear tests for 1989.[109] In early 1990 the Soviet government promised to conduct only 27 more tests at Semipalatinsk and then close the site in 1993, but that was not soon enough for the grassroots activists.[110] Ultimately the nuclear debate became caught up in the power struggle between "the center" (the Soviet government, ministerial, and Party apparatus in Moscow) and the republics. In December 1990, the Kazakhstan parliament banned nuclear-weapons testing on the republic's territory. In the wake of the failed coup in August 1991, the president of Kazakhstan closed the Semipalatinsk range.[111]

Anticipating the unavailability of the Semipalatinsk test site (every test there was being met with mass protest demonstrations), Soviet military officials had long been planning to move nuclear testing to the second and little used Novaia Zemlia site near the Arctic Circle. The grassroots activists were always one step ahead of them, however. From the very beginning of the Nevada movement, Suleimenov and his followers had expressed solidarity with the peoples of the north and demanded a global test ban, not simply the shifting of nuclear

107 "Soviet Miners Speak," interviews conducted by William Mandel, *The Station Relay*, 5, 1–5 (1989–91), p. 28; Peter Rutland, "Labor Unrest Movements in 1989 and 1990," *Soviet Economy*, 6, 4 (1990), reprinted in Ed. A. Hewett and Victor H. Winston, eds., *Milestones in Glasnost and Perestroyka: Politics and People* (Washington, DC: The Brook- ings Institution, 1991), pp. 287–325, at p. 315.
108 Interview with Thomas Cochran, Moscow, May 22, 1990.
109 Zheutlin, "Nevada, USSR," p. 11.
110 "Soviet Union to Close Testing Site," *Arms Control Today* (April 1990), p. 31.
111 *Arms Control Reporter*, pp. 608.B.208 and 608.B.216.

tests away from their "backyard." Domestic opposition to nuclear testing at Novaia Zemlia from local residents as well as deputies of the USSR Supreme Soviet was reinforced by international criticism of the plans to resume testing there. Finland, Norway, Sweden, Denmark, and Iceland all expressed concern. Greenpeace launched a campaign to interfere with the tests, sending a ship that was intercepted by the KGB but welcomed by local residents. A couple of weeks earlier the Soviet coast guard had seized a Norwegian ship with a crew of environmentalists who were trying to test for radioactivity in the area of the test range.[112]

Despite such widespread domestic and international opposition, the Soviet Defense Ministry managed to conduct a nuclear test, unannounced, on October 24, 1990 – its first in over a year, and, as it turned out, its last. Further plans for tests at Semipalatinsk and Novaia Zemlia were cancelled owing to popular opposition at the grassroots level and within the Soviet parliament.[113] In early October 1991, Mikhail Gorbachev declared a year-long moratorium on Soviet nuclear testing. Three weeks later, Boris Yeltsin banned nuclear tests on Russian territory for a year and specifically decreed that the Novaia Zemlia archipelago no longer be used as a nuclear test range.[114]

The counter-coalition: transnational and pronuclear

Despite the seemingly decisive victory of the antinuclear movement in shutting down the Soviet Union's two main test ranges and reinstating the unilateral test moratorium, the proponents of nuclear testing showed no sign of conceding. In February 1992, barely a month after the breakup of the Soviet Union, the Russian deputy minister for nuclear energy and industry began arguing for a resumption of nuclear tests following the end of Yeltsin's moratorium in October 1992. Viktor Mikhailov expressed concern about the potential "degradation" of the country's scientific expertise. He argued that "it is better for everyone to agree on a limited number of tests instead of a

---

[112] Shannon Fagan, "Target Novaya Zemlya: Journey into the Soviet Nuclear Testing Zone," *Greenpeace* magazine (January/February 1991), pp. 13–16; *Arms Control Reporter*, pp. 608.B.204–05.

[113] I. Sichka, "We Blast Without Warning," *Komsomol'skaia Pravda*, October 26, 1990; "Resolution Adopted on Novaya Zemlya Nuclear Test," TASS report, October 31, 1990 p. 1; "Arkhangelsk Leadership Protests Nuclear Tests," TASS report, October 31, 1990; all translations from the Foreign Broadcast Information Service, in *Daily Report: Soviet Union*, FBIS-SOV-90–210, 30 October 1990.

[114] *Arms Control Reporter*, pp. 608.B.220–21.

complete ban, because otherwise we might lose the level of [expertise] we now possess."[115]

The arguments of the Russian proponents of nuclear testing sound remarkably similar to those of their American counterparts – and not by coincidence. During the late 1980s Soviet advocates of nuclear testing were, like the Soviet proponents of strategic defenses, able to forge transnational alliances with US opponents of a test ban. They did so in some measure by taking advantage of the successful efforts of the pro-test-ban coalition to get nuclear testing and particularly verification back on the official Soviet–American arms-control agenda.

By demonstrating the feasibility of seismic verification and threatening to legislate an end to testing through congressional action, the test-ban coalition managed to get the Reagan administration to reverse its objection to a comprehensive test ban in principle. The administration agreed to undertake to negotiate a series of steps gradually limiting the number and size of tests, with the long-term goal of a total cessation (the Bush administration subsequently reneged on this commitment).[116]

The progress in seismic monitoring of nuclear testing that the NRDC–SAS project had achieved, combined with the Reagan and Bush administrations' preoccupation with Soviet cheating, helped to make verification a natural focus of official US–Soviet negotiations. The coalition of American and Soviet test ban proponents had actually paved the way for such negotiations by bringing US and Soviet weapons designers together for the first time to discuss verification at a conference in Moscow. The weaponeers got along remarkably well and seemed to sympathize with each other's desire to continue testing – much to the dismay of the conference organizers.[117] One thing that both sides could agree upon was that "joint efforts were needed to upgrade verification methods."[118] In the view of the weapons scientists, joint efforts at evaluating verification methods require continued nuclear explosions so that there will be something on which to base the evaluations. This approach coincides exactly with the one favored by the Reagan and Bush administrations. First with some reluctance, and then with increasing enthusiasm, Russian weapons

115 *Washington Post*, February 5, 1992, cited in the *Arms Control Reporter*, p. 608.B.225.
116 *Arms Control Reporter*, p. 608.B.191, citing various press reports from January 1990.
117 Discussions with Frank von Hippel of the FAS, Thomas Cochran of the NRDC, and Steve Fetter of the University of Maryland, in Moscow, Alma Ata, and Semipalatinsk, May 22–25, 1990.
118 TASS report, May 29, 1990, cited in the *Arms Control Reporter*, p. 608.B.199.

scientists began observing US nuclear tests in Nevada. In March 1992, twenty-three of them were on hand to observe the first US nuclear test of that year.[119] On their return home, they argued that carrying out the Russian–American agreements on verification required further nuclear tests.

Corporatist bargaining on nuclear testing

The Russian nuclear-testing lobby seemed to have achieved considerable success in influencing President Boris Yeltsin – thanks largely, it seems, to the efforts of Viktor Mikhailov. In January 1992, when Mikhailov was first deputy head of the Ministry of Nuclear Energy and Industry, he invited Yeltsin to visit the top-secret nuclear weapons laboratory at Arzamas-16. Mikhailov was searching for ways to keep his operations going. Rather than close the Novaia Zemlia test range, Mikhailov proposed to use it to conduct tests of "peaceful nuclear explosions." He suggested using the site as a disposal center to get rid of toxic materials such as chemical and nuclear weapons that were being reduced in connection with arms-control treaties. The idea would be to blow them up with nuclear explosives. Mikhailov apparently had a direct financial stake in such operations. His ministry was collaborating with a Russian corporation called CHETEK to sell disposal services to any interested customers. CHETEK was founded by weapons scientists at Arzamas-16 and originally funded by the Soviet Military-Industrial Commission. It financed some of the projects of the Ministry of Nuclear Energy.[120] The arrangement mixed private and state economic activities in a way that was becoming increasingly common in Russia in the early 1990s.

According to a Russian foreign ministry official, Mikhailov had considerable success in persuading Yeltsin of the merits of his proposals during a long, vodka-inspired discussion. Mikhailov presented three "treaties" for the president's signature: (1) to resume nuclear testing at Novaia Zemlia after the expiration of the one-year moratorium, thereafter conducting 3 or 4 tests per year; (2) to maintain the formerly closed nuclear research and test sites, such as Arzamas-16, under the central government's jurisdiction, in order to protect them from hardships of economic reform and from the interference of local

---

[119] *Arms Control Reporter*, p. 608.B.227.
[120] *Arms Control Reporter*, pp. 605.B.120–22, an extensive summary of research conducted by Canadian researchers.

authorities who might prefer to convert them to civilian activities; and (3) Mikhailov's own promotion to minister. Yeltsin signed all three.[121]

The Russian president's subsequent actions give this story the ring of truth. First, in February 1992, the month after his meeting with Mikhailov, Yeltsin instructed the ministry for nuclear energy and the joint high command of the Commonwealth of Independent States "to continue in 1992 the necessary work involved in preparing tunnels and wells for conducting underground nuclear tests on Novaia Zemlia at a rate of two to four per year, if the declared moratorium expires."[122] Second, Yeltsin signed a decree transferring Novaia Zemlia from the USSR defense ministry's Sixth State Central Test Site to the Russian Federation's control.[123] Finally, Mikhailov was promoted from first deputy to minister for nuclear energy. He became increasingly outspoken about the need to continue nuclear tests, relying on standard nostrums about "the need to maintain the country's defense sufficiency" as well as the newer arguments learned from his transnational allies in the United States: nuclear testing must continue in order to ensure proper verification of nuclear testing in compliance with current treaties.[124]

Alternative explanations

One possible alternative explanation for the shifts in Soviet policy on nuclear testing that does not emphasize the change in domestic structure might focus instead on the nature of the Russian–American relationship. From the late 1980s two trends seemed to coincide – a weakening in Russia's economic and political situation and an improvement in relations with the US. The US, especially during the Bush administration, consistently made promises to help the Soviet economy contingent on Soviet willingness to pursue policies congenial to the US.[125] By this argument, the Russian government saw no reason to push for a comprehensive test ban that the US opposed or even to maintain its own moratorium, because the US would continue testing with or without the Russians. Only when US policy changed

121 Discussion with Frank von Hippel, Princeton, April 24, 1992.
122 *Arms Control Reporter*, p. 608.B.226, citing *Nezavisimaia gazeta* [Independent Newspaper], March 24, 1992, and the Russian television news program *Vesti* of March 3, 1992.
123 Ibid.
124 *Rossiiskaia gazeta* [*Russian Newspaper*], quoted in the *Arms Control Reporter*, pp. 608.B.233–34.
125 Beschloss and Talbott, *At the Highest Levels*.

under the Clinton adminstration toward support for a test ban would the Russians decide not to resume testing. This explanation has much to recommend it, although it gives insignificant attention to the pressures on President Yeltsin from both the grassroots anti-nuclear activists and the nuclear establishment. Despite the important role of the United States, Russian testing policy often hinged on the delicate internal balance of pro- and anti-nuclear forces – a balance that emerged as a result of the change from a highly centralized, hierarchical domestic structure to a fragmented and fluid one.

Conclusion

The opening up of the Soviet system made it possible for transnational contacts to flourish. Paradoxically, however, the new circumstances meant that the particular transnational coalition of disarmament proponents that was so influential in the early Gorbachev years now had to compete with groups advocating very different policies. To the extent that transnational contacts give domestic groups more resources to influence their government, the new groups were often much better endowed than their predecessors. The public interest groups, peace activists, and university professors who made up the Western side of the transnational disarmament coalition typically did not dispose of the kind of resources available to, say, the Strategic Defense Initiative Office, the US government weapons laboratories, or TRW Corporation.

As a consequence, in part, of the disproportionate resources of the competing transnational actors, the old disarmament coalition often saw its prior achievements reversed. In May 1988, for example, in one of many such collaborative arms control initiatives, the Federation of American Scientists and the Committee of Soviet Scientists jointly proposed a ban on nuclear reactors in Earth orbit. The document was signed in Washington by Frank von Hippel on behalf of the FAS and Roald Sagdeev for the CSS.[126] Back in the USSR, the Soviet space-reactor community responded with newspaper articles promoting the importance of nuclear reactors in space and criticizing Sagdeev. Subsequently a Soviet delegation attended the annual US space-reactor conference in Albuquerque and offered their reactors for sale. Their

[126] *F.A.S. Public Interest Report*, 41, 9 (November 1988).

most enthusiastic customer was the SDI office of the Pentagon.[127] The leader of the Soviet delegation, Academician Nikolai N. Ponomarev-Stepnoi, was asked at the meeting about Sagdeev's opposition to nuclear reactors in Earth orbit. He said that he had met with Sagdeev before leaving Moscow and that Sagdeev "told me his opinion and I told him mine. And we were both so glad that we could tell each other our own opinion in our own country finally."[128] The scientist's coy remark illuminates the larger reality – that the structural changes induced by *glasnost'*, democratization, and market reforms, although supported and promoted by the transnational disarmament coalition, were a mixed blessing as far as its policy preferences were concerned.

In some cases, the change in domestic structure seems to have contributed to a change in the policy preferences themselves. Thus, Evgenii Velikhov, a hero of the transnational scientists' movement, became a much more ambiguous figure in the new conditions. He, too, began promoting the sale of nuclear space reactors to the US government – the Topaz model was developed at his Kurchatov Institute – even though the organization he founded (the Committee of Soviet Scientists) favored banning them.[129] In his efforts to find employment for scientists and international investment for enterprises of the former Soviet military-industrial sector, Velikhov has developed extensive contacts with representatives of US military contractors. He also may have modified his opposition to ballistic-missile defenses. In summer 1992, he invited Edward Teller and Lowell Wood of the Lawrence Livermore nuclear weapons laboratory for their first visit ever to Russia, ostensibly to discuss proposals for a global monitoring system to warn against missile attacks.[130] But Teller and Wood were well known as the most ardent proponents of Star-Wars missile defenses and they no doubt tried to persuade Velikhov of the merits of such systems and of the benefits of collaborating with US military technologists.

By mid-1993 the position of Russian proponents of collaborative development of ballistic-missile defenses and continued nuclear testing appeared to have been considerably weakened. The Clinton administration, unlike its predecessors, had come to embrace the

[127] William J. Broad, "US Moves to Bar Americans Buying Soviet Technology," *The New York Times*, March 1, 1992.
[128] von Hippel, "Arms Control Physics," p. 44.
[129] Bunn, "The ABM Talks," p. 23; Maxim Tarasenko, "Twinkle, Twinkle Little Topaz," *Bulletin of the Atomic Scientists*, 49, 6 (July/August 1993), pp. 11–13.
[130] Velikhov interview, July 29, 1992.

policies advocated by the transnational coalition of scientists. It bolstered proponents of the 1972 ABM treaty by supporting the "narrow" or "traditional" interpretation that the treaty "prohibits the development, testing and deployment of sea-based, air-based, space-based and mobile land-based ABM systems and components without regard to the technology utilized."[131] The administration's position on ballistic missile defense in general was more ambiguous. Although Secretary of Defense Les Aspin declared the "Star Wars era" over in early 1993, his administration created a Ballistic-Missile Defense Program as a successor agency to the SDI Office and requested $3.8 billion to fund it – the same amount that Congress had appropriated for SDI in the last year of the Bush administration.[132] In May 1994 a Pentagon delegation to Moscow tried to persuade the Russians to amend the ABM treaty to permit the development of theater ballistic-missile defense systems – part of a campaign likely to bolster the fortunes of some members of the Russian military-technical establishment.[133]

In the realm of nuclear testing the Clinton administration's decision to abide by the Congressional imposition of a US moratorium clearly undercut the Russian advocates of a test resumption. President Yeltsin welcomed the move and agreed to maintain the Russian moratorium.[134]

These developments reinforce the impression that changes in the Soviet/Russian domestic structure have exerted an important influence on the prospects for transnational actors to advance their policy goals. Under the old, highly centralized, hierarchical structure, Soviet scientists were able to persuade Mikhail Gorbachev to implement initiatives of unilateral restraint in nuclear testing and strategic defenses, despite the obvious US intention to pursue such programs vigorously. Under the new, post-1989 domestic structure, without a strong, centralized political authority backing them, the scientists found it difficult to compete with Russian proponents of nuclear testing and ballistic-missile defense – many of them lodged in the still-powerful institutions of the former Soviet military-industrial

---

131 Thomas L. Friedman, "US Formally Rejects 'Star Wars' in ABM Treaty," *The New York Times*, July 15, 1993, p. A6.
132 Ibid.
133 Stephen Foye, "US Defense Team Presses Mosocw on Cooperation," *Radio Free Europe/Radio Liberty Daily Report*, 87, (May 6, 1994) (electronic version). For views of some of the Russian military technologists, see Golubev *et al.*, "Proshloe i nastoiashchee Rossiiskikh sistem protivoraketnoi oborony."
134 *Arms Control Reporter*, p. 608.B.267.

sector. Only after major changes in US policy in 1993 did the political balance shift in favor of Russian transnational supporters of arms control and restraint. Without such strong external support, the transnational disarmament coalition is unlikely to regain the influence over Russian security policy that it enjoyed in the Soviet Union in the mid-1980s.

6 Mechanics of change: social movements, transnational coalitions, and the transformation processes in Eastern Europe

Patricia Chilton

Introduction[1]

At the Paris meeting of the Conference on Security and Cooperation in Europe (CSCE), called in November 1990 to mark a new departure in post-Cold War international relations, the leaders of the then thirty-four states of the old East and West blocs paid tribute to the people on the streets who, in the last few weeks of 1989, had changed the course of history.[2]

On the face of it, the role of "people power" was obvious. In country after country, popular pressure had forced totalitarian regimes to collapse or make transitions to democracy. In Poland, Hungary, East Germany, Czechoslovakia, Bulgaria, and Romania, supposedly strong governments disintegrated before spontaneous, unarmed demonstrations. The rapid de-legitimation of the single-party state went

An earlier version of this chapter appeared as an article in the journal *Democratization* 1, 1 (Spring 1994), pp. 151–81. The author wishes to thank all the participants in the Yale and Cornell workshops on transnational relations, especially Valerie Bunce, Peter Katzenstein, Stephen Krasner, David Meyer, and Thomas Risse-Kappen, for their advice and encouragement, and to acknowledge the support given in the early stages of this research by the Ploughshares Fund, San Francisco.

[1] The term "Eastern Europe" has been increasingly replaced by the terms "Central" or "East-Central Europe" since the end of 1989, though such terms were not widely comprehended or admissible before that date. For the sake of continuity, I use "Eastern Europe" throughout to designate the six non-Soviet Warsaw Pact countries: Poland, Hungary, East Germany, Czechoslovakia, Bulgaria, and Romania.

[2] President Bush, for instance, in his address to the CSCE summit: "We salute men of courage – Havel and Mazowiecki and Antall, here with us today – and all the other activists who took Helsinki's goals as solemn commitments and who suffered so that these commitments would be honored. And we salute all those individuals and private groups in the West who showed that the protection of human rights is not just the business of governments, it's everyone's business – nongovernmental organizations, the press, religious leaders, and ordinary citizens."

against all predictions.[3] But it happened, in a highly visible and unambiguous way, in front of the world's television cameras.

It is not so obvious, though, how these popular forces had managed to prevail, and whether their role was determining, or peripheral in comparison to other processes of transformation which were happening independently. It is equally not obvious whether the situations in the six countries were comparable, nor whether the differences in outcome were determined entirely by domestic politics, or by variables which transcended national boundaries.

In order to probe the impact of what are generally known as the new social movements[4] on the events of 1989, I have set out in this chapter to reassess the revolutions in Eastern Europe in the light of two independent variables, one domestic and one transnational, related to the existence of these social movements. The domestic variable identified here is the degree of civil society development apparent within each East bloc country prior to 1989. The transnational variable is the extent of coalition-building which had taken place, by 1989, between those elements of civil society which had developed in the East, and social movements outside, in the West. The dependent variable, meanwhile, is the particular form the regime transformation took in each case. This is clearly the most accessible area of information, and one which will be taken as a given in this chapter. Since there is ample knowledge about the immediate and more protracted outcomes of the 1989 events, those outcomes will only be briefly summarized here. The interesting question is whether the variation in outcomes can in any way be explained by the different levels of civil society development

---

[3] Important inferences for the analysis of international relations have not yet been drawn from the events of 1989. On the one hand, there has been a realist retrenchment represented by: John Lewis Gaddis, "Toward the Post-Cold War World," *Foreign Affairs* (Spring 1991), pp. 102–22; John J. Mearsheimer, "Back to the Future: Instability in Europe after the Cold War," *International Security* (Summer 1990), pp. 5–57; and Richard Pipes, "The Soviet Union Adrift," *Foreign Affairs* (Winter 1991), pp. 70–87. On the other hand, more thoughtful approaches have not confronted the problem directly, as in: Barry Buzan, Morten Kelstrup, Pierre H. Lemaitre, et al., *The European Security Order Recast: Scenarios for the Post-Cold War Era* (London: Pinter Publishers, 1990); and Richard H. Ullman, *Securing Europe* (Twickenham: Adamantine Press, 1991).

[4] See: Andrew Arato and Jean L. Cohen, "Social Movements, Civil Society and the Problem of Sovereignty," *Praxis International*, 4 (October 1984), pp. 266–83; Jürgen Habermas, "New Social Movements," *Telos*, 49 (Autumn 1981), pp. 33–37; Claus Offe, "New Social Movements: Challenging the Boundaries of Institutional Politics," *Social Research*, 52, 4 (Winter 1985), pp. 817–68; Alain Touraine, *The Voice and the Eye: An Analysis of Social Movements*, trans. Alan Duff (Cambridge: Cambridge University Press, 1981); R.B.J. Walker, *One World, Many Worlds: Struggles for a Just World Peace* (Boulder, CO: Lynne Rienner Publishers, 1988).

on the one hand, or the different levels of transnational coalition-building on the other.

I have chosen to focus in detail on the three very different cases of Hungary, East Germany, and Romania, and by comparing them to analyze the extent to which the variation between the outcomes can be explained by combinations of these domestic and transnational variables.[5] This may in turn illuminate the overall importance of the social movements, alongside the better-theorized impact of economic, political, and military variables. I argue that the capacity of social movements to form successful transnational coalitions is a determining factor with regard to the precise form of regime transformation in each country. Even though domestic structures may inhibit the activity of independent social movements, as they did in the majority of East bloc countries prior to 1989, transnational contacts may still be established between movements with sufficiently overlapping agendas. Where this occurs, weak social movements are empowered, and have a greater impact on regime transformation than might otherwise be expected.[6]

The dependent variable: regime transformation in Eastern Europe

The outcomes of the revolutions in the six Eastern European countries show major variations. Despite their coincidental timing and the superficial similarity displayed in their rejection of communism, there are significant domestic differences. Table 6.1 suggests a preliminary grouping of the six countries into three broad bands. This is based on a very simple classification of the outcomes according to two well-

---

[5] Recent thinking along similar lines is indicated by: Joseph A. Camilleri and Jim Falk, *The End of Sovereignty? The Politics of a Shrinking and Fragmenting World* (Aldershot: Edward Elgar, 1992); Friedrich Kratochwil, "The Embarrassment of Changes: Neo-Realism as the Science of *Realpolitik* without Politics," *Review of International Studies*, 19, 1 (January 1993), pp. 63–80; Andrew Moravcsik, "Introduction: Integrating International and Domestic Theories of International Bargaining," in Peter Evans, Harold Jacobson, and Robert Putnam, eds., *Double-Edged Diplomacy. International Bargaining and Domestic Politics* (Berkeley, CA: University of California Press, 1993), pp. 3–42; and Jan Aart Scholte, *International Relations of Social Change* (Buckingham: Open University Press, 1993).

[6] In essence, this argument picks up the challenge that "the impact of the popular upsurge upon the transition is clearer than the conditions for its emergence," and explores those conditions: Guillermo O'Donnell and Philippe C. Schmitter, *Transitions from Authoritarian Rule: Tentative Conclusions about Uncertain Democracies* (Baltimore, MD: The Johns Hopkins University Press, 1986), p. 55.

Table 6.1 *Variation in outcomes of the 1989 revolutions*

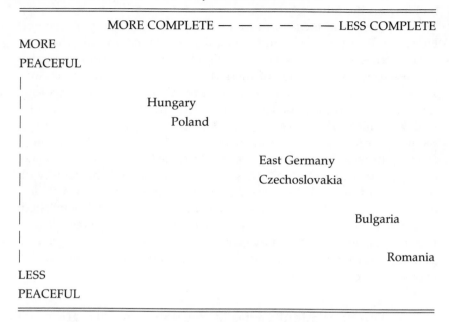

	MORE COMPLETE — — — — — — LESS COMPLETE
MORE PEACEFUL	
	Hungary
	Poland
	East Germany
	Czechoslovakia
	Bulgaria
	Romania
LESS PEACEFUL	

documented criteria. It is usually agreed that (a) the relative peaceful-ness of the popular revolutions, and (b) the completeness of the regime transformations, are features which characterize the outcomes as a whole. They are also among the most remarkable features of the 1989 revolutions. Nevertheless, a comparison between the cases must recognize that they occupy different spaces on a continuum from more to less peaceful, and from more to less complete. It also emerges that there is a strong positive correlation between these characteristics, with the more peaceful transitions coinciding with the more complete regime transformations. Thus the six cases may be distinguished, and provisionally grouped into three categories (see table 6.1).

On this scale, "more peaceful ... less peaceful" takes into account the violence of repression and intimidation, as well as the use of armed force by the state authorities and, in Romania at least, by some demon-strators. Similarly, "more complete ... less complete," referring to the system transformation, takes transformation of political culture into account, as well as the more obvious transition from unlegitimated single-party satellite state to sovereign multi-party parliamentary democracy. Thus the East German case does not qualify as the most complete – though some would argue that since the East German state has passed away altogether and been replaced by the West German state, this transformation is the most complete imaginable. The problem is that East Germans have not had time or opportunity to change their political culture from within. This is now showing up more clearly in the differentiated voting patterns of the two German populations in the 1994 elections, and in the resurgence of the former communist party at the polls.

Hungary and Poland experienced less violent confrontation between citizens and state during the period of transition, and achieved a more complete transformation of their domestic political structures than any of the other countries. Other factors, of course, distinguish them from the remaining four, not least the length of time their gradual transformations had been openly and legally under public discussion. There are also some differences between Polish and Hungarian parliamentary normalization: the Polish compromise is commonly considered to be slightly less modernized as yet than the Hungarian one.[7] Nevertheless, these two countries undoubtedly form a distinct group by comparison with the other four.

Czechoslovakia and East Germany, though they epitomized the "velvet revolutions" which made the events of 1989 so exceptional, had nevertheless experienced violent repression right up until the final collapse. Thus the confrontations with the state in autumn 1989 were still fraught with tensions, and uncertainties about the likelihood of violent crack-down. Also there are questions remaining about the completeness of the political transformation to date. Placing either of these regimes on this scale is problematic, because the transformation process lacks continuity at the level of political institutions. Czechoslovakia has now split into two Republics, and its future federative arrangements are uncertain, while in East Germany the new regime had scarcely emerged before it disappeared in the wider process of German unification. These largely extraneous factors make it difficult to measure how complete a regime transformation might have been within the boundaries of the original system. Beyond the level of political institutions, however, one could point to the continued process of political purging, and to the unresolved problems of the past, which have dogged both Czechoslovak and former East German

---

[7] This is the judgment of László Bruszt and David Stark, "Remaking the Political Field in Hungary: From the Politics of Confrontation to the Politics of Competition," in Ivo Banac, ed., *Eastern Europe in Revolution* (Ithaca, NY: Cornell University Press, 1992).

adaptation to post-communist political cultures. The transformation process could thus be classed as incomplete, at least in terms of political culture, even though the political institutions have been modernized.

Bulgaria and Romania share certain characteristics at the other end of the scale, though it is perhaps more accurate to locate the Bulgarian case somewhere between the East German and Czechoslovak and the Romanian one. Neither the Bulgarian nor the Romanian case is an example of complete transformation of regime by any standards, though there have been limited structural changes, and democratic forms of election in both countries. Moreover, the violence of the Romanian overthrow, and the number of civilian casualties, in that and subsequent clashes, have been unique among the regime changes of the six former Warsaw Pact/Soviet satellite countries. In this respect, Romania stands as the counter-case which may serve to indicate what the significant conditions for the nonviolent transformations of regime in the remaining countries must have been.

The independent variables: civil society development and transnational exchanges

Having made a preliminary classification of the Eastern European countries according to the outcomes of the 1989 events, we need to specify the independent variables to be looked at in order to explain these outcomes. The first, the domestic structure variable, is interpreted here as referring to the degree of civil society development within each country. The second, the transnational variable, refers to the extent of transnational coalition activity between social movements within the different Eastern European countries and comparable social movements in other countries, chiefly in Western Europe.

We should first define our use of the term civil society,[8] bearing in mind the understanding of the actors who popularized the term at this particular historical moment. In a totalitarian context, civil society

---

[8] It has become fashionable in Western commentary to denigrate the term "civil society," partly because of the elasticity of the concept, and partly because it challenges both realist and Marxist orthodoxies. I think it valuable to retain it here, not least because of its particular resonance in Eastern Europe, where it has functioned successfully both as a campaigning tool and as an instrument for analysis. A useful discussion of this problem is to be found in: Gordon White, "Civil Society, Democratization and Development: Clearing the Analytical Ground," *Democratization*, 1, 3 (Autumn 1994), pp. 375–90.

naturally defines itself in opposition to the state. It takes its meaning from being *not of the state*. In the broader context, state/civil society distinctions are not so sharp, but the concept still holds. Civil society exists through self-organized activity, not dependent upon the agency of the state for its initiation and day-to-day management, but on the free association of individuals. It is usually presumed to carry on within the legal framework of the state, or public law, though civil disobedience might cross this boundary. It is invariably defined in opposition to both military power and the use of force, those being the prerogative of the state.[9] Challenges to the state's authority which emanate from civil society are most likely to be legal or cultural ones (as with the American civil rights movement), rather than a direct attempt to seize political power.

Civil society has many different dimensions. These might include some, but not all, levels of political party activity; most pressure-group activity; commercial activity; cultural activity; much social welfare and self-help activity; and the work of voluntary associations, clubs, and charities. The definition can be as wide as all the normal nongovern-mental attributes of liberal pluralist democracy.[10] Our focus is on the political dimension, however, and on the specific meaning of the term for a new wave of social movements in Eastern Europe which in the 1980s saw "civil society" as an appropriate label for their brand of political activism. Put simply, it meant the formation of a women's movement which was not part of the ruling party structure; or the organization of a rock concert which did not have the approval of the party-state; or campaigning against nuclear weapons from outside the officially constituted peace movement. The thrust of this alter-native activity was to provoke party-states, which systematically excluded opposition, to react politically to politics. In a self-conscious and much theorized way, the social movements prepared a hostile political culture for the practice of opposition politics. Western social movements lacked such sharp distinction between state and civil society. Nevertheless, it is worth pointing out the difficulties experi-

---

9 Note, however, recent interest in the darker side of civil society – for example mafias, terrorism, and warlords – which organizes violence in parallel with the state.

10 Tomaz Mastnak, a leading civil society activist, offers one of the more subtle analyses of "the uncritical equation of civil society with democracy, freedom, pluralism" in his essay: "Modernization of Repression," in Vera Gáthy, ed., *State and Civil Society: Relationships In Flux* (Budapest: Ventura Publisher, 1989). He charts the restructuring of "the clash between civil society and the state" into "a clash between the traditional and democratic civil society," and illustrates both the historical validity of the term, and the dangers of taking it at face value.

enced by those Western movements trying to make contact with their counterparts in Eastern Europe during this period – difficulties with established institutions in the West, which led to some similar distinctions being made. Institutions which might otherwise have qualified as "civil society" – political parties, trade unions, and churches for example – frequently fought shy of supporting relatively unknown and unofficial social movement actors. More often than not, it was an unofficial group *within* a church, trade union, or party which took on the function of supporting social movements in the East, while the institutions themselves leaned more towards acceptance of the official communist party structures. This gave rise to conflicts in the West, between new social movements and "established" civil society, which were not unlike the conflicts in the East between new social movements and those reformers who preferred to work through the official party channels.

Civil society contacts between individuals or groups from two or more separate nation-states can be described as transnational coalitions. These would normally have some visibility (though this may sometimes be very low level indeed, like the *samizdat* exchanges between intellectuals in Eastern Europe before they became marketable by Western presses), and the capacity to generate products. Products may be ongoing activities, such as the long-term association of two groups to exchange news or to arrange visits (which was well established between East and West German partner parishes in the Lutheran church). Or they may be one-off events, such as the organization of a conference or speakers' tour, or the writing of a common text (like the *Helsinki Memorandum*[11]). Ideas and concepts are important products in this definition. Specific coalitions may not be durable, or transferable from a single event or issue to a wider context, but their capacity to generate ideas which are picked up by other groups is crucial.

The transnational actors we are looking at in Europe in the late 1970s and throughout the 1980s were a very specific set of social movements.[12] They can be defined as political associations outside the

---

[11] The *Helsinki Memorandum* is the short title given to the document: *Giving Real Life to the Helsinki Accords: A Memorandum, drawn up in common by independent groups and individuals in Eastern and Western Europe*, published by the European Network for East–West Dialogue (Berlin: April 1987). The text of this document was presented, prior to its publication, to the CSCE meeting in Vienna in December 1986.

[12] A list of the social movements active in the coalition should include at least: Charter 77 in Czechoslovakia, FIDESZ (Fiatal Demokraták Szövetsége: the Federation of Young

political apparatus of the state and, in the Western European countries, outside the established process of interest-group formation. In general, they can be classified as peace movements, human rights movements, green movements, democratic movements, movements within trade unions, movements within political parties, movements within churches, women's movements, and youth movements. All of the active groups were free associations of individuals organizing themselves around a political idea or statement of principle. Their programs varied greatly, but always combined elements from a common cluster of concepts which included peace, human rights, democracy, dealignment from the bloc system, environmental responsibility, and active citizenship. The *ad hoc* coalition these transnational actors had formed by the early 1980s had no name or juridical status, but can best be described as a "Peace and Human Rights Trans-National Coalition" (PHR-TNC). In effect, the PHR-TNC was a loose federation of smaller coalitions, many of which, like Interkerkelijk Vredesberaad (IKV: Dutch Inter-Church Peace Council)[13] in the Netherlands or European Nuclear Disarmament (END)[14] in Britain, had greater internal coherence and constitutional validity than the PHR-TNC itself. Indeed, the PHR-TNC owed its organizational existence to a small number of key coordinating groups such as these.

From an organizational perspective, these transnational actors formed networks. There was no single organization or centre of decision-making, but many different local, national, and international organizations, interconnecting with each other, on a voluntary basis. Cooperation was non-obligatory and non-hierarchical, but took place consistently over a period of several years. The networks were not stable. Degrees of affiliation, and relationships within the network,

Democrats) in Hungary, WiP (Wolnosc i Pokoj: Freedom and Peace) in Poland, *Schwerter zu Pflugscharen* and the congregations of the Evangelische Kirche in East Germany, the West German Green Party, the Dutch Interkerkelijk Vredesberaad (IKV: Inter-Church Peace Council), and all the affiliates of END (European Nuclear Disarmament) in Western Europe. A comprehensive history of these movements has yet to be written. But see: Thomas Rochon, *The Politics of the Peace Movement in Western Europe* (Princeton, NJ: Princeton University Press, 1988); James Hinton, *Protests and Visions: Peace Politics in 20th Century Britain* (London: Hutchinson, 1989); Jean-François Gribinski, *La Contestation anti-missiles des années quatre-vingt: une contestation pacifiste?*, Thèse pour le Doctorat de l'Université Paris II, December 1992.

13 The IKV was formed in 1966 as an ecumenical cooperative of nine denominations, including Protestants, Catholics, and Quakers.

14 END (European Nuclear Disarmament) was the London-based coordinating group formed with the END Appeal in 1980. It remained distinct from the END convention process, in which it was one of many participants, and from the much larger CND (the Campaign for Nuclear Disarmament) in Britain.

were changing all the time. There would always be one or more cores of entrepreneurial energy and coordinating strength, but these also changed over time.[15] If we try to identify the PHR-TNC at any point in its history, we find a large number of extremely heterogeneous associations, each of which has its own *raison d'être*, constituency, and working style.[16] Throughout the 1980s, the number of people concentrating solely on the PHR-TNC and maintaining the transnational exchanges across the East–West divide was fairly small, but they had good connections with a wide social base through their own informal networks.[17]

From an historical perspective, the PHR-TNC came about through the recognition, by wholly independent movements in the East and West of Europe, of the interdependence of their agendas. They came to this understanding by very different routes. In Eastern Europe, social movements were motivated primarily by immediate human rights demands, which had received fresh inspiration from the Helsinki Accords of 1975. Charter 77, the product of a group of Czechoslovak intellectuals (and the name given to their dissident movement), remains a key text[18] in this area:

> Charter 77 is not an organization; it has no rules, permanent bodies or formal membership . . . Like many similar citizen initiatives in various countries, West and East, it seeks to promote the general public interest . . . it wishes to conduct a constructive dialogue with the political and state authorities, particularly by drawing attention to various individual cases where human and civil rights are violated.[19]

---

15 Among the coordinating organizations which exercised core functions in the 1980s were: IPCC (the International Peace Communication and Coordination Centre) from 1981; the END Liaison Committee from 1982; the Network for East–West Dialogue from 1984; and the Helsinki Citizens' Assembly preparatory committee from 1988.

16 These ranged from the well-established organizations of Pax Christi and the International Society of Friends to alternative political parties like the German Greens, academic research institutes, publishing collectives, student organizations, peace camps, and the Jazz Sections of Charter 77 and other East bloc countries.

17 There is the French example of CODENE (Comité pour le désarmement nucléaire en Europe), a tiny umbrella organization, which nevertheless had 23 member groups, including a confessional youth group, the Mouvement Rural de la Jeunesse Chrétienne (MRJC), which had branches (government funded) in every secondary school in rural France.

18 Charter 77 is not so much a single text as a corpus of documents, though the January 1, 1977 *Declaration* is generally understood to be "the" Charter. For a full exposition of the texts and early history of the movement, see H. Gordon Skilling, *Charter 77 and Human Rights in Czechoslovakia* (London: George Allen & Unwin, 1981).

19 Charter 77, *Declaration* (Prague: January 1, 1977).

Charter 77's importance lay not only in the fact that it was representative of civil society initiatives burgeoning throughout Eastern Europe, but also in the fact that the Charter was a milestone in communication between social movements. While it was vigorously suppressed in Czechoslovakia, the text was promptly published in the West German *Frankfurter Allgemeine Zeitung*.[20] Contacts rapidly ensued with Komitat Obrony Robotników (Committee for the Defense of the Workers: KOR)[21] in Poland, and later with other East and West bloc movements.

In Western Europe, where even Charter 77 remained little known for several years, the social movements were motivated first and foremost by the crisis in strategic thinking which led NATO to its December 1979 decision on the deployment of US Cruise and Pershing missiles in Europe.[22] There was a widespread public perception that this strategy could not enhance the security of Europeans. Thus enormous popular pressure was brought to bear for the removal of this class of nuclear weapon – but not before social movement intellectuals had arrived at the conclusion that "European nuclear disarmament" meant including Eastern Europe too, and that in order to include Eastern Europeans they would have to have the right to speak as citizens in their own countries. This analysis appeared most cogently in the END Appeal[23] of April 1980, which can be seen as a key text in the history of the Western movement:

> We must act together to free the entire territory of Europe, from Poland to Portugal, from nuclear weapons . . . At the same time, we must defend and extend the right of all citizens, East or West, to take part in this common movement and to engage in every kind of exchange . . . exchanges between universities, churches, women's organizations, trade unions, youth organizations, professional groups and individuals.[24]

[20] January 7, 1977.

[21] KOR, a forerunner of Solidarnosc, published a number of joint documents with Charter 77, and a Czechoslovak–Polish meeting was held in September 1978.

[22] On the NATO 1979 decision, see Fred Halliday, *The Making of the Second Cold War* (London: Verso, 1983); Mary Kaldor, *The Imaginary War: Understanding the East–West Conflict* (Oxford: Basil Blackwell, 1990); E.P. Thompson, *Zero Option* (London: Merlin Press, 1982).

[23] The END Appeal was drawn up by a group of British intellectuals, and signed by counterparts in all of Western Europe. A few personal friends from East bloc countries were signatories, but most of the contacts were made subsequently.

[24] "*Appeal for European Nuclear Disarmament* launched on 28 April 1980," reprinted in E.P. Thompson and Dan Smith, eds., *Protest and Survive* (Harmondsworth: Penguin Books, 1980), pp. 223–26.

The consciously transnational strategy outlined here met with written responses from Charter 77, and from social movements in Hungary, Poland, and East Germany. From then on, the PHR-TNC existed. Over the following few years, the coalition's common "beyond the blocs" agenda, with its vision of a new united Europe, and dual theme of demilitarization and democratization, was elaborated in just such exchanges as had been envisaged in the END Appeal.[25]

The relationship between this "détente from below" and the persistence, in Europe at least, of policies of "détente from above" is paradoxical. Many of the contacts could not have been made without some relaxation of travel procedures agreed between East and West authorities. This was particularly true for the East–West German border, where the incremental benefits of the West German government's *Ostpolitik* continued to be reaped despite the tensions of renewed superpower confrontation. At the same time, many of the specific contacts which can be defined as social movement coalitions were made in spite of détente's failure rather than because of its success. Precisely those individuals likely to be invited by the coalitions to cross East–West borders were also the most likely to remain restricted in their freedom to travel. Easterners were systematically refused visas. Westerners with political contacts frequently found themselves turned back at the border, or placed under arrest. For these reasons, many of the most significant contacts were not meetings at all, but invitations, "empty chairs", and the exchange of ideas in *samizdat*.[26]

The relationship between the official Helsinki process and the so-called "Helsinki" groups[27] of civil rights campaigners in Eastern Europe is likewise paradoxical. The signing of the Helsinki Final Act in 1975 had been interpreted in many circles as an accommodation between East and West, entailing the abandonment of Eastern Europe, and confirming that the Yalta division of Europe would never be

[25] Jacques Rupnik charts the progression of this dialogue through other major documents – the Prague Appeal (1985), the *Helsinki Memorandum* (1986) – in Jacques Rupnik, "Central Europe or Mitteleuropa?," *Daedalus*, 119, 1 (Winter 1990), pp. 249–78. See also Jacques Rupnik, *The Other Europe* (London: Weidenfeld & Nicolson, 1989).

[26] "Empty chairs" were symbolically displayed at the Berlin (1983) and Perugia (1984) conferences when invited East bloc speakers were unable to attend; *samizdat* correspondence continued, however, and resulted in the Prague Appeal of 1985.

[27] Details of unofficial Helsinki monitoring groups can be found in Victor-Yves Ghebali, *La diplomatie de la détente: la CSCE, d'Helsinki à Vienne (1973–1989)* (Brussels: Etablissements Emile Bruylant, 1989), pp. 91–97; and Catherine Fitzpatrick, *From Below: Independent Peace and Environmental Movements in Eastern Europe and the USSR*, A Helsinki Watch Report, October 1987.

challenged "from above".[28] Alternative interpretations held that the Helsinki agreement contained the seeds of the destruction of the Soviet system, either because of the cooperative nature of the process set in train by Helsinki, or because of the normative effect of human rights provisions written into the Final Act.[29] The dissident movements in Eastern Europe used the Helsinki Final Act to legitimize their human rights demands. They also realized that without such movements, working to change the system "from below", the Helsinki Act was a dead letter. Significantly, one of the most important texts produced by the PHR-TNC in Europe during the 1980s was the *Helsinki Memorandum* of 1986, subtitled "Giving Real Life to the Helsinki Accords":

> Détente policy, to achieve permanent results, must have a firm basis not only on the governmental level, but within societies. Grass roots contacts and common activities between groups and individuals across frontiers can dissolve the structure of Cold War . . . Official détente policy should create a framework which encourages the process of "détente from below."[30]

"Détente from below" thus refers to two distinct but interlocking areas of new thinking. First, the bloc system of a divided Europe needed to be transformed before a number of divergent domestic goals could be achieved. Second, the system change could only be brought about by those same forces which were seeking social change. Governments, preferring stability, would naturally be resistant to both kinds of change. In other words, politically active citizens must be the agents of system transformation.

Social movements emerged independently in Eastern Europe in opposition to the repressive single-party state apparatuses identified

---

[28] George Ball, "Capitulation at Helsinki," *The Atlantic Quarterly*, 13, 3 (Autumn 1973), pp. 286–88; Patrick Wajsman, *L'Illusion de la détente* (Paris: Presses universitaires françaises, 1977); János Kis, "The Yalta Problem in the Mid-Eighties," *East European Reporter*, 1, 2 (1985), pp. 2–7; Milan, Šimečka "From Class Obsessions to Dialogue: Détente and the Changing Political Culture of Eastern Europe," in Mary Kaldor, Gerard Holden, and Richard Falk, eds., *The New Détente: Rethinking East–West Relations* (London: Verso, 1989), pp. 351–68.

[29] Ghebali, *La diplomatie de la détente*, p. 121, refers to the later Vienna provisions in particular as *modernes trompettes de Jericho* consolidating the collapse of the Eastern conception of the state. As a further illustration of this point, a story told to me by Russian negotiators who had been in Geneva in the early 1970s revealed rivalry between those engaged on the SALT (Strategic Arms Limitation Treaty) agreements claiming they would "end the arms race" and those engaged on the Helsinki agreements claiming they would "change the Soviet Union."

[30] *Helsinki Memorandum*, p. 4.

variously with communism, bureaucracy, and official elites. Inner migration into privacy has long been recognized as an attractive option in a totalitarian society. But a shared migration away from official politics and into parallel political structures based on emerging civil societies became a viable alternative from the late 1970s.[31] The new political culture grew in different national soils: political party formation in Hungary, trade unions in Poland, Protestant churches in East Germany, artists and intellectuals in Czechoslovakia. Peace movements and green politics in Western Europe also thought in terms of parallel institutions, creating "lateral" affinity groups of women, churches, lawyers, doctors, teachers, scientists, and musicians to share specialized knowledge and create communities with a measure of authority to challenge individual states on specific issues.[32]

These new social movements in both East and West were politically independent, not controlled by ideology or bureaucracy, and therefore "unofficial." Other features they tended to have in common were as follows: they communicated transnationally (often indirectly, *samizdat*-style); they entered into dialogue with comparable groups (often involving conflict and disagreement); they sought multiple bilateral contacts; and they challenged both their own and other governments. All sought to be a valid interlocutor of other groups in an international context, thereby acquiring legitimacy as actors on the international scene. This was crucial for the East bloc groups, since it invariably conferred some measure of legitimacy on their activities in a less penetrable domestic situation. Tactics like this had a tangible public relations effect, which meant that groups might win recognition, first through mutual attention and support, and then through media attention, higher profile activity, and increased popular support. Such tactics also had a sharp political effect, bringing independent social movements in the East bloc into fierce competition with the ruling communist party bureaucracies. Because the authori-

31 Václav Benda's notion of "parallel *polis*," Elemér Hankiss's "second society," and Adam Michnik's living "as if" (an idea which was reflected in the END Appeal: "We must commence to act *as if* a united, neutral and pacific Europe already exists") capture this transformation in political culture. See: Václav Benda, "The Parallel Polis," in H. Gordon Skilling and Paul Wilson, eds., *Civic Freedom in Central Europe: Voices from Czechoslovakia* (Basingstoke: Macmillan 1991), pp. 35–41; Elemér Hankiss, *East European Alternatives* (Oxford: Clarendon Press, 1990), chapter 3, "The Second Society, 1965–1985," pp. 82–111; and Adam Michnik, *Letters from Prison and Other Essays* (Berkeley, CA: University of California Press, 1985).

32 There are similarities here with the "epistemic communities" identified as international actors, in Peter M. Haas, ed., *Knowledge, Power, and International Policy Coordination*, special issue of *International Organization*, 46, 1 (Winter 1992).

ties had their own "peace committees," churches liaison groups, women's organizations, youth activities, ecological projects, and "citizens' initiatives," they therefore had their own representatives ready to discourse with Western counterparts on any issue. When these were passed over in favour of independents, who were beyond the control of party ideology and bureaucracy, it sent shock waves into the upper reaches of the party structures.[33]

Conferences which worked to bring together Eastern and Western Europeans in the same forum provided a locus for the development of valid interlocutor tactics in the 1980s. One such conference series was the annual END Convention process, launched in 1982,[34] which hosted hundreds of delegates each year in different European cities. The conferences themselves were almost secondary to their preparation. Annual conference preparation, lasting from the close of one event to the beginning of the next, was a continuous process of challenge. The issues that business focused on concerned the humdrum mechanics of conference organization: invitations, keynote speakers, themes, plenary platforms, membership, and travel. But all of these issues were politically charged. They generated debate within the movements about whom to select, and constant interchange between the organizers and officialdom about freedom of movement between countries.[35]

The nub of the problem was who were to be the valid interlocutors in Eastern Europe. Western organizers had to make plans for invitations, to issue invitations, and to follow through the practical arrangements for those invitations. Officially approved invitees were always available, for example through the official peace committees of the East bloc countries, anxious to confirm their own legitimacy as the valid interlocutors of Western peace movements. But the people the Westerners chose to invite as spokespersons of the civil societies in Eastern

---

[33] The amount of energy devoted to this competition by the bureaucracies has been borne out by the recent revelations of secret police files in East Germany, for example: Armin Mitter and Stefan Wolle, eds., *"Ich liebe euch doch alle!" Befehle und Lageberichte des MfS, Januar–November 1989* (Berlin: BasisDruck, 1990).

[34] Originally an offshoot of the END Appeal, the END Convention process took on a life of its own from its first international conference in Brussels in 1982. Its coordinating body, the END Liaison Committee, became one of the organizational cores of the PHR-TNC. Subsequent conventions were: Berlin 1983; Perugia 1984; Amsterdam 1985; Paris (Evry) 1986; Coventry 1987; Lund 1988; Vitoria 1989; Helsinki-Tallinn 1990; Moscow 1991; and, finally, Brussels 1992.

[35] Officials at the East German Embassy in London, for example, came to refer to the Coventry Convention as a watershed – "before" or "after" Coventry – in their dealings with the British public.

Europe were more often than not refused passports or visas to travel from the East. Westerners, on the other hand, who protested to the Eastern European regimes, risked having their own freedom of movement to travel in Eastern Europe curtailed. As a result, there were endless negotiations with officials, regular embassy contacts, frequent remonstrations and complaints.

Thus opposition groups whose very existence was denied at home (by refusing them legal registration, for example) gained legitimacy through their contacts with the outside world. Being heard, and listened to, by interlocutors in other countries ensured that the authorities at least took note of what they said. Therefore attaining the status of valid interlocutor in a transnational context made a difference domestically for many dissident groups. Sometimes this meant moral or material support, for example of underground presses and distribution systems.[36] Often dissidents were protected from harassment by the mere fact of being well known outside their own countries. Occasionally the Western movements mobilized support for specific groups or individuals:

> If Charter 77's spokespersons may not speak, without loss of freedom, to the Western peace movement, then I must make plain my view that our movement should break off any relations with Czech officialdom – including the official "Peace Committee" – and should certainly boycott their much advertized "Peace Assembly" in Prague next June. At the least, let us exact from them one small "human right" as the price of any attendance: let them release Ladislav Lis, and give to him the right to speak from the podium.[37]

Thus E. P. Thompson, in February 1983, demonstrated the strength of the transnational coalition to refuse cooperation with regimes and recognize the legitimacy of civil society representatives over the heads of their established governments. We have learned since how seriously this threat was taken by the regimes in question. For the civil societies, the less public space they had at home to exchange and elaborate ideas, the more important the transnational dialogue became. Participants in the dialogue remarked that they were primarily engaged in changing a belief system. The division of Europe was predicated on

[36] The Palach Press in London, for example, worked both ways, publishing underground material from the East bloc in the West, and redistributing it, with evidence of Western interest, throughout the East bloc countries.

[37] E.P. Thompson, "Letter to Prague [Václav Racek]", February 1983, reprinted in Jan Kavan and Zdena Tomin, eds., *Voices from Prague: Documents on Czechoslovakia and the Peace Movement* (London: Palach Press, 1983).

the belief that people could be kept from communicating by a wall, fence, or iron curtain. To achieve communication therefore was to begin to deconstruct those barriers, and transnational exchanges were seen both as the fulfilment of an aim and as an instrument of change.

On the first score, there is ample proof. The goal of communication was achieved through the engagement of independent political actors in an East–West dialogue. There were extensive contacts in the 1980s between social movements developing around peace and human rights issues in the Western European countries and a range of dissident and opposition groups in Eastern Europe.[38] The question is, to what extent the convergence between these new social movements in Western Europe and the emerging civil societies of Eastern Europe contributed towards the particular forms of transition which occurred in 1989. Through what mechanisms, and with what effect, did the transnational coalitions operate as instruments of change?

Our hypothesis can be summarized as follows. The transnational contacts were refracted by the level of civil society development in each of the Eastern European countries. Outcomes – such as the speed and extent of regime transformation, as well as the peacefulness of the transition – were therefore dependent on the varying state/civil society relationships in the domestic structures of those countries. We can further argue that the degree to which transnational contacts interacted with the development of independent civil societies in the East bloc countries had a significant impact on the precise form which the transition took in different countries. Where the six countries stand in relation to these variables is shown in table 6.2.

Situating the Eastern European countries on this grid is instructive. Hungary and Poland are again grouped together as the countries which combine a high degree of civil society activity and a high degree of transnational coalition activity, both of which are apparent well before 1989. Bulgaria and Romania, at least up until 1989, exhibit very low degrees of civil society development and transnational coalition making. None of the countries examined shows signs of high degrees of civil society development combined with lack of transnational coalition activity. But the cases of East Germany and Czechoslovakia do show a very unusual combination. Both show a very low development of civil society activity, but correspondingly high levels of trans-

---

[38] The most useful empirical work to date has been provided by Vladimir Tismaneanu, ed., *In Search of Civil Society: Independent Peace Movements in the Soviet Bloc* (London: Routledge, 1990).

Table 6.2 *Civil society and transnational coalitions*

Civil society development / Transnational coalition activity	HIGH	LOW
HIGH	Hungary Poland	East Germany Czechoslovakia
LOW		Bulgaria Romania

national coalition making. It is this peculiarity which forms the basis of our hypothesis that the social movements and their capacity to form transnational coalitions made a significant difference, particularly in situations where the civil societies were less developed.

In the following section, this hypothesis will be evaluated with regard to three Eastern European countries, one from each of the three groups in table 6.2. By comparing variations between these cases, it should be possible to give an accurate assessment of the effect of the transnational coalition variable. In doing so, we may come closer to providing insights into the mechanics of change in international political organization.

Mechanics of change: domestic variations

As we have seen from our earlier classifications, Hungary, East Germany, and Romania represent three quite different types of regime transition, despite much that they had in common in the 1989 events. Broadly speaking, Poland fits the Hungarian, Czechoslovakia the East German, and Bulgaria the Romanian model. Hungary and Poland belong to the negotiated, social contract mould, with independent social movements preparing themselves over a long period for the transfer of the state apparatus into their own (and other) hands. East Germany and Czechoslovakia both experienced sudden regime collapse and an extremely precarious velvet revolution, coming after some of the most severe repression of the decade. Romania and Bulgaria share some characteristics regarding the manner in which power was transferred, though they diverge on other scores. Both could be classified as *coups* rather than revolutions, and both are examples of incomplete regime transformation. The Romanian case is a particularly pure example of a regime collapse which was both catastrophic and arrested.

The following country by country accounts take the outcomes as given. They are not intended to be histories of the events, or causal accounts, but will examine in greater detail our earlier assertions as to the level of civil society and transnational activity in these three countries.

Hungary

The domestic structure of Hungary in the 1980s may be characterized as an already seriously weakened state,[39] faced with a sustained but low-key challenge from an active and relatively broad-based civil society. The regime had gradually grown quite distant from Moscow in its national policy-making, and the Hungarian Communist Party aimed actively at reforming itself from within. This ultimately led to a negotiated transition to democracy between the state apparatus and civil society.

With respect to civil society, we find a rich associative life already in the 1980s among professionals, intellectuals, business people, and the media, early evidence of transnational economic ventures, and concerted pressure from private and public spheres for improved European Community status.[40] The new thinking of the political clubs and social movements penetrated the party and trade-union structures from the early 1980s. Social movements involved in the PHR-TNC assumed important "dissident minority" positions within the new structures. While this activity enjoyed high visibility in the West, the coincidence of Western European and Eastern European dissident programs was only partial (the Hungarian movements were more attracted to democratic competition than demilitarization, for example), and "official" transnational contacts (political parties, unions, businesses, bureaucrats) predominated.

It is important, in the Hungarian example, to note the secondary role of this particular coalition (the PHR-TNC) in a context where civil

---

[39] Bruszt and Stark (in Banac, *Eastern Europe in Revolution*, pp. 14–15) argue against the view of "strong states" in Eastern Europe. I prefer to distinguish between the "weakened" states of Hungary and Poland, and the remaining "brittle but resistant" states whose collapse followed a catastrophe model.

[40] See John Pinder, *The European Community and Eastern Europe* (London: Pinter Publishers, 1991); and Judy Batt, *East Central Europe from Reform to Transformation* (London: Pinter Publishers, 1991).

society initiatives and transnational contacts were flourishing in all directions and in every walk of life. Political party formation and early moves towards economic modernization were clearly perceived as the most urgent areas by Hungarian reformers. In other words, the reforms sweeping ahead towards a fully fledged regime transformation did not need the input of the PHR-TNC whose impact we are assessing.

It would be reasonable to concede that it was the broader swathe of TNCs which enabled the PHR-TNC to prosper in Hungary. Because of the more liberal environment, it was easier to travel. Public meetings, even large and overtly political ones, were much less likely to be harassed. The 1980s saw the unimpeded mushrooming of political clubs, many of which were interested in the peace and human rights agenda.[41] Budapest became one of the easiest venues in Eastern Europe in which to organize events and international meetings. Hungarians could relatively easily participate in international events outside Hungary, compared with other Eastern European nationals. The independent Hungarian peace movement started by Ferenc Köszegi was one of the first to emerge from Eastern Europe.[42] Progress here was not smooth, however, and followed a pattern that recurred elsewhere in Hungarian politics. Mihaly Vajda's insider account of "enlightened absolutism"[43] conveys the problem of self-censorship and co-optation in Hungarian political life, which is precisely what happened to Köszegi's independent peace group.[44] That is, civil society initiatives were permitted, but at a price. And the price was compromise, forsaking the radical for the reform option.

In sum, the PHR-TNC seems to have been one element in a much wider transformation of Hungarian political culture, in which the state and civil society gradually agreed a framework for political reform

---

[41] Ferenc Miszlivetz, "Emerging Grassroots Movements in Eastern Europe: Toward a Civil Society?" in Vera Gáthy, ed., *State and Civil Society: Relationships In Flux* (Budapest: Ventura Publisher, 1989).

[42] Ferenc Köszegi and E.P. Thompson, *The New Hungarian Peace Movement* (London: Merlin Press, 1982).

[43] Mihaly Vajda, "The Crisis of the System in Eastern Europe and the Attitude of Hungarian Intellectuals," in Mihaly Vajda, *The State and Socialism* (New York: St. Martin's Press, 1981), pp. 123–31.

[44] The first attempt at an independent peace group was co-opted by the official Hungarian Peace Council. Interestingly, this Peace Council was also the first of the communist peace committees to apply for membership of the *un*official PHR-TNC, through the END Liaison Committee. It was also the first to be accepted, though the two events were separated by many years, and made up a sub-plot of the drama about who was to be the valid interlocutor for the coalition in the case of Hungary.

which re-legitimized and changed the state in the direction of liberal democracy.

Does that mean that the PHR movements and their TNCs were purely epiphenomenal in Hungary? Not entirely, since there were both domestic and transnational effects. Two important effects can be traced in Hungary itself. First, the PHR-TNC acted as a catalyst. In line with Vajda's analysis (that it was difficult even for intellectuals "to abandon the compromise and to criticize the basic power structure as well"), it appears that Hungarian political culture required a catalyst if it was to go beyond the likely compromise with reform communism which was on offer by mid-1988. That catalyst was certainly connected with the PHR-TNC. Bruszt and Stark point to key elements in the Hungarian negotiations from 1988 to 1989, elements which turned the tide in favour of resisting "political reforms of a compromised character that would have institutionalized some form of power sharing without questioning many of the basic prerogatives of the Communist Party in the political system."[45] FIDESZ (Fiatal Demokraták Szövetsége: Federation of Young Democrats) was one of the key elements in their view, and the Danube movement, which began as a single-issue environmental campaign against the Hungarian–Czechoslovak–Austrian dam project, was another. Garton Ash's eyewitness account of what he deems the turning point of the political debate also cites FIDESZ in the leading role.[46] But both FIDESZ and the Danube movement had been key participants in the PHR-TNC. FIDESZ in particular, though it was formally constituted only in March 1988, was rooted in the 1980s student politics of independent peace movements and transnational contacts.[47]

Second, the PHR-TNC program has survived in FIDESZ as part of democratic Hungary.[48] Without being an essential factor in the transition, it is now a substantial minority element of Hungarian party politics. FIDESZ, through its electoral success, ensures the continuity of the political program. Thus the domestic impact of the PHR-TNC was as a ginger group. That is, it spurred the new political forces into

---

[45] Banac, *Eastern Europe in Revolution*, p. 21.

[46] Timothy Garton Ash, "Budapest: the Last Funeral," in *We The People* (Cambridge: Granta Books, 1990).

[47] For a detailed account of these connections see: Miklós Haraszti, "The Beginnings of Civil Society: The Independent Peace Movement and the Danube Movement in Hungary," in Vladimir Tismaneanu, ed., *In Search of Civil Society* (London: Routledge, 1990), pp. 71–87.

[48] I am indebted to conversations with Julianna Matrai and Ferenc Miszlivetz for many insights into this process.

resisting compromises with the old structures, and therefore helped to ensure the completeness of the regime transformation process, while settling itself for a minority oppositional role.

But there are also two important effects outside Hungary. They can only be understood in relation to the networking function of the TNCs. First, the fact that the PHR-TNC flourished in Hungary, although secondary to the major party-political developments there, enabled elements of the TNCs in other parts of Eastern Europe to communicate more effectively. Meetings which were impossible in either West or other East bloc countries could often be held in Hungary, and the networks made full use of that. When the entire preparatory committee of the Helsinki Citizens' Assembly was arrested in Prague in June 1988, it reconvened in Budapest, and continued to plan its major international event in Prague. Second, there is the very specific transnational connection with the Hungarian community in Transylvania, to which we shall return when we come to the case of Romania. Here, especially, the Hungarian capacity to provide social movement rather than state support proved crucial.

Finally, we should bear in mind the important role of intellectuals in the transnational coalition building, and the major input of Hungarian ideas into that process. Konrad's "antipolitics,"[49] for example, had enormous resonance for social movements which were struggling to understand their own role as political actors. It gave a common theoretical thread to East and West experiences. At grassroots level, Hungarian members of the PHR-TNC played key roles in advancing the ideas of the coalition's core organizations. They were prime movers in persuading the END Convention to give voice to independents from the East, and in setting up the more focused East–West Dialogue Group as one of the coordinating bodies of the coalition in 1984. Later they promoted the foundation of the Helsinki Citizens' Assembly which took over this core function.[50]

In conclusion, the PHR-TNC was just one of many successful transnational coalitions in this case, and was probably not essential for the regime change, but played its part alongside others in the gradualist transformation that took place in Hungary. Moreover, the Hungarian

---

49 György Konrad, *Antipolitics* (New York: Harcourt, Brace, Jovanovich Publishers, 1984).
50 For background information on the Helsinki Citizens' Assembly, see: Patricia Chilton and Jiří Dienstbier, "The European Citizens' Assembly," in Robert Elias and Jennifer Turpin, eds., *Rethinking Peace* (Boulder, CO: Lynne Rienner Publishers, 1994), pp. 290–96.

PHR-TNC connection probably had its greatest impact outside the country, by influencing events in Czechoslovakia, East Germany, and Romania, the less penetrable states. The revolutions in these countries in the autumn of 1989 then had a feedback effect on the Hungarian transformation process.

East Germany

East Germany was characterized by a strong state and military and security apparatus, and by strict party discipline. Repressive measures against dissidents actually increased between 1987 and 1989, the Gorbachev reform years. But the state's resistance to reform, together with its dependence on Moscow for continued legitimation, led to a more complete collapse eventually. It also led to the passage of new people, including some of the social movement elements, into positions of power. However, this interim period was very brief. Indeed, it only lasted a few months in East Germany, compared with Czechoslovakia, where a similar pattern put the social movements into power for a more substantial period.

During the 1980s we can observe an unevenly emerging civil society, strong and well-organized only in the very limited sphere of the Protestant churches. Except for the final stages, this activity had a low visibility in the Western media. However, the East German dissident groups were well connected transnationally to churches, peace groups, and green parties, particularly in West Germany. Above all, we have evidence of a significant penetration of official structures by some of the ideas coming from below, in time to persuade the authorities to avoid a violent solution in 1989.

The most important thing to remember about the German case is how incredible it was to most observers at the time that such a massive challenge should be mounted against the repressive state apparatus, and achieve a revolution without bloodshed. It was in this connection that the transnational coalition between East German peace and human rights activists and their West European counterparts made a difference.

There were multiple links between the PHR-TNC and those domestic political forces mobilizing mass demonstrations against the East German government in 1989. In East Germany, as in Czechoslovakia, they emerged over many years. The opposition groups in Berlin and Leipzig (New Forum, Democratic Awakening, Democracy Now), like the Civic Forum in Prague, did not spring fully formed from the street demonstrations of 1989. They had been growing for more than a decade. Though they had been invisible to most observers, and had not called themselves a political party, or given themselves a name, they were "people who know and trust each other": people like Rainer Eppelmann, the Lutheran pastor who became minister for disarmament and defence in the first (and last) democratically elected East German government (and later a member of the German Bundestag for the Christian Democratic Party), Bärbel Bohley of the group Women for Peace, Gerd and Ulrike Poppe, of the Peace and Human Rights group. They, and others like them, had long worked with people they knew and trusted also in the West. Like the Charter 77 signatories in Czechoslovakia, they were fully integrated in the networking process we have described above. Silenced at home, they made their voices heard in a transnational forum.

This was the single most important function of the transnational coalition: to give people who could not be heard a voice. It is useful to bear this in mind in conjunction with other cross-border communication features, such as the Western, in particular West German, media. Western television was bound to have an impact because most of it was broadcast in the common German language. It certainly informed and motivated. But television did not listen to you. Unless individuals could communicate their critiques and ideas for change, they remained powerless to proceed to collective action.

To understand the German situation and the political climate in which the transnational contacts emerged during the early 1980s, one has to bear in mind the larger political context of US–Soviet relations.[51] The two Germanies were equally exposed to American and Soviet (nuclear) weapons facing each other across the inner-German border. In both countries, the social movements reacted similarly to the deployment of Intermediate-Range Nuclear Forces (INF). Peace movements in West Germany and their Eastern counterparts in the new independent peace groups and church initiatives felt equally threatened by the buildup. They also concurred in the assessment that there was a strategic corollary of the two superpowers which affected Central Europe. Both movements were convinced that, one day, the superpowers would fight a nuclear war on German soil. This conviction affected other European deployment countries, and was the basis

[51] See Thomas Risse-Kappen, *The Zero Option: INF, West Germany, and Arms Control* (Boulder, CO: Westview Press, 1988).

of the social movements' not merely moral but strategic response to the security question in the 1980s. The INF "Euromissile" crisis of 1979 therefore had a comparable impact on the two Germanies and both responded by producing social movements to protest against what they perceived as their allotted role in the strategy of the superpowers.

This commonality of cause was extremely important in stimulating transnational contacts. It provided a common ground for the social movements in both countries to understand each other.[52] However, it was every bit as important that the East German social movements developed autonomously, independently from the state institutions, and, in addition, independently from Western interference. Easterners were as sensitive to the charge of being "steered" by the West, as Westerners were to smears about being "manipulated" by the Kremlin. A diary entry for April 26, 1981, rings far more true than the conspiracy-theory fabrications on both sides. Following a news report on NATO doctrines, a small group of East German friends "talk into the night. A Utopian assembly. I picture hundreds, thousands, millions of such assemblies all across our continent."[53] This public concern found a protected space for the development of protest movements within the church. One of the most important texts of the PHR-TNC canon, the 1982 Berlin Appeal, emanated from the parish of Rainer Eppelmann. Robert Havermann, his co-author, then wrote a letter to the Western peace movements, which got through the Iron Curtain and constituted one of the first concrete proofs in the West that there were autonomous peace movements in the East.[54] It vindicated the strategy of the Western peace movements, as outlined in the END Appeal of 1980, to look for coalition partners in the East – similarly to the letters which found their way from Czechoslovakia to Berlin in

[52] The German case was unusual in having a peace movement orientation. Most of the Eastern European movements were primarily concerned with human rights, and approached peace issues with caution, since "peace" was also the slogan of the Communist regimes. See: Václav Havel, "Anatomy of a Reticence," intended for the Peace Congress in Amsterdam, in lieu of personal participation, and simultaneously for the international collection on European identity being prepared by Suhrkamp Verlag, *samizdat* translation by E. Kohak (Prague: April 1985).

[53] Christa Wolf, "Conditions of a Narrative," in *Cassandra: A Novel and Four Essays* (New York: Farrar, Straus & Giroux, 1984), p. 253. The reliability of this witness remains unaffected (indeed may be enhanced!) following allegations concerning Wolf's status as a Stasi informer.

[54] For texts, and further details, see John Sandford, *The Sword and the Ploughshare: Autonomous Peace Initiatives in East Germany* (London: Merlin Press, 1983); and Roger Woods, *Opposition in the GDR under Honecker, 1971–85: An Introduction and Documentation* (London: Macmillan, 1986).

213

1983 (from Jiří Dienstbier), and to Amsterdam in 1985 (from Václav Havel).

Reports of the END Appeal circulating at Kirchentag festivals held by the Evangelische Kirche in the summer of 1980 underscore the importance of the Protestant church for the transnational East–West dialogue. There were thousands of officially tolerated links at grass-roots level between the parishes in the two halves of Germany which had long provided financial as well as spiritual support to church groups in East Germany. Communication and travel were easier if people were ostensibly on church business. This was a lifeline to the new social movements. The peace movement TNC survived by "piggybacking" on the churches' TNC. Other groups were not organizationally cut off, either, given the networking methods employed. The women's groups, green groups, jazz groups, and others interconnected with the peace and human rights groups, and created confusing organizational structures which baffled the secret service monitoring of activities.[55]

For the social movements, there was no incompatibility between the moral and political dimensions of their activity. For the church hierarchy, there were problems. As a legitimized authority within the East German state, one of their functions was to serve as a safety valve, without allowing social protest to spill over and get out of hand. A delicate balance throughout the 1980s was this relationship between the enabling and the controlling effects of the church institution. On the one hand, the rich social implantation of the Protestant church in East Germany offered the new social movements valuable space for what was to become a political project. On the other hand, this project was spiritually and physically contained, within the churches, for the best part of the decade. Only in 1989 did the congregations literally spill out of church premises onto the streets.

Close observers[56] characterize 1989 as starting with a "springtime of new initiatives" in churches, peace groups, and communities. Then later the same ideas were picked up within the official structures themselves despite the resistance to them earlier. A small but significant number of individuals within the official structures were

---

55 Barbara Einhorn, "Where Have All the Women Gone? Women and the Women's Movement in East Central Europe," *Feminist Review* (Winter 1991), pp. 16–36; and Barbara Einhorn, *Cinderella Goes to Market: Citizenship, Gender, and Women's Movements in East Central Europe* (London: Verso, 1993), pp. 206–09.
56 I am particularly indebted here to interviews with Gert Weisskirchen and Paul Oestreicher.

genuinely sympathetic with the attempts they discerned to change the political culture. By late 1989, there was a deep split in the political class in East Germany, and the movement benefitted from it. A strong enough group emerged within the East German ruling party, the Sozialistische Einheitspartei Deutschlands (SED), arguing: "Look, it's impossible to fight these masses in a violent way, because then you'll have a Chinese solution on your hands, and how will you be able to carry that off?" This constituted the breakthrough. Thus, in autumn 1989, there was not only a mass movement longing for regime transformation, but one whose ideas had already penetrated the official state apparatus from below. This made it possible for such an enormous political upheaval to take place without bloodshed. In addition, West German parliamentarians who were involved with East German opposition groups talked to SED representatives. Churchmen who moved between the unofficial transnational coalition of social movements, and the "official" transnational body of the Churches Liaison Committee, followed a similar route towards persuading colleagues to argue against recourse to a Chinese solution in November 1989.

The question is whether all this activity made any difference in the actual collapse of the East German state. Was the German revolution not caused by the destabilizing effect of the mass emigration which started in the summer of 1989, and a state policy of trying to contain the problem by tinkering with the barriers? "The people voting with their feet" was a civil society phenomenon too, but very different from the transnational coalition. Opinion is divided among seasoned observers and historians as to whether the "leavers" or the "stayers" exerted the decisive pressure on the government in the last few months of 1989.[57] In my view, there is no contradiction. Both belong to the dialectic of a civil challenge to authoritarianism. The "leavers" opened up a public space in which the "stayers" could leave the church premises and stage the peaceful revolution. The "stayers" made it safe to leave.[58]

[57] Norman Naimark opts for the leavers, Timothy Garton Ash for the stayers: Norman M. Naimark, "*Ich will hier raus*: Emigration and the Collapse of the German Democratic Republic," in Banac, *Eastern Europe in Revolution*; Timothy Garton Ash, "Berlin: Wall's End," in *We The People*.

[58] Albert O. Hirschman, "Exit, Voice, and the Fate of the German Democratic Republic: An Essay in Conceptual History," *World Politics*, 45, 2, (January 1993), pp. 173–302. Hirschman concurs that in this case "exit (out-migration) and voice (protest demonstrations against the regime) worked in tandem and reinforced each other, achieving jointly the collapse of the regime."

We need to ask the counterfactual question. What might have happened if the PHR-TNC had not existed? There is nothing to suggest that the government would not have used force.[59] It could have hung on to power, and "failed to comprehend" for a considerable time. As in the past, too many would-be leavers might have failed, or been afraid to try. The moral intensity of the East German social movements contributed in no small part to breaking the cycle of fear, but their experience had other practical consequences. Without their long history of resistance to the authorities, supported by counterparts in other European countries, there would probably have been no breakthrough in communication with East German officials and no realistic assessment of the options coming from a significant minority. In addition, there would have been a lack of trust, a lack of organizing skills, and perhaps a lack of confidence in the movements' own political strength, if they had not already built up strong civil society networks.

The social movements in East Germany were effective in three ways. In overcoming fear, because of their moral dimension; in thwarting the security forces, because of their organizational style; and in influencing the decision by the regime not to use force, because of their transnational connections.

Without the social movements, then, it is probable that a full regime transformation would not have take place. A violent confrontation would have been likely, as in Romania. There might have been a partial transformation, as in Romania. But without the rapid buildup of a civil society empowered by its transnational contacts, a complete political transformation to a democratic system (some months ahead of German unification) would not have been possible.

Romania

Romania is the purest example of an extremely strong and repressive state apparatus and a very weak civil society. The state made up for its lack of popular legitimation by playing three contradictory cards: the security guarantees of the Warsaw Pact; the blessing of the West for its eccentric stand on Moscow foreign policy; and an authoritarian–

---

[59] On the contrary, it seems that Honecker's orders were indeed to use force, and that one of the turning points in the events was when Egon Krenz allowed himself to be persuaded by local people to reverse those orders in Leipzig on October 9, 1989. Shortly after this, on October 18, 1989, Honecker resigned, and Krenz succeeded him.

nationalist refusal of Soviet reformist leadership in its domestic policy. The violent overthrow of the regime depended on "traitors" within the party biding their time, and cashing in on the popular uprisings in East Germany and Czechoslovakia to effect a "soft coup" when spontaneous demonstrations started in Romania. This led to yet another system of authoritarian government under new leadership.[60]

Such civil society as existed in Romania lacked organizational bases. Social movements only formed political opposition groups after the 1989 coup. Transnational contacts only developed very late and they were not particularly strong on either the official or unofficial level. Moreover, there was no obvious overlap in the 1980s between the agendas of Romanian and Western dissidents. For example, Romania was no more a recipient of intermediate nuclear missiles in the East bloc than France was in the West (and both Romania and France were notable for their lack of strong independent peace movements). Furthermore, Romanian dissidence faced freakish domestic programs like de-villagification, which had no comparable manifestations in the West.

A key feature in this case was the lack of Romanian participation in the PHR-TNC prior to 1989. There are no Romanian signatories to the *Helsinki Memorandum* of 1986 (and no Bulgarian ones either). The lack of facilities for information and exchange between these countries and the rest of Europe is a direct but only partial explanation of this absence. Security was tight in Czechoslovakia and East Germany as well. Yet there are thirty-four signatures from Czechoslovakia and another forty-four from East Germany attached to this document, in addition to the forty-seven from Hungary and sixty-seven from Poland, which were easier to collect.

Romania is in many ways the counter case, with its marked absence of transnational activity during the 1980s. Of course, signs of an independent civil society were also absent in this case until much more recently. But Romania's major difference from East Germany, for example, is that there was no effective transnational network to penetrate official levels. As a result, even when the extraordinary brittleness of the regime was exposed, it proved more resilient than in the German case to genuine political transformation. The absence of either a well-developed civil society (as in Hungary) or of dissident movements embedded in transnational coalitions (as in East Germany)

---

[60] See Katherine Verdery and Gail Kligman, "Romania after Ceauşescu: Post-Communist Communism?," in Banac, *Eastern Europe in Revolution*.

resulted in the most violent case of regime change in Eastern Europe in 1989.[61]

The one transnational linkage which existed had an ambiguous impact on the events. There were strong links between the Hungarian community of Transylvania, in northwest Romania, and Hungary itself. Through the Hungarian connection, human rights violations reported against the ethnic Hungarian minority had been monitored in the West for some time. As in East Germany, the Protestant church in Transylvania had become the forum to protect, but also to contain, local protest. This protest spilled over into the community, fueled by the authorities' mistreatment of the popular Lutheran pastor, László Tökés. The fact that Tökés was Hungarian, and that the protest started in the Hungarian-dominated town of Timişoara, did not prevent this incident triggering the mass demonstrations of December 1989 in Bucharest. But the Hungarian factor, crucial though it was at a critical moment in time, did not constitute a solid foundation for transnational coalition-building in Romania. In this instance, Romanians adopted the Hungarians' cause as part and parcel of the general discontent with the regime. At the same time, however, there was enormous resentment among ethnic Romanians that they, as a majority, suffered more on balance than the minority Hungarians. Justified or not, this resentment was bound to marginalize over time any transnational coalition based on the Hungarian link alone.[62]

On the other hand, the examples that we have of Romanian dissidents in the 1980s tend to confirm that they had few connections with dissident transnational movements, but were rather courted by "official" representatives of foreign countries. It was the British ambassador, for instance, who sought to contact dissident intellectual Doina Cornea when she was threatened with imprisonment.[63] This kind of contact could be counterproductive, however, given the popular suspicion of foreign conspiracies. President Ceauşescu played on this to the bitter end, blaming the 1989 upheavals in neighboring countries on *"coups d'état* organized with the help of the scum of society with

---

61 Estimates of the number of people killed in the Romanian clashes vary from 64,000 – Prosecutor at the Ceauşescus' "trial," cited in Peter Cipkowski, *Revolution in Eastern Europe* (New York: John Wiley & Sons, Inc., 1991), p. 137 – to a Russian expert's 32! The true figure is probably around one thousand.
62 I am indebted to Iulia Traistaru for many insights on the dynamics of Romanian society.
63 H. Gordon Skilling, *Samizdat and an Independent Society in Central and Eastern Europe* (Basingstoke: Macmillan, 1989).

foreign support".[64] But Romania's intellectuals have traditionally been isolated in this way. The retreat of the bourgeoisie and intelligentsia into the private world, and their rejection (even contempt) of "politics," is a recurring theme among Romanians. Certainly, before 1989 there was no "parallel" world of dissidents and independents to migrate to.

Suspicion of foreigners even among disaffected Romanians was not surprisingly exacerbated by the fact that Ceauşescu himself enjoyed such good relations with the governments of Western countries. The regime's independent course from Moscow was not helpful to a break-through either, because it made the regime very resistant to the reforming trends in the Soviet Union. Moreover, Ceauşescu had a habit of claiming popular legitimacy through this display of independent foreign policy which the East German leader Honecker never had, having been visibly subservient to Moscow for so long. Military independence went along with this, albeit within the Warsaw Pact organization. The lack of Soviet military installations in Romania as compared with other Warsaw Pact countries was perhaps the key factor in isolating Romanian dissidents, by removing a potential common ground with the peace movements from Western Europe. It seems that there was insufficient commonality of cause for the PHR-TNC to function in Romania in the 1980s, or at any rate to overcome all the other barriers to establishing meaningful trans-national links.

The events at the end of 1989 resulted in a takeover by a relatively old guard of "dissident communist" elements within the existing state structure. There was not even a generational change. Adrian Marino describes how the "from below" revolution of December, led primarily by young people, was defeated by a "from above" revolution which aimed at preserving the old system with only a minimum of concess-ions.[65] The outcome was an enlightened authoritarianism compared with Ceauşescu's personal dictatorship, but any more fundamental political transformation was clearly arrested. This was reflected in the polls in May 1990, when the National Salvation Front was democrati-cally elected in Romania's first free elections.

---

64 Report of a Polexco meeting on December 17, 1989, cited in Martyn Rady, *Romania in Turmoil: A Contemporary History* (London: I.B. Tauris, 1992), p. 92.
65 Adrian Marino, *Dreptatea* (Bucharest daily newspaper), February 20, 1990, cited in Rady, *Romania in Turmoil*, p. 122. Pavel Campeanu, cited in Banac, *Eastern Europe in Revolution*, p. 125, also believed the old apparatus had sacrificed its ruler in order to retain control.

Would the results have been different if the PHR-TNC had flourished in Romania? One might speculate that there would have been some more solid alternatives to vote for, built with patience from the bottom up. A better answer might be to point to the signs that this process is now beginning in Romania, and following quite closely the pattern of the 1980s civil society-strengthening and coalition-building elsewhere in Eastern Europe.[66] The informal Group for Social Dialogue (founded on December 31, 1989), with a good transnational network, has helped to generate the Civic Alliance (in November 1990), which bears the hallmark of a serious political party-building venture. There is a strong sense in Romania now that transnational links are needed in order to forge the conditions for a new political culture, and that, even with free elections, the transition to non-Communism requires alternatives which have the credibility of being rooted in civil society.[67]

In sum, the Romanian experience of 1989 is the exception that proves the rule. In the absence of both civil society and strong transnational links, there was no regime transformation. The popular uprising in itself did not shift the party out of power, only the leader. Over and above this is the violence of the transition. This is particularly telling when compared with the eleventh-hour breakthrough in East Germany.

The transformation processes in Eastern Europe

From the time the PHR-TNC began in 1980, its leading members had enunciated three common and explicit goals: the ending of the Cold War, dissolution of the blocs, and nonviolent transition to democracy in Eastern Europe. Objectively, these goals were realized in 1989. The fact that most of the social movement activists who were so central in the Eastern European revolutions are now, once again, in opposition, should not be surprising. A distinctive feature of the new social movements was that their goal was not to seize power, but to shift the locus of power in totalitarian states. Moreover, the nature of these social movements is to be in opposition; not dissidents now, but still in opposition. While many of them would be surprised by the extent of

[66] Vladimir Tismaneanu, "The Revival of Politics in Romania," in Nils H. Wessell, ed., *The New Europe: Revolution in East–West Relations*, Proceedings of the Academy of Political Science, 38, 1 (New York: 1991), pp. 85–99.
[67] See Gail Kligman, "Reclaiming the Public: A Reflection on Creating Civil Society in Romania," *East European Politics and Societies*, 4, 3 (1990), pp. 393–439.

Table 6.3 *Transnational coalitions related to outcomes*

		Cases		Outcomes
+CS	+TNC	Hungary Poland	(a)	Gradual transition Nonviolent transfer of power Major structural changes Social movements co-opted (and otherwise re-marginalized)

−CS	+TNC	East Germany
		Czechoslovakia
			(b)	Rapid regime collapse
				Nonviolent transfer of power
				    (but serious confrontation)
				Major structural changes
				Social movements assuming
				    some prominence in the
				    period of transition

−CS	−TNC	Romania
		Bulgaria
			(c)	Sudden regime collapse
				Violent confrontations
				Limited structural changes
				Social movements virtually
				    absent until later in the
				    process

+CS	−TNC	None		

The signs + and − in the above diagram are not used as absolutes. They refer to the existence of higher and lower degrees of domestic civil society activity (CS) and transnational coalition activity (TNC) in the different country groups.

their achievements in 1989, few of them would be surprised that flaws soon appeared in the replacement systems, and that the social movements were better placed to point these out than others. All the more remarkable is the prominence achieved by social movement activists in the immediate aftermath of 1989, especially in the cases of East Germany and Czechoslovakia.

Causal connections are difficult to prove where massive social and political change occurs. Events on this scale have multiple and complex causes, and it would be wrong to attribute sole responsibility for outcomes to social movements merely because the outcomes corresponded with their goals. In any case, the specific coalition we are looking at, the PHR-TNC, was only one of the transnational actors influencing the events of 1989. Nevertheless, empirical evidence suggests that there are connections, and comparing similar cases allows us to make some theoretical generalizations.

Table 6.3 offers a model which relates the social movement variables considered earlier to the outcomes of regime transformation in the different Eastern European countries. There are three types represented: (a) cases with a high degree of civil society activity in the domestic environment and a high degree of transnational coalition activity; (b) cases with a low degree of civil society but a high degree of transnational coalition-building based on the limited civil society activity that does exist; and (c) cases where both civil society and transnational coalitions are very limited.[68]

A fourth theoretical possibility, which does not occur empirically in this sample of regimes, would be a high degree of civil society development and a low degree of transnational activity. It is predictable that such a combination is unlikely to occur, given that a highly developed civil society is unlikely to be contained by formal nation-state boundaries. Should the state strive to contain it, civil society would suffer repression, thus reducing its activity to a low level to match the degree of containment. The lack of convincing examples of the high civil society/low transnationalism combination, even beyond the countries considered here, is in itself a confirmation of the theory.

It can be seen from table 6.3 that there is a correspondence between the three case types and the nature of the regime change. Thus the social movement variables correlate with factors which define the outcomes: factors such as the level of violence of the transition, the speed of the transition, the completeness of the regime transformation, and the involvement or not of civil society actors (at least temporarily) in the new regimes. More importantly, however, table 6.3 indicates the conditions under which TNCs become significant. Clearly the most interesting cases are East Germany and Czechoslovakia: in these cases there was only a limited development of civil society, but a high degree of transnational coalition-building. Indigenous civil society activity may have been intense, but it was strongly controlled or repressed domestically, and isolated from mainstream political life, whether in broad structures like the East German Protestant church or

---

[68] In principle, the CS/TNC factors could be quantified if an appropriate metric could be defined. This is not the purpose of the present chapter, but see the tables established for measuring Tolerance (compare CS) and Integration (compare TNC) in Roland Bleiker, Doug Bond, and Myung-Soo Lee, "Unification From Below? German Unity and its Implications for Korean Unification Dynamics," paper presented at the ISA Convention in Atlanta, GA, April 2, 1992.

in narrow ones like Charter 77 in Czechoslovakia. In these cases, the legitimizing effect of the transnational coalitions was crucial in determining the outcomes.

A strong argument can thus be made for the impact of transnational coalitions in these cases. Without the PHR-TNCs, and their capacity to raise the status of unofficial social movements to that of valid interlocutor, these movements would not have achieved either the public prominence, or the penetration of official structures, which were the necessary preconditions for the nonviolent regime collapse in 1989.

While such a strong case for transnational effects can only be made for East Germany and Czechoslovakia (and, in the German case, events related to unification quickly took over), these two were historically the key countries in the autumn of 1989. Without the success of the German and Czechoslovak velvet revolutions, Bulgaria and Romania would not have registered the jolt they did into at least transitional regimes, and Poland and Hungary would not have normalized their own regimes and their relations with the West (and with the Soviet Union) as swiftly and smoothly as they did.

In Hungary and Poland the PHR-TNCs had only a minimal influence – mainly on the structure of the oppositions emerging in the new pluralist democracies – because other civil society TNCs were already well developed. Hungary's wide range of commercial exchanges, and Poland's links with Western Europe through the Roman Catholic church and the established trade union bureaucracies, had opened up the political opportunity structure in the early 1980s. The cooptation process which followed legitimized dominant movements like Solidarnosc, but left the alternative movements like the Wolnosc i Pokoj (WiP) group (the Freedom and Peace branch of Solidarnosc) with more marginal functions than their counterparts in East Germany or Czechoslovakia. In Bulgaria and Romania, civil society TNCs only began to have influence *after* the initial regime collapse (and are actually growing in importance in both these countries as the only means of building the new social movements and political parties needed to challenge the transitional regimes). But in East Germany and Czechoslovakia, the PHR-TNCs were crucial in determining both the manner of the transition and the likelihood that successful democratic structures would replace the de-legitimized regimes.

223

Conclusion

Our argument is that components of the domestic structures (nature of the state and degree of civil society) affected the degree of TNC activity, and its impact on the regime transition. At the same time, TNCs affected civil society, and its capacity to bring about nonviolent change. TNCs contributed to the 1989 transformation processes in terms of the manner and extent of the regime change. They did so in varying degrees, depending on differences in the domestic structures, namely the strength of civil society in each country.

But the question of the impact of TNCs on the events of 1989 cannot and should not be divorced from other explanations. Neither the series of events as a whole nor any of the national regime transformations can be accounted for in a mono-causal way. Explanations of the 1989 events based on economic factors, political leadership factors, and military factors are complementary in some way to our attempt to assess the impact of the civil factors. None is convincing as a simple explanation in itself.

Economic arguments are not incompatible with our attempt to explain the transformation from the bottom up. The drive towards economic liberalization and integration into the global economy, for example, is experienced at the level of the individual citizen and at the level of communities, and is in many ways connected with aspirations to enhance personal autonomy. A one-dimensional argument that the collapsing economies of the Communist bloc forced a change of regime without other agents of change is flawed, however. It does not take account of the discrepancies between economic hardship and ripeness for revolution in the different Eastern European cases (East Germany was less threatened by economic collapse than was Romania, for example). Besides, the old regimes could have carried on for a considerable time (with less disruption than the reforms brought), had it not been for other forces pressing towards transformation.

Political leadership arguments have to be qualified, too. The presence and policies of Gorbachev undeniably made possible events in Eastern Europe that would have provoked heavy-handed reactions from the Soviet administration in an earlier era. However, Gorbachev did not (indeed, he could not) force the East bloc satellites to reform. The forces of change came as much from within the domestic societies as from the outside. Soviet retrenchment, and the Gorbachev phenomenon, were both well under way by 1987, but they showed no signs of weakening either the East German or the Romanian state in the short term. Also international opinion, at official levels, was more concerned with keeping the lid on what it suspected might be destabilizing change, rather than encouraging it. Thus it is at least theoretically possible that the Eastern European Communist parties could have stayed in power, if the social movements had not been there to catalyze the transition.[69] If one compares the East German and Romanian cases, the social movements were probably the ingredient that made the difference between the two outcomes. And if one concludes that the social movements had an impact here, one also has to recognize that their project was in train before Gorbachev took over the stewardship of the Soviet bloc.[70]

Military arguments are also interesting when they can be combined with civil society accounts. It is only when they are presented in isolation from other factors that they appear improbable. The common argument that military confrontation, and the West's superiority in the arms race, forced Soviet political-military elites to back down and to admit their errors is not wholly convincing. It does not fit the facts either of Soviet intentions or of the dynamics of the military economy. It is more compelling to assume that the military build-up, and the state's apparent inability to provide security for its citizens, forced some serious new thinking on all sides, not least in civil society, and that this in turn had an effect on foreign policy and military thinking.[71] This becomes all the more interesting when it is matched against the West's experience of military build-up, which in the 1980s provoked public and expert disquiet, to an extent that these began to impact on policy.[72]

Transnationalism takes account of coalitions of non-state actors across national borders. Regime transformation on the scale experienced in Eastern Europe during 1989 entails the development of transnational legal norms and of a transnational political culture. A

[69] I am indebted to M.J. Peterson for remarks leading to this formulation.
[70] There are questions that could be asked here as to which way the new thinking was flowing in the mid-1980s.
[71] Researchers at the Institut für Internationale Politik und Wirtschaft der DDR (IPW: East German Institute for Politics and Economy), for instance, fed seminal papers on concepts of military balance and sufficiency into Warsaw Pact discussions, and work is now being done on this and other institutes as epistemic communities.
[72] See, for example, the acknowledgement made of social movement influence on nuclear weapon policy (both Soviet and American) in Jonathan Haslam, *The Soviet Union and the Politics of Nuclear Weapons in Europe, 1969–87* (Ithaca, NY: Cornell University Press, 1990), p. 117.

precondition for these developments, according to our findings, was a certain level of transnational activity, involving actors from civil society, citizens' groups, and non-governmental organizations. Specific transnational coalitions, focusing on peace and human rights, fulfilled these conditions in key areas of Europe in the 1980s. Where these transnational coalitions were absent, there was no development towards democracy and human rights. While these transnational activities alone were not a sufficient condition for the events of 1989 to unfold, they were a necessary condition, particularly in those cases in which domestic civil societies were underdeveloped.

7 Ivory, conservation, and environmental transnational coalitions

Thomas Princen

Environment, development, trade

Five hundred years ago, 10 million elephants populated Africa's forests and savannas, from the shore of the Mediterranean almost to the tip of Cape Good Hope.[1] Although estimates vary, today's elephant population is believed to be one-twentieth of that figure. Recently, in just one decade, the elephant population dropped nearly 50 percent, from an estimated 1.3 million in 1979 to 625,000 in 1989.[2] At this rate, the elephant could be extinct in many parts of Africa by the end of the century.[3]

Although habitat loss is the greatest long-term threat to the elephant, the principal immediate cause of elephant deaths in recent years has been poaching. After the Second World War, the demand for and price of ivory rose sharply, making poaching a very lucrative business. In the 1970s, many people invested in ivory as a hedge on worldwide inflation. Prices for raw ivory in Japan, Hong Kong, and Europe, the major ivory-consuming areas, rose from between $3 and $10 a pound in the 1960s to $50 a pound by the mid-1970s. In the 1980s, ivory sold for as much as $200 a pound. At the same time, Hong Kong

[1] *World Wildlife Fund Letter*, 1989, "A Program to Save the African Elephant," no. 2, p. 1.
[2] Sarah Fitzgerald, *International Wildlife Trade: Whose Business Is It?* (Washington, DC: World Wildlife Fund, 1989), p. 62.
[3] As a so-called keystone species, the loss of the elephant would probably reverberate throughout the ecosystem with ecological and social costs. Elephants are a major force in maintaining biological diversity in the African savanna and forests, playing a major role in the dynamic savanna–woodland balance. Commercial livestock economies also benefit from healthier herds as elephants expand grasslands and reduce the incidence of the tsetse fly. Douglas H. Chadwick, "Elephants – Out of Time, Out of Space," *National Geographic*, 179, 5 (May 1991), p. 25.

improved its ability to mass-produce ivory carvings.[4] Consequently, international ivory trade and thus, elephant killing, skyrocketed. According to one estimate, poachers were killing 200–300 elephants a day.[5]

The decline in elephant populations can be characterized as having two interactive components. One is local, where property rights to elephant harvesting and maintenance are inadequately designated and enforced. The second is international, where high income growth has led to high demand for a precious commodity (ivory). Demand creates significant rents but, due largely to the skewed distribution of those rents (i.e., to manufacturers and retailers), the rate of extraction exceeds what would be socially optimal – namely, a sustainable yield.[6] This demand combines with fluid trade patterns among producers, intermediaries, and consumers,[7] to skew economic rents away from African states and primary harvesters.

The local and international forces driving the elephant to extinction are interactive in that local producers (hunters, pastoralists, and other peasants and their communities) still garner enough of the rents relative to their income to create the incentive to harvest. In addition, when range state governments attempt to protect wildlife by excluding local people, those people become hostile to such practices and treat wildlife as a menace, not a resource. Put differently, compo-

---

[4] Fitzgerald, *International Wildlife Trade*, p. 65.   [5] *The Economist*, July 1, 1989.
[6] For estimates of those rents and their distribution among African producers and foreign manufacturers and consumers, see Edward B. Barbier, Joanne C. Burgess, Timothy M. Swanson, and David W. Pearce, *Elephants, Economics and Ivory* (London: Earthscan Publications, Ltd, 1990).
[7] Barbier, Burgess, Swanson, and Pearce, *Elephants, Economics and Ivory*, document the elaborate and shifting patterns in ivory trade: first, a substantial amount of raw and worked ivory, legal and illegal, is traded within Africa itself before it leaves the continent: "the intra-Africa trade is both extremely elaborate and difficult to trace. Often it revolves around trade routes that facilitate the transformation of illegally acquired ivory from one African country into 'legal' exports of worked and raw ivory from another country" (p. 40). To illustrate, for many years, Burundi had just one elephant but, in 1986, Burundi produced 23,000 tons of ivory, all carefully documented as originating in the country (p. 34).
The second pattern of trade occurred outside of Africa. For example, Hong Kong, the largest raw ivory importer, received only 30 percent of its imports directly from producing countries (p. 54). For many years, a major intermediary was Belgium. When Belgium joined CITES in 1984 and began to impose trade controls (p. 62), trade dropped drastically and shifted to countries like Macau. When CITES imposed a ban on all wildlife trade with Macau in 1986, the trade shifted to Singapore and Taiwan and when these were closed off it shifted to Dubai and the United Arab Emirates. None of these countries had any significant history in ivory carving or trading. Traders, mostly Asians, were simply able to keep one step ahead of trade restrictions (pp. 71–75).

site discount rates – from primary harvesters to traders to ultimate consumers – can be high enough to drive a species like the elephant to extinction, eliminating the resource for all users in the long run.

Governments, both of producer and consumer states, intergovernmental bodies, and environmental transnational coalitions (ETCs) have attempted to reverse the trend towards elephant extinction. One approach has been to break the destructive trade links, hence, the ivory trade ban imposed by the Conference of the Parties to the Convention on International Trade in Endangered Species of Wild Fauna and Flora (CITES) in October 1989.[8] Another has been to strengthen domestic management practices. In the end, as most participants seem to agree, a combination of the two will be necessary to ensure the elephant's survival.

This chapter focuses on the role ETCs have played in this process. In particular, I ask how ETC strategies have had differential impacts on two range states, Kenya and Zimbabwe. I argue that those impacts are (1) direct, via the historical and contemporary influence ETCs have had on each state's conservation policies; and (2) indirect, via their influence on public perceptions of wildlife destruction and the resulting changes in international demand for ivory. I show that as ecological and social conditions deteriorated in Africa generally, these impacts created contradictions within the ETCs that the trade ban only partially – or temporarily – resolved. Finally, I conclude that these impacts may have also spurred a significant reassessment within both states regarding wildlife policy, a reassessment that, over time, may have long-term environmental and developmental consequences.

As will be seen, assessment of the transnational environmental community's relations with two states reveals how, in general, differences in domestic structures determine the policy impact of transnational actors. A country with a state-dominated domestic structure (Zimbabwe) is more impervious to direct transnational penetration than a state with weak domestic structures (Kenya). But this case suggests that access to the weak state only ensures the transnational actors' ability to support and make modest changes in existing policies (especially if those policies evolved historically in concert with trans-

---

[8] For a detailed account of the domestic and international determinants of the trade ban, see the chapter, "The Ivory Trade Ban: NGOs and International Conservation," in Thomas Princen and Matthias Finger, *Environmental NGOs in World Politics: Linking the Local and the Global* (London: Routledge, 1994), pp. 121–59.

national activities). If fundamental policy change is required – as when a species is threatened by a complex set of economic and social factors – then access means little. In addition, this case suggests that domestic impact varies with the international strategies adopted by the transnational actors. It is here that a strategy that leads to a uniform international action such as a trade ban can support one domestic policy and thwart the other. It is here that transnational activity can actually serve to pry open a strong state (Zimbabwe), forming coalitions with domestic actors which can, in turn, influence that state's international policy-making.

Environmental transnational coalitions

ETCs fall into one of two categories, what I will term the "professional" and the "public opinion" ETCs.[9] Members of the professional ETC have a long-term, in-country presence. They are highly professional either as scientists or as program specialists. They work primarily with the state to create and manage protected areas for wildlife, parks and preserves. They engage in research, public education, and monitoring and they fund special projects. Africa, in particular, has a long history of such work both under colonial and post-independence administrations.

The professional ETC also works out of country and, in fact, member organizations are often based in the North. There they raise funds, conduct research, educate Northern publics, and work with international agencies. On the elephant question, the relevant coalition includes the World Wildlife Fund (WWF), the International Union for the Conservation of Nature and Natural Resources (IUCN; now called the World Conservation Union), Trade Records Analysis of Flora and Fauna in Commerce (TRAFFIC), the Wildlife Trade Monitoring Unit, Wildlife Conservation International and others. This ETC has strong links to intergovernmental bodies such as the United Nations Environment Programme (UNEP) and the CITES Secretariat and also works with trade associations. The coalition is highly integrated; members

---

[9] The usual dichotomy is the conservationists and the preservationists or the natural resource users and the animal rights proponents. Although the "professional" versus "public opinion" designation roughly corresponds to these dichotomies, I choose these terms to highlight their political approaches as opposed to their environmental philosophy.

often share staffing and office space and attend many of the same meetings.[10]

The second type of coalition, the public opinion ETC, is more diffuse and fluid in its composition but not necessarily any less influential. It is made up largely of preservation and animal rights organizations that band together on a given campaign (e.g., save the seals, save the elephant) but mostly operate independently. It relies on high-visibility campaigns designed to sway public opinion and specializes in specific animals or ecosystems but readily adopts other issues when they gain (or have the potential of gaining) the public's attention. Seeking immediate victories, they are not organized to promote, much less implement, long-term solutions. They target publics that tend to be responsive to emotional appeals or that can sway key governmental decisions. They do little at the level of local resource utilization nor at the level of international organization (although many attend CITES biennial meetings). They are often more dependent on membership for funding than the professional ETC which procures funds from governments, foundations, and corporations.

On the elephant question, a loose coalition of preservation-oriented non-governmental organizations (NGOs) emerged. They included such groups as Friends of the Animals, Greenpeace, the Humane Society, Defenders of Wildlife, the Environmental Investigation Agency, and Amnistie pour les Elephants.

[10] Several examples illustrate the high degree of integration within this coalition, the strong links to intergovernmental bodies, and connections with trade organizations. First, WWF-International shares offices with IUCN in Gland, Switzerland. TRAFFIC, although it has independent non-governmental organization (NGO) status in CITES meetings, is considered an arm of WWF and is located in WWF offices worldwide. Second, when the 1989 Conference of the Parties to CITES passed a resolution to create a panel of experts to review proposals to downlist the elephant, the resolution stipulated that the panel would be established with the recommendations of TRAFFIC, IUCN, and UNEP (*TRAFFIC Newsletter*, December, 1989, p. 2). Third, to assist African governments in preserving their elephant populations, the African Wildlife Foundation, the European Economic Community, IUCN, TRAFFIC, US Fish and Wildlife Service, the CITES Secretariat, Wildlife Conservation International, Wildlife Conservation Monitoring Centre, and WWF formed the African Elephant Conservation Coordinating Group to develop an Action Plan (African Elephant Conservation Coordinating Group, "African Elephant Action Plan," March 1990, 4th edn) which became a key document in the follow-up to the October 1989 uplisting. Fourth, the CITES-run Ivory Unit was initially financed by the ivory division of the Japan General Merchandise Importers Association. Those funds were channelled to the CITES Secretariat via WWF-Japan and WWF-International (CITES Secretariat, "Interpretation and Implementation of the Convention: Trade in Ivory from African Elephants, Operation of the Ivory Trade Control System," document 7.21, Lausanne, Switzerland, October 9 to 20, 1989, pp. 1–20).

Thomas Princen

State conservation policies – comparing Kenya and Zimbabwe

In Africa, the primary interaction between range states and ETCs has been to promote the establishment of parks and preserves. Parks were products of European policies in the colonial era and state development policies in the post-independence era.[11] In fact, one can discern a trend of "increasing externalisation of control over environmental resources" from rural communities to central colonial governments, especially from the 1940s on and then, with growing environmental concern in the 1970s, a renewal of state intervention (this time by post-independence governments), much of it financed from outside Africa.[12] Much of the financing and the political impetus for these policies came from private, non-governmental groups, the predecessors of today's ETCs.

The antecedents to Northern-based ETCs can be found in the scientific and naturalist expeditions of the late eighteenth century.[13] Prior to this time, European interests were driven by the demand for slaves and commodities such as ivory. The period of African exploration was first characterized by scholarly inquiry and included naturalists, geographers, and ethnographers as well as non-specialists fascinated with the nature and peoples of the continent. Some of the more prominent expeditions were funded by the private British organization, the Association for Promoting the Discovery of the Interior Parts of Africa or, more commonly, the Africa Association.[14] These scientifically oriented travels set the stage for government sponsored exploration where the primary concern was trade.[15] The Scottish missionary, David Livingstone, was probably the most prominent in this breed of explorers. Livingtone's early exploits were privately funded, namely by the London Missionary Society and the Royal Geographic Society. Later, the British government supported his work,

[11] In fact, in East Africa the amount of land absorbed into protected areas has more than doubled since independence. J. Terrence McCabe, "A New Paradigm for Conservation and Development in Tanzania," in "Progress and Priorities in African Conservation History: A Symposium," *Forest & Conservation History*, 35, 4 (October 1991), pp. 188–91.
[12] John McCracken, "Introduction" to Part Three, "Conservation Priorities and Rural Communities," in David Anderson and Richard Grove, *Conservation in Africa: People, Policies and Practice* (Cambridge: Cambridge University Press, 1987), p. 189.
[13] This account of ETC antecedents derives largely from Jonathan S. Adams and Thomas O. McShane, *The Myth of Wild Africa: Conservation Without Illusion* (New York: Norton & Co., 1992).
[14] Ibid. p. 11.   [15] Ibid. p. 13.

232

especially as he promoted commerce along with missionary and geographic goals.

A second set of antecedents to the Northern-based ETCs was the European hunters of the late nineteenth and early twentieth centuries. They shared a passion not only for hunting as sport but for wildlife and wildlands. Many hunters also collected specimens for scientific study working with, for example, the Royal Geographic Society. With respect to wilderness protection, hunters, conservationists, and nature lovers shared common ground and, in fact, were often one in the same person. Theodore Roosevelt was among the most prominent as both safari hunter and promoter of wildlife conservation.

Despite European hunters' concerns for wilderness protection, however, their hunting practices were major factors in the decline of wildlife throughout the continent.[16] As wildlife declined, Europeans tended to blame native practices and, being vocal and politically active, lobbied their home governments for game laws and protected areas. The first game legislation introduced by the British was in 1822. Hunters, conservationists, and nature lovers also lobbied for international protection of wildlife. The first such agreement was the Convention for the Preservation of Wild Animals, Birds, and Fish in Africa. When most parties failed to ratify the agreement, the growing preservationist lobby in England succeeded in promoting game reserves in the colonies. For example, the Society for the Preservation of the Fauna of the Empire (SPFE) was formed at the turn of the century to bring together colonial officials, hunters, naturalists, and the gentry to pressure the British government.[17] This collection of people interested in wildlife was not unlike that which makes up the World Wildlife Fund today except that hunters played a major role in the SPFE.

The SPFE's primary goal was to enhance hunting for Europeans and its primary means was to exclude native Africans. The SPFE's call for game reserves – generally opposed by European settlers because reserves took up valuable farmland – and for national parks gained momentum in the 1930s. The famous Serengeti National Park, for example, traces its roots to a report prepared for the SPFE. That report proposed nine national parks for the five British colonies.

---

[16] By the first years of the twentieth century, much of southern Africa had lost its wildlife heritage to European hunters. Adams and McSchane, *The Myth of Wild Africa*, p. 30

[17] Ibid. p. 46.

By the 1950s when the British government had eradicated the tsetse fly and when cattle were increasing in numbers – two factors that upset ecosystems, thus threatening wildlife – the SPFE, now the Fauna Preservation Society (FPS), took a lead role in implementing its earlier parks proposal. The Serengeti became a major focus for study, for expansion, and for international attention promoted by conservationists who sought to exclude native peoples entirely. These efforts became the pattern for the rest of the century including the deliberate undermining of multiple-use conservation areas where native residents would have a share in the management of and the proceeds from wildlife use.

In sum, private groups and individuals representing scientific, naturalist, and hunting interests were significant actors in the evolution of domestic conservation policies in British East Africa. Neither natives nor European settlers were able to oppose these groups' efforts to erect game reserves and national parks despite the direct threats to livelihood such protected lands presented. The emphasis on protection and exclusion of resident peoples was common throughout the colonies.

Divergences in domestic policies and, subsequently, the impacts of international policies and transnational activities, were determined by other factors, however: the domestic structures of the respective colonies and independent countries. Two countries, Kenya and Zimbabwe, exemplify the differences between East Africa and southern Africa and, hence, the impact of the new international political space created by the ivory trade ban. In these countries, conservation policies can be seen as part of an overall settlement and development pattern in the colonial and early post-independence periods. If such policies were successful in these periods,[18] they clearly were not in the 1980s. Land-use conflicts heightened by political instability raised new questions about the sustainability – biologically and politically – of such policies.

The rapid decline in elephant numbers was, therefore, a symptom of a larger set of forces, some domestic, some international. Caught in all

---

[18] Subsistence farmers and pastoralists who were expelled from the land and prevented from hunting wildlife as supplements to their diet and income, did not see these conservation policies as successful. Some of those who would otherwise be engaging in traditional sustainable utilization were consequently labeled poachers by the international community. Many poachers also came over the border from neighboring countries, especially Somalia. Somalia has challenged Kenya's right to its northern territory which is occupied by ethnic Somalis.

of this were the ETCs, especially the professional ETC, which had invested heavily in supporting and influencing state wildlife policies. An examination of the development of the domestic structures that contributed to these policies sets the African context of transnational environmental politics.

Kenya

The British colonization of Kenya in 1892 began a process of Europeans wresting control of and access to wildlife from native peoples. National parks began in the 1930s and intensified in the 1950s and thereafter. Designed to protect wildlife for expatriate tourism, the creation of parks required the expulsion of resident or nomadic peoples and, once established, their exclusion from local land and wildlife uses. The tradition of parks concentrated foreign attention on wildlife, often ignoring both the ecological and social effects of parceling out protected areas.[19]

With respect to wildlife use, the colonial state claimed ownership of all wildlife and issued hunting licenses at prices villagers could not afford. This destroyed local customs whereby village chiefs owned all wildlife on behalf of their tribe. Colonial game laws were designed in part to eliminate hunting by the Wata and grazing by the Masai. According to two critics of traditional conservation, however, compared to the Europeans,

> the Wata were more effective hunters, made better use of the animals they killed, and caused their prey to suffer less. The view that the Wata were barbaric, however, pervaded colonial Africa, and it was enshrined in many of that era's conservation laws. Those laws ... broke down the African conservation ethic, which begins with the integral role wildlife has always played in African life.[20]

As for the Masai, a UNESCO report on the status of East African wildlife concluded that the, "marvelous fauna [of the Serengeti] were being gravely threatened, ... largely by the rapidly increasing Maasai"

---

[19] Critiques of the park system in Africa are numerous; see, for example, Adams and McShane, *The Myth of Wild Africa*; Anderson and Grove, *Conservation in Africa*; Patrick C. West and Steven R. Brechin, eds., *Resident Peoples and National Parks: Social Dilemmas and Strategies in International Conservation* (Tucson, AZ: University of Arizona Press, 1991).

[20] Adams and McShane, *The Myth of Wild Africa*, p. 33.

and their cattle.[21] Scientific evidence was lacking, however, prompting others to conclude that wild animals were not being destroyed, "especially given the evidence of pastoralism in the area for at least the preceding 2,500 years."[22] Nevertheless, the myth of cattle destroying wildlife persists to this day. Archaeologist David Collett concludes that

> while both the economics of tourism and the desire to preserve wildlife have played a part in the development of National Parks and Game Reserves in [Kenya's] Maasailand, it is the covert power of the [colonial and post-independence] administrative image of the Maasai that has provided the most sustained justification for these policies.[23]

Adams and McShane sum up the effect of parks and hunting policies:

> The traditional system provided for communal needs and interests as well as conservation. Colonial game laws did not.
>
> Both colonial and post-independence governments actively inhibited the ability of rural Africans to take control over their own lives. The damage has been at once spiritual and economic; villages have gradually fallen away from the economic mainstream, and now depend on urban centers for goods and services (e.g., food, clothing, and shelter) they once provided for themselves. African governments and international donors alike treat rural people in Africa like children.[24]

Kenya's independence in 1963 brought a period of economic growth and optimism, at least until about 1983. As a "pro-Western" country, political stability and economic growth made Kenya a favorite recipient of foreign aid. Although factionalism along tribal lines and presidential patronage characterized the political system under President Jomo Kenyatta, a governance system emerged that engaged virtually all levels of society. For example, local self-help development organizations proliferated during the 1960s and 1970s. Elected officials would advance their political careers by assisting these organizations and civil servants at the district and national levels assisted with projects. These organizations "established clear norms of social interaction between state and society as well as within local communities."[25]

---

[21] David Collett, "Pastoralists and Wildlife: Image and Reality in Kenya Maasailand," in Anderson and Grove, *Conservation in Africa*, p. 144.

[22] Ibid. p. 145.   [23] Ibid.

[24] Adams and McShane, *The Myth of Wild Africa*, pp. 163–64.

[25] Joel D. Barkan, "The Rise and Fall of a Governance Realm in Kenya," in Goran Hyden and Michael Bratton, eds., *Governance and Politics in Africa* (Boulder, CO: Lynne Rienner, 1992), p. 177.

Upon Kenyatta's death in 1978, Vice President Daniel arap Moi assumed the presidency amid a growing number of problems. These included the world coffee boom that ended in 1979, the rise in the price of imported oil, the world recession in 1981 and 1982, and severe droughts in 1979–80. Add to these the fastest growing population in the world, declining per capita income in the rural areas, and heavy migration to the cities and Moi had little choice but to reorient government policies drastically. His approach was to consolidate virtually all power in his hands, creating a highly personalized presidency and a diminution of local authority.[26] He also encouraged more private ownership of land where, among other effects, small farming would supplant pastoralism.

Under these conditions, it is not surprising that rural peoples resented wildlife policies that excluded them from valuable land (whether for farming, grazing, or hunting) and that returned few benefits to their communities. For some, so-called poaching was merely a return to traditional practices necessitated by the failure of the central government to meet their needs.[27] For others, such as the Masai, it was a protest. Whichever it was, with Moi's consolidation of power, declining numbers of elephants, and mounting pressure at home and from abroad to protect the tourist industry, Moi launched a high-profile anti-poaching campaign. To do this, he appointed the renowned anthropologist, Richard Leakey, to head Kenya's Wildlife Service and gave him considerable power to reform an agency with a history of corruption going back to colonial times. Leakey immediately began weeding out corrupt officials and raised park rangers' wages. He developed plans to fence in huge areas of protected land despite the enormous cost and the facts that no fence can stop a determined elephant, and that fences disrupt migrations and hence the very ecosystem they are supposed to be protecting. The fences did, however, serve as "powerful symbols of the traditional method of conservation in Africa."[28]

In a highly publicized display, Leakey also put the torch to twelve

[26] Barkan, "The Rise and Fall of a Governance Realm in Kenya."

[27] Richard Bell, a biologist born and raised in Africa, distinguishes poaching from hunting: "I don't actually like the word 'poacher' when applied to someone from the local community; it has connotations of some faceless force of evil. In fact, the local poacher is usually a well-known, highly skilled man, admired for the way he beats what is seen as a repressive system ... Professional poaching by outsiders is altogether different ..." Quoted in Sue Armstrong and Fred Bridgland, "Elephants and the Ivory Tower," *New Scientist*, 26 August 1989, p. 41.

[28] Adams and McShane, *The Myth of Wild Africa*, p. 58.

tons of ivory worth $3 million on the market. With that, he imple-
mented a shoot-to-kill policy against poachers, providing his wardens
with automatic rifles and helicopter gunships.[29] He also went abroad
to secure funds. WWF and other NGOs assisted by providing funds
and equipment for the anti-poaching campaign and by sponsoring his
promotional tours.

Moi's approach was thus an extension and an intensification of a
historically well-established pattern of wildlife conservation in Kenya
– namely, to exclude local peoples, concentrate authority (and revenues) with the state, and promote foreign consumption of wildlife
values. At the time, there was a growing awareness among both
conservation and development specialists that local communities had
to be involved in wildlife management as an integral part of both
conservation and development. But Moi's predicament and his choices
at the national level left him little room. He could not devolve authority to the local level for wildlife protection at the same time – he was
consolidating power on all other issues. Moreover, he needed immediate results to reassure the international community that he was serious
about restoring order and providing a safe place for investment and
tourism.

Moi's predicament had, in turn, its parallel within the ETC.
Although groups like WWF have long espoused the principle of local
participation, their primary point of access for wildlife conservation
has been the relevant wildlife or parks agency. When human populations were low and the government could provide communities with
basic services (in part funded by tourism), that was indeed a "winning
coalition." But conflicts arise when such agencies are viewed by the
public as law enforcement and paramilitary organizations whose
primary goal is to protect visitors from local peoples. Thus, to the
extent that the professional ETC aligned itself with such agencies and
supported their conservation policies, the ETC was unable to promote
community-based conservation programs. Moreover, it had little
choice but to support the anti-poaching campaign and, eventually, the
international effort to ban the ivory trade.

Kenya was thus a weak state with respect to wildlife management in
the sense that the state could do little to stem misuse of what was

---

[29] Adams and McShane see the anti-poaching campaign as a war for Kenya's economic
survival, "Tourism rises and falls on the shifting attitudes of a few well-off residents of
Europe, North America, and Japan. Thus far, Kenya has exploited the myth of wild
Africa by making it accessible. The challenge facing Leakey and the rest of KWS
[Kenya Wildlife Service] is to keep that myth alive" (*The Myth of Wild Africa*, p. 69).

otherwise deemed a state resource. It could neither harvest the resource nor protect it from poaching. In addition, access to domestic institutions by transnational actors was easy, as it had been since colonial times. With the resource under pressure, Kenya could only appeal to the international community for increased assistance and more tourism.

Zimbabwe

Although independent Zimbabwe – formerly Southern Rhodesia – emerged out of a British colonial past similar to Kenya's and has an abundance of wildlife resources,[30] at least two factors distinguish its conservation and development policies.

First, in Zimbabwe, white settlers played a dominant societal role throughout the colonial and independence periods. Although a small minority, the number of white settlers was considerably greater than that in Kenya. Moreover, "unlike Kenya ... Zimbabwe ... was governed for more than a century by white settlers who were intent upon remaining in charge";[31] and, unlike Kenya where many colonists were poor farmers or adventurers, those who settled in Zimbabwe came to stay and build a new society, bringing with them a long tradition of scientific management.[32] The implication was that although Zimbabwe's conservation policy followed a pattern common to British colonial Africa, one guided by exclusion and control of local peoples, it was also able to adapt to conditions peculiar to Zimbabwe, including the drive for economic self-reliance.

A second distinguishing factor was the isolation Zimbabwe experienced during white rule and civil war and, to a lesser extent, as a self-proclaimed Marxist state. Under such conditions, Zimbabwe had to develop its own infrastructure and its own means of economic development. For example, Zimbabwe has a national conservation strategy which Zimbabweans themselves developed with local private and public support. This contrasts with other developing countries

---

[30] Contrary to conventional international development wisdom, wildlife is one of the most productive uses of land in Africa, particularly in arid regions. By one estimate, wildlife tourism in Kenya produces $100 per hectare and sport hunting $10/ hectare while cattle ranching in Zimbabwe's semi-arid pasture *costs* the economy $4/hectare. Adams and McShane, *The Myth of Wild Africa*, p. 172.

[31] Kenneth Ingham, *Politics in Modern Africa: The Uneven Tribal Dimension* (London: Routledge, 1990), p. 201.

[32] Interview, October 6, 1992, Calestous Juma, Director, African Centre for Technology Studies, Nairobi, Kenya.

where, typically, international conservation organizations and aid agencies with expatriate consultants fund and write such plans.[33]

The implication for conservation policy is that, unlike Kenya which, after independence, continued to rely on foreign assistance and tourism to modernize, Zimbabwe took a more independent path to exploiting its resources.[34] What is more, with a protracted war (from roughly 1963 to 1980) and sanctions, tourism, especially nature viewing (as opposed to safari hunting), was not a viable development strategy. As a result of these factors, Zimbabwe has had little inter-action with international conservationists and little development of tourism, certainly much less than Kenya. Rather, with respect to wildlife, it has pioneered wildlife management techniques that exploit the resource for many purposes, including revenue for both the central government and local communities.

Thus, independent Zimbabwe has taken a dual track towards wild-life management. One approach, similar to Kenya's, was to intensify law enforcement and strengthen the protected areas to encourage expatriate hunting and, to some extent, touring. It also encouraged private commercial operations that raise wild animals for safari hunting, meat, skins, and trophies. The number of these ranches has grown steadily since the early 1970s, bringing in significant foreign exchange.[35]

The second track was to incorporate local peoples not just as tour guides and park wardens (as in Kenya) but as stewards of the wildlife areas. The first method retains authority with the state but returns revenues to communities that incur the costs (e.g., destroyed crops) of living with and protecting wildlife. An example is the state-run ranch management program for elephants that provides water and pro-tected habitat. When the population exceeds the estimated carrying capacity, rangers cull entire herds. The animals are processed for skin, meat, and ivory and a portion of the revenues are channeled to the local communities. As a result, elephant populations have increased from their low of four to five thousand in the late nineteenth century to some 50,000 today.[36]

---

[33] Adams and McShane, *The Myth of Wild Africa*, pp. 242–43.
[34] Interview, Calestous Juma.
[35] Adams and McShane, *The Myth of Wild Africa*, p. 169.
[36] Some critics dispute these numbers or the reasons for the population increase. For example, biologist William Clark argues that Zimbabwe has encouraged elephants to migrate to its territory by making artificial watering holes where they are counted as a

The second method of incorporating local peoples was actually to transfer wildlife ownership rights. The approach can be traced to the successful commercial operations which prompted the government to pass the Parks and Wildlife Act of 1975 giving landowners the right to exploit wildlife on their own land for their own benefit. Although the Act was aimed primarily at the commercial farmers, with independence, it had a major impact on communally owned land, which comprises roughly 45 percent of Zimbabwe and is home to much of the country's wildlife. Each of the country's sixteen district councils – an administrative body that has authority over roughly 100 villages – could be designated the landowner under the Act.[37]

Although the potential of this new-found (or, historically speaking, recovered) authority went unrealized for some ten years, in 1988 two district councils were actually granted the authority to manage their own wildlife in a program called CAMPFIRE – Communal Areas Management Progamme for Indigenous Resources. Rowan Martin, the deputy director of wildlife, describes the preliminary results: "Two years ago in Zimbabwe we started letting people, for the first time, own the game on their land. Now they're asking for it to be stocked with impala, not goats. That has to be a good thing, because nobody comes to Africa to see goats."[38] Possibly more significantly, rural communities are beginning to come to the Department of National Parks and Wildlife Management for help – in effect, transforming the department from a law enforcement agency to one that provides technical assistance.[39]

Although the CAMPFIRE program has had its problems, it illustrates alternative approaches to international conservation, including the role of the professional ETC. For example, WWF works with a local NGO, the Zimbabwe Trust and with the University of Harare's Center for Applied Social Sciences which has long studied the role of rural communities in wildlife conservation. Rather than merely funding and training game wardens, which it continues to do in Kenya, WWF has begun to train the district councils in negotiating contracts with commercial wildlife operators.

In sum, Zimbabwe can be characterized as a strong state with respect to wildlife management. Its corporatist past has contributed to

population increase and then slaughtered. Quoted in Princen and Finger, *Environmental NGOs in World Politics*, pp. 147–48.
[37] Adams and McShane, *The Myth of Wild Africa*, pp. 176–77.
[38] Quoted from Armstrong and Bridgland, "Elephants and the Ivory Tower," p. 39.
[39] Adams and McShane, *The Myth of Wild Africa*, p. 242.

an emphasis on local self-reliance making direct access by transnational actors difficult. It has begun to take on fundamental issues of
land use and property rights, including the rights to wildlife for all
uses. Whereas British colonial Africa and the successor independent
states all claimed ownership of wildlife, only Zimbabwe has begun to
experiment with transferring those rights to private property owners
and to local communal authorities. It has also promoted state-run
ranch and culling operations.

As a result, poaching is a minor problem and elephants (and other
wildlife) are thriving.[40] In addition, the economic effect with respect to
the ivory trade appears to be to capture much of the economic rents.
Comparing revenues in 1985 received by harvesters in Africa with the
revenue of raw ivory in Japan, the ultimate consumer, Zimbabwe's
revenues to harvesters were $63–76 per kilogram (compared with, for
example, Zaire's' $7 per kilogram) and Japan's value was $85–99 per
kilogram.[41]

The social effect of devolution of control to the local level appears to
be to strengthen state–society relations, again, in contrast to Kenya's
response to conservation problems. Zimbabwean Martin explains that
conservation programs can succeed if the people who own the land
can take control of it. If the land is communally owned, as in much of
rural Africa, institutions must exist that allow those communities to
utilize their markets: "Government bureaucracies will kill conservation outside the parks, as will international restrictions."[42] Thus,
Zimbabwe also stands in contrast to Kenya by showing little incli-
nation to privatize communally held lands.[43] The effect is to avoid
disrupting ecological relationships (e.g., migratory patterns) and cultural norms (e.g., communal land use) and yet exploit the income and
dietary potential of the land and its wildlife.

Finally, at the international level, trade bans promoted by the ETCs,
presumably to help countries like Kenya, will hurt efforts like those in
Zimbabwe to marry local needs to the sustainable use of wildlife
resources. How, then, can the interactions between ETCs and range
states be explained, especially the impact on those states' ability to
pursue, or adapt, their conservation and development policies?

[40] Minister of Natural Resources and Tourism, September 22, 1989, press conference,
"Ivory Trade: The Zimbabwe Position," Department of National Parks and Wildlife
Management, Harare, Zimbabwe, pp. 1–9.
[41] Barbier, Burgess, Swanson, and Pearce, *Elephants, Economics and Ivory*, pp. 15–16.
[42] Paraphrased by Adams and McShane, *The Myth of Wild Africa*, p. 171.
[43] Stoneman and Cliffe, *Zimbabwe: Politics, Economics and Society*, p. 62.

ETC–state interactions and their differential impacts

The evolution of conservation policies in Kenya and Zimbabwe can thus be explained in part by colonial and post-independence state practices which, in turn, were influenced by early nature and game-oriented groups. These policies have had an internal logic whereby Kenya has relied heavily on a foreign presence to the exclusion of local wildlife and wildlands use and Zimbabwe has managed and culled its wildlife populations and begun to shift property rights away from the state to local communities. Despite their internal logic, however, both policies were vulnerable to outside pressures, in part mediated by the two ETCs.

Kenya, dependent on tourism and hence on a positive international image, was vulnerable to changes in public perceptions, whether they be perceptions of declining wildlife or declining political stability.[44] In addition, to the extent that high prices for ivory drove both local people and bordering peoples to poach, Kenya was vulnerable to market forces as anti-poaching operations were a drain on government resources.

Zimbabwe, on the other hand, was dependent on the ivory trade for management and local development revenues. Consequently, it was vulnerable to changes in consumer preferences for ivory and to changes in international regulation of ivory trade. Its efforts to manage its wildlife sustainably by shifting the rewards and devolving the authority to the local level could be thwarted by an international move to label ivory consumption an immoral act or to uplist the African elephant to Appendix I in CITES, thus banning all trade in elephant products. Thus, the public opinion ETC was Zimbabwe's biggest threat. And if the public opinion ETC could enlist the professional ETC and a few key consumer states like the US and Japan (in that order) in the cause to "save the elephant," Zimbabwe's conservation policy would be severely hurt.

It should be added that Zimbabwe was also indirectly vulnerable to the ivory trade via the decimation of elephant populations in neighboring states. That is, to the extent that illegal transshipment (from,

---

[44] To evaluate just how important the elephant was to the tourist industry, in a report entitled, "The Viewing Value of Elephants," Gardner Brown and Wes Henry calculated the non-consumed value of elephants in Kenya to be $25 million per year; cited in Barbier, Burgess, Swanson, and Pearce, *Elephants, Economics and Ivory*, pp. 18–19.

say, Zaire) requires legal harvesting and shipping, Zimbabwe was, by allowing or failing to halt illegal shipments, abetting the decline in the elephant elsewhere. Zimbabwe could develop indigenous and self-contained wildlife management policies and sell the products abroad, but, given that neither live elephants nor harvested tusks respect national boundaries, Zimbabwe's policies could not be entirely divorced from regional realities of poaching and population decline.[45]

In short, from the perspective of the ETC generally, what was good for one state – a ban on ivory trade for Kenya – was highly detrimental to the other. The different impact of a ban posed a dilemma for the professional ETC. Although there are divisions within the professional ETC, there is a growing consensus that wildlife conservation can no longer be separated from human needs and economic development. The specifics may vary, but conservationists in the field generally agree that local communities must be involved in wildlife conservation – that is, involvement that is more meaningful than servicing foreign-operated safaris or nationally-owned viewing lodges.[46] Richard Bell, a biologist born and raised in Africa, puts it this way:

> The institutional nature of conservation was established during the colonial period; it has strong paternalistic and racist elements to it, and is itself a large part of the problem.
>
> What has happened is that the control of natural resources has been progressively taken away from rural communities by central government bureaucracies; the benefits flowing from them have also been progressively concentrated in national treasuries. In effect a wall has been erected between rural communities and the resources among which they live.[47]

Even if the professional ETC acknowledges this reality, it knows that, to be effective, it must develop good relations with all range states regardless of their specific management practices.[48] WWF, for example, has had programs in both Zimbabwe and Kenya. Its dilemma arises when the conservation issue becomes increasingly inter-

---

[45] Although elephants do migrate, most populations in Africa are contained within national boundaries.
[46] For further arguments for local involvement and local control over wildlife resources, see Anderson and Grove, *Conservation in Africa*; Barbier, Burgess, Swanson, and Pearce, *Elephants, Economics and Ivory*; R.H.V. Bell, "Conservation with a Human Face," in Anderson and Grove, *Conservation in Africa*; Adams and McShane, *The Myth of Wild Africa*; West and Brechin, *Resident Peoples and National Parks*.
[47] Quoted in Armstrong and Bridgland, "Elephants and the Ivory Tower," p. 39.
[48] Interview, Michael O'Connell, World Wildlife Fund, Washington, DC, 1991.

nationalized, both from trade and from heightened public opinion (brought on largely by the public-opinion ETC).

Given this dilemma, the rapid decline in elephant populations, and the increasingly desperate political and economic conditions within Africa as a whole in the 1980s, the professional ETC became largely ineffectual in the field. WWF could translate public concern into greater financial support for park management including anti-poaching operations. But, as argued above, both domestic and international conditions can easily overwhelm such efforts. Field support was just not enough. The professional ETC also had to step up its efforts to restrict trade but, in so doing, not cross that threshold whereby trade restrictions would damage key experiments in Zimbabwe and elsewhere.[49] It was a difficult balancing act, one not resolved until WWF finally joined the call for a ban in June 1989, shortly before the CITES meeting in October that considered and eventually decided to uplist – that is, to give greater protection to – the African elephant.

WWF's support of the trade ban was arguably a key factor in building the momentum in 1989 to the October meeting. The public opinion ETC had been advocating a CITES uplisting for at least a decade but to little effect.[50] Studies were conducted to verify population levels and, at the request of several African countries, a CITES-run quota system was established. But the studies were inconclusive until the mid-1980s (although some proponents of a ban claimed the trends were clear much earlier) and the quota system was flawed by the provision that exporting states could set their own "quota" without regard to sustainable levels of harvesting. To the consternation of much of the public opinion ETC, the professional ETC supported the quota system and, in fact, contributed substantially to the studies.

WWF's reversal and siding with the public-opinion ETC elicited

[49] Zambia's experiments are based on safari hunting rather than culling thus maintaining (or encouraging) a tourist industry while still seeking revenues from hunting, including presumably, the sale of ivory and other wildlife products. Adams and McShane, *The Myth of Wild Africa*, pp. 161–67.

[50] Biologist Bill Clark, in a dispute with WWF and its position on elephants over the years, wrote in a private letter: "At the 1979 CITES meeting in Costa Rica, I circulated documents calling for a transfer of the species to Appendix I and a halt to the ivory trade. I was ridiculed by, among others, WWF. I persisted through subsequent CITES meetings, and elsewhere, for ten difficult years. And through that period, it became increasingly obvious to me that the most serious obstacle to my efforts was the triumvirate of WWF, IUCN and TRAFFIC." Quoted in Princen and Finger, *Environmental NGOs in World Politics*, p. 149.

vigorous denunciations from the southern African range states. Such a reaction suggests the influence ETCs have on international and national conservation policies. At a press conference in September, 1989, when a ban was virtually assured, Zimbabwe's Minister of Natural Resources and Tourism explained that:

> elephant products such as ivory, skin and meat have earned Zimbabwe about Zimbabwe $20 million in direct exports since 1980 ... This has assisted in conservation and placed a high value on elephant.
>
> The international community should be aware that successful conservation of elephant will inevitably lead to ivory production. If we were not to manage elephant, it would be naive to believe that they would stop producing ivory. Greater numbers would die naturally, more would be killed as problem animals, and illegal hunting would increase.
>
> ... As many as 50 observers from local NGOs and District Councils are going to the CITES Meeting in Switzerland to support Zimbabwe. Publications on the Zimbabwe conservation philosophy have been prepared by the NGOs. All of this is very encouraging for government and we have no doubt where our duties lie. We cannot allow international conservation politics to divert us from our primary responsibility to the citizens of Zimbabwe.[51]

The Zimbabwe minister went on to explain the sequence of events and the role of the ETCs leading to the proposed ban:

> Certain non-governmental organisations, based mainly in East Africa, took it upon themselves to initiate a major study of the ivory trade last year. Before completing or publishing their work, they went to the international press and persuaded international NGOs that they should call for a world ban on the ivory trade. Under political pressure, a number of Western governments introduced a moratorium on trade.[52]

Finally, the minister stated that Zimbabwe and a number of other southern African governments had devised a common marketing strategy, but the plan was kept confidential so as not "to give certain NGOs the opportunity to derail them before the CITES Meeting."[53]

---

[51] Minister of Natural Resources and Tourism, "Ivory Trade: The Zimbabwe Position," pp. 2–3.

[52] Ibid. p. 4.

[53] Ibid. p. 5. As further evidence of the influence of ETCs, at a meeting of producer states in July 1989 members of the public opinion ETC were present as observers but effectively harassed the southern African states. A member of the London-based Environmental Investigation Agency said, "We'll be crawling round the world going

To assess the impact on state policies of these transnational activities and the resulting trade ban, it is important to note that governments monitor international developments on a continuous basis and begin to react, as in the ivory case, when the momentum builds toward a new regulatory regime. In other words, to assess the domestic response to an evolving regime, it is not sufficient to look only at policies that emerge after formal legislation is enacted. In addition, in looking forward, one must account for lag times associated not only with bureaucratic and legislative processes but with the slow evolution of norms and ideas and, especially regarding conservation policies, with the biophysical conditions that mitigate against rapid and drastic policy changes. Thus, conservation policies that have a long social history and significant biological determinants – for example, large protected herbivores can wreak havoc if they are suddenly abandoned – can not be easily reversed. With these considerations in mind, one can expect only marginal policy changes in Kenya and Zimbabwe in the immediate aftermath of the ivory trade ban. In the long-term, by contrast, the ban may compel substantial changes domestically and internationally.

Kenya attributes the decline in the rate of killing of elephants (which began in mid-1989, shortly before the CITES meeting that banned ivory trade) to intensified efforts by its newly created agency, the Kenya Wildlife Service (KWS) under the directorship of Richard Leakey; to the increased effectiveness of protection operations; to global awareness of the elephant problem; and to the various national moratoriums on ivory trade that went into effect before the ban.[54] The last two factors were driven by the ETCs which suggests that Kenya's

through the dustbins of these organisations to see where their ivory is coming from." Quoted in Armstrong and Bridgland, "Elephants and the Ivory Tower," p. 39.

John Turner, Director of the US Fish and Wildlife Service in the Bush administration led the US delegation to the 1992 biennial meeting of CITES. He speaks of the tremendous influence environmental groups, especially the well-funded animal rights groups, have on the proceedings and in their publicity campaigns, especially in Europe. Personal communication, October 26, 1992. Adams and McShane attack such groups on their own, self-proclaimed, turf, namely, ethics: "The ethical standards which support the argument for animal rights do not apply in Africa. Some people in the animal rights movement argue that it is only a matter of time before African culture 'evolves' to a point where Africans will accept the value of strict preservationism. Not only does this attitude endorse the imperialist assumption that Western culture is more advanced, it also implies that the West has a moral duty to intervene until Africans recognize the folly of their ways." *The Myth of Wild Africa*, p. 167.

[54] "Elephant Conservation Plan: Kenya," Kenya Wildlife Service, Nairobi, Kenya, October 1991.

new policy of intensified protection, although partly domestic in origin, evolved in step with international efforts and were mutually reinforcing.

For example, the ban brought increased international assistance whereby the KWS increased personnel in its protection unit from 465 men before the ban to 523 after the ban. Observers appear to agree that, without the ban, such efforts would have been inconsequential in the face of overwhelming demand and poaching.[55] Also, had the ban not taken place, it is doubtful whether Kenya could have maintained such expensive protective operations.

In fact, a second and, possibly, long-range effect of the ban on Kenya, is that prominent people in the conservation community, including parks authorities, have begun to question the sustainability of exclusionist, paramilitary, and expensive wildlife policies. On financial grounds alone, let alone social, political, and ecological, the ban and subsequent huge investments in policing are unlikely to be maintained, especially if the international community, its main source of funds for aid and tourism, loses interest or suffers an economic downturn.[56]

In Zimbabwe, the primary effects of the trade ban have been to intensify efforts to educate the international community about conservation realities in Africa and to organize regionally to create a producers' cartel in ivory. Zimbabwean officials discovered that the best-laid plans, however sophisticated sociologically and biologically, can not indeed be divorced from the perceptions and the politics of the international community. This is especially true when those plans depend on international trade. Consequently, Zimbabwe has, since the ban, launched a major public-relations campaign to educate environmentalists about the pitfalls of exclusionist approaches and the potential of approaches that respect resident peoples and the environment alike. They are working with mainstream NGOs like IUCN.[57]

The idea of a producers' cartel had been developing for some time but, because trade was profitable – and sustainable under Zimbabwe's management programs – there was little incentive to pursue it. After the ban, however, Zimbabwe and other southern African nations, due to their continuing wildlife management programs, have growing

---

55 Interview, John S. Williams, demographer, the World Conservation Union (IUCN), 1992.
56 Telephone interview, Catherine Allen, IUCN, Washington, DC, January, 1993.
57 Ibid.

elephant populations that need to be culled. So these countries have stepped up their efforts to organize such a cartel. A first strategy was to obtain a partial downlisting of the elephant under CITES, in effect, separating themselves from those countries who had poaching problems and who, through the trade ban and international pressure, shut down the ivory trade worldwide. Although the US initially supported the plan, these countries were not successful in the 1992 Kyoto Conference of the Parties to CITES. There is currently talk of these countries withdrawing from CITES and pursuing the cartel plan independently and in collaboration with non-CITES parties and, possibly, with Japan, which has floated the idea of resuming trade in ivory.[58]

Conclusion

State responses to rapid environmental decline can take the form of unilateral restrictions (e.g., on hunting or on trade) or multilateral agreement (e.g., regional or global). The ivory trade case suggests that neither response can be understood separate from the transnational economic and political forces affecting the resource and the domestic structures of the producer states. The decline in the African elephant was at once a problem of inadequate management and investment by range states on the one hand and high demand and fluid trade patterns on the other. Transnational alliances among environmental organizations arose (in collaboration with intergovernmental organizations) to counter these patterns. The initial strategy of tightening trade regulation and promoting anti-poaching efforts proved inadequate in the face of domestic troubles and high international demand. A trade ban became the last resort.

As shown, the initiation of and momentum toward the ban was heavily influenced by, first, the public relations ETC and, then, the professional ETC. For a "weak" state like Kenya, access to domestic institutions by transnational actors was easy, as it had been since colonial times. Consequently, the events leading to the ban and the ban itself reinforced existing wildlife policies. At the same time, Kenyan officials and conservationists appear to have been forced to reassess the full, long-term social and environmental costs of paramilitary approaches that are expensive and exclusionist. Here, then, access to and alignment with governmental actors did not help because

[58] "MITI to Propose Renewed Ivory Trade," *Nikkei Weekly*, (Tokyo, Japan), August 1, 1992.

fundamental *shifts* in policies, not the reinforcement of longstanding policies, were needed.

For a state-dominated country like Zimbabwe that was beginning to experiment with devolving wildlife authority and wildlife benefits to the local level, the ETC could gain access only indirectly, that is, via the international institution, CITES. The instrument was necessarily uniform and blunt – a ban, which jeopardized Zimbabwe's domestic efforts to make fundamental policy shifts. The ban also forced countries like Zimbabwe to reassess their foreign policies with respect to the conservation community and to neighboring range states.

The impact of transnational activity including the eventual ban therefore varied with the vulnerabilities of domestic wildlife and development policies. The differential impact was due, in part, to the domestic and societal structures in which the ETC operated and in which international regulations had their impact. Kenya and Zimbabwe may be similar on many counts, but the development of their respective institutions and societies was significantly different, particularly with respect to the ability of the state to shift economic rents to those who live with wildlife. Given the key role local communities play in wildlife conservation in African states, the divergence in state policies toward local property rights over wildlife and wild (or communal) lands was a major determinant of the effects of the interactions among ETCs, range states, and the international wildlife trade regime.

In the early years of independence, Kenya showed signs of strengthening community-based development and, in fact, the first attempt to integrate local people's needs with conservation began in Kenya in 1960.[59] But the stresses of the 1980s pushed Kenyan policies toward greater enforcement and greater exclusion. Local resentment translated into poaching and increased encroachment on protected lands. Consistent with its colonial and post-independence past, Kenya could do little but appeal for international support and clamp down on violators. Consequently, first the public-opinion ETC and then the professional ETC were willing partners – and access was easy.

In Zimbabwe, the pre-independence apartheid policies and long civil war and eventual independence led to a different approach to

---

[59] The project failed for many of the reasons outlined above. The Game Department was the major obstacle, in part because of the dominant conservation philosophy and in part because it insisted on receiving all revenues. Adams and McShane, *The Myth of Wild Africa*, p. 162.

government and local resource management. Leaders used the state for personal self-aggrandizement much less than in Kenya and, despite racial and income inequities, a consensus of sorts emerged from a corporatist past that emphasized local self-reliance, making direct access by transnational actors difficult. The ETCs thus had little effect on these policies (with the exception of the one WWF project) but neither could they insulate Zimbabwe and its experiments with local control of wildlife from the effects of the global ban on ivory trade. In fact, promoting the ban at the international level was the only way – albeit indirect – to influence Zimbabwe's policies. As it turned out, the effects were perverse at least in the short term as Zimbabwe's experiments in sustainable practices were put in jeopardy. In the long term, the ETC's strategy may pay off because the ban, in effect, helped to pry Zimbabwe open, especially to selected members of the professional ETC. There is some evidence now that Zimbabwe is welcoming groups like WWF and IUCN to assist with community-based conservation programs.[60] It is likely that one reason is to build a transnational coalition to counter the one that emerged in 1989 and led to the ban. Zimbabwe has also stepped up its public education efforts to convince the international community of the wisdom of its programs.

As for specific impacts and policy changes, it should be stressed that little in the way of conservation resembles, say, state responses to the oil shocks of the 1970s. Wildlife and wildlands are not critical to states in the same way that oil is (at least, in the immediate term). In addition, the combination of bureaucratic inertia and biological reality means that states cannot change course when international conditions suddenly change. Kenya's wildlife policies have been dependent on tourism and foreign perceptions, Zimbabwe's on managing and culling herds of elephants who continue to eat and reproduce. Neither country could stop or change course rapidly: if Kenya allowed local hunting, say, it would lose its tourists; if Zimbabwe stopped culling, wildlands and farms alike would be overrun by elephants.[61]

For all these reasons, one must expect policy responses that are nuanced and gradual in their evolution. Some conservationists in Kenya are questioning the long-term viability of high-cost enforcement and many in Zimbabwe are reassessing their relations with the

---

[60] Michael Sutton, World Wildlife Fund memorandum, Washington, DC, June 25, 1990.
[61] Precedents do exist for such ecological and human devastation by elephants and other grazers when humans have managed populations inappropriately.

international conservation community. It may be many years before anyone knows what the full impact of the trade ban will be on wildlife policies in Africa.

A growing consensus is emerging within the international conservation community that recognizes that solutions to global environmental problems such as species loss must be tailored to conditions at the level of the ecosystem and the local community. Sweeping measures like bans can provide short-term amelioration, but they must be tied to the conditions that resource users face on a day-to-day basis. But if there is a consensus about wildlife conservation and human needs, what is less well recognized is that trade patterns and transnational environmental politics are also major determinants of environmental outcomes. The two – conservation/development with local control on the one hand and transnational economic and political relations on the other – cannot be separated for either analytic or prescriptive purposes. Linking the two – local tailoring and global economic management – is a daunting task. But this case suggests that at least two lessons can be derived for the future of interactions among transnational environmental groups, producer states, and the relevant international resource regime.

One lesson is that simple measures like trade bans may be necessary to break destructive trade patterns and to provide a breathing spell to devise long-term solutions.[62] But such bans may also harm those states and communities that are doing the most to find sustainable means of economic development and conservation. The second lesson is that transnational efforts that focus only on state-run or even community-based projects will be vulnerable to larger political and economic forces. Simultaneous and coordinated efforts (e.g., between the professional and public-opinion ETCs) to address these forces will be necessary.

Finally, this case mostly confirms the propositions set forth by Risse-Kappen in the introduction to this volume. At the same time, it suggests that, when causal patterns are complex, they are difficult to sort out. This is especially true when the impact of transnational actors

[62] For an argument to explain the appeal and utility of a ban based on notions of focal points, bureaucratic decision-making, and the science/policy interface, see the chapter "The Ivory Trade Ban: NGOs and International Conservation," in Princen and Finger, *Environmental NGOs in World Politics*. For discussion of the need for simplified approaches, especially for implementation, see Oran R. Young, *International Cooperation: Building Regimes for Natural Resources and the Environment* (Ithaca: Cornell University Press, 1989), p. 234.

is mediated by both domestic and international factors and when biophysical and social conditions make for profound changes on the ground.

Where the ETC was able to penetrate the weak domestic structure of Kenya and had a long history of building and maintaining coalitions to promote one policy – that is, conservation through exclusion – it could not adjust to intrasocietal conflicts over resource use. Its inability to adjust appears to be associated with the strength of the previous coalitions as well as with the inability of governmental actors to adjust, given its dependency on foreign support.

Concomitantly, the ETC's *indirect* penetration of the state-dominated country, Zimbabwe, with a world-wide trade ban had perverse effects in the near term. In the long term, with penetration facilitated by these perverse effects, the ETC appears to be building winning coalitions for non-exclusionist policies.

Although in this chapter I did not investigate in detail TNA inter-actions with international institutions, this study does suggest that a highly institutionalized trade regime centering around CITES facil-itates transnational activities, especially TNA's ability to gain access to state-dominated countries like Zimbabwe. In this instance, ETCs were instrumental in the creation of the wildlife trade regime in the early 1970s and are now critical to its maintenance. They were also instru-mental in promoting the trade ban.[63] Thus, whereas the ETCs had relatively few channels into Zimbabwe prior to the ban, their success with the ban forced such access.

---

[63] See the chapter, "The Ivory Trade Ban: NGOs and International Conservation," in Princen and Finger, *Environmental NGOs in World Politics*, for evidence of the trans-national NGO role in CITES.

Conclusions: So what?

8 Power politics, institutions, and transnational relations

Stephen D. Krasner

Introduction

Neorealism has the great analytic virtues of parsimony and heuristic power. But even its most forceful proponents do not claim that it provides a complete description and analysis of international politics or foreign policy.[1] For neorealism, states, understood as unified rational actors that embody the capabilities within a given territory, are the ontological givens. Systemic outcomes are a function of the distribution of power among states. The only analysis that neorealism can offer for the foreign policy of a specific state is based on the power capabilities of that state and the overall distribution of power in the system. Neorealism has little to say about transnational relations. For that matter it has little to say about domestic politics either.

If, however, emphasis is given not to states as unified rational actors, but rather to another critical aspect of realism, the assumption of anarchy, then transnational actors must be a natural component of a sovereign state system. By definition, transnational relations could not occur in an empire; that is, a political system in which there is only one supreme political authority. All interactions in such a system must be domestic. Transnational actors can only exist in a system in which there are mutually exclusive multiple centers of political authority. If there is anarchy, if there is no supreme political authority, then transnational phenomena will almost certainly be present. Only if states

This paper has benefitted from the comments of Thomas Risse-Kappen, the anonymous reader for Cambridge University Press, and the other participants in this project.
[1] Kenneth Waltz, "Reflections on *Theory of International Politics*: A Response to My Critics," in Robert O. Keohane, ed., *Neorealism and Its Critics* (New York: Columbia University Press, 1986), pp. 331–32.

were completely autarkic, or if all interactions across borders were conducted by official state functionaries, would there be no transnational actors.

Power affects transnational relations in two different ways. First, transnational actors can be seen as a manifestation of the institutional structures of states, especially the most powerful states. The character of transnational actors will reflect the institutional environment within which they must function and the most important component of this environment is states. In this specification the state or polity is understood as a set of institutional relationships that include formal governmental institutions, civil society, and the rules that govern interactions between them.[2] Power means that the structures of some institutions (those that are weaker) must be isomorphic with others (those that are stronger).

This institutional perspective is ontologically distinct from realist and neo-realist arguments, because, while it emphasizes the importance of power, it takes institutional structures rather than actors as the units of analysis. This formulation is consistent with the position taken by several of the authors in this project, especially Risse-Kappen, who understand domestic structures and transnational actors to be interacting in a complementary way. It differs from their perspectives, however, in emphasizing the relevance of power: the state (here understood as a set of institutionalized relationships) is the strongest actor in the sense that other actors must conform to its structure. Furthermore, not all states are equal: the institutional structures of the most powerful states have the greatest influence on the institutional arrangements of transnational actors.

The second way in which power is relevant is more conventional: transnational relations can be analyzed in terms of relational power. Behavior and outcomes are a function of the capabilities of different actors, both public and private. In this formulation the state is defined as a set of central decision-making organizations and actors.[3] This conceptualization, which has generally been labelled statist, is consist-

---

[2] See, for instance, Peter Katzenstein, *Small States in the World Economy* (Ithaca, NY: Cornell University Press, 1985) and the discussion by Thomas Risse-Kappen in his introduction to this volume.

[3] Using the term "state" both for central decision-making organizations and for basic institutional structures does create semantic confusion. The clearest usage would be to limit the term "state" to central decision-making institutions and personnel, and to use the term "polity" for institutional structures. This usage, however, is not widely accepted.

ent with traditional realist perspectives. Both statism and realism are analytic traditions that fall within a larger Machiavellian or power-politics paradigm that takes actors rather than institutional structures as the units of analysis and which understands politics as a struggle over the distribution of resources or even over life and death. Neo-realism sees states as unified rational actors and ignores internal divisions; statism defines states as central decision-making organizations that must confront both internal and external challengers. Central decision-makers attempting to secure their preferences must interact with domestic and transnational actors, as well as other states.[4] Outcomes are a function of the relative power of actors.

States, understood as central decision-making organizations and personnel, will be indifferent to some kinds of transnational flows, unable to block others even if they would like to do so, and encouraging to still others. States will be unconcerned about many kinds of flows. Most governments would not care about travelling circuses, or if they did care about travelling circuses, they might not be much concerned with transmission of fashion for tableware, or the extent to which styles of cooking were affected by developments in other countries, even though such considerations could preoccupy many of their citizens.

Even if states did make an effort to control their borders fully, and certainly the Soviet Union made such efforts at various points in its history, it is unlikely that it would be fully successful. The Soviets and other countries were never able to obstruct completely transnational information flows such as international radio transmissions, even though they protested that such flows were a violation of state sovereignty and they attempted to jam foreign signals. Even for more tangible flows, such as goods and people, it has been difficult for states to control their borders fully. For instance, hundreds of thousands of illegal immigrants and billions of dollars-worth of illegal drugs move across American borders every year. Smuggling is an old and well practiced profession.

Finally, there will be some kinds of transnational flows that central decision-makers will encourage. The Soviets were happy to receive information about the American nuclear bomb program from Klaus

---

[4] See, for instance, Stephen D. Krasner, *Defending the National Interest* (Princeton, NJ: Princeton University Press, 1978); Peter Evans, D. Rueschemeyer, and T. Skocpol, eds., *Bringing the State Back In* (New York: Cambridge University Press, 1985); Robert Putnam, "Diplomacy and Domestic Politics: The Logic of Two-Level Games," *International Organization*, 42, 3 (Summer 1988), pp. 427–60.

Fuchs and other spies. They sanctioned foreign involvement in Soviet economic activity after the inauguration of the New Economic Program in the late 1920s, just as many countries in the contemporary environment, especially in developing areas, have encouraged direct foreign investment (DFI). Soviet officials sought to procure certain kinds of foreign goods, often those that the United States and its allies attempted to prevent them from having. At various times the Soviet Union, possibly the most closed major state that the world has seen, promoted the activities of transnational actors; the Comintern was founded by Lenin in 1919 to coordinate the activities of communist parties in other countries and subvert non-communist governments.

Many states have encouraged transnational outflows not only of their products but sometimes even of their people. It may be easier to expel an unwanted group such as an ethnic or religious minority, to turn the group into a transnational actor, than to contain or persecute such a group within the borders of the state. The option of expulsion is not available to empires and internal exile may be more expensive than creating international refugees.

In sum, transnationals may frustrate or promote the objectives of state actors. In conflicts between the state (central decision-making organizations) and multinationals, state actors have formidable resources. They win often, but not always.

Institutional structures and transnational actors

The institutional structures of transnational actors must reflect the institutional environment within which they function. The most important component of that environment is the sovereign state. State structures influence not only the avenues through which transnational actors must operate, but the very nature of these actors themselves. The way in which any individual transnational actor is organized may vary across states because the transnational must accommodate itself to different state structures. More powerful states, that is, polities with more resources, will have the greatest influence on the institutional structures of other entities including transnationals.

Organizations that exist in institutionally complex environments can enhance their likelihood of survival by fitting in, by becoming isomorphic with the institutions with which they must interact. Isomorphism enhances legitimacy and access to resources. States are the most important organizations in the environment of transnational actors.[5]

Isomorphism can be the result of coercion, competitive pressures, or concerns about legitimacy. Legal requirements are the most obvious form of coercion. American law, for instance, prohibits bias based on ethnicity and mandates affirmative action for groups that have been historically disadvantaged. In contrast, Japan has no affirmative action program for its Korean minority which has been excluded from many commercial and bureaucratic opportunities. Firms in the United States both transnational and domestic are legally compelled to have affirmative action programs; firms in Japan, whether domestic or transnational, are not.

Competitive pressures encourage organizations to become more similar because they can function more efficiently if they are more alike. In a state with a fragmented decision-making structure and many points of access effective political action requires that private actors, including transnationals, also be organized to take advantage of multiple points of access. In a corporatist political structure foreign investors must become members of peak associations if they hope to influence public and private policy.

Organizations also become more similar because they adopt established norms to enhance their legitimacy and access to resources. These norms can emanate from many sources including other transnationals and international organizations as well as states. Given the influence of the values of some large states on the expectations and attitudes of many public and private actors, however, there will be a strong incentive for the organizational form of transnational actors to conform with these state norms.[6]

For transnational actors coercion (especially formal legal requirements) and competitive pressures, will lead to variations in institutional forms across states. Transnational actors will organize themselves differently in different countries. They may arrange themselves as bribe givers in one place, lobbyists in another, and diplomatic emissaries in still a third.

---

[5] John W. Meyer and Brian Rowen, "Institutionalized Organizations: Formal Structure in Myth and Ceremony," in Paul J. DiMaggio and Walter W. Powell, eds., *The New Institutionalism in Organizational Analysis* (Chicago: University of Chicago Press, 1991), p. 53.

[6] Paul J. DiMaggio and Walter W. Powell, "The Iron Cage Revisited: Institutional Isomorphism and Collective Rationality in Organization Fields," in DiMaggio and Powell, eds., *The New Institutionalism in Organizational Analysis*, p. 66.

The need to conform to norms and expectations, as opposed to responding to coercion, may or may not lead to cross national variations in the organizational structure of a given transnational actor. Normative expectations can be generated from several different sources. The institutionalized norms of a transnational actor might be endogenous to that actor, or they might reflect the values of a host country, or the values of a particularly powerful national state, most probably the state within which the transnational actor has most of its operations. If the organization's own internal norms are particularly powerful, then there might be little variation in institutional structure across states. In contrast, if the norms of host countries are determinant, then transnational actors will organize themselves differently in different countries.

The institutional structures of the Catholic church, that most enduring of transnational actors, reflect both competitive incentives emanating from national states, and norms and expectations that are derived from the church itself. In the medieval period the church claimed, and often had, authority which stretched across political boundaries and overawed secular rulers. But the church lost its prerogatives and power during the struggles that characterized the Renaissance and Reformation. The church has come, like some mini-state, to occupy a defined piece of territory, the 108 acres of Vatican City. The church sends formal emissaries, papal nuncios, as diplomatic representatives to secular rulers. The church divides the whole earth into mutually exclusive territorial units that are linked in a vertical chain from the parish priest to the Holy See. Most of these units are based on lines of political authority – cities, regions, or countries. This organizational structure reflects competitive incentives: the church must interact with the secular state to carry out its pastoral mission effectively, and therefore it has a great incentive to mimic some aspects of state's organizational structure. The church cannot secure territorial access without the approval of states. While such access has been generously granted in some cases it has been denied in others.[7]

At the same time, however, other institutional structures of the church are endogenously generated or reflect historical compromises that were made under very different institutional circumstances. Some states claim the right to control ecclesiastical appointments under

---

[7] Ivan Vallier, "The Roman Catholic Church: A Transnational Actor," *International Organization*, 25, 3 (Summer 1971), pp. 480–85.

agreements with the church that were made hundreds of years ago; for other states such claims would be antithetical to their constitutional structure.[8] The Holy See maintains direct relations with pastoral priests through curial officials. It proselytizes non-Catholics through hierarchically structured missionary orders. The Pope is selected by the international College of Cardinals. Curial affairs, missionary activities, and papal selection are all dictated by rules and norms of the church that have only been tangentially affected by sovereign states.

The Catholic church is an example of an organization in which competitive pressures have led to institutional isomorphism with states while the need for institutional legitimacy has been satisfied in several different ways. The incentive to mimic state structures has affected some aspects of the church's own organizational arrangements while other institutional formations are explicable only in terms of autochthonously generated norms and rules. Hence, even the Catholic church with a long history that antedates the modern international system of sovereignty cannot be understood as if it were somehow a free floating actor simply bargaining with various public officials. The church's own institutional structures reflect the coercive, competitive, and normative pressures for isomorphism with states.

Multinational corporations, the most prominent kind of transnational actor in the contemporary world, arose in an institutional setting in which states were already firmly established. Unlike the Catholic church they do not have an institutional history and internally generated rules and norms that reflect environments as different as the Roman Empire, the Middle Ages, the Renaissance, the Reformation, and the first era of European global expansion in the sixteenth and seventeenth centuries. Competitive incentives and state coercion, usually legal, have compelled multinational corporations to organize in ways that allow them to interact effectively with national states. Some multinationals have been created and owned by states. At a minimum, most corporations must have the approval of the state to secure territorial access, without which they could not operate at all. More fundamentally, the very existence of multinationals depends upon property rights that are created and maintained by states. Corporations must have a stable legal environment that recognizes among other things, private property, limited liability, and impersonal ownership.

[8] Vallier, "Catholic Church," pp. 486–87.

263

Variations in institutional arrangements and regulations across states will inevitably place some constraints on the ability of corporations to operate as fully integrated businesses. The more curbs that are placed on the rights of the corporation to allocate capital, labor, technology, intermediate goods, and final products across national boundaries, the more a supposedly transnational company becomes a collection of national subsidiaries, perhaps with the same name, but with limited operational integration. The fewer the constraints, the more a transnational corporation can operate as a single global entity making decisions without regard to national boundaries.

Given the variations in taxation and legal rules, transnational corporations must, inevitably, adjust their activities to accommodate particular national conditions, both formal and informal. The affiliates of foreign banks in the United States must operate within the limitations imposed by the Glass Steagall Act on unified banking. All of the different rules that affect employment practices, sexual harassment, environmental safety, and health insurance, impact on multinational corporations as well as on purely national firms. The social-security payments and charitable contributions of Toyota's assembly facility in Kentucky do not follow the same pattern as those of its parent in Toyota City. Toyota's American subsidiary is not organized like comparable GM, Ford, or Chrysler plants, but it is not organized like Toyota's Japanese factories either.

In addition to variations in national rules that affect both domestic and foreign companies in the same way, receptivity to foreign investors and the extent to which such investors are treated differently from national firms has also varied across countries. Simon Reich has pointed out that Britain and the United States have encouraged access and accorded national treatment. Both the United States and the United Kingdom have generally avoided discrimination in favor of national firms, although the United States does impose restrictions on foreign investors in some sectors, including communications, transportation, and the exploitation of natural resources on public lands. In contrast, France has followed a policy of limited access and discriminatory intervention. Germany has allowed access but discriminated in favor of German firms. In the mid-1970s Germany explicitly adopted laws to prevent the foreign takeover of strategically important industries, including autos.[9]

[9] Simon Reich, "Roads to Follow: Regulating Direct Foreign Investment," *International Organization*, 43, 4 (Autumn 1989), pp. 543–84.

In Japan, as in France, it has been difficult for foreign companies to secure access, and when they have entered they have been treated differently as a result of both government policy and private *keiretsu* practices. This is true for American companies despite the fact that Japanese multinationals have had more or less unconstrained access to the US market. Japanese transnational corporate investment in the United States tends to be wholly owned and these subsidiaries engage in very high levels of intra-corporate trade or trade with the other firms in the same *keiretsu*. In contrast, direct foreign investment in Japan is both much smaller and concentrated in minority-owned affiliates that engage in relatively little external trade.[10] Legal, administrative, and corporate barriers have made the level of transnational activity in Japan lower than in other industrialized countries. The public and private institutional structures in Japan are very different from those in the United States and, as a result, the level and nature of transnational corporate activities are also very different.

Aside from legal and administrative constraints, competitive incentives will lead corporations to organize and operate differently in different countries. Katzenstein and Tsujinaka point out that the preferred form of political activity by Japanese corporations with interests in the United States is multiple channel lobbying: Japanese companies hire American lobbyists and lawyers to press their case throughout Congress and the bureaucracy. In contrast, American firms with interests in Japan have little direct access to the Japanese political system. They must rely on high-level intervention by the American government to promote and protect their interests. Corporate political activity is different because domestic political structures are different. Japanese companies in the United States act like American companies. American companies in Japan, lacking direct access to the Japanese bureaucratic and political process, cannot act like Japanese companies.

Transnational actors must adapt to national institutional structures, at least if the state they are interacting with is powerful; that is, capable of unilaterally affecting the objectives of the transnational actor. The liberal perception of global interdependence sweeping before it all variations in national behavior is empirically wrong.

Incentives to adjust to national institutions are not as consequential

---

10 Dennis J. Encarnation, "A Common Evolution? A Comparison of United States and Japanese Transnational Corporations," *Transnational Corporations*, 2, 1 (February 1993), pp. 20–27; Robert Z. Lawrence, "Japan's Different Trade Regime: An Analysis with Particular Reference to *Keiretsu*," *The Journal of Economic Perspectives*, 7, 3 (Summer 1993): 3–20.

when transnational actors confront weaker states. Thomas Princen notes that when there was conflict, major wildlife organizations chose the policies preferred by private and public actors in more powerful states over those advocated by governments in weaker African states. The leaders of these associations believed that the success of their efforts depended on their ability to influence policy-makers in the industrialized world, rather than on their leverage on states within which ivory was harvested. The World Wildlife Foundation did not re-organize itself to become more institutionally isomorphic with the state structure of Zimbabwe. Norms emanating from the industrialized West, such as the conviction that killing any potentially endangered animal is bad, were more compelling than norms embraced within African states, such as the view that wildlife should contribute to the well being of the local population.

In the contemporary world transnational fascist and racist organizations are weak; this would hardly be the case if Germany had won the Second World War. Multinational corporations are strong, a reflection of the legal provisions and economic organization of the most powerful states in the international system. Had the United States rather than the Soviet Union collapsed in 1991, the role of transnational corporations would surely be much more modest. Private foundations such as Ford and Rockefeller, as well as politically sponsored foundations such as the Friedrich Ebert Stiftung, have active international programs. Their very existence is based on legal institutions and national norms in the United States and the Federal Republic of Germany.[11] In the nineteenth century missionary groups were important transnational actors. These groups reflected the proselytizing ethos of many Christian denominations in Europe and the United States that could flourish because these countries endorsed religious toleration.[12]

Aside from their influence on the institutional arrangements of transnational actors, state actions often account for the very existence of such actors in the first place. While the Catholic church antedates the modern international order, almost all other transnational actors developed in the context of an already established system of political sovereigns, and some of these actors were purposefully spawned by

---

[11] On the Ford Foundation see Peter D. Bell, "The Ford Foundation as a Transnational Actor," *International Organization*, 25, 3 (Summer 1971), pp. 465–78.

[12] James A. Field, Jr., "Transnationalism and the New Tribe," *International Organization*, 25, 3 (Summer 1971), p. 362.

states. The early European trading companies such as the British East India Company were developed to operate across borders because the state did not have the capacity to do so on its own. Nineteenth-century international finance was closely linked with political and security concerns and heavily influenced by official policy, especially in France and Germany.[13] The British Petroleum Company was originally established by the British government to secure oil reserves in the Middle East that could be used to fuel the British navy. American companies were admitted to the Turkish Petroleum Company only because of pressure from the United States government on Britain and France at the conclusion of the First World War. The largest French and Italian energy companies, both of which operate internationally, are state owned. The Firestone Rubber Company's involvement in developing rubber plantations in Liberia was the result of encouragement from Herbert Hoover while he was Secretary of Commerce in the Coolidge Administration.[14] The international communist movement, including some specific organizations such as the Comintern, was supported by the Soviet Union. Libya, Syria, Iraq, and Iran have sponsored transnational terrorist organizations.

In sum, states have powerfully influenced the institutional structure and even the existence of many transnational actors. Almost all transnational actors rely on stable property rights that are created and enforced by states. They must conform with the legal stipulations of different national governments. Competitive pressures encourage transnational actors to organize in ways that allow them to interact effectively with states, especially powerful states. Powerful states are also the source of legitimating and rationalizing myths that can influence the rules and norms adopted by transnational actors themselves. Few transnational organizations could function without becoming institutionally isomorphic with the different states within which they conduct their affairs.

Transnational actors and relational power

Although states, especially powerful states, can create transnational actors in the first place and stimulate them to become institutionally

[13] Herbert Feis, *Europe, the World's Banker, 1870–1914* (New York: Norton: 1965), pp. 120–22, 167–69; Janice Thomson, *Mercenaries, Pirates, and Sovereigns: State-Building and Extraterritorial Violence in Early Modern Europe* (Princeton, NJ: Princeton University Press, 1994).

[14] Hoover was afraid that the British would establish a world rubber cartel.

isomorphic, this does not mean that public officials will always prevail when there are differences between their preferences and those of transnationals. Much of the literature on transnational relations has focused on the threat that they pose to sovereignty, where sovereignty refers to government control rather than to an institutionalized structure in which political authority is based on exclusive control over a defined territory. States – now understood as central decision-making organizations and actors – and transnationals are inevitably involved in a bargaining relationship. States may lose; they may accept transnational actors even though they would have preferred to exclude them entirely or allowed their involvement only on more restrictive terms. But states may also win; they may secure resources that enhance their capabilities and control over their own domestic population or other states or transnationals.[15]

Different transnational actors possess distinct kinds of resources. Religious organizations can offer legitimacy; transnational corporations can bring wealth; private foundations can transmit knowledge and money; and arms traders can provide military power. States also can have different kinds of assets including the sophistication of civil servants, the ability to offer financial incentives, and the competence to monitor agreements. All states, however, even the smallest and the poorest, possess one sometimes critical prerogative: the right to grant legitimate territorial access.[16]

The outcome of bargaining between states and transnational actors will depend on the balance of interests and capabilities. Other things being equal, the more important it is for an actor to operate legally within the boundaries of a specific country, the greater the leverage of political authorities. For instance, a company engaged in mineral exploitation needs access to the territory of specific countries where deposits are located; a company engaged in assembling clothing can operate anywhere where there is cheap labor and transportation. The state – that is, central decision-makers – has more leverage over natural-resource developers than over garment manufacturers.

Transnational activities can be most problematic for state control when the right to grant territorial access cannot be effectively exercised, or is of little importance because transnational actors have other

---

[15] For a discussion of the multiple issues involved in bargaining between transnationals and states see Barbara Haskel, "Access to Society: A Neglected Dimension of Power," *International Organization*, 34 (Winter 1980), 89–120.

[16] Samuel P. Huntington, "Transnational Organizations in World Politics," *World Politics*, 25, 3 (April 1973), pp. 333–68.

options, or is irrelevant altogether. Many kinds of transnational flows can occur without the physical presence of transnational actors within a country. International radio transmissions offer one obvious example. Transmitters located in one country can broadcast signals that reach many others. It is difficult for receiving states to block or jam incoming signals. Senders can not only operate on many different frequencies, they can also choose frequencies that are close to those in the target state. The target would interfere with its own stations if it obstructed international transmissions. Jamming may also increase the curiosity of potential listeners who need only relatively cheap receivers to tap foreign broadcasts. The effort by many states in the Soviet bloc to impede transnational broadcasting failed.[17]

Broadcasting is an example of a situation in which the most important resource available to all states, the right to grant territorial access, could not be effectively exercised because it was too difficult to block the transborder incursions of electromagnetic waves. Power capabilities, which were derived from the relative ease of sending as opposed to impeding signals, favored senders. States did loose sovereignty, here understood as the *ability to control* transborder flows (as opposed to sovereignty understood as an *institutional arrangement* defined by territoriality and exclusion of non-national authority); they were unable to control the flow of information across their national borders.

While international capital flows are not quite as disembodied as electromagnetic waves, the volume and ease of global movements has undermined the ability of states to control their own macro-economic policies. States might be able to restrict the flow of financial assets across their borders but only at the cost of jeopardizing their ability to provide capital for their own domestic borrowers. Banks, both domestic and international, are linked in a single global market involving massive amounts of funds that are only loosely controlled by national monetary authorities. The growth of international capital markets and the difficulty that national authorities have in monitoring and restraining flows has compromised the ability of even the very largest states to conduct an independent monetary policy.[18] Transnational

---

[17] Rutger Lindahl, *Broadcasting Across Borders: A Study on the Role of Propaganda in External Broadcasts* (Lund, Sweden: C.W.K. Gleerup, 1978), p. 115; Jonathan Eyal, "Recent Developments in the Jamming of Western Radio Stations Broadcasting to the USSR and Eastern Europe," Radio Liberty Research RL 419/86 (November 7, 1986), p. 2.

[18] Michael Webb, "International Economic Structures, Government Interests, and International Coordination of Macroeconomic Adjustment Policies," *International Organi-*

radio broadcasts and international capital movements have weakened state sovereignty because one major bargaining chip available to states, the ability to withhold territorial access, has been of limited relevance.

Much of the earlier literature on transnational corporations focused on the inability or unwillingness of states to regulate the conditions under which transnationals would operate within their borders. Even if access was critical for the transnational, the state failed to exercise its right to specify the terms under which it would take place. In the dependency literature, multinationals were treated as part of a global capitalist system that, at best, limited Third World states to dependent development and, at worst, condemned poorer countries to impoverishment. Multinationals were instruments of exploitation. They were the mechanism through which the resources of the poor were transferred for the benefit of the rich. According to dependency theory, transnational corporations could corrupt domestic politics by allying with the indigenous bourgeoisie. Their activities were abetted by the military and economic aid programs of their home countries and ultimately backed by the covert or overt use of force.[19] The bargaining position of host country Third World governments was very weak and was weakened even further by the penetration of transnational actors.

Concerns about the power of multinationals was not limited to analysts focusing on the Third World. Europeans also pointed to the danger of American multinationals. Large American companies were seen as dominating the European market because of their superior size, technology, and access to capital and markets. European countries accepted these investments because they feared that they would be worse off without them, or they were pressured by the United States government, or they were ignorant of the threat posed by American domination.[20]

More generally, in their edited volume Keohane and Nye noted that transnational relations could challenge state control. Transnationals could change attitudes, increase the ability of some states to affect

---

zation, 45 (Summer 1991). The classic statement of this argument is Richard N. Cooper, *The Economics of Interdependence* (New York: McGraw Hill, 1968).

[19] Peter Evans, *Dependent Development* (Princeton, NJ: Princeton University Press, 1979); Enzo Faletto and Fernando Henrique Cardoso, *Dependency and Development in Latin America* (Berkeley, CA: Berkeley University Press, 1979).

[20] Theodore H. Moran, "Introduction: Government and Transnational Corporations," in T. Moran, ed., *Government and Transnational Corporations* (London: Routledge, 1993). The most well-known statement of European anxiety is Jean Jacques Servan-Schreiber, *The American Challenge* (New York: Athenaeum, 1968).

developments in others, and contribute to the emergence of private foreign policies that oppose or impinge on state policies.[21] Raymond Vernon's *Sovereignty at Bay*, also published in 1971, was much more nuanced than the title intimates but it did suggest the difficulty that any central decision-makers including those in the most powerful states, might have in regulating companies that operated in many different countries. For Vernon, as for others, the basic assumption was that the economic advantages offered by multinationals was a powerful incentive for host country governments to admit them into the country, but at the same time, the ability of each individual government to regulate the activities of such companies was constrained by the resources and global options available to corporate managers.

Many contemporary discussions of transnationals share the concerns about state control that dominated the earlier literature. The ability of transnationals to adopt institutionally isomorphic structures can make them even more politically influential in host countries. A number of American observers have argued that large Japanese companies are corrupting the American political process. Japanese transnationals have spent very large sums on lobbying in the United States and they have achieved significant victories.[22]

Hence, states may set the rules of the game within which transnationals operate, but that does not mean that states will always prevail in specific conflicts. In the United States, as Risse-Kappen argues, fragmented institutions and weak policy networks facilitate political involvement for transnationals and, one might add, trans-

---

[21] Robert O. Keohane and Joseph S. Nye, Jr., "Transnational Relations and World Politics: An Introduction," *International Organization*, 25, 3 (Summer 1971), p. 337.
[22] See Pat Choate, *Agents of Influence* (New York: Knopf, 1990) for a critical assessment of Japanese lobbying. For figures for expenditures by foreign actors in the United States as well as anecdotal information about penetration of the American political system see *New York Times*, November 2, 1993, p. 1, c. 2. In one of the most well-known cases of successful lobbying Toshiba avoided major sanctions after it was revealed in 1987 that one of its subsidiaries, Toshiba Machine Tool had, along with a Norwegian firm, exported equipment that probably allowed the Soviet Union to produce submarine propellers that reduced the likelihood of sonar detection. Toshiba Machine Tool was banned from the American market and Toshiba itself was banned from bidding on US government contracts for three years (although there were numerous exceptions), but the company preserved its $5–10 billion market in the United States. Toshiba spent several million dollars on a lobbying effort that involved hiring major American law and public relations firms, mobilizing the 4,100 employees in its American subsidiaries, and securing the support of US high technology companies that used Toshiba components. See Stephen Dryden, "The Battle of the Sumo Lobbyists," *Regardies, The Business of Washington*, 9 (September 1988), pp. 49 ff.

nationals that are both clever and rich can do well within such a domestic structure.

There are also, however, some compelling examples of situations in which transnational corporations and activities have enhanced the capabilities of states. In all of these cases the importance of territorial access has been a necessary, if not a sufficient, condition for the exercise of state power.

The exploitation of raw materials is an arena where access is critical. Oil, gold, copper, and tin do not migrate across international boundaries. Multinational corporations cannot develop these resources without permission from the state. This does not necessarily mean that states will always do well. Industries exploiting raw materials are usually highly concentrated. Corporations control sector specific assets that make it difficult, if not impossible, for host-country governments to operate entirely on their own, although over time the bargaining position of states has improved. In the first few decades of the twentieth century, many potential raw material exporting states had limited administrative capacity, technical skills, capital, and market knowledge. They were dependent on resources that could only be provided by transnational actors, and were happy to receive modest payments for exploration rights that might never yield commercially valuable deposits. After discoveries were made, however, and large non-fungible capital expenditures put in place, the bargaining power of states improved. Once states developed greater technical and economic knowledge and secured more capital the position of the transnational actor became even weaker. Changes in the benefits for states, derived from what Raymond Vernon referred to as the obsolescing bargain, were dramatic.[23]

The ability to control territorial access coupled with growing technological sophistication, market knowledge, and capital has, for instance, enhanced the power of oil-exporting states. Tax rates for oil rose from 50 percent to 92 percent after 1970.[24] Saudi Arabia, Kuwait, Brunei, and Abu Dhabi are among the richest countries in the world with regard to per capita income. Especially for Saudi Arabia, material wealth has augmented international influence. The Saudis have bankrolled other states and political movements in the Islamic world. While this has not

---

[23] Raymond Vernon, *Sovereignty at Bay: The Multinational Spread of US Enterprises* (New York: Basic Books, 1971), pp. 46–53; Theodore H. Moran, *Multinational Corporations and the Politics of Dependence: Copper in Chile* (Princeton, NJ: Princeton University Press, 1974).

[24] Moran, "Introduction," p. 5.

always resulted in desirable outcomes, as exemplified by Iraq's invasion of Kuwait, Saudi Arabia is more influential than it would have been had the major international oil companies not engaged in discovery, exploitation, and sales, as well as the training of Saudi nationals and the payment of staggering sums to the government. Saudi Arabia's level of sovereign control has been enhanced not undermined.

Civil aviation is another area where the importance of territorial access has enlarged the capabilities of many states. Passenger planes need airports. Large passenger planes need large airports. It is easy to monitor take-offs and landings and the allocation of gates. Since the military effectiveness of aviation was demonstrated in the First World War, claims to sovereign control over the airspace above national territory have been mutually accepted.[25] The critical importance of territorial access has made it possible for almost all states, even those with limited material resources and technological capability, to develop their own national airlines. In most cases passenger traffic has been shared more or less equally between the airlines of the sending and receiving countries.[26]

The impact of direct foreign investment in manufacturing on state control is not straightforward. The importance of territorial access varies depending upon the motivation of the investor. DFI can be stimulated by many factors including entry into specific markets, access to technology, anxiety about import restrictions, and utilization of cheap domestic labor for export production. Host-country governments may also have a number of different concerns including technology transfer, industrial development, employment, and exports. Negotiations may include, if only implicitly, local groups and the home-country government, not just the transnational corporation and host-country officials. Governments can do well if territorial access is important for corporations, state actors are insulated from societal influence (at least influence from transnationals), and bureaucracies are competent.

Into the 1970s, Japan used its administrative and regulatory powers to encourage transnational corporations to transfer valued technology

---

[25] This is not to say that the rule is always honored. The United States engaged in extensive air surveillance of the Soviet Union through overflights before the development of satellites. These planes, however, did not land in the Soviet Union, at least not voluntarily.

[26] Stephen D. Krasner, *Structural Conflict: The Third World Against Global Liberalism* (Berkeley, CA: University of California Press, 1985), chapter 8.

to Japanese companies. Companies capitulated because they wanted access to the large and rapidly developing Japanese market. For instance, despite the fact that IBM had organized itself as a yen-based company in the 1950s to avoid ministry of international trade and industry (MITI) foreign-exchange controls, MITI officials made it clear that the company's operations would be frustrated unless it shared technology with Japanese firms. MITI's vice minister stated that: "We will take every measure possible to obstruct the success of your business unless you license IBM patents to Japanese firms and charge them no more than a 5 percent royalty."[27] IBM capitulated, sold the patents, and accepted MITI administrative guidance on sales levels in exchange for the right to manufacture in Japan.

Texas Instruments (TI) encountered similar problems. In 1964 the company tried to form a subsidiary but was rejected when it refused to make integrated circuit patents available to Japanese companies. When conditions for direct foreign investment were liberalized in 1967 TI applied again, but MITI did not act for thirty months. Finally, MITI allowed the company to form a 50–50 joint venture with Sony in exchange for offering non-exclusive licenses on integrated circuits to all members of the Japanese industry. After three years TI was permitted to buy out Sony and establish a wholly owned subsidiary. The long delay facilitated the development of the Japanese semi-conductor industry.[28]

Thus, Japan was able to bargain effectively with transnationals. Japan used transnational actors to advance state objectives. The importance of territorial access was the necessary condition for the success of this policy. Without, however, the administrative and technological competence of bureaucrats and corporate officials, Japan's objectives would not have been realized. The Japanese state had more rather than less control over both domestic actors and international competitors as a result of negotiating with transnational corporations.

Mexico, a country both smaller in terms of economic size and less technologically sophisticated than Japan, has also bargained effectively with transnational coalitions (TNCs). Mexico was interested in developing a competitive automobile industry. Lacking the ability

---

27 Chalmers Johnson, *MITI and the Japanese Miracle: The Growth of Industrial Policy, 1925–1975* (Stanford, CA: Stanford University Press, 1982), p. 247.
28 Discussions of Texas Instruments' experience can be found in Michael Borrus, J. Millstein, and J. Zysman, *US–Japanese Competition in the Semiconductor Industry: A Study in International Trade and Technological Development*, p. 69; Chalmers Johnson, *MITI*, p. 285; *Wall Street Journal*, August 13, 1967 and April 29, 1968.

to create such an industry from purely national resources, Mexico sought investment from American companies. As a condition, however, of access to the Mexican market, the government success-fully insisted that the companies export vehicles to the United States even though it would have been cheaper to produce them north of the border.[29]

The United States also enjoyed some success in encouraging direct foreign investment in manufacturing by threatening to block access to the American market. Without anxieties generated by various American import restrictions, including voluntary export restraints on automobiles, the huge investments made by Japanese companies in the United States could hardly be explained. The largest Japanese automobile companies have all established assembly plants in the United States, providing benefits for American workers and possibly technological spin-offs for American producers.[30] The American government never had a coherent plan for revitalizing the US auto industry.

The bargaining power of the state is much weaker if territorial access is not important. If investment is undertaken primarily to take advan-tage of cheap labor that can be used to produce components for export, the state will not have much leverage. The greater the homogeneity of labor across countries and the less the cost of transportation and communication, the greater the number of options available to the TNC. If production can take place in any one of a number of countries, the ability to grant entry to any one country will not be worth much. Access to international markets will be intermediated by companies. The leverage of the corporations will be particularly great if com-ponents are produced in a number of different countries, no one of which could assemble a final product.

In sum, changes in technology have threatened state control in many areas. In some cases technology has facilitated disembodied transnational movements such as radio transmissions and capital flows. In other cases technology has diminished the importance of geographic location by either reducing transportation costs or stan-dardizing capital equipment so that it can be employed by semi-skilled

---

[29] US Congress, Office of Technology Assessment, *US–Mexico Trade: Pulling Together? Pulling Apart?* ITE-545 (Washington: US Government Printing Office, 1992), pp. 132–50.

[30] For a positive assessment of the impact of the joint Toyota GM plant in Fremont, California, see the testimony of Dorothy Christelow before the US Congress, Joint Economic Committee, Hearings, *Japan's Economic Challenge*, December 4, 1990.

workers in many different countries. Nevertheless, the bargaining power of states remains formidable in those cases where transnational actors must have territorial access to specific countries. States with large markets and technologically sophisticated labor forces can bargain effectively with multinational corporations.

Furthermore, it is not evident that the long-term trend is toward greater erosion of state control. Until the nineteenth century all major states were dependent upon mercenaries, i.e.. transnational actors, to put an effective army in the field.[31] Until Britain reformed its fiscal institutions at the end of the seventeenth century, no major state was able to finance its own affairs, including war fighting, without relying on international bankers.[32] Transnational ideas were much more consequential for authority in the sixteenth century when the Protestant Reformation transformed political and religious life across Western Europe, than any set of ideas has been in the twentieth century.

From the conclusion of the Napoleonic Wars to the 1960s states expanded their sovereignty. States increased their taxing powers and military capability. At least for a period after the Second World War, they could conduct independent macroeconomic policies. Especially for the United States, the ratio of exports and imports to gross national product was low (about 8 percent until the 1970s) and its bargaining leverage across a wide range of issue areas was very high.

During the last two decades technology has eroded control even for the very largest states by compromising their ability to conduct an independent monetary policy and globalizing the production of some manufactures. The impact of technological change on state capability is not, however, unidirectional. The industrial revolution made states stronger. The technological/information revolution made states, on balance, weaker, contrary to the fears so compellingly expressed in Huxley's *Brave New World* and Orwell's *1984*. Ever higher levels of material prosperity may yet increase the relative importance of non-tradeable services, reducing the importance of multinational corporations and again providing states with greater levels of control.

[31] Janice E. Thomson, "State Practices, International Norms, and the Decline of Mercenarism," *International Studies Quarterly*, 34, 1 (March 1990), pp. 23–48.
[32] Douglass C. North and Barry R. Weingast, "Constitutions and Commitments: The Evolution of Institutions Governing Public Choice in Seventeenth Century England," *Journal of Economic History*, 49 (1990) pp. 803–33; Paul Kennedy, *The Rise and Fall of the Great Powers: Economic Change and Military Conflict from 1500–2000* (New York: Random House, 1987).

Conclusion

Transnational actors and transnational relations have generally been viewed as phenomena that are antithetical to realist conceptualizations or beyond the scope of realist analysis. This is because the ontological assumptions of neorealism treat states as the only unproblematic actors in the international system. Liberal transnationalism arguments, in contrast, have promiscuously embraced any actor that might be consequential, including multinational corporations, religious assemblies, ethnic groups, international financiers, terrorist organizations, drug smugglers, states, and international organizations. Realism, however, offers an obvious reason to expect the presence of transnational actors. If multiple sovereign territorial units (states) and anarchy are defining characteristics of the international system, then there will almost certainly be transnational actors, because interactions across borders will not be limited to states alone.

Moreover, realism is only one specific articulation of a broader paradigm – power politics – which analyzes outcomes as a manifestation of the power and conflicting interests of actors. From a power-politics perspective, which understands states as rational central decision-making organizations and personnel (a position that has generally been labelled statism), transnationals can be understood as one of a number of actors with which states or rulers must relate. Statism, realism, and neorealism are all manifestations of a power politics paradigm which is actor oriented and which sees politics as a struggle over valued resources.

Private and public actors are locked in a bargaining relationship. States may be indifferent, encouraging, or antipathetic to the activities of transnationals. When there are conflicts between the state, comprehended as a set of central decision-making organizations and personnel, and transnationals, outcomes will depend upon power. Power can be operationalized by investigating the relative opportunity costs of change for the protagonists. Many factors such as financial resources and bureaucratic capability, as well as domestic pressure from private-interest groups, could influence the calculations of central decision-makers. For transnational actors, one critical issue is whether or not they must secure legally recognized territorial access, a juridical prerogative possessed by all states, even the smallest and least developed. In some areas, such as raw materials exploitation and civil aviation, access is essential. In others, such as international broadcasting, it is irrelevant. If territorial access is important for transnationals, then states will have bargaining leverage; if it is not, the position of central decision-makers, even in very powerful countries, will be weak.

Liberal observers have argued that there has been a fundamental deterioration in the level of state control which can be attributed primarily to technological changes in communications and transportation. These changes have made it possible for transnationals to operate in a wide range of venues and have reduced the importance of territorial access to any specific or small set of countries. This argument is historically myopic; states were more dependent on transnational actors, at least through the eighteenth century, than they are now; they could neither fight nor finance without relying on mercenaries and international bankers. Nevertheless, the ease of movement of information and goods since the Second World War has compromised the ability of states to conduct independent monetary policies and to regulate some manufacturing activities.

The future, however, has rarely been a linear extrapolation from the past and further technological change may actually enhance rather than reduce national autonomy. Rousseau argued in his *Constitutional Project for Corsica* that Corsica should aim for a self-sufficient existence based on agricultural prosperity. Marx's idealization of communism, with individuals fully actualizing all of their potential depended, in practice, upon the kind of material prosperity that only further technological progress can bring. If the future is characterized, for instance, by robotic machines and cheap and limitless energy from fusion, solar, or some other source, there will be less need for the transnational flow of goods.

In analyzing bargaining between transnationals and states from a power-politics perspective, the basic institutional structure of the actors is taken as given and independent. The discussion starts with actors. There is no attempt to explain how actors came to exist in the first place or why they assume particular institutional forms. For the power-politics paradigm in either its realist or statist form questions like the following do not arise: why is international commerce organized by multinational corporations in the twentieth century while it was organized by merchant trading companies in the seventeenth? Why does sovereign lending take place through international financial institutions in the late twentieth century as opposed to bilateral lending which characterized the nineteenth century?

There is, however, a second and very different conceptualization of

278

the way in which power is consequential for transnational actors. If states are understood not as central decision-making organizations and personnel but rather as institutional structures or polities, then the basic institutional structure of transnationals will be influenced or even determined by the institutional characteristics of states, because states are the most consequential units that transnationals encounter. Power here is related to the fact that it is states or polities that structure the basic environment within which transnationals must function: the nature of the legal system; the specification of legitimate organizational forms (in the contemporary world multinational corporations are acceptable, but mercenary armies are not); the determination of acceptable modes of political action (giving money to political parties in the United States is permissible, giving money to voters is not). In this perspective, institutional structures not actors are the units of analysis, an ontological stance that is inconsistent with conventional actor-oriented power politics approaches including both realism and statism, but which does, nevertheless, focus on power. It is the institutional structure of states which has the most important influence on the institutional characteristics of other actors, including transnationals.

There are powerful motivations for transnationals to organize themselves in ways that are compatible with state institutions. Coercive incentives, especially legal regulations, competitive incentives, and normative legitimacy encourage transnationals to become institutionally isomorphic with states. The organizational form of transnationals will vary across countries, because different countries have different legal rules, domestic political structures, and normative values. The more powerful the state, the more important it is for the success of the transnational actor, the more compelling these pulls to isomorphism will be. Even the very existence of certain kinds of non-state international actors reflects state institutions. In a world dominated by Nazi regimes, Amnesty International would not exist. If the Soviet Union had won the Cold War, multinational corporations would hardly be seen as formidable entities.

In sum, state power can be understood in two different ways. First, more powerful states (with the state understood as an institutional structure or polity) set the basic rules and define the environment within which transnationals must function. Second, if states are understood as actors, more precisely as central decision making organizations, then the relative capabilities of states and transnationals determine the outcome of specific disputes.

Structures of governance and transnational relations: what have we learned?

Thomas Risse-Kappen

The chapters in this volume demonstrate that transnational relations matter in world politics and that we cannot explain state behavior in crucial issue-areas without taking the cross-boundary activities of non-state actors into account. Matthew Evangelista and Patricia Chilton illustrate, for example, that transnational relations contributed to the change in Soviet security policy and to the transformation processes in Eastern Europe and, thus, to the end of the Cold War. David Cameron argues that institutionalized transnational and trans-governmental actors were crucial in the negotiations leading to the treaty on European Economic and Monetary Union (EMU) which is supposed to institute a common currency in Europe by the end of the decade.

But the chapters in this volume also show that there are important limits to the impact of even powerful transnational actors. Cal Clark and Steve Chan show that the contribution of multinational corporations (MNCs) to economic growth in East Asia depends on state strength in conjunction with a Confucian culture. Peter Katzenstein and Yutaka Tsujinaka demonstrate that American MNCs needed support from the US state in order to penetrate Japanese markets. Matthew Evangelista shows that the impact of US-Russian transnational coalitions on Russian arms control policy decreased when the country's domestic structure changed. Thomas Princen argues that the success of environmental International Non-Governmental Organizations (INGOs) might sometimes be counter-productive for their goals, if they neglect the domestic conditions in their "target states."

In sum, this volume does not confirm some arguments of the earlier

For helpful comments to a draft of this chapter I am most grateful to M. J. Peterson, Janice Thomson, and various contributors to this volume.

debate on transnational relations that interdependence among societies is becoming all-pervasive thereby diminishing the role of the state in international relations. Nor, however, does this book substantiate the claims by realist critiques of the earlier debate that powerful states always win confrontations with transnational actors. Stephen Krasner, who argues from a power-politics perspective in this volume as Robert Gilpin did in the 1971 Keohane and Nye book, readily acknowledges this point.[1] The findings of this book move the controversy beyond sterile debates between "state-centered" and "society-dominated" approaches to world politics toward a new appreciation of the interaction between states and transnational actors.

This chapter proceeds in three steps. First, I summarize the findings of the empirical chapters in light of the propositions developed in the introduction. The chapters confirm the proposition that institutional structures of governance – both domestic and international – mediate the impact of transnational actors (TNAs) on state policies. At the same time, these institutional structures also influence the very nature of these TNAs. The propositions about TNA access hold up pretty well against the empirical evidence, while the arguments about coalition-building have to be modified. In particular, the empirical findings point to the significance of culture and norms.

Second, I address alternative explanations for the outcomes in the various case studies. Obvious candidates include the realist emphasis on international material structures, focus on inter-state bargaining as opposed to transnational relations, and domestic politics accounts. Structural realism does not seem to speak to the questions asked in this volume (but see Krasner's chapter for a broader perspective focusing on power politics). Emphasis on inter-state bargains or domestic politics also appears to be insufficient in explaining the evidence. I then argue that domestic structures and international institutions are more significant in mediating the impact of TNAs on state policies than issue-area or actor characteristics.

Third, I relate the arguments of this book to broader debates in the field of international relations and identify areas of future research. The findings clarify some issues in the study of ideas, domestic structures, and international institutions. The approach also contributes to

---

[1] See Robert Gilpin, "The Politics of Transnational Economic Relations," in Robert O. Keohane and Joseph S. Nye, Jr., eds., *Transnational Relations and World Politics* (Cambridge, MA: Harvard University Press, 1971), pp. 48–69.

integrating international and domestic levels of analysis to explain foreign policy behavior.

Transnational actors, domestic structures, and international institutions: the findings

The starting point of this volume has been that the earlier debate on transnational relations failed, not because transnational actors are irrelevant, but because previous studies largely asked the wrong questions.[2] First, the concept itself was defined too vaguely. This book concentrates on regularized contacts among specific transnational actors – from exchanges between human rights and peace groups (Patricia Chilton's chapter), between US and Soviet intellectuals and scholars (Matthew Evangelista's chapter), to transgovernmental coalitions (chapters by Peter Katzenstein and Yutaka Tsujinaka, and David Cameron), INGOs (Thomas Princen's chapter) and MNCs (chapters by Katzenstein and Tsujinaka and Clark and Chan).

Second and more important, the controversy was too often framed as one between "state-centered" versus "society-dominated" approaches to world politics. The chapters in this volume suggest overwhelmingly that the interesting question is not whether transnational relations would somehow make the state system irrelevant, but how transnational relations interact with states. As Stephen Krasner reminds us, transnational relations would not even exist if there were no territorially bound units in the international system, i.e., states. As a result, we can now safely put the old controversy between "statist realism" and "societist liberalism" to rest. Liberals are correct in pointing out that transnational relations are causally consequential in world politics. Realists rightly insist that states remain central and sometimes even dominant actors in international relations. But both realists and liberals often use the notion of the state in a confusing way by failing to differentiate between the state as an institutionalized

---

[2] See the introductory chapter to this volume for details. It is a pity that the more sophisticated approach by Robert O. Keohane and Joseph S. Nye, Jr., in *Power and Interdependence* (Boston: Little, Brown, and Co., 1977) was rarely used to guide empirical research. Ten years later, Keohane and Nye acknowledged that they had "only partially incorporated the liberal emphasis on institutions, interdependence, and regularized transnational contacts into a sophisticated, systematic analysis of process and structure in world politics" ("Afterword," in Keohane and Nye, *Power and Interdependence*, 2nd edn. [Glenview, IL: Scott, Foresman, and Co., 1989], pp. 245–67, 267).

structure of governance and the state as an actor, i.e., the national government.

The central proposition of this volume (see introduction) is that structures of governance – domestic and international – determine:

1 important actor characteristics of TNAs;
2 TNA strategies to influence policies in their "target" states;
3 TNA impact on these policies.

But structures of governance not only constrain TNA activities, they also enable them. The case studies demonstrate that successful TNA are not confined to only influencing particular policy decisions. While Evangelista's analysis emphasizes arms control choices as the primary TNA effect, the transnational community of arms control experts also influenced the general direction of the new Soviet foreign policy, i.e., state goals and preferences.[3] Thomas Princen argues that transnational groups of environmentalists brought the issue of elephant preservation on to the state agenda, affected national preferences in African states, and had a crucial impact on creating an international regime banning ivory trade.[4] Katzenstein and Tsujinaka as well as Cameron also find TNA influence on state interests with regard to Japanese foreign policy and European integration. Patricia Chilton demonstrates that transnational alliances were instrumental in the transformation processes of domestic structures.[5]

---

[3] For further evidence see Robert Herman, "Soviet New Thinking: Ideas, Interests, and the Redefinition of Security", PhD dissertation, Cornell University, forthcoming; Thomas Risse-Kappen, "Ideas Do Not Float Freely. Transnational Coalitions, Domestic Structures, and the End of the Cold War," *International Organization*, 48, 2 (Spring 1994), pp. 185–214.

[4] Princen's case study confirms that TNAs and INGOs based on collective principled beliefs can have similar agenda-setting effects as "epistemic communities" based on collective causal beliefs. On the latter see Peter Haas, ed., *Knowledge, Power, and International Policy Coordination*, special issue of *International Organization*, 46, 1 (Winter 1992). On the role of INGOs in the creation of the ivory trade ban see also Thomas Princen and Matthias Finger, "The Ivory Trade Ban: NGOs and International Conservation," in Thomas Princen and Matthias Finger, *Environmental NGOs in World Politics: Linking the Local and the Global* (London: Routledge, 1994), pp. 121–159.

[5] Her findings confirm evidence on the impact of transnational human rights networks in Latin America and South Africa. See, for example, Alison Brysk, "Social Movements, the International System, and Human Rights in Argentina," *Comparative Political Studies*, 26, 3 (1993), pp. 259–85; Alison Brysk, "Acting Globally: Indian Rights and International Politics in Latin America," in Donna Lee Van Cott, ed., *Indigenous Peoples and Democracy in Latin America* (New York: St. Martin's Press, 1994); Kathryn Sikkink, "Human Rights, Principled Issue-Networks, and Sovereignty in Latin America," *International Organization*, 47, 3 (Summer 1993), pp. 411–41; Audie Klotz, *Protesting Prejudice: Apartheid and the Politics of Norms in International Relations* (Ithaca, NY: Cornell University Press, 1995). For further evidence on the East European case see Daniel Thomas,

In sum, a truly interactive relationship between states and trans-national relations emerges. Cameron's chapter in particular shows that this interaction is not confined to the domestic level, but also pertains to the relationship between international institutions and trans-national actors.

How domestic structures and international institutions influence transnational relations

Stephen Krasner argues most explicitly in this volume that domestic structures – i.e., the political institutions, civil society, the links between the two, and the political culture – not only determine TNA impact but also influence their very nature. He claims that "the institutional structures of the most powerful states have the greatest influence on the institutional arrangements of transnational actors" (p. 258). Even the Catholic church as a transnational actor that pre-dates the modern inter-state system adapted to a world of mutually exclusive territorial units – states. Toyota in the US is differently organized from Toyota in Japan. American companies in Japan adjusted to the symbiotic relationship between the Japanese bureaucracy and the business community (chapter by Katzenstein and Tsujinaka).

While the empirical chapters do not explicitly address Krasner's point, they contain evidence to underscore the argument that TNAs adapt to the institutional structure of the state within which they operate. The difference between Western European social movements and those in the state-controlled societies of the former Communist Eastern Europe is particularly striking in this context (Chilton's chapter). While both exemplify non-traditional forms of interest representation, the Western European movements had their own organizations, offices, regular meetings and the like. The Eastern European movements relied on personal contacts, irregular meetings, underground literature, and other ways of communication in an environment where public opposition was illegal. The transnational exchanges across the East–West divide were themselves influenced by the state-controlled and authoritarian domestic structures in the East.

"When Norms and Movements Matter: Helsinki, Human Rights, and Political Change in Eastern Europe, 1970–1990," PhD dissertation, Cornell University, 1995. For a similar study pertaining to environmental issues see Rodger A. Payne, "Rethinking Global Interdependence: Transnational Relations and Political Structure," manuscript, University of Louisville, Kentucky, October 1994.

They were largely informal and took place rather irregularly or outside so-called "official" meetings with state representatives.

In the case of the European Union (EU), David Cameron observes that the fragmented structure of the German political institutions – particularly the nature of coalition governments and the independence of the *Bundesbank* – is conducive to transnational and transgovernmental activities by German actors within the EU. German state officials rarely speak with one voice in the EU, partly because the German domestic structure facilitates such practices.

The chapters also confirm the proposition (see the introduction) that the institutionalization of the inter-state relationship – from cooperative agreements to regimes and international organizations – has a strong effect on transnational relations. Strongly institutionalized and cooperative inter-state relations are represented in this volume by the US–Japanese security alliance (chapter by Katzenstein and Tsujinaka) and the EU (Cameron's chapter). As Cameron points out, the European Union not only enabled transnational coalitions to flourish, but even institutionalized them (Committee of Central Bankers, Monetary Committee). The EU then delegated authority to them in monetary matters and in preparation of the Economic and Monetary Union (EMU).

One specific type of transnational actor which is conspicuously absent in the other chapters appears to be crucial in both cases – *transgovernmental* alliances among state officials. They confirm a proposition of early regime theory that international institutions enable practices whereby state representatives act independently from their national governments, build coalitions with like-minded officials from other countries, and then use these alliances to strengthen their own bargaining leverage at home.[6] A study of the transatlantic security relationship also supports the proposition. Transgovernmental coalitions emerged as a major tool by which European governments influenced American foreign policy.[7]

These findings challenge the assumption that interactions within

---

[6] See, for example, Robert O. Keohane, "The Demand for International Regimes," in Stephen Krasner, ed., *International Regimes* (Ithaca, NY: Cornell University Press, 1983), pp. 141–71, 162–66. Unfortunately, regime analysis did not develop this line of argument further, but concentrated on what Andrew Moravcsik called "inter-governmental institutionalism." See his "Negotiating the Single European Act," *International Organization*, 45, 1 (1991), pp. 651–88.

[7] See Thomas Risse-Kappen, *Cooperation Among Democracies. The European Influence on US Foreign Policy* (Princeton, NJ: Princeton University Press, 1995).

international institutions must be conceptualized as inter-state bargains. This seems to be the less the case, the stronger the institution. The EU, for example, can neither be understood as primarily an intergovernmental nor a supranational institution (Cameron's chapter). Rather, transnational and transgovernmental coalition-building of like-minded officials bargaining with other alliances within the normative framework provided by the institution appears to better characterize the interaction patterns within highly integrated regimes and organizations. If so, three consequences emerge, one methodological and two theoretical:

1 Network analysis as developed in organizational theory should provide a better tool to study the interactions within international institutions than the traditional focus on inter-governmental bargaining.[8]

2 Highly institutionalized structures of international governance create a political space challenging the state system and national sovereignty "from above," but in a way that is different from traditional notions of centralized and hierarchical supranational institutions. Rather, de-centralized structures of multi-level governance emerge in which actors are no longer motivated by their particular national loyalties and identities, but by collective principled and causal beliefs as well as by the goals of the institution.[9]

3 It does not appear to be sheer coincidence that transgovern-

[8] For reviews of the state of the art see Renate Mayntz, "Policy-Netzwerke und die Logik von Verhandlungssystemen," in Adrienne Héritier, ed., *Policy-Analyse*, Politische Vierteljahresschrift-Sonderheft 24 (Opladen: Westdeutscher Verlag, 1993), pp. 39–56; Fritz W. Scharpf, "Positive und negative Koordination in Verhandlungssystemen," ibid., pp. 57–83; R.A.W. Rhodes and D. Marsh, "New Directions in the Study of Policy Networks," *European Journal of Political Research*, special issue on *Policy Networks*, 21, 1–2 (February 1992). For an application on international organizations see Andreas Nölke, *Geberkoordination für die Länder Afrikas südlich der Sahara. Analyse eines interorganisatorischen Netzwerkes zwischen bi- und multilateralen Entwicklungshilfeagenturen*, PhD Dissertation, University of Konstanz, February 1993.

[9] The difficulties of current scholarship in identifying the nature of the European Union is instructive in this context. See, for example, Stanley Hoffmann and Robert O. Keohane, "Institutional Change in Europe in the 1980s," in Robert O. Keohane and Stanley Hoffmann, eds., *The New European Community* (Boulder, CO: Westview, 1989), pp. 1–39; G. Marks, "Structural Policy and Multilevel Governance in the European Community," in A. Cafrung and G. Rosenthal, eds., *The State of the European Community* (Boulder, CO: Lynne Rienner Publ., 1993), pp. 1–30; Moravcsik, "Negotiating the Single European Act"; Wolfgang Wessels, "Staat und (westeuropäische) Integration. Die Fusionsthese," in Wolfgang Kreile, ed., *Die Integration Europas*, Politische Vierteljahresschrift-Sonderheft 23 (Opladen: Westdeutscher Verlag, 1992), pp. 36–61.

mental networks are particularly relevant within the regimes and organizations of the "democratic peace" such as NATO, the EU, or the American–Japanese security relationship. As I argue elsewhere, these institutions are based on common identities among the actors pertaining to democratic values, norms, and rules of decision-making which transcend identities based on national boundaries.[10]

At the other end of the spectrum are hostile and largely conflictual inter-state relations such as the Cold War between East and West (chapters by Chilton and Evangelista). It is probably not coincidental that transnational relations are only weakly institutionalized in these two cases and entirely informal in Chilton's case. The contacts among European peace and human rights groups across the Iron Curtain emerged *after* the European governments had established the détente process and the Helsinki regime of the Conference on Security and Cooperation in Europe (CSCE) was in place. Some degree of inter-state cooperation was necessary to enable even these limited trans-societal contacts.[11] It is also unlikely that the alliance for a nuclear test ban between the US Natural Resources Defense Council and the Soviet Academy of Sciences would have been possible without the improvement in the US–Soviet relationship in the mid-1980s (Evangelista's chapter). Even then the US tried to hinder the coalition's activities.[12]

In sum, the empirical case studies contain evidence to support the proposition that domestic structures and international institutions influence the very nature of transnational relations. Transnational and transgovernmental activities would not exist without states enabling them in the first place. But Stephen Krasner's argument goes one step further. Domestic structures not only influence the institutional structures of many TNAs. Powerful states also become the source of many

---

[10] See Risse-Kappen, *Cooperation Among Democracies*. My thinking on these issues owes a lot to a project on norms and international security organized by Peter Katzenstein and the Social Science Research Council. See Peter Katzenstein, ed., *Norms and International Security* (New York: Columbia University Press, forthcoming).

[11] Some European actors had this in mind when they promoted détente. Egon Bahr, one of the architects of German *Ostpolitik*, argued back in 1963 that inter-state détente in Europe was to provide access to the closed societies of Eastern Europe thereby gradually undermining the grip of the Communist regimes on their societies. He called this "change through rapprochement." See Egon Bahr's speech at the Evangelische Akademie Tutzing, July 15, 1963, in Boris Meißner, ed., *Die deutsche Ostpolitik 1961–1970* (Cologne: Wissenschaft & Politik, 1970), pp. 45–48. On the impact of the Helsinki process on East European dissident movements see Daniel Thomas, *When Norms and Movements Matter*.

[12] For details see Philip Schrag, *Listening to the Bomb* (Boulder, CO: Westview, 1989).

norms that transnational actors promote. Had Nazi Germany won the Second World War, contemporary TNAs would advance very different values, while today's human rights INGOs promote the norms of the Western states that dominate world politics.[13] It is true that most TNAs examined in this volume originated in the Western culture and support values and norms consistent with Western liberal polities.

The question arises, though, what is cause and what is effect. It might well be that Western TNAs are particularly successful because their ideas conform to the values and norms of the most powerful states in the world. But it is also possible that these states are powerful because TNAs promote and spread their ideas. Western dominance in the world would then be a function not so much of Western material capabilities, but of the persuasive power of Western liberal ideas spread and diffused by transnational actors.[14] It is noteworthy in this context that Communist ideas promoted by transnational actors, such as the international Communist movement, fell by the wayside with the end of the Cold War and in parallel to the decline and final collapse of the Soviet Union. Western ideas, however, have survived the decline of American hegemony pretty well.

Moreover, even powerful states have to deal with the transnational actors whose existence they enabled in the first place. Institutional isomorphism and ideological consistency between states and TNAs does not prevent the latter from influencing the former, as numerous examples in this volume demonstrate.

How domestic structures mediate the policy impact of transnational actors

I argue in the introduction that domestic structures determine both the accessibility of states to TNA and their ultimate policy impact. In general, the proposition seems to hold up well against the empirical evidence.

With regard to TNA access, Katzenstein and Tsujinaka compare Japanese MNCs in the US with US MNCs in Japan and demonstrate

---

[13] This line of reasoning follows Samuel Huntington, "Transnational Organizations in World Politics," *World Politics*, 25 (April 1973), pp. 333–68. The argument is also very close to a concept of hegemony emphasizing both material power and cultural norms. See, for example, Robert Cox, "Social Forces, States, and World Orders: Beyond International Relations Theory," in Robert O. Keohane, ed., *Neorealism and its Critics* (New York: Columbia University Press, 1986), pp. 204–54.

[14] I owe this point to discussions with Daniel Deudney and G. John Ikenberry.

that TNA access is easier, the "weaker" the political institutions and the "stronger" the society. While the Japanese companies had no problem penetrating the open American political system, American companies needed support by the US state to gain market access in Japan. Chan and Clark confirm for Asia that state strength is strongly correlated with limitations on MNC access, with South Korea and the Philippines representing the two ends of the spectrum. Singapore stands out as a state-dominated domestic structure pursuing an economic growth strategy which relied on foreign investments. But MNC access was heavily regulated in this case, while the "weak" Philippine state did not have this capability.

Evangelista confirms the latter point for other TNAs and a different issue-area. In the case of the former Soviet Union, TNA access to the political system depended on the leadership's willingness to listen to outside advice. Prior to Gorbachev's entry into office, the transnational exchanges between American arms controllers and Soviet "institut-chiks" as well as natural scientists were largely irrelevant for Soviet foreign policy, because the group did not reach the top decision-makers. The situation changed under Gorbachev, but TNA access was still state-controlled. Only when the Soviet domestic structure was transformed by *perestroika* and *glasnost* was TNA access no longer a problem.

Chilton's case study also supports the argument. In the case of the Eastern European dissidents, transnational contacts could not be established with Romania, the most totalitarian state, and were almost forced into illegality in East Germany and Czechoslovakia, but were less problematic in Poland and Hungary which were also the least state-controlled of the Communist societies.

But TNA access does not equal policy impact. One could even argue that access and TNA impact are inversely related. The more difficult it is for transnational actors to penetrate the institutions of their "target state," the stronger the policy impact seems to be, once access is achieved. This counter-intuitive finding is supported by various case studies. As Evangelista demonstrates, TNA access essentially equaled policy impact in a state-controlled system such as the former Soviet Union under Gorbachev. Once the top leadership decided to listen to the transnational coalitions, their influence on Soviet arms control policy was significant. The point is also confirmed by Princen's analysis of the INGO role in ivory management in Zimbabwe. Clark and Chan show with regard to Singapore that the MNC contribution to

289

economic growth strategies became significant, since the government both recruited and regulated direct foreign investments.

But the impact of the transnational actors depended in both cases on the compatibility of their goals with state policies.[15] Gorbachev was at least pre-disposed to foreign policy change, while Singapore's government needed MNCs to implement its growth strategy. Unlike Gorbachev, the Chinese leadership was not pre-disposed toward arms control and, thus, emerging transnational ties among Chinese scholars and the US arms control community did not have much impact.[16] But leadership susceptibility toward TNA goals is not always a pre-condition for TNA influence in state-controlled domestic structures. TNA objectives and state goals were incompatible in the East European cases where TNA impact represented a direct challenge to state rule over society (Chilton's chapter).

At the other end of the spectrum are society-dominated systems and "weak states." According to the hypothesis, TNA access should be easy in these cases, while policy impact is expected to be more difficult given the requirements for building "winning coalitions" with like-minded domestic actors who constantly face countervailing forces. Here, a more complex picture emerges from the case studies. Evangelista confirms the argument by showing that it was increasingly difficult for the transnational arms control community to influence policies in post-Soviet Russia. The more the political system opened up and democratized, the more countervailing coalitions emerged. Yeltsin had to listen to a variety of domestic actors and could not impose the transnational coalition's views on society.

A case study pertaining to US arms control policies also confirms the proposition. The same transnational alliance which was so successful in influencing the transformation of Soviet security policy under Gorbachev, was less effective in moving the Reagan and Bush Administrations toward vigorous arms control efforts in response to the Soviet moves, since it lacked the ability to build "winning coalitions" in the public and in Congress.[17]

But TNAs can adjust to the domestic structure of the "target state" and overcome the hurdles of building large "winning coalitions." Katzenstein and Tsujinaka show how Japanese corporations in the US

---

[15] I thank M. J. Peterson for pointing this out to me.

[16] See Alastair I. Johnston, "Is There Learning in Chinese Arms Control Policy?," paper prepared for the American Political Science Association Annual Conference, New York, September 1–4, 1994.

[17] See Risse-Kappen, "Ideas Do Not Float Freely," for details.

successfully adjusted to the American domestic structure and, through extensive lobbying efforts in Congress, defeated attempts at protectionist legislation.

Their findings are also instructive with regard to Japan where a strong state is balanced by a strong society in a system of "reciprocal consent" which makes both access and policy impact difficult to achieve for TNAs. In the economic area, US MNCs used the American government to pressure the Japanese into opening their markets. But the process which Katzenstein and Tsujinaka describe cannot be conceptualized in an inter-state framework. *Gaiatsu* means that Japanese domestic actors who shared the US view, effectively used American pressure to change the coalition patterns. US MNCs also successfully adjusted to the Japanese domestic structure by developing ties to the bureaucracy, to business leaders, and by targeting media and public opinion. This pattern was even more effective in the security area in which American coalition-building with domestic Japanese actors served to increase Tokyo's profile in national defense.

These findings suggest that the need to build "winning coalitions" with domestic actors as a condition for TNA impact is particularly relevant in society-dominated and corporatist domestic structures. Moreover, TNA goals have to be compatible with the preferences of important domestic actors, either in society or, as in the case of state-controlled or state-dominated systems, in the top leadership itself. In other words, they need coalition partners inside the country who either share their goals or can be persuaded to do so.

Other case studies in this volume appear to confirm statist arguments against the liberal transnationalist literature of the 1970s.[18] The "weakest" state investigated in this volume is probably Kenya. As Thomas Princen argues, INGOs failed to achieve their goal of stabilizing the elephant population in the country. The reason for this failure was not that the INGOs were unable to form "winning coalitions," but the lack of state capacity to implement and enforce its own anti-poaching laws. Lack of state capacity and rent-seeking state actors also explain why MNC access did not stimulate economic growth in the Philippines (chapter by Clark and Chan).

So far, the propositions developed in the introduction appear to be confirmed. But some empirical findings do not fit the assumptions. Cal

---

[18] See Peter Evans, D. Rueschemeyer, and T. Skocpol, eds., *Bringing the State Back In* (Cambridge: Cambridge University Press, 1985); Ulrich Menzel and Dieter Senghaas, *Europas Entwicklung und die Dritte Welt* (Frankfurt/M.: Suhrkamp, 1986).

Clark and Steve Chan point out, for example, that the case of Hong Kong defies the model. While Hong Kong has a centralized decision-making apparatus and a low degree of social pressure, it cannot be regarded as a state-dominated domestic structure, since there is a general political consensus on a "minimalist" state role in economic activities. A consensual political culture constraining the state role is more significant in this case than organizational features of the political institutions.

The example, then, confirms the suggestion that it is necessary to incorporate *political culture* in a modified domestic structure concept. Indeed, Cal Clark and Steve Chan find a strong correlation between a consensual Confucian culture and economic growth, while more clientelist and fragmented cultures in Asia appear to inhibit economic performance. The comparison between the Philippines ("minimalist" state, clientelist culture), Hong Kong ("minimalist" state, consensual culture), and Singapore (interventionist state, consensual culture) is particularly instructive. All three states allowed MNCs in, but only Singapore regulated direct foreign investments heavily. The impact of the MNCs on economic growth was negative in the Philippine case, but positive in the cases of Hong Kong and Singapore despite almost opposite state policies. As Clark and Chan argue, the Confucian culture molded the MNC impact in both cases for the purpose of national development.

Katzenstein and Tsujinaka also find cultural variables significant in the US–Japanese relationship. The Japanese culture of "reciprocal consent" leads to a rather immobile decision-making process and serves as a major obstacle for TNA access and impact but can be overcome through the mechanisms of *gaiatsu*.[19] One could add that the American cultural consensus of "individualist pluralism" and of limited government intervention in society serves to facilitate the "buying" efforts of Japanese lobbyists. A comparison of American and German responses to the Gorbachev revolution in foreign policy also showed that cultural differences played a role in explaining the variation in impact of transnational activities promoting "common security" and a positive Western reaction to Gorbachev.[20]

But these findings do not yet allow for firm conclusions. They serve

---

[19] For further evidence on the normative structure of Japan's polity see Peter Katzenstein and Nobuo Okawara, *Japan's National Security* (Ithaca, NY: Cornell University Press, 1993).

[20] See Risse-Kappen, "Ideas Do Not Float Freely."

as a plausibility probe for the proposition that political culture matters. We do not know much about its independent effects as opposed to other components of domestic structures. In the cases of Japan, the US, and Germany, culture and formal organizational variables reinforce each other and are, thus, difficult to disentangle. It is unlikely that formal organizational features of political institutions will survive over a long period of time if they are not backed by a societal consensus embedded in the political culture (except for oppressive states). We also need more studies such as the Philippines–Hong Kong–Singapore comparison in the Clark and Chan chapter to determine the role of political culture in comparison to other parts of the domestic structure.[21]

In conclusion, the empirical findings confirm the central proposition of this volume that domestic structures mediate, refract, and filter the policy impact of transnational activities. Most important, the evidence validates the assumption that the state–TNA relationship must be conceptualized in an interactive manner. But the case studies also suggest that the ability to form "winning coalitions" with domestic actors is only one reason for the success or failure of TNA in influencing state policies and that the norms embedded in the political culture have to be taken more seriously in domestic structure models.

States and transnational actors: who wins?

The earlier debate on transnational relations devoted much energy to the subject of whether states or TNAs win direct confrontations between the two.[22] Some argued that state control over outcomes was a losing proposition given the proliferation of transnational relations and complex interdependence, while others maintained that national governments could easily prevail over TNAs if they chose to do so. While the empirical chapters in this volume do not address the issue directly, they nevertheless speak to it. A much more complex picture than simple dichotomies emerges.

[21] For an attempt at using cultural variables to explain variation in military doctrines see Elizabeth Kier, *Images of War. Culture, Politics, and Military Doctrine* (Princeton, NJ: Princeton University Press, forthcoming). See also Thomas Berger, "Norms, Identity, and National Security in Germany and Japan," in Katzenstein, ed., *Norms and International Security*, forthcoming.

[22] See, on the one hand, Gilpin, "The Politics of Transnational Economic Relations," on the other Joseph S. Nye, Jr., and Robert O. Keohane, "Transnational Relations and World Politics: A Conclusion," in Keohane and Nye, *Transnational Relations and World Politics*, pp. 371–97, 372–74. See also Keohane and Nye, *Power and Interdependence*.

Rather than diminishing state control over outcomes, TNAs seem to depend on a minimum of state capacity in the particular issue-area in order to be effective. TNAs need the state to have an impact. TNA activities sometimes help creating such state capacities in the first place, as Princen argues with regard to INGOs and ivory management in Zimbabwe. The same holds true for other environmental issues where pressure by INGOs and transnational "epistemic communities" led to an increase in state capacities to regulate the market, both domestically and through the creation of international regimes.[23] Stephen Krasner points out in this context that the rich Middle Eastern states owe their power largely to MNC activities engaged in the exploitation of oil. Finally, as Katzenstein and Tsujinaka show, US–Japanese transgovernmental security relations considerably strengthened rather than weakened the Japanese state role in national defense.

But there are also counter-examples in which transnational relations considerably weakened state control over outcomes. Increased capital mobility and the revolution in telecommunications have had enormous effects on the ability of states to control the flow of money and information (Krasner's chapter). In the human rights area, transnational activities appear to have generally weakened state control over society. As Patricia Chilton argues, transnational links among dissident, peace, and human rights groups were crucial for the development and evolution of civil society in Eastern Europe contributing to the peaceful revolutions in 1989. TNA impact was greatest in East Germany and Czechoslovakia, while it was less relevant in Poland where strong domestic organizations such as Solidarnosc and the Catholic church already existed.[24] Chilton's findings on TNA impact in the human rights area are similar to evidence pertaining to Latin America.[25] Another example for decreased state autonomy *vis-à-vis* society concerns the democratization of security policies in various

---

[23] See, for example, Peter Haas, *Saving the Mediterranean* (New York: Columbia University Press, 1990), Peter Haas, ed., *Knowledge, Power, and International Policy Coordination*; for INGO efforts in this issue-area see Princen and Finger, *Environmental NGOs in World Politics*.

[24] One could add, though, that transnational contacts had been relevant in Poland during an earlier time-period than the one investigated in Chilton's chapter. It is not clear whether *Solidarnosc* could have survived in 1980/81 without massive Western aid, channeled to Poland through the transnational links of the Catholic Church and others.

[25] See Brysk, "Social Movements, the International System, and Human Rights in Argentina"; Sikkink, "Human Rights, Principled Issue-Networks, and Sovereignty in Latin America." See also Thomas, "When Norms and Movements Matter."

Western European countries, particularly Germany, as a result of transnational peace movement activities during the early 1980s.[26]

Thus, both "statism" – the state always wins, and crude "societism" – the society-world erodes the state system, are equally disconfirmed by the findings. Purposeful TNAs cannot achieve their goals in the absence of a minimum of state autonomy *vis-à-vis* society. State actors frequently rely on TNAs to gather information, monitor other states' behavior, define their preferences, and change policies. And even the "strongest" states are vulnerable to TNA influence under certain conditions.

But state *capacity* defined as the ability to extract resources from society and to regulate societal interactions in a given issue-area needs to be distinguished from state *autonomy vis-à-vis* society. Expanded state capacities with regard to environmental policies, for example, do not necessarily imply decreased societal control over state policies. The evidence presented here seems to suggest that transnational relations reduce state autonomy *vis-à-vis* society, if they affect it at all. Other things being equal, transnational relations appear to strengthen society in its relations to the state. As concerns state capacity, however, the findings vary from issue to issue depending on both TNA goals and state responses to them.

These considerations then lead to a new answer to the question of who wins in confrontations between national governments and TNAs. Stephen Krasner argues that the more important it is for TNAs to operate legally within the boundaries of a given country, the more bargaining leverage governments have. The empirical chapters in this volume evaluate the proposition to some degree, though implicitly. MNCs happen to be the type of transnational actors investigated in this volume with the least impact on state policies and the most difficulties to penetrate state borders, as Katzenstein and Tsujinaka, and Clark and Chan show with regard to Japan, South Korea, and India. In each of these cases, the political institutions are strong, centralized, and supported by a "statist" political culture. As a result, governments have a greater capacity to control territorial access than

---

[26] Cf. Thomas Rochon, *Mobilizing for Peace: The Anti-Nuclear Movement in Western Europe* (Princeton, NJ: Princeton University Press, 1988); Thomas Risse-Kappen, *Die Krise der Sicherheitspolitik. Neuorientierungen und Entscheidungsprozesse im politischen System der Bundesrepublik Deutschland, 1977–1984* (Mainz-Munich: Kaiser, Grünewald, 1988).

in cases of fragmented political institutions in polities emphasizing pluralism and free-market capitalism such as the US (chapter by Katzenstein and Tsujinaka; see also chapter by Clark and Chan concerning the Philippines). Another example confirming Krasner's point appears to be the security area where, in the nineteenth century, states acquired the monopoly over the use of force in the international environment during a long battle with pirates, mercenaries, and other transnational actors.[27] In this case, the states won the ultimate control over territory including the high seas.

Idea-based TNAs, however, do not necessarily require legal territorial access to further their goals, as the example of coalitions among human rights groups in Eastern and Western Europe shows (Chilton's chapter). The same holds true for the public opinion INGOs advocating an ivory trade ban (Princen's chapter). Once the logic of persuasion and communication prevails, state control over territory becomes less relevant and TNAs might "win" even confrontations with powerful and strong states. The end of the Cold War is a case in point.[28]

A somewhat counter-intuitive picture emerges that state actors are particularly able to "win" against TNAs whose power capacities depend on material resources and require territorial access, while confrontations between governments and idea-based as well as information-based TNAs depend primarily on the latter's capacity to build "winning coalitions" inside the country or to mobilize international support for their goals. One could then answer the "who wins?" question with the proposition that TNAs are the more likely to prevail in conflicts with national governments, the less they require territorial access to achieve their goals and the less state-dominated the domestic structure of the "target state." In other words, Gilpin's original answer to this question might still hold, but might be less and less relevant, the more world society is populated by TNAs other than MNCs and pirates.[29]

---

[27] See Janice Thomson, *Mercenaries, Pirates, and Sovereigns: State-Building and Extraterritorial Violence in Early Modern Europe* (Princeton, NJ: Princeton University Press, 1993).

[28] See Daniel Deudney and G. John Ikenberry, "The International Sources of Soviet Change," *International Security*, 16 (Winter 1991/92), pp. 74–118.

[29] Gilpin, "The Politics of Transnational Economic Relations." See also Gilpin, *US Power and the Multinational Corporation* (New York: Basic Books, 1975). Moreover, Gilpin's argument might even become less relevant with regard to MNCs, the more production patterns are globalized.

How international institutions mediate the impact of transnational actors

The second major proposition put forward in the introduction held that international institutions also mediate the policy impact of trans-national actors. First, strongly institutionalized inter-state relation-ships facilitate TNA access to the political arena of the "target state." Second, TNAs promoting the norms incorporated in the institution should be in a stronger position than other actors with regard to the ability of forming "winning coalitions."

The two chapters dealing explicitly with the propositions strongly support them. First, as argued above, the findings presented by Cameron, and Katzenstein and Tsujinaka confirm that international institutions facilitate the emergence of transgovernmental coalitions. Second, they also support the argument that TNAs working in the framework of international institutions gain comparatively easy access to the decision-making processes of the participating states. This is particularly important when domestic structures do not normally provide TNAs with multiple channels into the political systems. In the American–Japanese case, the comparison between the less institution-alized economic issue-area and the dense network of the security alliance is particularly instructive (Katzenstein and Tsujinaka). In the economic area, TNA access proved comparatively difficult given the Japanese domestic structure. Within the framework of the highly institutionalized US–Japanese security alliance, however, strong trans-governmental ties developed. The findings closely resemble trans-governmental coalition-building in the Anglo-American "special relationship" as well as in the German–American alliance.[30]

These transgovernmental alliances were causally consequential. In the case of US–Japanese security relations, the transgovernmental network gradually increased Japan's role in national defense. With regard to the transatlantic alliance, transnational and transgovern-mental coalition-building enabled the Europeans to influence American foreign policy, both the definition of interests and specific decisions.

As David Cameron shows in detail with regard to the EU, the process leading to the most significant development in European

---

[30] For details see Risse-Kappen, *Cooperation Among Democracies*; Thomas Schwarz, *America's Germany. John J. McCloy and the Federal Republic of Germany* (Cambridge, MA: Harvard University Press, 1991).

integration in recent years, the decision to institute an Economic and Monetary Union (EMU) with a common currency, cannot be understood without reference to institutionalized transnational and transgovernmental actors representing neither their governments nor the European Commission. TNAs were causally consequential throughout the evolution of EMU, from the Delors Committee to the Committee of Central Bank Governors and the Monetary Committee. In addition, specific non-governmental actors such as the president of the German Bundesbank at the time, Karl Otto Pöhl, provided transnational entrepreneurial leadership in much the same way as described by Oran Young for environmental regime-building.[31]

Cameron's findings are confirmed for a different issue-area in the EU. Harald Müller has shown how nuclear non-proliferation policies of several EU member states have been strongly affected by the emergence of a transgovernmental coalition of foreign ministry officials working in the framework of the European Political Cooperation.[32] This group and their advisors, a transnational "epistemic community," developed an internal policy consensus which they used to promote changes in the national non-proliferation policies of various countries. Upshots of the network's activities were the French decision to join the non-proliferation regime as well as the German tightening of export controls.

In the human rights and environmental issue-areas, INGOs and other transnational coalitions frequently monitor regime compliance, reveal violations by state governments thereby creating international publicity, and empower domestic actors to raise their voices. As a result, improvements in the human rights records of states have been reported for both Eastern Europe and Latin America.[33]

In sum, transnational and transgovernmental coalitions appear to

---

[31] See Oran Young, "Political Leadership and Regime Formation: On the Development of Institutions in International Society," *International Organization*, 45, 3 (Summer 1991), pp. 281–308; Oran Young, *International Governance. Protecting the Environment in a Stateless Society* (Ithaca, NY: Cornell University Press, 1994).

[32] See Harald Müller, ed., *A European Non-Proliferation Policy* (Oxford: Clarendon Press, 1987); Harald Müller, ed., *How Western European Nuclear Policy Is Made. Deciding on the Atom* (London: Macmillan, 1991).

[33] For details see Brysk, "Social Movements, the International System, and Human Rights in Argentina"; Brysk, "Acting Globally: Indian Rights and International Politics in Latin America"; Sikkink, "Human Rights, Principled Issue-Networks, and Sovereignty in Latin America"; Thomas, *When Norms and Movements Matter*; Princen and Finger, *Environmental NGOs in World Politics*. On environmental regimes see also Oran Young and Gail Osherenko, eds., *Polar Politics. Creating International Environmenal Regimes* (Ithaca, NY: Cornell University Press, 1993).

constitute principal agents promoting, interpreting, and enforcing regime norms, rules, and decision-making procedures. Their impact seems to be particularly relevant in instances of institutional and integrative as opposed to distributive bargaining.[34] At the same time, regime norms empower and legitimize their activities thereby increasing their impact on state policies. Transnational and transgovernmental polities emerge in highly institutionalized international regimes and organizations whose actors develop a collective identity internalizing the regime norms. At the same time, these networks also participate in the domestic polities where they can use the regime norms to promote compliant behavior. While these norms may be contested in the domestic discourses, regime-promoting transnational coalitions are usually in an advantageous position, since they can claim to be authoritative interpreters of what constitutes appropriate behavior in compliance with the regime. This does not necessarily mean that they win every domestic debate, but the congruence of their demands with the norms embedded in international institutions should facilitate their policy impact.

These findings suggest that Putnam's "two-level game" model linking domestic politics and international negotiations needs to be amended.[35] Putnam's original framework conceptualized state governments as the only actors linking the international with the domestic level, even though Andrew Moravcsik has added transnational and transgovernmental alliances to it. If these TNAs can both affect the domestic "win-sets" and the inter-state negotiations, as this volume argues, they would by-pass national governments (understood as unitary actors). One could then argue that Putnam's level I of inter-state negotiations is not populated by state governments, but by cross-cutting transnational and transgovernmental alliances and that this is the level where the original bargains are struck. Since international regimes are still *inter-state* institutions, however, the state does not simply disappear from the framework. Rather, state governments have to sign on to the original agreements which then have to be ratified through the processes of domestic politics (Putnam's level II).

---

[34] For a discussion see Young, *International Governance*, pp. 81–139.

[35] See Robert Putnam, "Diplomacy and Domestic Politics: The Logic of Two-Level Games," *International Organization*, 42, 3 (Summer 1988), pp. 427–60; Peter Evans, Harold Jacobson, and Robert Putnam, eds., *Double-Edged Diplomacy. International Bargaining and Domestic Politics* (Berkeley, CA: University of California Press, 1993). For the following see Andrew Moravcsik, "Integrating International and Domestic Explanations of World Politics: A Theoretical Introduction," in ibid., pp. 3–42, 31–32.

This suggests that we need to conceptualize this process as a "three-level game" whereby level I represents the realm of transnational/transgovernmental bargaining, level II the sphere of intra-governmental as well as inter-state bargaining over the negotiating results on level I, and level III the area of domestic politics.[36] Cameron's chapter on the process by which the EMU came about represents a good illustration of this model. Bargaining outcomes accomplished at level I can well be rejected on levels II and III. The first Danish referendum against the Maastricht treaties is an example of level III rejection, while several instances of level II opposition can be found in Cameron's chapter. Another prominent example pertains to the famous "walk in the woods" deal between the US and the Soviet chief negotiators during the negotiations on Intermediate-range Nuclear Forces (INF) in 1982 which was rejected by both home governments, before it could even reach level III.[37]

Despite the INF case, however, it should be noted that transnational and transgovernmental *negotiations* on level I (as opposed to TNA impact on inter-state bargaining which is far more common) are rather rare in world politics and probably confined to already highly institutionalized inter-state relations. Even in these cases transnational actors need domestic and governmental coalition partners in order to get their agreements supported and ratified. Moreover, the emergence of transgovernmental alliances in particular is likely to depend on fragmented and de-centralized political institutions as in the cases of the US and Germany (see chapters by Cameron, and Katzenstein and Tsujinaka).

Alternative explanations

Two types of alternative explanations to the account presented so far come to mind. First, it could be argued that the findings can be better explained by more conventional approaches to international relations, such as realism, inter-state bargaining, or domestic politics. TNA impact might then be epiphenomenal. Second, one could maintain that there are alternatives to the two variables which supposedly mediate the impact of transnational actors – domestic structures and

[36] For a similar argument emphasizing alliances among states see Jeffrey Knopf, "Beyond Two-Level Games: Domestic-International Interaction in the Intermediate-Range Nuclear Forces Negotiations," *International Organization*, 47, 3 (Autumn 1993), pp. 599–628.

[37] For details see Strobe Talbott, *Deadly Gambits* (New York: A. Knopf, 1984).

international institutions. Here, differences in issue-areas and TNA properties come to mind.

Realism, inter-state relations, and domestic politics

At least three alternative explanations challenge the findings of significant TNA impact in the various chapters. First, structural realists could argue that the *distribution of power* in the international system accounts by and large for the outcomes. Second, the findings involving international negotiations might be explained more easily on the basis of *inter-state bargains* as compared to transnational relations. Third, the outcomes could be accounted for by *domestic politics* alone.

Realism appears to challenge the accounts of most chapters in this book. In the case of the European EMU, one could argue that giving up economic and monetary sovereignty to a supranational institution was the price to be paid by the EU members to contain the new power of a united Germany. But if that was the purpose, why did the Federal Republic itself agree to give up its powerful Deutsche Mark? Alternatively, one could maintain that the Germans decided to accept EMU because they knew that their economic clout would prevent undesirable policies by the supranational institution. But this only begets the question why the other EU members then accepted EMU and, thus, German hegemony in disguise? Either the Germans or the other Europeans (or both) acted irrationally, given these lines of reasoning. Moreover, as Cameron points out, there was no unified German position on EMU, but various German government officials participated in distinct transgovernmental coalitions promoting different proposals.

In the US–Japanese case, the by-and-large successful American pressures toward the opening of Japanese markets and the increase in Tokyo's defense spending could ultimately be explained by the power asymmetry between the two countries in conjunction with the Japanese security dependence on the US. While this argument might provide a preliminary answer, it does not account for the different strategies which the US used in the two issue-areas ("bullying" versus "binding"). Moreover, if the power asymmetry between the two countries determines the outcomes, the successful attempts by Japanese companies in the US to prevent protectionist legislation are hard to explain.

Concerning East Asian developmentalism, it is not so much realism but dependency theory which appears to present an alternative explanation based on the power structure of the international system. As Cal Clark and Steve Chan point out, the cases of successful economic growth in Hong Kong and Singapore despite heavy doses of direct foreign investments in these countries are hard to reconcile with the theory.

With regard to Moscow's arms control policy, realism might explain the structural pressures on the Soviet Union to change course (economic decline in conjunction with a costly arms race).[38] But the content, the scope, as well as the timing of the Gorbachev response to these structural conditions appear to be outside the range of a realist account.

As to the transformations in Eastern Europe, one could argue that they resulted primarily from the revocation of the Brezhnev doctrine by Gorbachev and the Soviet refusal to back the Communist regimes with Red Army tanks. The change in Soviet policies toward Eastern Europe certainly represented a necessary condition for the revolutions. But, as Patricia Chilton points out, Gorbachev did not force the Eastern European states to reform. The change in Soviet behavior also cannot account for the considerable variation in the transformation processes in terms of both speed and the degree of violence involved.

Thus, realist explanations appear to be mostly indeterminate with regard to the policy changes investigated in the empirical chapters. As structural realists such as Kenneth Waltz have long recognized, the approach does not offer a theory of foreign policy.[39] Realism points to structural constraints and opportunities which states face in the international system, but it does not provide satisfactory explanations for particular state choices in *response* to these conditions. This book deals with such choices and uses the concept of transnational relations to gain leverage in the study of comparative foreign policy.

But why embark on the rather complex and tedious task of identifying transnational actors and their policy impact if the evidence

38 See Kenneth Oye, "Explaining the End of the Cold War: Morphological and Behavioral Adaptations to the Nuclear Peace," in Richard N. Lebow and Thomas Risse-Kappen, eds., *The End of the Cold War and International Relations Theory* (New York: Columbia University Press, 1995). For a critical discussion of such explanations see Matthew Evangelista, "Internal and External Constraints on Grand Strategy: The Soviet Case," in Richard Rosecrance and Arthur Stein, eds., *The Domestic Bases of Grand Strategy* (Ithaca, NY: Cornell University Press, 1993), pp. 154–78.
39 See Kenneth Waltz, "Reflections on *Theory of International Politics*: A Response to My Critics," in Keohane, *Neorealism and Its Critics*, pp. 322–45, 331. See also Keohane, "Realism, Neorealism, and the Study of World Politics," ibid., pp. 1–26.

can equally well be explained as resulting from inter-state bargaining? One could argue, for example, that the EMU resulted from *inter*governmental rather than *trans*governmental negotiations analogous to Moravcsik's account of the Single European Act.[40] Cameron does not argue that intergovernmental bargaining was irrelevant for the process leading to EMU. But his findings suggest the necessity to differentiate between stages in the decision-making process. In this case, an *intergovernmental* institution delegated authority to *transnational and transgovernmental* actors that had already worked in monitoring the European Monetary System (EMS). The intergovernmental Council of Ministers later signed on to the agreements achieved among the transnational actors.

Concerning US–Japanese relations, it could be argued that the American state successfully pressured Japan to open its markets to foreigners and to increase its defense expenditures. But emphasis on inter-state bargaining misses the point made by Katzenstein and Tsujinaka that the US state was only brought into the picture by American MNCs when the latter failed to gain access to Japan given the peculiarities of the country's domestic structure. In other words, TNAs transferred the issue on the inter-state level in the first place.[41] The mechanisms of *gaiatsu* where Japanese domestic actors use outside pressure for coalition-building purposes also cannot be adequately conceptualized in the framework of inter-state relations. They are not just domestic, either, since transnational and foreign influences impact upon coalition-building processes. Finally, emphasizing inter-state relations does not explain why the American state plays an important role in furthering US–MNC interests in Japan, while Japanese firms apparently do not need their government to pursue their interests in the US. The variation can be accounted for by the difference in domestic structures.

With regard to Moscow's arms control policy under Gorbachev, it could be argued from a "peace through strength" perspective that the accommodationist policy was forced upon the Soviet Union by tough Western bargaining behavior during the Reagan years. The problem is that Moscow still faced choices how to respond to Reagan's policies, particularly the Strategic Defense Initiative (SDI). As Evangelista

[40] Moravcsik, "Negotiating the Single European Act."
[41] Janice Thomson also argues that a major impact of transnational activities consists of transferring issues from the domestic to the inter-state level. See her *Mercenaries, Pirates, and Sovereigns*.

points out, the initial Soviet answer to SDI was to respond with a vigorous arms buildup of both offensive and defensive weaponry. Only when the transnational coalition weighed in, did it convince the leadership that an expensive arms race was counterproductive.

In sum, emphasizing inter-state rather than transnational relations either fails to explain the particular policy decisions in the various case studies or appears to be as indeterminate as realism. This leaves *domestic politics* as a final alternative explanation. One could argue that economic growth in Asia, the change in Soviet arms control policy, the regime transformation in Eastern Europe, and ivory management in Africa can be sufficiently explained by the internal dynamics of domestic coalition-building processes and that recourse to transnational relations is unnecessary.

Two different arguments emerge from the chapters. First, Clark and Chan, and Chilton suggest that domestic explanations appear to be sufficient in some cases. South Korea, for example, achieved high economic growth without much direct foreign investment, while the Philippines could not use MNCs to further development. Only in Hong Kong and Singapore did MNC access contribute to economic growth. As Clark and Chan point out, state strategies in conjunction with a Confucian culture mediated the impact of MNCs to promote economic development. Regarding the transformation in Eastern Europe, the comparison between Poland/Hungary and East Germany/ Czechoslovakia is instructive. Chilton argues that the processes in the former two countries can be satisfactorily explained on domestic grounds, mainly by the evolution of civil society. Only in the cases of East Germany and Czechoslovakia, with a very limited degree of civil society development, does reference to transnational exchanges add to the explanation.

Second, Evangelista and Princen do not suggest that domestic politics was insignificant in their cases. Both chapters come to similar conclusions, namely that the transnational actors promoted new ideas which did not originate in the domestic environment of the political systems. In the case of elephant preservation, TNAs set the international agenda, helped the states to manage ivory, and, later on, changed the international environment in which the African states acted through the creation of an international regime. Concerning Soviet arms control policy, the transnational coalitions promoted specific proposals which fell on fertile grounds among the Gorbachev leadership given its receptivity to new ideas.

In sum, none of the chapters suggests that domestic politics was insignificant. In some cases, its impact is overwhelming, so that recourse to transnational activities does not add to the explanation. In most instances, however, domestic politics provides the framework in which TNAs operate and influence policies. The interaction of domestic politics and TNA activities accounts for the outcome in most cases examined in this book.

Issue-areas and actor characteristics

The chapters in this volume looked at variation in *domestic structures* and *international institutions* to account for the differential policy impact of transnational actors. There might be other variables accounting for differences in TNA impact.[42]

One could argue, for example, that the specific nature of the *issue-area* is equally or even more important than domestic structures and international institutions in filtering the policy impact of transnational actors. For example, transnational activities might be less relevant in issue-areas such as security – "high politics," while "low politics" areas such as environmental and economic issues would be more susceptible to TNA influence. It has been argued, for example, that state control over outcomes in American foreign policy is considerably stronger with regard to defense as compared to economic issues.[43] Following this line of reasoning, one could then hypothesize that TNA access to political institutions should be more difficult in the security area than, say, in the economic or environmental issue-areas. But TNA impact following successful access might be greater in security policy than concerning economic or environmental issues, since less societal actors are involved in the former as compared to the latter issue-areas. Moreover, economic and environmental questions frequently involve re-distributive issues and it is, therefore, more likely that transnational actors face countervailing coalitions in these issue-areas.

The empirical chapters do not test this proposition systematically (except for Katzenstein and Tsujinaka who compare two issue-areas). But the findings suggest that differences in domestic structures are in general more significant than variations in issue-areas. Evangelista's

[42] I thank Kathryn Sikkink for alerting me to some of the following points.
[43] See, for example, G. John Ikenberry, David A. Lake, Michael Mastanduno, eds., *The State and American Foreign Economic Policy* (Ithaca, NY: Cornell University Press, 1988); Stephen Krasner, *Defending the National Interest* (Princeton, NJ: Princeton University Press, 1978).

and Chilton's chapters deal with two issue-areas – security and human rights – in which state autonomy from societal pressures should be particularly great.[44] Both show that there was substantial variation in TNA impact resulting from differences in domestic structures – the Soviet versus the Russian political systems and the differences between Poland/Hungary and East Germany/Czechoslovakia. If issue-area characteristics were more important than domestic structures, the variation in TNA impact should have been less significant.

Cal Clark and Steve Chan show, with regard to the economic issue-area of "low politics," that state intervention in the Asian capitalist economies covers the entire spectrum from *laissez-faire* policies, as in the Philippines and Hong Kong to state capitalism, as in Singapore. MNC access and impact varied enormously according to the differences in domestic structure, in particular political culture, which appears to be counter-intuitive if the determining factor is the capitalist economy. The variation in their findings resembles the evidence reported by Evangelista and Chilton.

David Cameron's findings on the EMU are similar to the case of European nuclear non-proliferation policies (see above). Causally consequential transgovernmental networking within the EU does not differ much from the interaction patterns in the transatlantic relationship or the US–Japanese security alliance (chapter by Katzenstein and Tsujinaka).[45] The common denominator in these cases is the high degree of institutionalization in the inter-state relationship, while differences in issue-areas appear insignificant.

These findings do not imply, however, that the nature of the issue-area is completely irrelevant for TNA impact, just that the conventional wisdom about "high" versus "low politics" is probably wrong. As Stephen Krasner points out, issues involving state control over territorial access should increase governmental leverage over TNAs (see chapters by Clark and Chan, and Katzenstein and Tsujinaka for evidence). Moreover, TNA, particularly INGO, impact in the framework of international institutions should increase, the more issues pertain to institutional rather than distributive bargaining (compare chapters by Cameron and Princen versus chapters by Clark and Chan, and Katzenstein and Tsujinaka). Both propositions have not been systematically tested in this volume, but merit further scholarly attention.

---

[44] In the human rights area, this is only true for authoritarian states, of course.
[45] See Müller, *A European Non-Proliferation Policy*; Müller, *How Western European Nuclear Policy Is Made*; Risse-Kappen, *Cooperation Among Democracies*.

Finally, Katzenstein and Tsujinaka show that domestic structures sometimes vary depending on the issue-area. Their evidence is counter-intuitive to the conventional wisdom on the differences between the economic and security realms. As one would expect, the American state appears to be "weak" concerning economic issues, but "stronger" regarding the security realm. The Japanese state, however, is so "weak" in national defense that it has been called an "incomplete state,"[46] while nobody doubts its capacity to regulate the economy. Katzenstein and Tsujinaka report for the economic relationship between the two countries what one should expect for the security area, namely some degree of inter-state bargaining, while transnational and transgovernmental interactions are more common in the security alliance. The variation cannot be accounted for by some general differences between the two issue-areas independently from specific domestic structures. Rather, the difference results from Japanese post-war history and a domestic structure which provided the state with a strong capacity in the economic realm, while severely constraining it with regard to national security.[47]

In sum, one should not expect the same TNA impact on state policies across issue-areas in a given country. But it is probably impossible to generalize about TNA influence by just looking at the specific content of the issues involved and ignoring either domestic structures or the particular international institutional environment in which TNAs and states operate.

If it is unlikely that issue-area characteristics as such affect the policy impact of TNA, more than domestic structures or international institutions do, what about TNA properties themselves? As argued above, the organizational structure of TNA, is often a function of the institutional and domestic structure in which they operate (see also Krasner's chapter) so that the question would be nonsensical. But apart from that, one could posit that MNCs affect policies differently from INGOs or loose transnational coalitions. Two possibilities come to mind. First, different types of transnational actors might use different pathways to influence policies. Japanese MNCs might achieve their goals in the US by lobbying Congress (chapter by Katzenstein and Tsujinaka), while human rights INGOs might target the State Department and other

---

[46] For further evidence see Katzenstein and Okawara, *Japan's National Security*.

[47] On this point see also Thomas Berger, "From Sword to Chrysanthemum: Japan's Culture of Antimilitarism," *International Security*, 17, 4 (Spring 1993), pp. 119–50.

executive agencies directly.[48] In the case of the state-controlled domestic structures of the former Communist countries, transnational networks of arms control experts influenced the top leadership in Moscow (Evangelista), while human rights networks spoke to dissidents in civil society (Chilton). The proposition that transnational actors can use several functionally equivalent causal pathways to affect policies and that the pathway chosen depends on their goals, does not contradict the argument presented in this book. Rather, one would expect TNAs to pick the most effective pathway to achieve a policy impact in a given domestic structure.

Second, one could argue that TNAs influence state policies differently, depending on their power and the degree of their institutionalization. One would then assume that – other things being equal – transnational actors have the greater impact on state preferences and policies, the more they command (material) power resources and the more they are institutionalized. As a result, MNCs and INGOs should be more influential than loose coalitions of transnational actors such as those among the Soviet "institutchiks" and Western arms controllers.

The chapters in this volume do not systematically evaluate the proposition, since they do not compare the policy influence of different types of TNA (except for Katzenstein and Tsujinaka). But the overall evidence does not support the argument that TNAs' material power or their degree of institutionalization is particularly significant with regard to policy impact. As to the latter, it did not matter much whether MNCs, INGOs, transgovernmental alliances, or loose transnational networks were involved. The stronger state autonomy *vis-à-vis* society in the particular issue-area, the more difficult TNA access became no matter how strongly institutionalized the internal organization of the actors. The same holds true for their policy impact as a function of state capacity, on the one hand, and coalition-building requirements, on the other.

As to the power resources available to TNAs, three types of transnational actors have been investigated in this volume. First, the power of MNCs stems from their economic capacities. However, it did not help them much when pitched against "strong states," even among less developed countries (chapter by Clark and Chan). In the case of

---

48 See Kathryn Sikkink, "The Power of Principled Ideas: Human Rights Policies in the United States and Western Europe," in Judith Goldstein and Robert O. Keohane, eds., *Ideas and Foreign Policy. Beliefs, Institutions, and Political Change* (Ithaca, NY: Cornell University Press, 1993), pp. 139–70, 153, 167–68.

society-dominated domestic structures such as the Philippines, MNCs were repelled by the weakness of the state. The chapter by Clark and Chan confirms what the "statist" literature has always argued – the assumption that powerful MNCs usually win against weak states is a myth.[49] The only case reported in this book in which material resources might have made a difference in enhancing the influence of a transnational actor concerns the role of the German Bundesbank in the process leading to EMU (Cameron's chapter). One could argue that Karl Otto Pöhl, the head of the Bundesbank, acted as a charismatic transnational leader in the negotiations and, at the same time, brought the bank's structural power – its control over monetary policy in Europe – to bear.[50]

Second, other TNAs investigated in this volume did not command economic resources, but gained their strength through the persuasive power of principled ideas and values.[51] The transnational social movements in Europe are cases in point (Chilton's chapter). Their ideas resonated with the peoples of Eastern Europe, thus undermining the legitimacy of the Communist regimes (the "power of the powerless," as Vaclav Havel put it). In the case of environmental INGOs concerned about elephant preservation, their impact did not result so much from the persuasive strength of their ideas in Africa, but from their ability to influence Western public opinion. They used the strong societies in highly industrialized nations to affect policies in Third World countries.

A third group of TNAs combined principled ideas with knowledge-based claims, as for example, the transnational arms control community (Evangelista's chapter).[52] Their policy impact resulted from the fact that Gorbachev and Shevardnadze shared their values and then

---

[49] See Peter Evans, "Transnational Linkages and the Economic Role of the State: An Analysis of Developing and Industrialized Nations in the Post-World War II Period," in Evans *et al.*, *Bringing the State Back In*; Hartmut Elsenhans, *Nord-Süd-Beziehungen* (Stuttgart: Kohlhammer, 1984), pp. 84–94.

[50] On "structural" and "charismatic" leadership in institutional bargaining see Young, "Political Leadership and Regime Formation."

[51] On these types of power resources see Joseph S. Nye, Jr., *Bound to Lead* (New York: Basic Books, 1990).

[52] I hesitate to use the term "epistemic community" for these actors given the emphasis on "*recognized* expertise and competence" and "*authoritative* claim to policy-relevant knowledge" in Haas's definition (my italics). See Peter Haas, "Introduction: Epistemic Communities and International Policy Coordination," in Peter Haas, ed., *Knowledge, Power, and International Policy Coordination*, pp. 1–35, 3. The expertise of the arms control community was only "recognized" in specific circles and their knowledge claims were contested, both in the former Soviet Union and in the West.

accepted their knowledge claims. Indeed, there is not much empirical evidence that knowledge alone constitutes a power base. Even the findings presented in the special issue of *International Organization* on "epistemic communities" do not suggest that knowledge claims make a difference in the absence of collectively held principled ideas. The primacy of values over knowledge is further confirmed by studies on human rights issue networks who do not claim any significant "knowledge," but nevertheless seemed to have quite an impact (Chilton's chapter).[53]

In sum, the evidence in this volume does not suggest that the policy impact of TNAs varies systematically with the types of actors involved. The chapters show that *actor strategies* were more important for TNA success or failure than actor properties or the resources they command to further their goals. Actor strategies varied as a consequence of the domestic structures in which they operated, while it was irrelevant whether the TNAs in question were MNCs, INGOs, social movements, or loose coalitions. US MNCs chose different strategies to gain market access in Japan than Japanese MNCs in the US (chapter by Katzenstein and Tsujinaka). Dissident groups in Eastern Europe equally adjusted to the domestic conditions of the repressive states in which they operated (Chilton's chapter). The transnational arms control community lobbied Congress in the US, while it targeted the top leadership in the former Soviet Union (Evangelista's chapter).[54] In each of these cases, the domestic structure of the "target state" determined the strategy chosen by "successful" TNAs.

Conclusions

The evidence presented in this book can be summarized as follows. First, transnational relations matter in world politics and the earlier debate of the 1970s closed the book on the subject prematurely. Second, institutionalized structures of governance – domestic and international – mediate the policy impact of transnational actors. The "state world" and the "society world" need each other.[55] The weaker

---

53 See also Brysk, "Social Movements, the International System, and Human Rights in Argentina"; Klotz, *Protesting Prejudice*; Sikkink, "Human Rights, Principled Issue-Networks, and Sovereignty in Latin America"; Thomas, *When Norms and Movements Matter*.
54 See also Risse-Kappen, "Ideas Do Not Float Freely."
55 On these notions see Ernst-Otto Czempiel, *Weltpolitik im Umbruch* (Munich: Beck, 1991).

the "state" domestically *and* internationally and the weaker international institutions, the less relevant are TNAs. But the states also need TNAs – to achieve economic growth, to gain new policy-relevant ideas, to create international institutions, and to monitor regime compliance. Third, if we concentrate on domestic structures and international institutions as major variables that determine the policy impact of TNAs, we appear to gain more explanatory leverage than by emphasizing international power structures, inter-state bargaining, domestic politics, or issue-area and actor properties.

These findings contribute to several debates in contemporary international relations theory. First, there is renewed interest in the role of principled and causal ideas in foreign policy.[56] Research in this context has directed attention to the role of non-traditional social actors – "epistemic communities," social movements, INGOs, and others – in promoting ideas in a variety of issue-areas. The current state of the art has established that ideas matter, but little is known with regard to the conditions under which they fail or succeed in inducing policy change. Cognitive theories can tell us a lot with regard to the micro-level, i.e., how and under what conditions individual leaders are receptive to new values and knowledge.[57] But these approaches risk over-estimating the role of individuals in policy change, because leaders' freedom of maneuver is itself a function of the institutional structure in which they operate.

The proposition explored in this book, that variation in domestic structures and international institutions mediates the policy influence of TNAs, is, therefore, relevant for the debate about ideas and foreign policy in general. Various chapters in this volume (Chilton, Evangelista, and Princen) concentrate on agents of change – transnational

[56] See, for example, Emanuel Adler, *The Power of Ideology: The Quest for Technological Autonomy in Argentina and Brazil* (Berkeley, CA: University of California Press, 1987); Goldstein and Keohane, *Ideas and Foreign Policy*; Ernst Haas, *When Knowledge Is Power* (Berkeley, CA: University of California Press, 1990); Peter Haas, *Knowledge, Power, and Policy Coordination*; John Odell, *US International Monetary Policy: Markets, Power, and Ideas as Sources of Change* (Princeton, NJ: Princeton University Press, 1982); Kathryn Sikkink, *Ideas and Institutions: Developmentalism in Brazil and Argentina* (Ithaca, NY: Cornell University Press, 1991).

[57] See, for example, George Breslauer and Philip Tetlock, eds., *Learning in US and Soviet Foreign Policy* (Boulder, CO: Westview, 1991); Jack S. Levy, "Learning and Foreign Policy: Sweeping a Conceptual Minefield," *International Organization*, 48, 2 (Spring 1994), pp. 279–312; Janice G. Stein, "Political Learning by Doing: Gorbachev as uncommitted thinker and Motivated Learner," *International Organization*, 48, 2 (Spring 1994), pp. 155–84; Sarah E. Mendelson, "Internal Battles and External Wars: Politics, Learning, and the Soviet Withdrawal from Afghanistan," *World Politics*, 45, 3 (April 1993), pp. 327–60.

expert communities, social movements, and INGOs – promoting new ideas. The findings confirm that domestic structure approaches used in conjunction with cognitive theories go a long way in establishing the conditions under which ideas matter in foreign policy.

However, this volume does not yet fully take advantage of the social constructivist turn in recent international relations theory.[58] Analyzing the role of non-traditional transnational actors who promote principled or causal beliefs requires taking communicative rather than instrumental rationality and the logic of persuasion rather than the logic of cost-benefit calculations more seriously. The US-Soviet arms control community, the Eastern European dissident movements, and the INGOs promoting an ivory ban probably achieved their policy impact, because they succeeded in persuading others that their goals were worth pursuing and that the advocated policies were the appropriate means to achieve them. We need to know more about coalition-building through persuasion and communication thereby transforming actors' interests and preferences as opposed to assembling winning coalitions held together by exogenously given and instrumentally defined preferences.

Social constructivism is also relevant concerning the second area of research to which this volume contributes, the study of domestic structures and international institutions. Domestic structure approaches have so far concentrated on formal organizations and institutional features of the state.[59] In a similar way, regime analysis has emphasized the formal structure of international institutions such as their rules and decision-making procedures in order to determine regime effectiveness and goal achievement.[60] This and other studies suggest that the "new institutionalism" emphasizing communication,

---

[58] I prefer the term "social constructivism" for what others have called "reflectivism" or "interpretive" approaches. See, for example, Peter Katzenstein, ed., *Norms and International Security*; Friedrich Kratochwil, *Rules, Norms, and Decisions* (Cambridge: Cambridge University Press, 1989); Harald Müller, "Internationale Beziehungen als kommunikatives Handeln," *Zeitschrift für Internationale Beziehungen*, 1, 1 (1994), pp. 15–43; Thomas Schaber and Cornelia Ulbert, "Reflexivität in den Internationalen Beziehungen," ibid., pp. 139–169; Alexander Wendt, "Anarchy is what States Make of It: The Social Construction of Power Politics," *International Organization*, 46, 2 (1992), pp. 391–425.

[59] On the state of the art see Matthew Evangelista, "Domestic Structures and International Change," in Michael Doyle and G. John Ikenberry, eds., *New Thinking in International Relations Theory* (forthcoming).

[60] On the state of the art in regime analysis see Harald Müller, *Die Chance der Kooperation* (Darmstadt: Wissenschaftliche Buchgesellschaft, 1993); Volker Rittberger, ed., *Regime Theory and International Relations* (Oxford: Oxford University Press, 1993); Young, *International Governance*.

collective understandings, identity, and norms of appropriateness has to be taken more seriously. This book represents a first step in modifying the domestic structure concept by incorporating political culture. More theoretical and empirical work is necessary on the precise relationship between the formal structure of political institutions and the ideas embedded in the political culture. The most promising avenue for future research seems to study those cases in which formal organizational structures and political culture do not simply reinforce each other, but where tensions between the two appear (see the case of Hong Kong in the chapter by Clark and Chan).

The third debate to which this volume contributes concerns the study of comparative foreign policy, namely the interaction of domestic politics and international relations. There is a growing consensus in the field that the grand theories of international relations – whether realism, liberalism, or institutionalism – cannot account for the variation in foreign policy behavior in response to international structural conditions. Most analysts agree that approaches emphasizing the *interaction* of domestic and international factors appear to be most promising toward a theory of comparative foreign policy.[61] This volume complements the analysis of "two-level games" by pointing out another – transnational – pathway to study the interaction between domestic politics and international relations.

In conclusion, this book argues out that the interaction between structures of governance – domestic and international – on the one hand, and non-state actors, on the other, is worth studying empirically rather than engaging in fruitless debates whether states or TNAs are more important in world politics. Our endeavor can, of course, only be one step in showing how transnational relations matter. But the book has accomplished its task if it convinces skeptical readers that we need to bring transnational relations back in, if we want to understand international relations.

---

[61] For reviews of the literature see Moravcsik, "Integrating International and Domestic Explanations of World Politics"; Harald Müller and Thomas Risse-Kappen, "From the Outside In and the Inside Out. Domestic Politics, International Relations, and Foreign Policy," in David Skidmore and Valerie Hudson, eds., *The Limits of State Autonomy: Societal Groups and Foreign Policy Formulation* (Boulder, CO: Westview, 1993), pp. 25–48.

Index

CAMBRIDGE STUDIES IN INTERNATIONAL RELATIONS